KU-149-788

Bach's Cycle,
Mozart's Arrow

SIMPSON

IMPRINT IN HUMANITIES

The humanities endowment
by Sharon Hanley Simpson and
Barclay Simpson honors
MURIEL CARTER HANLEY
whose intellect and sensitivity
have enriched the many lives
that she has touched.

Bach's Cycle, Mozart's Arrow

An Essay on the Origins of Musical Modernity

KAROL BERGER

University of California Press

BERKELEY   LOS ANGELES   LONDON

The publisher gratefully acknowledges
the generous contributions to this book provided
by the Music Endowment Fund of the University of
California Press Foundation and by Stanford University.

University of California Press, one of the most distinguished university
presses in the United States, enriches lives around the world by
advancing scholarship in the humanities, social sciences, and natural
sciences. Its activities are supported by the UC Press Foundation and by
philanthropic contributions from individuals and institutions. For more
information, visit www.ucpress.edu.

University of California Press
Berkeley and Los Angeles, California

University of California Press, Ltd.
London, England

© 2007 by The Regents of the University of California

Library of Congress Cataloging-in-Publication Data

Berger, Karol, 1947–
    Bach's cycle, Mozart's arrow : an essay on the origins of musical
modernity / Karol Berger.
        p.   cm.
    Includes bibliographical references and index.
    ISBN 978-0-520-25091-8 (cloth : alk. paper)
    1. Music—18th century—History and criticism.   2. Bach, Johann
Sebastian, 1685–1750—Criticism and interpretation.   3. Mozart,
Wolfgang Amadeus, 1756–1791—Criticism and interpretation.
    I. Title.
ML195.B47 2007
780.9'033—dc22   2006029140

Manufactured in the United States of America

16   15   14   13   12   11   10   09   08   07
10 9   8   7   6   5   4   3   2   1

This book is printed on Natures Book, which contains 50% post-
consumer waste and meets the minimum requirements of ANSI/NISO
Z39.48–1992 (R 1997) (Permanence of Paper).

For Anna

and for my fellow travelers,
Andrzej and Wojciech

ma già volgeva il mio disio e 'l *velle,*
sì come rota ch'igualmente è mossa,
   l'amor che move il sole e l'altre stelle.

             Paradiso XXXIII.143–45

Considerate la vostra semenza:
fatti non foste a viver come bruti,
ma per seguir virtute e canoscenza.

             Inferno XXVI.118–20

Contents

Illustrations

Introduction

The change that is the subject of this book is well captured when you place two paintings side by side—Nicolas Poussin's *Il ballo della vita humana* (*A Dance to the Music of Time*) of ca. 1639–1640 and Giandomenico Tiepolo's *Il Mondo Novo* (*The New World*) of 1791 (Figures 1 and 2). The earlier of the two abounds in circular images: bodies move along circular orbits to the music of Time's lyre. Poussin's time is cyclical, ruled by the sun's daily rising and setting, the annual succession of recurring seasons, turns of the wheel of fortune—all the eternal cycles that govern human life. Tiepolo, by contrast, observes from behind a thoroughly modern crowd assembled to gawk at a spectacle made possible by the newest technological medium (shortly to be featured also in *Faust II*)—a magic lantern displaying the exotic marvels of "the new world." These humans are not subject to an eternal, unchanging order. On the contrary, they are children of a unique historical moment, their gaze fixed on a dimly imagined future, a new, emerging world. Tiepolo's time is linear, progressive, oriented toward the future (one might go further and say that Tiepolo contemplates the human condition not with the awe that Poussin had shown but with detached irony). It is the shift from Poussin's to Tiepolo's view of time that will be my subject here.

The generation of Europeans from after the fall of Napoleon, whose memories reached back to the days of the ancien régime, shared the sense of having lived through the most profound upheaval and transformation in human history. This sense is the leitmotif running through Chateaubriand's *Mémoires d'outre-tombe*, where it found its perhaps most unforgettable expression. "The old men of former times," Chateaubriand wrote in 1822,

FIGURE 1. Nicolas Poussin, *A Dance to the Music of Time*, ca. 1639–40. By kind permission of the Trustees of the Wallace Collection, London.

were less unhappy and less isolated than those of today: if, by lingering on earth, they had lost their friends, little else had changed around them; they were strangers to youth, but not to society. Nowadays, a straggler in this life has witnessed the death, not only of men, but also of ideas: principles, customs, tastes, pleasures, sorrows, opinions, none of these resembles what he used to know. He belongs to a different race from the human species among which he ends his days.[1]

The leitmotif received its pithiest formulation in the preface of 1833: "I've seen the beginning and the end of a world."[2] And Chateaubriand was hardly alone. In an article originally published in *Heidelberger Jahrbücher* in the winter of 1817–1818 Hegel spoke of "the last twenty-five years, possibly the richest that world history has had, and for us the most instructive, because it is to them that our world and our ideas belong."[3] Nearly two centuries later—and this despite the seemingly still more profound disruptions Europe experienced after 1914—this conviction, whether expressed with Hegel's sobriety or voiced in Chateaubriand's sonorous tone of somber melancholy, still rings true.

FIGURE 2. Giandomenico Tiepolo, *The New World*, 1791. Museo del Settecento Veneziano, Ca' Rezzonico, Venice. Photo: Scala/Art Resource, N.Y.

Ernst Robert Curtius opens and closes his 1948 meditation, titled *European Literature and the Latin Middle Ages,* with some thoughts on the temporal shape and limits of his subject.[4] The development of European literature, he thinks, is marked by two caesuras. The first was "the fallow period of decline which extended from 425 to 775" and separated the ancient from the medieval world. The second caesura is where we still find ourselves today: "A new period of decline begins in the nineteenth century and reaches the dimensions of catastrophe in the twentieth." Elsewhere he posits that this new period began around 1750.[5] Here Curtius follows the English historian G. M. Trevelyan, who in his *English Social History* of 1944 proposed extending the medieval period into the eighteenth century up to the Industrial Revolution, which "changed human life more than did the Renaissance and the Reformation."[6] (This notion of the "long Middle Ages" extending to the Industrial Revolution is, by the way, still alive in Jacques Le Goff's 1985 book *L'imaginaire médiéval.*)[7] Similarly, for Curtius, "a break with the more than millennial European literary tradition also makes its appearance in England about 1750." Elsewhere he elaborates: "The middle of the eighteenth century witnessed not only the beginnings of that great economic change which is termed the Industrial Revolution. It saw also the first powerful revolt against cultural tradition, which is marked by Rousseau."[8]

Curtius cannot quite make up his mind as to what to call the times that followed Antiquity. "But does it make sense to call the period from 400 to 1750 the 'Middle Ages'?" he asks. "Obviously not." He affirms elsewhere that "medieval forms of life subsist until about 1750, to put it roughly" and concludes that "we need not bother to find a name for this period. But if we try to consider it as a cultural unit, we may get a better understanding of our past." As for the times that followed, although he is as aware as anyone that it is customary to call the age the "Modern Period," Curtius declares that "historians in times to come will presumably set our age down as the 'Period of Technique.'"[9] Ultimately we, too, need not bother with the name. What matters is the underlying vision of the shape of historical time.

Of the two caesuras that mark the development of European literature, the more recent one is also the more important, profound, and catastrophic. In spite of the interregnum that separated the ancient and the medieval worlds, Curtius believed that those two worlds maintained an underlying continuity: "the substance of antique culture was never destroyed." If "the bases of Western thought are classical antiquity and Christianity, . . . the lesson of the Middle Ages is reverent reception and faithful transmission of a precious deposit" so as to maintain the continuity of the tradition from its "founding hero," Homer, to its "last universal author," Goethe. For the modernity of the last two centuries, by contrast, not only is the "break with the more than millennial European literary tradition" defining but it also threatens to be definitive (though of course one cannot know that for sure): "The nineteenth century produced a type of writer who championed revolutionary ideas and revolutionary poetry. That is a feature which betrays an age of disintegration, to use the formula of Toynbee. It may amount to what he called 'a refusal of mimesis.' But the equilibrium of culture will be preserved only if those disrupting forces are balanced by new ways of stating and adapting the legacy which has been entrusted to us by the past."[10]

Curtius explicitly opposed his dark vision of modernity to the inherited optimistic notion of progress: "The decisive change that the nineteenth and twentieth centuries have brought about in the world was accomplished through industry and technique—both of which were at first hailed as 'progress' but are now manifestly powers of destruction as well." He wanted to distance himself from those who saw the "Modern Period" beginning around 1500, because "to assume that a period begins shortly before or shortly after 1500 depends upon also admitting, at least tacitly, that the Modern Period, up to 1914, was a realization of progress—in the direction of enlightenment and democracy (England and France) and in the direction of the national state (Germany and Italy). This belief in progress was refuted by the world wars of the twentieth century."[11]

It is understandable that this dark vision was widely shared in the late 1940s, as was the view that the origins of the recent European collapse reach back into the eighteenth century, if not earlier (think of Adorno and Horkheimer, or, for that matter, Heidegger, figures seemingly as politically

distant from Curtius and from one another as can be). Whether we still find
this pessimistic outlook persuasive today, after half a century of undeniable
progress, is a question that need not detain us here. What matters and survives intact, whether we give it a dark, bright, or neutral coloring, is the belief that something fundamental and decisive happened in the late eighteenth
century; that history, and not only the history of literature, at that point
took a decisive turn, new and more decisive than any taken earlier; and that
this turn was marked both by the beginning of an unprecedented and more
or less continuously accelerating economic growth, fueled by new science
and technology, and by political democratic revolutions in America and
France. Whether we are optimists or pessimists, whether we like our world
or abhor it, we still locate its origins in the political, economic, social, and
cultural developments of the late eighteenth century. It is then that our
modernity was born.

———

This view that the late eighteenth century marks the arrival of modernity
may be a commonplace among historians of politics, economics, society, culture, literature, and art but, with the significant exception of those influenced
by Adorno, it is not widely shared by music historians.[12] Unlike the much
narrower notion of early twentieth-century musical modernism, modernity
is not a concept that figures often in our vocabulary. On the rare occasions
when it does, the birth of modern music is located not around 1750 or 1800
but around 1600. Leo Schrade, for example, called Monteverdi the "creator
of modern music" in his 1950 book on the composer, and an important current journal, *Early Music History*, in delimiting its scope in the subtitle *Studies in Medieval and Early Modern Music*, suggests that post-medieval music must be "early modern." But these are exceptional cases: in the standard
usage of our music history texts, to say nothing of our concert life, twentieth-
century modernism is the only "modern" music there is.

   To be sure, we do commonly recognize that an important stylistic change
occurred some time around, roughly speaking, the middle of the eighteenth
century, when the "baroque" was replaced by the "classical" style. But we
do not claim that this change was different in kind, more fundamental, let
alone catastrophic, than the stylistic revolution that preceded it and transformed the "Renaissance" into the "baroque" style. And while we often
agree with Friedrich Blume, who did not consider the next stylistic transition, that between the "classical" and "romantic" styles, to be in the same
league and proposed a single "classic-romantic" period (on the grounds that
no truly fundamental changes in compositional technique occurred between,

say, 1740 and 1907), we certainly do not see the mid-eighteenth-century revolution as more thoroughgoing than the one effected by Schoenberg and Stravinsky around the time of the Great War—quite the contrary.

To get a sense of the exceptional, epoch-making character of late eighteenth-century musical innovations we need to go back to the second decade of the nineteenth century, to E. T. A. Hoffmann's landmark essays "Beethoven's Instrumental Music" and "Old and New Church Music."[13] Hoffmann would probably not object to Blume's notion of a single classic-romantic period, since for him the two terms do not contradict each other: Haydn, Mozart, and Beethoven are all romantics, and they are also new music's classic authors, its Homers and Virgils. More important, their "new art, whose earliest beginnings can be traced no further back than the middle of the eighteenth century," is also identified as being "modern" (Mozart and Haydn are "the creators of modern instrumental music")[14] and separated from the music of their predecessors by a wide gulf. That earlier, premodern music—like painting or poetry, with which more often than not it was combined—was a mimetic art. It imitated something specific and definite, the emotion of the subject who delivered the text. What defines new music is its separation from language and hence from the mimesis of anything definite, anything in particular. New music's "only subject-matter," Hoffmann famously declared, "is infinity." All of earlier music's "precise feelings" are abandoned in favor of "an inexpressible longing."[15]

What accounts for this difference of vision? Why can Hoffmann see an epochal break, nothing less than the birth of musical modernity, where we see no more than one stylistic renovation among many? In part, obviously, because we are aware of the later developments that Hoffmann could not know; our understanding of these later developments colors our interpretation of what happened in the eighteenth century. (Those at mid-twentieth century tended to consider the undermining of music's tonal and metric framework, begun fifty years earlier, a change of such fundamental significance that all preceding changes in music history paled by comparison. Today we are more inclined to see the Schoenbergian and Stravinskian expressionisms as contingent stylistic developments rather than inevitable revolutions, and hence more likely to consider them as episodes within a longer story.) Less obviously, perhaps, we also tend to concentrate exclusively on stylistic matters, on compositional means. The essentials of the mid-eighteenth-century innovations lie, for us, in the demotion of thorough-bass from its central role in composition to the margins of performance practice; the full emancipation of instrumental music; and the development of formal thinking based on the interplay between tonal planning and thematic argumentation. Hoffmann was as aware of these technical innovations as we are, but he did not put them at the center of the story he was telling. What was decisive for him was not the renovation of compositional means but the new aims that these means were expected to serve. His emphasis was on music's subject matter and content, as well as on the new ambition to embody in music infinite totality and longing rather than definite emotions. For him the means used to satisfy this ambition were of secondary importance.

How would the evolution of music during the eighteenth century begin to look if we were to take our methodological cue from Hoffmann and considered music in terms of aims rather than means? This is the subject I shall explore in the present book. For Hoffmann what was essential about modern music was what might be termed, with a nod to Curtius and Toynbee, the "refusal of mimesis." Although I think that Hoffmann put his finger on a centrally important point here, I shall not make this the focus of my investigation. Instead, I would like to concentrate on a change in the shape of musical time, on the demotion of what might be called, now with a nod to Stephen Jay Gould, "time's cycle" in favor of "time's arrow."[16]

For those of us brought up in the European art music tradition, Scott Burnham's book *Beethoven Hero* was a reminder of how much our expectations and values continue to be informed by assumptions derived from the key works of Beethoven's heroic style, not least among them the Fifth Symphony.[17] The particular assumption I am interested in here, however, goes beyond the confines of the heroic style and underlies virtually all of the classical Viennese instrumental repertory that was for Hoffmann the paradigm of musical modernity. The assumption is, simply, that in music the temporal order in which events occur always matters.

There can be little doubt that it does matter in the Viennese sonata genres. The disposition of events in a sonata (or string quartet, symphony, concerto), the temporal order in which they appear, is essential: to tamper with it is to drastically change, or destroy, the meaning of the work. The temporal positions of the main and second subjects, or of exposition and recapitulation, cannot be swapped at will. To experience such works with understanding one has to register, however dimly, that the material being developed has earlier been exposed, or that what is now being recapitulated has already, in some form, been heard before. The interpolation of the Scherzo material in the Finale of the Fifth Symphony does not make much sense unless one is aware of its having appeared earlier.

This much is obvious. What is less obvious is that not all music works this way. The Viennese classics have shaped our musical expectations and values to such an extent that we expect these values to inform any music we encounter. Carolyn Abbate's argument against plot-centered, as opposed to narrator-centered, understanding of musical narrative exemplifies how widespread the assumption is that all music must be essentially temporal, that the disposition of events in time always matters in music: since all music is temporal, Abbate argues—that is, since music always has a temporal arrangement of events or "plot"—it is all "narrative," and hence applying the term, taken in this sense, to music is redundant.[18] But for music written a mere half century before the Viennese classics this assumption of the primacy of the temporal disposition of events is invalid.

Try a simple thought experiment. Those who listen with understanding to a sonata movement by Haydn, Mozart, or Beethoven always know where within the movement they find themselves, what has happened since the beginning, and what must still come before the movement can end. Most important, we can anticipate long in advance the moment when the piece will end. This does not happen when listening with understanding to a Bach fugue. Here we do not really care how much longer the piece will go on. In fact, more often than not, Bach goes out of his way to announce the ending emphatically a few measures ahead, so that its arrival will not be completely unexpected. In a fugue, unlike in a sonata, we are usually not sure where we are within the piece, nor does understanding what goes on at any given moment depend on such awareness (as it emphatically does in a sonata movement). This contrast is not just due to differences between the two genres, sonata and fugue. The same contrast obtains between Bach and Mozart concerto movements: in a Mozart concerto movement the moment of the ending can, and is, anticipated almost from the beginning; in a concerto movement by Bach it is not, and cannot be, anticipated until the final ritornello gets under way. In a Bach concerto movement the meaning of any given event does not essentially depend on its temporal position within the movement. It is important to recognize that a given segment belongs to a ritornello, but it does not much matter whether the ritornello in question is the second, third, or fourth (and, in fact, one never knows in advance how many ritornelli to expect). In a Mozart movement an event can be understood only if one knows where in the temporal order it occurs. Dahlhaus's point with regard to Beethoven's *Tempest* sonata (that "the theme is not so much the object of a musical discourse as a mere substrate of a process which imparts meaning to the music by providing that substrate with formal functions") is valid with regard to music of the Viennese classics generally.[19]

What I claim in this book, in short, is that in the later eighteenth century European art music began to take seriously the flow of time from past to future. Until then music was simply "in time"; it "took time"—events had somehow to be arranged successively, but the distinction between past and future, "earlier" and "later," mattered little to the way the music was experienced and understood. From that point on music added the experience of linear time, of time's arrow, to its essential subject matter. Music could no longer be experienced with understanding unless one recognized the temporal ordering of events.

My second central claim is that this change in the shape of musical time was not a development internal to music alone but rather, with the onset of modernity, part of a larger transformation in the way educated Europeans began to conceive of time: just as their experience and image of historical time shifted from cyclical to linear, composers dropped the predominantly cyclical model of time in favor of a predominantly linear one.

This is not a claim about causality; I do not presume to explain why music changed the way it did, certainly not by invoking some mysterious workings of the *Zeitgeist*. Rather than worrying about the causes of the change, I simply register the structural homology between the shapes of the historical and musical times, and note its consequences. Perhaps the causes and the consequences are not too far apart in cases like this one: New musical means—to follow Hoffmann's line of thought—are adopted to realize new aims. But whether these new musical means were specifically developed to realize the new aims or whether, evolving independently of these aims—which seems more likely—they later adapted to them remains an open question.

Hegel famously claimed that art "only fulfils its supreme task when it has placed itself in the same sphere as religion and philosophy, and when it is simply one way of bringing to our minds and expressing the *Divine*, the deepest interests of mankind, and the most comprehensive truths of the spirit," albeit by means specific to it, that is, by embodying these truths in sensuous images.[20] Modern music's newfound ability to embody the experience of linear time made it a suitable vehicle for bringing to contemporary minds some of their deepest interests. Definitive of modernity are narratives of secular universal history, whether conceived in liberal terms of progressive continuity or in egalitarian terms of revolutionary breakthrough. Once the transcendent divine has been brought down to earth and made immanent in the historical march of mankind toward a utopian future, composers who were at all interested had the means to capture such themes in musical narrative.

Mozart has shown how this might be done in the transition from dark archaic minor to bright modern major in the trial scene in *The Magic Flute,* and in the general trajectory of the opera from darkness and confusion to light and clarity (a trajectory commonly read, from the early 1790s on, as a political allegory of the recent events in France). Beethoven's translation of such progressions into purely instrumental terms in his Fifth Symphony gave music one of its most beloved "archetypal plots" for more than a century afterward. It is only proper that the Fifth served as the main focus of Hoffmann's interpretation of musical modernity. That he was not fully taken in by its triumphalism, that he found its insistent vehemence to be ultimately self-undermining, is a tribute to his uncannily sensitive musical and historical antennae. But whether confident, hesitant, or self-defeating, symphonic narratives of this sort were simply not possible before the advent of musical modernity, with its emphasis on the experience of linear time.

To make plausible my claim that the experience of linear time became centrally important to European art music only in the later eighteenth century, I focus this book on Bach and Mozart, the former cast in the role of a late representative of the premodern ways of shaping musical time, the latter representing an early case of a fully developed modern approach to musical temporality. With each composer I consider examples of both vocal and instrumental music, probing characteristic ways of shaping time particular to each genre.

Although the choice of Mozart as an early representative of the fully elaborated modern approach to musical time is not likely to encounter much opposition (even if some readers would make the more obvious choice of Beethoven and others would root for Haydn), casting Bach as the representative premodern is bound to raise eyebrows and needs to be explained. To forestall potential misunderstanding, let me emphasize that my choice in no way implies that Bach was unaware of the possibilities of projecting linear temporal developments in his music or that he was uninterested in exploring such possibilities—or even, more generally, that he was not aware of up-to-date trends in the music of his time or eager to exploit them.[21]

The circle of fifths is, well, exactly that: a trajectory—broken by one diminished fifth to confine it within a single diatonic scale and thus keep it from modulating—that, if followed long enough, will get you back to where you had started from. But it was the exploitation of this trajectory in Italian instrumental ensemble music from about the time of Bach's birth that, paradoxically, laid the foundation for projecting a sense of linear forward propulsion in music then and in the future. As Richard Taruskin recently argued, "it was precisely in Corelli's time, the late seventeenth century, that the circle of fifths was being 'theorized' as the main propeller of harmonic motion, and it was Corelli more than any other one composer who put that new idea into telling practice." The idea, in essence, consisted in relating all the scale degrees within a key, as well as all the keys within a movement, to a single tonal center, and measuring the distance of a degree or key from the center by chains of fifths. "The fully elaborated [tonal] system's birthplace was the Italian music of the 1680s." Corelli and his imitators harness the circle of fifths "to drive a dynamically unfolding form-generating process."[22] Whether on the local level of a single phrase, or on the global level of the whole movement, the establishment of a tonal center, the deviation from it, and the resulting drive to regain it, gave their music unprecedented forward propulsion and goal-directed momentum.

Bach's fascination with these techniques and his willingness to learn from his Italian predecessors and contemporaries, Vivaldi in particular, is well established. Taruskin himself shows how, in the Organ Toccata in F (BWV 540, probably from the Weimar years, 1708–1717) Bach detaches a cadential preparation from its resolution, "dramatically delaying the arrival of the keenly anticipated stable harmony." "Bach's Toccata," Taruskin continues, "is one of the earliest pieces to so dramatize the working out of its form-building tonal functions." And he concludes:

> Bach deserves enormous credit for sensing so early the huge emotional and dramatic potentialities of the new harmonic processes, and for exploiting them so effectively. . . . By harnessing harmonic tension to govern and regulate the unfolding of the Toccata's form, he managed to invest that unfolding-to-completion with an unprecedented psychological import. Thanks to this newly psychologized deployment of harmonic functions—in which harmonic goals are at once identified and postponed, and in which harmonic motion is at once directed and delayed—"abstract" musical structures could achieve both vaster dimensions and a vastly more compelling emotional force than any previously envisioned.[23]

All of this is undeniable. Just as the transition from premodern to modern worldview and the resulting shift in prevailing attitudes toward time, motion, and change—which, we shall shortly see, provide the context for the musical transformation that is the subject of this book—took a long time to be accomplished, so too the transition from premodern to modern attitudes toward musical time was the work of many generations: the practice that came to its full maturity in Vienna in the 1780s may well have had its roots in Rome of the 1680s. It is also undeniable that Bach himself took interest in this practice and contributed to its development. If we were looking for a pure, uncontaminated representative of the cyclical time in music, someone like Ockeghem would serve our purposes better than Bach.

All the same, there is a good reason for choosing Bach, not Ockeghem, to articulate our story. Bach was the last great composer in the canon to have served primarily as a church musician—and arguably the last one to have made the musical embodiment of the church's outlook his main business. Like his church, he was fully aware of the linear unfolding of human biographical and historical time, and, also like his church, he believed this time to be enveloped by God's eternity, subordinated to it, made relative by its absoluteness. In a number of central instances, I shall argue here, his music displays a double temporality, developing unquestionably up-to-date goal-directed momentum but relativizing and subordinating its forward propulsion to a sense of cyclical or entirely timeless stasis worthy of his medieval predecessors. It was this sort of double temporality that Wagner captured in his apt image of a Bach fugue as "a crystal flying like a bullet." Bach's preference for God's eternity over human time is all the more dramatic precisely because he was able to capture the linear drive in his music. My point, in short, is not to deny his music's linearity but to show how, repeatedly, the linearity there is relativized, seen from the absolute perspective of eternity.

By the same token, given my goals in this study, it will not be necessary to compare how the two composers approached the same musical genres. Rather, I will need to compare their respective attitudes to musical time as seen in those genres that were centrally important to them. The generic centers of gravity in Bach's and Mozart's oeuvres overlap only rarely and then imperfectly. It is possible to compare the dramaturgy of the passion with that of opera, and I do so in Chapter 3, but differences between the genres must not be overlooked. Similarly, one might compare a Mozart fugue with those of Bach (as Edward Lowinsky has done), but one should not forget how different the role of the genre was in Bach's and Mozart's respective universe.[24] There is at least one genre, however, that greatly interested both composers in a similar way: the concerto; here is the area where a direct comparison is in order and produces telling results. As I demonstrate in Chapter 4, Mozart's central preoccupation in his concertos was to tell a coherent story, and this required that he pay attention to the temporal order in which he presented his ideas. Nothing could have been further from Bach's mind. As Laurence Dreyfus has shown, Bach's central preoccupation in his concertos was to see how many interesting permutations might be derived from the materials of the ritornello; the order in which to present these permutations was of secondary importance.[25]

The subject of Chapter 1 is the opening chorus of the St. Matthew Passion. The chorus is based on a da capo aria text, and its shape makes sense only against the background of the generic conventions that govern Bach's da capo arias; I therefore begin by reconstructing these conventions. Heard against the background of these conventions, the chorus can for the first time be seen to possess an extraordinary conceit, namely, an ending that conflates into a single phrase what normally is presented in successive ones. It makes simultaneous what should be successive—abolishing the succession of past, present, and future in favor of the simultaneity of the present and thus neutralizing the flow of time in favor of the eternal Now.

Chapter 2 offers a close reading of an instrumental composition, the first fugue from the first volume of the *Well-Tempered Keyboard*. Here I show that what is of interest in a piece of this sort—to the composer, player, and listener alike—is the invention of subjects capable of many interesting and varied contrapuntal treatments rather than a specific temporal order in which such treatments occur. To be sure, a fugue combines the atemporal and the temporal, but it is the atemporal dimension that really matters. Given that music is a quintessentially temporal art, there is something peculiar in Bach's evident desire to neutralize time—to make it relatively unimportant, as in the fugue, or abolish it altogether, as in the Passion's opening chorus. The desire is clearly neither limited to those two pieces nor marginal in Bach's oeuvre as a whole. What matters to Bach in most of his music, whether vocal or instrumental, is not the linear flow of time from past to future, beginning to end. Rather, time is made to follow a circular route or neutralized altogether.

In Chapter 3 I return to the Passion's opening chorus to ask why it is here, before the story of the Passion even gets under way, that Bach wants to abolish time. I will demonstrate that in the Passion, time (or, strictly speaking, the two temporalities of story and storytelling) is nested within the structurally and ontologically more primordial timeless eternity (the temporality of contemplation) embodied, as it happens, in what is musically the work's most substantial layer. Since the contemplators' role is to teach us, the audience, by example, to show us the proper hermeneutic behavior, one of Bach's aims in the Passion is to attenuate the temporal distance between the world of the story and our world. Thus not only the opening chorus but the Passion as a whole is marked by the wish to neutralize time, to render insignificant its relentless flow from past to future. More important still, the story of humanity that is the implied context of Jesus's story possesses the same complex temporality, the same embedding of the linear flow of time within the framework of eternity that we find in Bach's setting. The linear time of human earthly history is not infinite; it had a beginning and will come to an end. "Before" and "after" there is God's infinite time, eternity. It is this fundamental structure of irreversible time embedded in eternity, of man's time suspended in God's time, that Bach replicates in the Passion. God's time, the time without irreversibility, is better than human time because it allows permanence. It is precisely because God's eternity is better than the irreversible time of humanity that Bach, as did so many of his predecessors, prefers it in his music too. We can see this not just in the Passion but in much of his music in general, instrumental and vocal. For Bach, the name of what most truly endures was "God"; hence music, based on the supposedly eternal rules of harmony, could serve as a metaphor for God. But whereas Bach still saw harmony as a metaphor for God, Goethe (who now makes his first appearance in the book and who will play an important role in my story from now on) speaks already from the other historical shore, from the world in which metaphors are all we have. In this new world, our world, it is God who has become the metaphor for harmony.

The four Mozart chapters, reversing the order of the Bach chapters, start with instrumental music. One of the central claims in this book is that at some point between early and late eighteenth century, between Bach and Mozart, musical form became primarily temporal, and that the center of attention for musicians—composers, performers, and listeners alike—shifted toward the temporal disposition of events. I attempt in Chapter 4 to demonstrate this point at its most abstract, by considering the temporality of the instrumental genre that was of central importance to Mozart, the concerto allegro. Following a path similar to that of Chapter 1, I begin by reconstructing the generic norms that governed Mozart's concerto allegros and then offer a detailed reading of an individual movement against the background of these norms. Among Mozart's instrumental genres the concerto stands out for its profusion of melodic invention. In these concerto allegros the main focus of interest is the order in which melodic ideas are presented within each of the three tellings of the story—opening ritornello, exposition, and recapitulation—making each of the tellings progressively more complete and logical. The point is to tell an amusing, moving, and coherent story, a story with a beginning, middle, and end, and to tell it not once but three times, with each successive version clarifying and closing the gaps in the preceding one. Mozart's instrumental forms may have their ancestry in the circular baroque patterns of the concerto and the binary dance, but they transform these patterns so as to straighten the temporal cycle into an arrow. The recapitulation is not simply a return; it is, rather, the necessary outcome, the final act of closing gaps and reconciling differences between the earlier versions of the story. And the fundamental premise of Mozart's playing is that the linear flow of time from past to future matters: listeners do not get the point of what they hear unless they pay attention to the temporal order in which the ideas are presented.

These observations apply equally to Mozart's instrumental movements and to the way he shapes individual numbers in his operas. Not that the presence of a text and a dramatic action is ever a negligible factor: the arias and ensembles are not simply sung sonatas. In Chapter 5 I offer detailed readings of several celebrated ensembles—specifically the *Figaro* Sextet, the *Idomeneo* Quartet, the *Don Giovanni* Quartet, the first-act *Figaro* Trio, and the *Don Giovanni* Sextet—to show the distance Mozart could put between himself and traditional formal patterns when the dramatic occasion so required, to show, that is, that linear, future-oriented time can acquire a variety of highly individual shapes.

The discussion of the *Don Giovanni* Sextet with which Chapter 5 ends becomes the springboard for a more detailed general consideration of the entire opera in Chapter 6. Just as in the part of the book devoted to Bach two chapters of formal compositional analyses gave way to a consideration of broader issues, theological and philosophical, allowing us to unlock the significance of the formal shapes we had discovered, so here, in the Mozart part, the two formalist chapters are followed by my attempt to position the analytic conclusions in intellectual contexts that will reveal their significance. Don Giovanni, the embodiment of limitless desire, is one of perhaps only two mythical figures born of the modern age (the other being Faust), a figure of the liberal Lockean strand within modernity that accepts and celebrates our endlessly acquisitive stance. Absolute, unlimited freedom, however, defeats any attempt to create a coherent self or a community. So far I have considered only two temporal possibilities, that of existing in God's eternity or that of existing in human linear time that extends from past to future. Don Giovanni, as Kierkegaard brilliantly recognized, shows that there is a third possibility: he lives only in the present, refusing to acknowledge the links that connect the present with past and future, the links on which the coherent individual and collective identities of those around him are built. His is a story of how the foundations of human individual and collective autonomy were laid. It is a story that bears comparison with that of *The Marriage of Figaro,* on the one hand, and of the Passion, on the other. It also bears comparison with the story of Goethe's Faust, a figure driven by will to power rather than merely erotic desire but whose peculiar mode of temporal existence is nevertheless closely related to that of Don Giovanni, as is his aspiration to absolute freedom.

If *Don Giovanni* explores the liberal, individualist component of the modern outlook, *The Magic Flute*, which is the subject of Chapter 7, probes modernity's democratic, communitarian aspirations. The subject of *The Magic Flute* is the revolution in values that occurred when the old regime, in which power was in the hands of the old, was replaced by a new order, in which the young were able to make their own autonomous choices; it is (to speak with Ivan Nagel) about the passing of mercy and the arrival of autonomy. It is also the work in which modern instrumental music acquires its own foundation myth. The abstract, autonomous subject of modern politics, no longer a mere "prince" but rather a universal "man," finds his own medium in the new, abstract, autonomous art. Beethoven will take up the fundamental structure of this myth in a number of works, *Fidelio* and the Ninth Symphony among them.

Separating the chapters devoted to Mozart from those devoted to Bach stands a lengthy Interlude that is at once the physical and intellectual center of this book. The Interlude tells the story of the transition from the premodern Christian moral-political outlook to the modern post-Christian worldview. Here I provide a larger context for the musical developments I discuss elsewhere in this book, a context for understanding how we got, in a mere sixty years, from a work like the St. Matthew Passion to a work like *Don Giovanni*. Whereas the musical chapters can be read and understood on their own, the Interlude presents the perspective from which the music is seen here. I shall not attempt to summarize its content, beyond indicating that the story it tells is the story of the emergence of human autonomy and a consequent transformation in the fundamental experience and understanding of how time is shaped. This is the story of how we, educated Europeans, exchanged time's cycle for time's arrow, and why. In their thinking about both the moral and the natural realms, the moderns shifted the balance of their esteem decisively from eternity, rest, and immutability—which had been privileged by the ancients and by the medieval Christians—toward time, motion, and change. Modernity, scientific as well as moral-political, is at bottom an attempt to emancipate linear time.

Framing the whole book are a Prelude and a Postlude, glimpses into what happened before and after the main story told here. Similarly to the shift in moral-political, as well as scientific, outlook that separated the moderns from their ancestors and that I outline in the Interlude, the shift in the fundamental attitudes toward musical time traced in the Bach and Mozart chapters did not occur suddenly within the few decades separating the two composers. Rather, both shifts extended over several centuries; they had long prehistories and afterlives that reverberate to this day. At most one can see the later eighteenth century as a time when the process of change accelerated. Hence the need for the retrospective glance of the Prelude and the prospective one of the Postlude.

The Prelude offers an interpretation of Monteverdi's *L'Orfeo*, a work that captures conflicting attitudes toward an early stage of emerging modernity. Suspicion as to the validity of the modern project, I point out there, predates 1914. From early on—from the beginning, really—modernity was shadowed by self-doubt and anxiety. These found early expression in the question that drove the quarrel of the ancients and moderns (the musical version of which quarrel has been raging since the middle of the sixteenth century): can we equal, let alone surpass, the cultural achievements of the ancients? Monteverdi's *L'Orfeo* was a vote of confidence for musical modernity. But it was a half-hearted sort of confidence, affirming the values of modern harmony only as a consolation prize for the early modern subject defeated in his quest for autonomy. Almost two centuries had to pass for modern self-confidence to grow sufficiently to allow us to imagine a successful quest for autonomy, an Orpheus who triumphs in life, as in Mozart's *The Magic Flute*, rather than in death.

The Postlude, in turn, shows to what extent this self-confidence, which culminates in *The Magic Flute*, was undermined as the Revolution failed to achieve its democratic goals. The traditional image of Beethoven as the tone poet of the heroic Revolutionary and Napoleonic history, while not false, is, I argue here, one-sided. The Beethovenian abstraction out of time is the obverse of the Beethovenian heroic quest and its temporal teleology. Music had no sooner acquired its "classical" ability to represent linear time than it began "romantically" to undermine and question it by exploring moments of timelessness. Similarly to Rousseau's writing, Beethoven's composition is torn between the ideal of engagement in the historical social world and the wish to disengage from it, to escape into the private refuge beyond or within. In Beethoven's Ninth Symphony the ideal of engagement in the historical social world of an emancipating autonomous humanity is nostalgically commemorated as an infinitely postponed utopia, thus transcending in a complex way the simple opposition of cyclical and linear time.

L'Orfeo, or the Anxiety of the Moderns

Oh! pour voir un moment, une seule fois, la nature divine,
complète, l'idéal enfin, je donnerais, toute ma fortune, mais j'irais
te chercher dans tes limbes, beauté céleste! Comme Orphée, je
descendrais dans l'enfer de l'art pour en ramener la vie.
—FRENHOFER IN BALZAC, "Le chef-d'oeuvre inconnu"

CHROMATICISM AND MONODY, the two main new musical means developed in the late sixteenth century by those who dreamed of bringing ancient music back to life, only rarely come together in Monteverdi's *L'Orfeo*, where, for the most part, the monody stays chastely diatonic. All the more pregnant are the moments when they do meet, and nowhere more so than at Eurydice's parting words, when, struck by Orpheus's unlawful glance, she is condemned to "go back to the shades of death" (Torn'a l'ombre di morte), one of the opera's most vividly realized moments. "Ah, too sweet a sight, and too bitter . . ." (Ahi vista troppo dolce e troppo amara . . .), she says (Example 1), making no distinction between the sight in front of her eyes and that in front of his, and her melodic line just manages to hold to the diatonic outline of the G-Dorian frame.[1] But it is a struggle, and she almost loses grip at the caesura (at the word "dolce"), where her chromatic passing g♯' is supported by the equally chromatic upper-neighbor e♮ in the bass. (The fluidity of the sixth scale step is characteristic of Dorian mode at this time, but in the context one tends to hear the e♭ as the diatonic step. Regardless, the choice of the "hard" version of the step for "dolce" and of the "soft" one for "amara" compounds the verbal oxymoron with a musical one.) The same g♯' against e♮ threatens again to dissolve the diatonic modal frame at "misera," as Eurydice turns her attention now unambiguously to herself (it is hard to undermine the modal stability more profoundly than by inflecting the final), and again it is with great effort that she regains her grip on the frame, resting first on the fifth scale step as she names what she is about to lose, "vita," and then on the first as she names what is even more precious to her than life, her "consorte." Orpheus sees her obscured by a shadow ("but what eclipse, alas, obscures you?" [Ma qual Eclissi oime v'oscura?]), and as

EXAMPLE 1. Claudio Monteverdi and Alessandro Striggio, *L'Orfeo*, Act 4, Eurydice's "Ahi vista troppo dolce e troppo amara"; with analytic sketch

her body evaporates into a cold shade, the musical coherence of her diction, too, threatens to dissolve, going in and out of tonal focus.

The monodist learned from the madrigalist: one of the most common ways of introducing chromatic progressions in the madrigal was to juxtapose two triads a minor third apart, with both triads, or at least the lower one, being major. In the *chiaroscuro* of modal clarity overshadowed by chromaticism Monteverdi found the aural equivalent of Annibale Carracci's representation, ca. 1600, of the scene in the fresco medallion of the Farnese Gallery depicting the firm outline of a female body beginning to be transformed into rising mist (Figure 3), or of Bernini's 1624 *Apollo and Daphne* in the Borghese Gallery, where the female body transmutes into the bark of a laurel tree (Figure 4).

I am mixing my myths deliberately here. Two stories dominate the first decade or so of opera history: the story of Orpheus and Eurydice told by the Florentine poet Rinuccini and performed in Florence with music mostly by Peri in 1600, and with music by Caccini in 1602 (the same story in a version told by the Mantuan poet Striggio was performed with Monteverdi's music in Mantua in 1607); and the story of Apollo and Daphne, again told by Rinuccini and performed with music by Peri and Corsi, now mostly lost, in Florence in 1598, and with music by the Florentine composer Marco da Gagliano in Mantua in 1608.

The story Monteverdi set was well known to his audience from the fourth book of Virgil's *Georgics* and the tenth and eleventh books of Ovid's *Metamorphoses*.[2] The poet-musician Orpheus, a son of the sun-god Apollo and a Muse, perhaps Calliope, and an artist so effective that he "drew by his singing wild beasts" (trasse al suo cantar le fere), has no sooner won the heart of the nymph Eurydice and, surrounded by singing and dancing nymphs and shepherds, begun to celebrate their wedding than he learns of the sudden death of his bride. Armed with his "golden lyre" (aurea cetra), Orpheus descends to the underworld, puts to sleep with his "beautiful song" (bel canto) the "mighty spirit" (possente spirito) guarding the entrance (a somewhat ambiguous feat for a singer, this), and enters the Dantean "city of sorrow" (città dolente) in search of "one glance" (un . . . sguardo) of the "serene eyes" (luci serene) of his beloved. There he arouses the pity of Proserpine, who pleads with Pluto to allow Orpheus to bring Eurydice back to the living, provided he refrain from casting "a single glance" (un solo sguardo) at her before they reach the exit. But Orpheus's exaltation of his "omnipotent lyre" (cetra onnipotente) is premature. The temptation to see "the sweet light of the beloved pupils" (de l'amate pupille il dolce lume) proves too strong; he turns around and sees the "sweetest eyes" (dolcissimi lumi). Eurydice is lost "through too much love" (per troppo amor), or, as the Chorus of Spirits explains, because "Orpheus conquered hell and then was conquered by his emotions" (Orfeo vinse l'inferno e vinto poi/Fu da gl'affetti suoi), whereas "worthy of eternal glory is only he who will have victory over himself" (degno d'eterna gloria/Sia sol colui ch'avrà di se vittoria).

FIGURE 3. Annibale Carracci, *Orpheus and Eurydice,* ca. 1600. Farnese Palace, Rome. Photo: G. Schiavinotto, Edizioni dell'Elefante.

Orpheus returns alone to the now deserted scene of his wedding, where only Echo hears his solitary laments. Nymphs and shepherds dance no more, as Orpheus dedicates his "lyre and song" (la mia cetra e 'l canto) to the shade of his departed wife.[3] Eurydice was the only woman worthy of praise, he declares, and never again will love pierce his heart.

FIGURE 4. Gianlorenzo Bernini, *Apollo and Daphne*, 1622–24. Galleria Borghese, Rome. Photo: Alinari/Art Resource, N.Y.

The story has not one ending but two. According to Striggio's printed libretto, which the audience at the première had in their hands and which thus probably represents what they saw and heard, Orpheus managed to escape, at least temporarily, the Bacchantes whom he had enraged with his misogyny.[4] In 1480 an earlier Mantuan Orpheus, that of Poliziano (well known to Striggio, as Barbara Hanning and Nino Pirrotta, among others, have demonstrated), was not so lucky: the Bacchantes caught and dismembered him.[5] On that earlier occasion the final Bacchanal on stage (to be followed by a court ball) served as a transition back to the heterosexual order threatened by Orpheus's misogyny. Silke Leopold has suggested that Striggio might have had something similar in mind, as his *favola* was presented in the Carnival season,[6] but a ball to follow the Bacchanal seems unlikely, given the exclusively male academic audience for whom the 24 February 1607 première was intended (complementing the almost certainly all-male cast) and the constricted performance quarters (the "narrow stage" [angusta Scena] that Monteverdi mentions in the dedicatory letter of the first edition).[7] No matter: by giving the last word to the Bacchantes, Striggio, no less than Poliziano, provided a corrective to his hero's male self-sufficiency.

Lest it seem I have succumbed to the academic fashion of outing famous musicians, I should point out that viewing the bereaved Orpheus as a threat to heterosexuality had some currency in Renaissance thought.[8] When Poliziano staged his *Favola d'Orfeo* in Mantua in 1480 he found there, in the *Camera Picta* of Castello di San Giorgio, three scenes from the myth of Orpheus painted by Mantegna by 1474, among them the scene of Orpheus killed by the Maenads (Figure 5). (Mantegna was the only great Italian painter of the fifteenth century to be interested in the myth.)[9] It is also very likely that Mantegna chose the subject of Orpheus's being beaten and killed by the women of Thrace for an engraving or drawing. This image no longer exists, but we have an idea of what it was like from an anonymous North Italian engraving generally considered to be derived from it (Figure 6). This engraving, in turn, is closely related to the celebrated drawing of 1494 by Dürer, likewise known to have been derived from the Mantegna (Figure 7). (Both the Dürer drawing and the North Italian engraving were the subject of a small but characteristically wide-ranging and thought-provoking 1906 study by Aby Warburg, who linked them to Poliziano's play and demonstrated that their "pathetic formulae," a key Warburg concept, depended on ancient representations of the scene.)[10] A running boy in the Mantegna— and other images derived from it—is there to remind us of Orpheus's rejection of the love of women. And in case we miss the point, Dürer adds a scroll with the inscription "Orfeuss der Erst puseran" (Orpheus the first homosexual [or pederast]).[11] But this as an aside only: it is not my aim here to fill gaps in ongoing research into the construction of gender in Monteverdi's operas.[12]

Monteverdi's published score of 1609, in any case, provided an alternative ending.[13] Here Orpheus's father, Apollo, descends in a cloud, advising

FIGURE 5. Andrea Mantegna, *Orpheus Killed by the Bacchantes*, ca. 1470–74. Camera Picta, Castello di San Giorgio, Mantua. Photo: Quattrone.

his son not to be a slave to his passions ("it is not, it is not the advice of a generous breast to serve one's own passion" [Non è non è consiglio / Di generoso petto / Servir al proprio affetto]); he then bestows immortality on him and promises that in heaven he will contemplate the "resemblances" (sembianze) of "the sweet rays" (i dolci rai) of his beloved in the sun and stars. The whole point of music, after all, as her allegorical figure in the Prologue herself had explained, was to "attract . . . souls to the sonorous harmony of heaven's lyre" (à l'armonia sonora / De la lira del ciel . . . l'alme invoglio).[14] (Orpheus's lyre, Gaffurio tells us, was the image of the "heaven's lyre," of the harmony of the spheres, with each of its seven strings standing for one of the seven planets.[15] Indeed, the ancients thought that the lyre, invented by Hermes and given by him to Apollo, from whom it passed on to Orpheus, was after the latter's death placed by Zeus among the constellations.)[16] A double ascension, followed by nymphs and shepherds singing and dancing again, ends Monteverdi's opera: "Thus goes he who does not recoil at the call of an immortal god, thus obtains grace in heaven he who here below tested hell" (Cosi và chi non s'arretra / Al chiamar di Nume eterno / Cosi gratia in ciel impetra / Che qua giù provò l'inferno).[17]

Rinuccini gave his *Euridice* a *fine* even more *lieto* than this, since he al-

FIGURE 6. Anonymous North Italian artist, *The Death of Orpheus*, ca. 1480. Hamburger Kunsthalle, Hamburg. Photo: Bildarchiv Preussischer Kulturbesitz/Art Resource, N.Y.

lowed his Orpheus to leave the underworld with his wife—appropriately so, given that the drama was a contribution to the celebrations accompanying the wedding of Maria de' Medici to Henri IV of France.[18] (No one seriously doubts, by the way, that the Rinuccini-Peri version of the story was known to both Striggio and Monteverdi.)[19] Less unambiguously happy was the ending of Rinuccini's *Dafne*, where Apollo, smitten by love for the chaste nymph Daphne is left empty-handed, or worse, embracing rough bark, after she flees his advances by getting herself metamorphosed into a laurel tree.[20] All Apollo can do at the end is to render himself a service similar to the one we have seen him offering his son and to transform the erotic fiasco into a poetic triumph. Daphne's tree will be forever green, immortality of sorts, and crowns made of its branches and leaves will be worn as a sign of honor. Apollo himself will wear one, thus unmistakably identifying himself as a poet to an audience whose cultural memory included Petrarch's being crowned with laurel on the Capitol in 1341, as well as numerous representations of their most famous poets so crowned. (In the Preface to his setting of *Dafne*, Marco da Gagliano wrote of the figure of Ovid, who in Rinuccini's drama is the Prologue personified: "His dress must be suitable for a poet, with a laurel wreath on his head, a lyre by his side, and the bow

FIGURE 7. Albrecht Dürer, *The Death of Orpheus*, 1494. Hamburger Kunsthalle, Hamburg. Photo: Bildarchiv Preussischer Kulturbesitz/Art Resource, N.Y. Photo: Christoph Irrgang.

in his hand." The composer then specified the same attributes for Apollo
and gave detailed instructions on how in the final lament Apollo should
crown himself with laurel.)[21]

It has often been observed that the central figures of the early Florentine
and Mantuan operas, Orpheus and Apollo, were musicians, or poet-musicians.
It has even been suggested, by Pirrotta and others, that musicians were chosen to justify the novelty of an entire play's being sung, rather than spoken, on stage.[22] This, however, could not have been the only, or even the main,
reason for the choice: verisimilitude in representing the stories would be the
least of one's worries if the stories themselves were of people going in and
out of hell, ascending to heaven, or being translated into trees. Whatever motivated the choice of these particular early operatic heroes, the effect of the
choice is obvious: a poet-musician as the central figure of the new poetic-
musical genre ensures that the early operas are intensely self-reflexive. They
are meditations on the dilemmas faced by poet-musicians in general and on
the opportunities and perils of the new genre in particular.

What has not often been observed is that the two myths have more than
their hero type in common. Both heroes suffer the same kind of misfortune:
neither can attain the nymph who is the object of his desire. Moreover, they
both fail in a similar way, at the moment of near-consummation. The same
sort of catastrophe occurs in both stories: just as the hero is about to embrace
his nymph, she turns into something utterly unembraceable. (Orpheus even
has to suffer this kind of fiasco twice, as if his wedding day were a rehearsal
for the definitive failure at the exit from Hades.) And both heroes are similarly consoled at the end—consoled not on earth, but in heaven. Orpheus is
offered immortality and contemplation of the eternal "resemblance" of celestial bodies to his beloved's eyes. Apollo, himself already immortal, is consoled by the contemplation of the eternally green laurel tree.

What is the significance of this particular figure—that of a failed lover
on earth consoled by the artist's immortality in heaven—at the center of
early opera? Dazzled by the final apotheosis, some commentators like to
speak of *L'Orfeo* as celebrating the triumph of music.[23] If this seems excessive, it is not only because Orpheus's apotheosis and Neoplatonic escape
from earthly passion are not really a reward for his musicianship at all.[24] It
is also because the heavy price paid for triumph is conveniently forgotten.
What sort of a triumph is it that kills the beloved and renders the lover unfit
for life on earth? Likewise unconvincing is the opinion of devotees of a more
suspicious hermeneutics who find Monteverdi's revised ending entirely hol-
low, a shallow, pragmatic compromise, with courtly conventions perhaps.[25]
These commentators remember Orpheus's failure to bring Eurydice out of

Hades and see in his final apotheosis nothing but a spurious cover-up. Presumably they would find Orpheus's dismemberment, on or off stage, more to their taste, offering truth in the place of starry-eyed consolatory illusions.

We have, then, two ways of reading the story. We may choose to emphasize Orpheus the lover, in which case his is a story of unmitigated disaster and Monteverdi's ending incongruous—or worse, mendacious. Or we may concentrate on Orpheus the poet-musician, in which case Monteverdi's ending is credible, or at any rate not incongruous, especially if we keep in mind that it does not commit us to overlooking the price the hero pays for his apotheosis. (And how could we overlook the price? Thoughts of immortality can never be extricated from thoughts of death. Not only because, finite beings that we are, we would not bother with immortality if it were not for death. More crucially, for us, death is the presupposition of immortality.) The latter reading offers the advantage of being consistent with the charitable and courteous hermeneutic principle that encourages us to declare a text corrupt or incoherent only when all else fails; in this particular case the advantage is that it allows us to take Monteverdi's ending seriously.

It is also a considerably less literal, more allegorical, reading. If Orpheus-Apollo is the creative artist, the nymph he pursues must be more than just an object of erotic desire; she must be the figure of artistic vision itself. This reading conceives the tragedy of Orpheus-Apollo as more than an amorous misadventure, framing it as the tragedy of an artist who comes close to capturing the vision he pursues, only to see it slip through his fingers at the instant of realization. Unable to capture his vision fully in the here and now, his consolation is a double immortality: his and that of his vision in the eternal beyond, where his vision is made permanent, like an evergreen tree, or like celestial bodies, and where he can expect the immortality of fame. (Note that in the dedicatory letter to the first edition of the score, Monteverdi expressed the hope that his opera "may be as durable as humankind" [che sia per esser durabile al pari dell'humana generatione].)[26]

We would have, then, in *L'Orfeo*, an allegory of the inherently tragic situation of the artist, an instance of an understanding of the artist's situation that was natural, inevitable even, given the generalized idealism of Platonist inspiration that, as Erwin Panofsky has demonstrated, dominated early modern art theory.[27] If the true object of the work of art was the Idea in the mind of the artist, a slippage was bound to occur at the moment of realization, just when the purely mental was about to be embodied, because the real was not likely to live up to the perfection of the ideal.

This tragic vision of the artist's situation was destined for a long life in the modern period. It is still present as late as 1955 in Maurice Blanchot's essay "The Gaze of Orpheus," a reading of the myth through the prism of concepts and images derived from German metaphysics, from Hegel, Schopenhauer, and Heidegger. "The act of writing begins with Orpheus's gaze," Blanchot proposes. For Orpheus,

> Eurydice is the limit of what art can attain; . . . she is the profoundly dark point towards which art, desire, death, and the night all seem to lead. . . . His *work* is to bring it [this "point"] back into the daylight and in the daylight give it form, figure and reality. Orpheus can do anything except look this "point" in the face, look at the center of the night in the night. . . . He can draw it upwards, but only by keeping his back turned to it. . . . this is the meaning of the concealment revealed in the night. But in the impulse of his migration Orpheus forgets the work he has to accomplish, and he has to forget it, because the ultimate requirement of his impulse is not that there should be a work, but that someone should stand and face this "point" and grasp its essence where this essence appears.

Blanchot goes on to spell out the point of story explicitly: "The Greek myth says: one cannot create a work unless the enormous experience of the depths . . . is not pursued for its own sake." But the artist's pursuit of the vision, the metaphysical insight, the pursuit that is the condition of his art, is also a guarantee of his inevitable failure: "The work is everything to Orpheus, everything except that desired gaze in which the work is lost, so that it is also only in this gaze that the work can go beyond itself, unite with its origin and establish itself in impossibility."[28]

The myth's longevity should not surprise us. Orpheus's story stays remarkably close to our everyday experience of loss, be it loss of a loved one to death, or, more generally, loss of anything that once mattered to us but has since drowned in the incessant flow of time. A deceased parent may appear to us in a dream, a once intense experience may unexpectedly resurface in memory, but, no matter how much we cherish such moments, they are also inherently frustrating and unsatisfactory; there is always something "more" that eludes us. In such moments we are all "artists" vainly attempting to capture and give permanence to an irretrievable phantom.

Stripped of its original mythical-allegorical clothing, this understanding of the artist's situation was given particularly compelling form by Proust in his description of the death of Bergotte, one of the key set pieces of his novel.[29] On 24 May 1921, one of the last occasions he left his home, Proust, mortally ill, visited a Jeu de Paume exhibition of Dutch paintings that included Vermeer's *View of Delft,* on loan from The Hague.[30] The visit prompted him to imagine the death of his own Orpheus. Bergotte, the great and celebrated writer, long reclusive and gravely ill, old and tired, reads in a newspaper that "a little patch of yellow wall" in the Vermeer, then on exhibit in Paris, "was so well painted that it was, if one looked at it by itself, like some priceless specimen of Chinese art, of a beauty that was sufficient in itself." Not being able to recall the spot in "a picture which he [like Proust] adored and imagined that he knew by heart," Bergotte drags himself to the exhibition and, indeed, notices for the first time "the precious substance of the tiny patch of yellow wall." Subject to attacks of giddiness, "he fixed his eyes, like a child upon a yellow butterfly which it is trying to catch, upon the precious little patch of wall. 'That is how I ought to have written,' he said. 'My last books are too dry, I ought to have gone over them with several coats of paint, made my language exquisite in itself, like this little patch of yellow wall.'" Unsure whether he is dying or suffering from a simple indigestion, "he repeated to himself: 'Little patch of yellow wall, with a sloping roof, little patch of yellow wall,'" just as the fatal stroke overtakes him.[31]

It is said that after Orpheus was dismembered by the Bacchantes, his severed head floated down the river Hebrus still repeating Eurydice's name. The modern Orpheus dies murmuring the name of the vision of artistic perfection long pursued but ultimately as elusive as a yellow Nabokovian butterfly. Like Monteverdi, Proust's narrator reflects on the consoling double immortality of the artist and his vision, beginning a long meditation that is the late modern secular version of the Platonist artistic ideology and from which I select only a few key thoughts:

> Everything is arranged in this life as though we entered it carrying the burden of obligations contracted in a former life; there is no reason inherent in the conditions of life on this earth that can . . . make the talented artist consider himself obliged to begin over again a score of times a piece of work the admiration aroused by which will matter little to his body devoured by worms. . . . All these obligations . . . seem to belong to a different world . . . of those unknown laws which we have obeyed because we bore their precepts in our hearts . . . —those laws to which every profound work of the intellect brings us nearer.

The one form of "resurrection" conceivable to Proust's narrator is the Horatian one whereby "among future generations, the works of men . . . shine." Lights shining in the night promise permanence to both artists. In heaven's shining stars Orpheus is allowed to contemplate the resemblance to Eurydice's eyes. As for Bergotte, Proust's parting image must bring a gasp of recognition to anyone who has seen how Parisian booksellers like to arrange individual titles in their shop windows in groups of three, the central copy showing its spine and the two flanking ones displaying the front cover: "They buried him, but all through the night of mourning, in the lighted windows, his books arranged three by three kept watch like angels with outspread wings and seemed, for him who was no more, the symbol of his resurrection."[32]

———

Explicit self-interpretation of the sort provided by the story of the death of Bergotte is, of course, absent from Monteverdi's ending of the story of Orpheus. A direct confirmation of my interpretation is not likely to be found, but an indirect one is not difficult to imagine. One need only consider how the stories of Orpheus and Eurydice, of Apollo and Daphne, were understood in the tradition within which the authors of early operas worked. Historians of art and literature confirm what the preceding leads us to suspect: first, that in Renaissance Italy the two myths were often treated as practically interchangeable; second, that Orpheus-Apollo, the poet, or poet-musician, was the figure of the creative artist at his most sublime and noble; and third, that Eurydice occasionally transcended her role of the love object to become a figure of wisdom or art pursued by the artist.[33]

Orpheus's career in Renaissance Italy began where it ended, in Florence and Mantua in the 1460s and 1470s. In Florence, Marsilio Ficino cast Orpheus in the role of the philosopher-poet to be imitated and identified with. In Mantua, Mantegna inaugurated Orpheus's Renaissance pictorial career as the figure of the creative artist, and Poliziano gave this figure a poetic-dramatic life and put it on stage. But while artists between 1470 and 1520 liked to visualize Orpheus as playing to the animals in serene harmony with nature, an image still recalled in *The Magic Flute*, Giorgione in Venice simultaneously developed a more tragic picture of Orpheus, one centered on his loss of Eurydice.[34] Giorgione's painting is lost, but a seventeenth-century copy by David Teniers (Figure 8) reveals that it was dominated by a portrait of the artist (quite possibly a self-portrait),[35] his instrument in hand and crowned like Apollo with laurel, tortured by the remembrance of the fatal moonlit moment at the gates of Hades shown in the background, with Orpheus at the extreme right turning toward a spectrally white Eurydice shadowed by an infernal spirit or Hermes.[36] More than anything else it is this lost image of Giorgione that marks the birth of the allegory of the inherently tragic situation of the artist of which *L'Orfeo* is a later instance.

It would be interesting to know how Giorgione interpreted the myth of Apollo and Daphne, but, although we know that he did represent the subject,

FIGURE 8. David Teniers the Younger, after Giorgione, *Self-Portrait as Orpheus*, ca. 1640. Suida-Manning Collection, New York.

FIGURE 9. Dosso Dossi, *Apollo*, ca. 1524. Galleria Borghese, Rome. Photo: Scala/Art Resource, N.Y.

neither the painting nor a copy or description survives.[37] We are, however, amply compensated with the great *Apollo* by Giorgione's Ferrarese admirer Dosso Dossi, an obviously closely related sublime image of the artist showing the tragic moment of loss in the background (Figure 9). Here the passionate musician identifies so closely with the figure of his art that the gesture of his right hand, prolonged by a wooden bow, echoes the gesture of Daphne's hands turning into wooden branches.

The early operas do more, however, than merely repeat the interpretations of Giorgione and Dosso in a different medium. For Rinuccini, Striggio, and the composers who set their texts, Daphne and Eurydice were bound to stand for something more specific than art in general. Early opera was the principal fruit of a half century of intense speculation on the nature of ancient music and the effort to bring ancient music and its fabled power over the emotions back to life. Elsewhere I have characterized these speculations and efforts as resulting in nothing less than the early modern paradigm shift, whereby both aims and means of musical practice were transformed.[38] Let me briefly recall the main components of this revolution, beginning with the aims.

The post-1550 shift consisted in the increased prominence and practical relevance accorded the ancient idea that music could make humans feel various changeable passions and thus form a person's enduring character (*ethos*)—this as an alternative and challenge to the previously dominant and equally ancient idea of music as the sounding, sensuous embodiment of the intelligible harmony of simple numerical ratios (*harmonia*). By 1550 it was increasingly believed that the latter aim had been fully accomplished by early sixteenth-century Franco-Flemish vocal polyphony, the *ars perfecta*, "to which nothing could be added" (as Glarean put it), and codified by Gioseffo Zarlino in his *Le Istitutioni harmoniche* of 1558. The more adventurous musicians—such as Nicola Vicentino, who initiated the musical version of the quarrel of the ancients and moderns in *L'antica musica ridotta alla moderna prattica* (1555), and above all Vinzenzo Galilei in *Dialogo della musica antica, et della moderna* (1581)—those musicians humanistically inspired by the growing understanding of ancient music and its role in ancient tragic theater, now began to turn their attention toward ever more vivid representation of the passions of the singing subject. Thus by the first decade of the seventeenth century the Monteverdi brothers could famously (in declarations accompanying Claudio's *Il quinto libro de madrigali a cinque voci* of 1605 and *Scherzi musicali* of 1607) speak of not one but two competing practices: the first being the harmonic one, conservatively aimed at embodying in sound the immutable eternal intelligible order obtaining in the universe God had created; and the second being the mimetic one, progressively devising novel ways of representing the passions of the singing characters, and subordinating even harmony to this aim. (It is a noteworthy, and potentially confusing, feature of this contrast that the more conservative first practice was nevertheless understood as characteristic of the "moderns," since it made use of musical means—polyphony, counterpoint—thought to have been unknown to the ancients, whereas the progressive second practice, which proposed to revive not only the aims but also the means attributed to ancient music, was the practice of the new "ancients.") The most important difference between the two competing ideas of music was that in the mimetic conception language was an essential component of music, which consisted, as Plato taught, of *harmonia, rhythmos,* and *logos,* whereby harmony and rhythm were subservient to the words that in specifying the represented passions justified the harmonic-rhythmic means; in the harmonic conception, by contrast, music consisted of *harmonia* alone (or at most, of *harmonia* and *rhythmos*), and language was an accidental attribute, not needed to justify the autonomous abstract logic of sound relations.

The shift in music's aims, the emergence of a plurality of aims, could not but have an impact on the means by which these aims were realized. In two areas, in particular, theorists, working side by side with composers and occasionally even ahead of them, took an active and creative role in developing new musical means while trying to breathe new life into ones thought to be ancient. One such area was that of radical chromaticism. For Vicentino, the most prominent early advocate of the subordination of harmony to passions, the best hope for recapturing the miraculous ethical power of ancient music was to go beyond the confines of the diatonic system, and this not so much because non-diatonic resources were used by ancient musicians as because they were not used by modern ones and thus were fresh and able to produce strong effects.

The other area of theoretical invention and initiative was monody. As in the case of non-diatonicism, turning away from Netherlandish polyphony was advocated by some late sixteenth-century Italians in the spirit of a humanistic revival of ancient music and its ethical force. In a 1572 letter to Galilei, Girolamo Mei affirmed that the aim of ancient musicians "was not the sweetness of the consonances to satisfy the ear (since there is no testimony nor any evidence by the authors about the use of these in their singing) but the complete and efficacious expression of everything he wanted to make understood . . . by means and through the aid of high and low sounds . . . accompanied with the regulated temperament of the fast and slow."[39] Inspired by Mei, Galilei and his Florentine Camerata friends concluded that if modern vocal music were to abandon the aim of sensuous pleasure for the higher one of ethical efficacy, it had also to abandon polyphony for monophony. Passions were represented in a melody by appropriately chosen vocal range and rhythm and tempo. Polyphony not only made words difficult to follow but, worse, it set the same words in contradictory fashion, giving them different ranges and rhythms in different voices.

In the late discourses appended to his counterpoint treatise, Galilei modified somewhat this radically anti-polyphonic stance and began to advocate supporting vocal melody with the accompaniment of instrumental consonant harmonies whose highest line doubled the melody. It was not just, he now conceded, that instrumental consonances pleased the ear but that "the musician, with variety of intervals and in particular of consonances, communicates to the intellect all the passions of the soul, especially shaped appropriately by the text."[40]

Ideas of this sort resulted in viable new styles and genres of composition. Their permanent legacy was to provide even the most ambitious art music with a textural alternative to the classical equal-voiced polyphony of the high Renaissance, an alternative that assumed a functional differentiation between the soprano melody and the supporting chordal accompaniment as well as polarization of the soprano and bass parts. Thus the plurality of practices—the most important achievement of the period—involved not only a plurality of aims but also a corresponding plurality of means and, not the least among them, a plurality of textures.

Central among the many and complex reasons for the early modern paradigm shift was undoubtedly the desire to revive the reputed ethical power of ancient music. As was programmatically stated by the title of the treatise that inaugurated the whole process, "ancient music" was to be "brought back to modern practice" (*L'antica musica ridotta alla moderna prattica*), brought back by modern musicians from the oblivion, as Eurydice was to be brought back by Orpheus. To take the self-reflexive character of the early Florentine-Mantuan opera seriously is to recognize not only the figure of the modern poet-musician in Orpheus and Apollo but also the figure of ancient music, ardently pursued for the past half century, in Eurydice and Daphne. In this reading, early operas allegorize and dramatize their own birth, or, more generally, dramatize the efforts to bring back the passionate-ethical aims and various means—dissonant, figurative, chromatic, above all, monodic—of ancient music.

—

The fact that allegorical readings of such figures were not unknown in Renaissance culture, and may even be found in Monteverdi's proximity, validates this approach. One example comes from the Florentine Neoplatonic circles that played a central role in the prehistory of efforts to bring back the aims and means of ancient music, as well as in the prehistory of *L'Orfeo*. From the start Ficino associated Orpheus with the idea of recovering ancient music. In his *Vita Marsilii Ficini* Giovanni Corsi reported: "He set the hymns of Orpheus and they say that he sang them with wonderful sweetness to the lyre in the ancient manner." Poliziano, a fellow Florentine Neoplatonist, explained the significance of this early monodic singing when he claimed that Ficino's lyre, "far more fortunate than the lyre of Thracian Orpheus, has called back from the underworld the true . . . Eurydice, that is, . . . Platonic wisdom."[41]

Another example comes from Rubens, Monteverdi's fellow artist and, from about 1600 to 1608, his colleague at the Gonzaga court. The painter's knowledge of classical culture was exceptional, even for his time. The erudite French scholar Nicolas-Claude Fabri de Peiresc wrote in a 1622 letter that "in matters of antiquity principally, Rubens' knowledge was the most universal and remarkable" he had ever seen.[42] When in 1636–1637 he sketched the decorations for La Torre della Parada, the royal hunting lodge near Madrid, the painter included among many other subjects episodes from both the story of Apollo and Daphne (now at the Musée Bonnat in Bayonne) and that of Orpheus and Eurydice (now at the Kunsthaus in Zurich).[43] We learn what such stories meant to him from a letter of 1 August 1637 to Francis Junius, the librarian to Thomas Howard, Earl of Arundel, acknowledging the receipt of Junius's recently published book on ancient painting, *De Pictura Veterum* (Amsterdam, 1637), which he highly praised.[44] "This book of yours," Rubens wrote, "is truly a rich storehouse of all the examples, opinions, and precepts which, relating to the dignity and honor of the art of painting, scattered everywhere in ancient writings, have been preserved to our day." He continued:

> But since those examples of the ancient painters can now be followed only in the imagination, . . . I wish that some such treatise on the paintings of the Italian masters might be carried out with similar care. For examples or models of their work are publicly exhibited even today. . . . Those things which are perceived by the senses produce a sharper and more durable impression, require a closer examination, and afford a richer material for study than those which present themselves to us only in the imagination, like dreams, or so obscured by words that we

try in vain to grasp them (as Orpheus the shade of Eurydice), but which often elude us and thwart our hopes. We can say this from experience; for how few among us, in attempting to present in visual terms some famous work of Apelles or Timanthes which is graphically described by Pliny or by other authors, will not produce something that is insulting or alien to the dignity of the ancients?

Not only does Rubens implicitly conflate here the Eurydice and Daphne myths; more important, he explicitly casts Eurydice in the role of the ancient painting forever escaping the grasp of the modern artist. And, incidentally, he affirms, slyly, the worth and dignity of modern painting even while professing, sincerely, no doubt, his veneration for that of ancient times.

In short, if they can serve as figures of ancient wisdom or ancient painting ardently pursued by the modern philosopher or artist, our nymphs can certainly also stand for the ancient music that modern musicians have, for decades now, attempted to capture and bring back.

—

And this is where the "anxiety" of the Prelude title comes in. More is at stake in early opera than the generalized anxiety of the Platonizing artist who fears that the ideal vision will forever, like Daphne or Eurydice, slip from his grasp. The operas also dramatize the anxiety of the early moderns in their relationship to the ancients, the fear that the project of bringing back ancient music may be somehow not viable, doomed for reasons akin to those that would lead Rubens to consider the project of bringing back ancient painting to be doomed. Unlike ancient architecture, sculpture, and letters, ancient painting and music did not leave enough traces to make any project of reconstruction secure. A musical "rebirth," a renaissance, would forever have to remain questionable in a way that went beyond the worries expressed in the literary "quarrel of the ancients and the moderns," beyond the anxiety of the early moderns as to whether their literary achievements could withstand comparison with those of the ancients. Moreover, musicians had to worry about whether they really knew with what to compare their achievements, since there were no actual monuments but only the shadows the monuments cast in ancient theoretical and philosophical discussions of music's emotionally potent aims and means. Like Eurydice behind Orpheus in the underworld, ancient music could not be perceived directly and seemed to melt into thin air under the scholar's glance. For a musician, *L'Orfeo* suggests, the comparison with the ancients, which was a central component of the early modern self-image and self-understanding, was particularly fraught and elusive. If early operas dramatize the effort to bring back ancient music, Eurydice's final recitative, a musical discourse on the verge of dissolving into incoherence and unintelligibility, makes audible how this effort unravels.

In his *The Legitimacy of the Modern World* Hans Blumenberg observed: "For the constitution of the modern age, it is not the Renaissance that is exemplary; on the contrary, it is the opposition encountered by the fundamental Renaissance thesis of the unsurpassability of ancient literature, from the seventeenth century onward."[45] Indeed, in the final analysis *L'Orfeo* leaves us with doubts as to the Renaissance thesis of the unsurpassability of ancient music. If Striggio's libretto called into question the confidence with which Vicentino announced the project of bringing back ancient music, Monteverdi's revised ending suggested a perspective from which the failure or near-failure of the project did not have to be seen as unsurpassable tragedy. If the ending does represent "the triumph of music," it is a triumph of the *prima* over the *seconda prattica,* that is, of modern over ancient music, of music understood as "nothing but harmony" (Zarlino's words) over music that subordinated harmony to the aim of expressing the passions of the speaking subject.

Already in the opera's Prologue, the allegorical figure of Music announces that, while she is capable of inspiring "the most frigid minds . . . now with noble anger and now with love" (le più gelate menti . . . hor di nobil' ira et hor d'Amore), her real, ultimate point is to "attract . . . souls to the sonorous harmony of heaven's lyre" (à l'armonia sonora / De la lira del ciel . . . l'alme invoglio). This order of values is explicitly confirmed in Monteverdi's ending. At the end of Act 4 the Chorus of Spirits criticizes Orpheus for allowing himself to be "conquered . . . by his emotions" (vinto . . . dagl'affetti suoi). Now Apollo himself tells his son not to be a slave to his passions ("it is not, it is not the advice of a generous breast to serve one's own passion" [Non è non è consiglio / Di generoso petto / Servir al proprio affetto]), while Orpheus admits that the very same passions that the Music of the Prologue had boasted of being able to inspire, anger and love (the passions that in 1638 will be the subject of Monteverdi's *Madrigali guerrieri, et amorosi*), have brought him, "with extreme suffering, to a desperate end" (a disperato fine / Con estremo dolore).[46] For Orpheus, to ascend to heaven is to leave behind the life of mutable passions for the life of eternal harmony, the shifting quicksands of the *seconda* for the consoling stability of the *prima prattica.*

Note that neither the figure of Music in the Prologue nor Monteverdi at the end advocates taking shortcuts, bypassing passions altogether to go directly for harmony. They do not thereby repudiate the second practice but,

FIGURE 10. Giorgione, *Christ Carrying the Cross*, 1508–9. Scuola Grande di S. Rocco, Venice. Photo: Cameraphoto Arte, Venice/Art Resource, N.Y.

rather, accord it its proper place, as a necessary stage on the road to the final goal of heavenly harmony. Take another look at Giorgione's Orpheus. The anguished self-portrait of the artist bears remarkable similarity to the painter's *Christ Carrying the Cross* in the Scuola Grande di San Rocco (Figure 10).[47] The association of Orpheus with Christ was a commonplace already in late antiquity: the poet's descent to and return from hell was bound to be seen as a prefiguration of Christ's.[48] If Giorgione alludes to this tradition, it is to suggest that the poet's passion is as indispensable a price of his quest for beauty as Christ's suffering is of the salvation of mankind.[49] The Spirits, Apollo, Eurydice herself reproach Orpheus for his excess of passion: "Then thus you lose me through too much love?" (Cosi per troppo amor dunque mi perdi?), she asks at her second death.[50] (Similarly, Apollo kills his nymph through too much love.) But no one suggests that Orpheus might have earned his heavenly immortality without taking the *via dolorosa* of passion first. No one, surely not Monteverdi, would want to give up on the broadening of music's expressive range brought about by the second practice. Nonetheless, the final emphasis on, and confidence in, harmony as transcending passions is unmistakable. The story of *L'Orfeo* is the story of how early modern music overcame the anxiety crisis caused by the Renaissance obsession with the shade of *l'antica musica*.

All the same, the ultimate irony here is inescapable. If this denouement seemed, to an early seventeenth-century musician, an expression of his recovered confidence in the values of modern music, it is likely to strike us, rather, as showing loss of nerve. This is because we see clearly something that at the beginning of the seventeenth century could have been perceived only dimly, if at all. Schematically put (and this is the schema I plan to flesh out in this book), the main job of art before it became fully modern in the late eighteenth century was to give sensuous embodiment to the eternal—cosmic or divine—order and truth. Since that time, by contrast, the tendency has been to use art to proclaim human autonomy; for the moderns, for us, art is mainly a tool of self-affirmation. That is why to us Orpheus is bound to look like a Tamino, or a Walther, who failed. What Monteverdi might have experienced as a vote of confidence in the powers of modern harmony we are likely to experience as a defeat of the early modern subject in his quest for autonomy and self-affirmation.

PART I

Bach's Cycle

1   The Arrested Procession

Those who heard Bach lead performances of his St. Matthew Passion during Good Friday Vespers at St. Thomas's in Leipzig in 1727 (and later, in 1729, 1736, and perhaps around 1742) probably had a printed libretto available to them.[1] To be sure, this would have included neither the text of the gospel (Matthew 26–27) nor the words of the independent Lutheran chorales that Bach periodically interpolated into the evangelist's story. But it would have allowed listeners to follow the free poems that framed the story and occasionally punctuated it, as well as the chorale texts (and in the case of No. 30, "Ach, nun ist mein Jesus hin," at the beginning of Part 2, a verse from the Song of Solomon 6.1) that Bach had intertwined with the free poems to form a single dialogical whole.[2] No exemplar of such a libretto actually survives, but Carl Friedrich Zelter saw one from 1729 in Berlin a hundred years later, when his pupil Mendelssohn famously revived the work, and a libretto of this sort exists for Bach's Christmas Oratorio.[3] Moreover, we can get an idea of what the St. Matthew Passion libretto must have looked like from its 1729 Leipzig reprint in a five-volume collection of poetry by the Passion's librettist, the Leipzig writer Christian Friedrich Henrici, who published under the pen name Picander.[4]

In this reprint from two years after the première service—where Picander would have noticed that Bach opened his Passion with a concerted choral movement—the opening poem is labeled "Aria" and given a "Da Capo" direction at the end (Figure 11). Picander also gave the label "Choral" to the church hymn embedded in the aria (the first stanza of a 1531 song by Nikolaus Decius based on the Latin "Agnus Dei"), and he named the personages exchanging thoughts in the aria "Die Tochter Zion und die Gläubigen" (The Daughter Zion and the Faithful), marking their respective portions of the

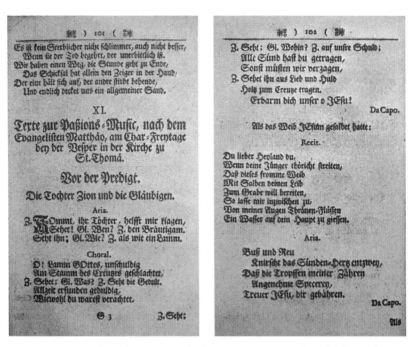

FIGURE 11. Picander [Christian Friedrich Henrici], *Ernst-Scherzhaffte und Satyrische Gedichte* (Leipzig, 1729), 2:101–2; facs. in Alfred Dürr, *Kritischer Bericht*, 73.

text with the abbreviations "Z." and "Gl." With these directives the poet invites composers of his text to set the opening movement as an aria for a female voice (or at any rate a voice of higher tessitura, since one assumes all public singers to have been male). Bach interpreted the invitation with some freedom, giving the words of the Daughter Zion not to a soloist but mostly to the first of his two four-part choirs (both choirs sing the last two lines of the B section, the first line of the da capo, and the Daughter's final response in the da capo) and not bothering to revise the singular "mir" (me) in the first line to a more appropriate plural "uns" (us). But he accepted the poet's suggestion that the Daughter's aria be accompanied by a choir of the Faithful—Bach gives the words of the Faithful to the second choir—and that another choir sing the chorale—Bach sets the chorale monophonically and gives it to a group of sopranists, labeling the autograph part for this group "Soprano in Ripieno."[5] Rather than singing in duet with her, the Faithful accompany the Daughter's aria. In their conversation she has the essential text, takes the initiative, exhorts them. They merely respond to her insistent orders ("Sehet!" [See!] or "Seht ihn!" [See Him!]) with short questions

("Wen?" [Whom?], "Wie?" [How?], "Was?" [What?], "Wohin?" [Where?]). In short, in Bach's setting of Picander's opening aria the first choir assumes the main role of the Daughter Zion, the second choir the accompanying role of the Faithful, and a separate group of sopranists sings the chorale. Bach blurs this generally clear distribution of roles toward the end of the setting (where the second choir joins the first in the role of the Daughter) and in the instrumental ritornelli, where the separate orchestras that accompany each choir play together, though not always in unison.

The libretto is informative (especially considering that the intended audience might have had access to it, too) because it provides information missing even in the autograph or a carefully edited score. Because the libretto establishes the two protagonists, Bach needed two separate vocal forces to set the opening number.[6] The libretto also clarifies why Bach gave the Daughter's text to a four-part choir rather than to a soloist. The Passion tells the story of the pivotal turning point of human history. From the start, therefore, the tone needs to be set high. The effect of epic monumentality that Bach undoubtedly sought to create here is not one that a solo, even one accompanied by a choir, could have provided. But does it then follow that allowing the Daughter to speak in the first person singular was an oversight? This is unlikely, for Bach elsewhere did not hesitate to revise the libretto when he thought necessary. In the opening number, for example, Picander's Aria is written in trochaic tetrameter, except for the last verse of the middle section; Picander shortens this to a trimeter ("Holz zum Kreuze tragen"), but Bach corrected it to regular tetrameter ("Holz zum Kreuze selber tragen").[7]

There is even stronger evidence that Bach's decision not to change the Daughter's "mir" to "uns" was deliberate. The opening number is not the only one in which the Daughter Zion and the Faithful appear in Picander's Passion. They reappear, with the Daughter now called simply "Zion," at the end of Part 1 (marked "Vor der Predigt" [before the sermon] in the libretto); at the beginning and end of Part 2 ("Nach der Predigt" [after the sermon]); and once within each Part, for a recitative-aria pair. The numbers are as follows:

1. "Kommt, ihr Töchter, helft mir klagen"

19. "O Schmerz! hier zittert das gequälte Herz"

20. "Ich will bei meinem Jesu wachen"

27a. "So ist mein Jesus nun gefangen"

27b. "Sind Blitze, sind Donner in Wolken verschwunden"

30. "Ach, nun ist mein Jesus hin"

59. "Ach Golgatha"

60. "Sehet, Jesus hat die Hand"

67. "Nun ist der Herr zur Ruh gebracht"

68. "Wir setzen uns mit Tränen nieder"

Nos. 19–20 are a recitative and aria for the tenor of the first choir as Zion, accompanied by the second choir as the Faithful. No. 27a is an aria for the soprano and alto of the first choir as Zion, accompanied by the second choir as the Faithful. This is followed in No. 27b by the two choirs singing together (though not always in unison) the text that Picander seems to give to both the Daughter and the Faithful: in the libretto, No. 27a is labeled "Aria à 1," and the words of the two protagonists are marked, as before, "Z." and "Gl."; No. 27b is marked simply "à 2" without any indication of who speaks the text, which suggests that whereas No. 27a is primarily Zion's aria, with the Faithful providing the customary accompaniment, the essential text in No. 27b is to be spoken by both protagonists. No. 30 is an aria for the alto of the first choir as Zion, accompanied by the second choir as the Faithful. (Originally Bach must have planned to give Zion's part to the bass rather than the alto: this is done in Altnickol's copy of the early version of the score and in the first twenty-eight measures, subsequently corrected, of the autograph score that preserves the revised version.) Nos. 59–60 are a recitative and aria for the alto of the first choir as Zion, accompanied (in the aria only) by the second choir as the Faithful. No. 67 is a recitative for the bass, tenor, alto, and soprano of the first choir, taking Zion's words in turn and accompanied by the second choir as the Faithful. No. 68 is an "Aria Tutti," as the libretto labels it, for both choirs singing the same text together, though again not always in unison. The libretto's "tutti" suggests that whereas usually Zion and the Faithful are given separate words in a dialogue, here at the end of Part 2, as in No. 27b at the end of Picander's Part 1, they join in speaking the same text.

Apart from the endings of Picander's two Parts (Nos. 27b and 68), which Bach set for both choirs singing the same text together (though not always in unison), he retains the distribution of roles established in No. 1. Zion always has the principal text and is always impersonated by singers of the first choir, though not always by all four voices singing together, as they do in No. 1. Rather, her words are given to a single voice—to the tenor in Nos. 19 and 20, to the alto in Nos. 30, 59, and 60—or to a soprano-alto duet (No. 27a). Even in No. 67, which calls on all four voices, they appear successively rather than jointly. The Faithful, on the other hand, always have an accompanying role and are always impersonated by the second choir. The blurring of clear role distribution that can be observed toward the end of No. 1, where both choirs together sing a common text, becomes a structural feature of the Passion as a whole when, in the numbers that end each of Picander's two Parts (Nos. 27b and 68), Bach again gives both choirs the same text. The last section of No. 1 thus anticipates the two protagonists' merging in the two endings. It is clear that Bach's decision to use two separate choirs was dictated by Picander's two protagonists, for the two choirs engage in dialogue only in those numbers that involve the Daughter Zion and her fellow Faithful. The remaining independent (that is, non-Gospel) movements of the Passion are either Picander arias (with or without preceding recitatives) or traditional chorales. The arias, which feature singular protagonists only, are set for voices from either the first or the second choir but never for both choirs at the same time; the chorales, with their plural protagonists, are always set for both choirs singing in unison (this is true even of the chorale fantasia No. 29 ["O Mensch, bewein dein Sünde groß"], the number that Bach removed from the second version of the St. John Passion when he revised the St. Matthew Passion in 1736 to provide a suitably monumental ending for Part 1, where he doubled the cantus firmus–carrying sopranos by adding soprano in ripieno and the organs): none of these texts offers an occasion for the kind of genuine dialogue where the two choirs, whether complete or not, whether singing the same text or not, could, by not singing in unison throughout, mark their individuality as they do in the Zion-Faithful numbers.

The text of the opening movement clearly establishes that the Daughter Zion is a single person (she speaks in the first person singular) and that the Faithful are many (she addresses them in the plural). This is confirmed in the subsequent Zion-Faithful numbers that provide verbal clues such as personal pronouns. There are two exceptions, two seeming inconsistencies: Nos. 19 and 67, where the Faithful speak in the first person singular. The first instance can be explained easily, for here the Faithful are singing a chorale, where such usage is common. The second instance I cannot explain, leaving us with one inconsistency in the Faithful's use of the first person singular. Zion, however, is always singular, even when her role is shared by two or four voices. It was clearly no oversight, therefore, that Bach did not revise Picander's text and accepted Zion's saying "mir" in the opening number.

—

Picander's labeling the opening number "Aria" consequently ceases to be a puzzle: this is indeed an aria of the Daughter Zion, accompanied by the Faithful and a chorale cantus firmus. But what did Bach do with the poet's directive to give the aria "Da Capo" form?

Bach's understanding of the generic conventions governing da capo form can be reconstructed.[8] Recitatives aside, Bach set almost all of Picander's poetry, the basis for much of the musical substance of the Passion, in da capo form. Nos. 27, 30, and 60 are the only exceptions. The remaining fourteen poems, whether so marked in the libretto or not, are all set as da capos:[9]

1. "Kommt, ihr Töchter, helft mir klagen"

6. "Buß und Reu"

8. "Blute nur, du liebes Herz"

13. "Ich will dir mein Herze schenken"

20. "Ich will bei meinem Jesu wachen"

23. "Gerne will ich mich bequemen"

35. "Geduld"

39. "Erbarme dich"

42. "Gebt mir meinen Jesum wieder"

49. "Aus Liebe will mein Heiland sterben"

52. "Können Tränen meiner Wangen"

57. "Komm, süßes Kreuz, so will ich sagen"

65. "Mache dich, mein Herze, rein"

68. "Wir setzen uns mit Tränen nieder"

All of these poems, the fourteen set in da capo form and the three exceptional ones, are labeled "Aria" in Picander's libretto and almost all are also so labeled in Bach's autograph. The only exceptions are the opening and closing numbers of the Passion: No. 1, which is unlabeled, and No. 68, marked "il Choro finale." I shall return to these two exceptions, but the twelve labeled arias suffice for a preliminary reconstruction of Bach's conception of the generic norms of the da capo aria. (A full reconstruction would, of course, require an examination of all of Bach's extant da capo arias.)

At least one feature belongs to the da capo (ABA) form by definition: the opening portion of the poem must return at the end. But in Bach's Passion there are two kinds of the form. In the first, the return of the opening section is set to the same music as upon first presentation, a literal da capo that Bach never writes out; instead, he marks the repeat in the customary way with a "da capo" directive at the end of the B section of the aria—or, if he does not want the repeat to start at the top of the A section, with a "dal segno" directive where he wants the repeat to start—and a fermata that tells musicians where to end the A section; this applies to Nos. 6, 8, 13, 23, 52, and 65, as well as the exceptional No. 68.[10] In the second kind the textual return is musically modified, a varied da capo, which has of course to be written out; this applies to Nos. 20, 35, 39, 42, 49, and 57, as well as the exceptional No. 1. The main difference between the two kinds is simply that in the literal da capo the A section must for obvious reasons not only begin but also end in the tonic key, whereas in the varied da capo it ends in the tonic key in the return but not the first time around.

In these two distinct types of the form, each is characterized by a set of normal procedures. The A section of the literal da capo form opens and closes with single-phrase instrumental ritornellos in the tonic key; these frame two vocal phrases, also in the tonic and both setting the complete A text, with the first closely reproducing the opening ritornello. In the B section two modulating phrases each set the complete B text. In the varied da capo form the opening A section presents a single-phrase instrumental ritornello in the tonic key, followed by a single vocal phrase that sets the A text and modulates from the tonic to the mediant or dominant key; in the return of the A section the order of the two phrases is reversed, and the vocal phrase either stays in the tonic or modulates back to it from the key in which the B section ended. The B text is set as a single modulating phrase. The difference between the way the central section is shaped in the two versions of da capo form corresponds to the difference between their outer sections. The literal da capo form is more spacious. Not only is its entirety circular but its outer sections create their own smaller circles. It follows that the central section should be more expansive, too. The varied da capo, on the other hand, is more concentrated; it forms a single circle, and, accordingly, its central section is also more compact. Each of these two basic patterns allows for a great variety of expansion, contraction, and other sorts of deviation from the norm, the variety being limited only by the composer's imagination. It is in considering the final and, especially, the opening choruses in Bach's Passion against these norms that their individuality will become most immediately apparent.

⸺

Let us begin by briefly considering how Bach adapted the norms that govern the A section of the literal da capo form to what he required for the final chorus, No. 68, "Wir setzen uns mit Tränen nieder," which, like the opening chorus, appears in Picander's libretto as an "Aria" with a "Da Capo." The opening ritornello (mm. 1–12) follows the norm in being a single phrase closed with a full cadence, but already in the first part (mm. 1–8) Bach exceptionally undertakes a modulation from i to III and punctuates the phrase with a half cadence in III before confirming the new key in the second part (mm. 9–12). He uses the same music again to set the A text (mm. 13–24), after which he rewrites the ritornello (mm. 25–36) so as to reverse its tonal relations: now the first part (mm. 25–32) modulates from III to i and is punctuated with a half cadence in the home key, whereas the second part (mm. 33–36) confirms the home key ending with a full cadence made memorably poignant by the leading-tone accented appoggiatura sounding against the minor tonic chord. The A section closes with the rewritten ritornello music set again to the A text (mm. 37–48). As a result the dissonant appoggiatura marks the final measure of the work: Bach never forgets that this is a story of suffering.

What this A section retains from the norm of a literal da capo is the content of four phrases, two instrumental and two vocal ones. What is different is, first, the order in which the phrases occur (the ritornellos alternate with the vocal phrases instead of framing them); second, the complete musical identity of both vocal phrases with the preceding instrumental ones; third, the corresponding motivic content of the two ritornellos; and fourth, the modulating rather than stationary tonal plan. Thanks to the last three features—this double-mirrored movement from tonic to mediant key and back—and despite the unusual placement of the second ritornello, Bach retains, in fact strengthens, the section's circular shape.

Let us now return to the opening chorus, a movement whose formal complexity by far surpasses that of all other movements in the Passion, including all the material that involves Zion and the Faithful.[11] Keeping in mind the generic and formal expectations set up by the libretto, as well as what we know of Bach's norms, let us then consider this chorus as a da capo aria.

The first phrase (mm. 1–17), which presents a single-phrase instrumental ritornello in the tonic key, certainly conforms to the expectations of that form (for all references to the opening chorus, see chapter appendix, pp. 61–88). The internal structure of the phrase is reminiscent of classical antecedent-consequent construction; whereas a half cadence punctuates the antecedent in m. 9, the consequent, whose first four measures reproduce the first four of the antecedent almost literally but a fifth higher, closes with a full cadence. The two orchestras play in unison almost throughout, separating only in mm. 14–15 for a brief antiphonal exchange of echoes—a glimpse of the two-choir dialogue to come. Otherwise the texture consists essentially of

EXAMPLE 2. Bach, St. Matthew Passion, No. 1 (opening chorus), mm. 1–2, reductive sketch of Flute II/Oboe II and Violin I

three melodic voices—Flute I/Oboe I, Flute II/Oboe II, and Violin I—over the continuo bass. The essential melodic content is the two-part counterpoint between Flute II/Oboe II (mm. 1–2^4) and Violin I (mm. 1^2–2^3), which is imitated a fifth higher by Flute I/Oboe I and Violin I in mm. 2^3–4^2. (The superscript numbers indicate the beat within the measure.) In the consequent the two-part counterpoint is presented first by Violin I (mm. 9–10^4) and Flute I/Oboe I (mm. 9^2–10^3), a fifth higher than originally and in double counterpoint, that is, with the originally lower line now on top. This is then repeated yet another fifth higher by Flute I/Oboe I and Flute II/Oboe II (mm. 10^3–12^2), with the originally lower line back on the bottom again.

As the ritornello in an aria epitomizes the musical-expressive content of the A section, the motivic material described above deserves further examination (Example 2). The counterpoint (Violin I, mm. 1^2–2^3) is a free inversion of the main motif (Flute II/Oboe II, mm. 1–2^4): the motif makes an incomplete chromatic ascent from the first scale step up a fourth before descending to the diatonic third step (minor third when the motif is first presented, and major third when it is imitated); the counterpoint makes an incomplete chromatic descent from the first scale step down a fourth. The E-minor tonal identity of the opening two (or, for that matter, seventeen) measures is never in doubt, but from the start the chromatic saturation (and especially the accented sharpened third in the upper voice) is striking, particularly when grating against the stationary tonic pedal point in the bass. This music does not delay announcing that its central subject is suffering, passion. And the long-held stationary bass announces something else: the epic scope of the story to be told.[12] (In their own way, the opening measures of the St. John Passion, too, make the same two points right from the start.)

Like the opening orchestral ritornello, the first vocal phrase (mm. 17–30) behaves normally enough, suggesting (incorrectly, it will soon turn out) that we may be hearing a literal da capo: it closely follows the ritornello's punctuation and motivic content, setting what may be the complete A text in the tonic key (chapter appendix, pp. 65–69). At this point the two ensembles separate, to allow the first choir to assume the role of the Daughter Zion while the second impersonates the Faithful. As in the ritornello, the phrase is divided by a half cadence (m. 26) and closed by a full one (m. 30, albeit with the third rather than the prime in the soprano); this time, however, the phrase is less balanced: the content of the first half sentence (mm. 17–26) corresponds closely to that of the antecedent of the ritornello (mm. 1–9), but the second half sentence (mm. 26–30) does not follow the ritornello's consequent. Instead, the two choirs immediately begin a rapid homophonic dialogue reminiscent of the single occasion toward the end of the ritornello when the two ensembles separated (mm. 14–15).

The initial impression that this might be a literal da capo is dispelled by the second vocal phrase (mm. 30–38; chapter appendix, pp. 69–72), which suggests, rather, a varied da capo. Again the phrase sets what seems to be the A text and modulates to the relative major key. Both in punctuation and in motivic content the phrase is a condensed variant of the preceding one. (Note the abbreviated half phrases and resulting acceleration: as the spacious incises of the ritornello give way, by the second part of the second phrase, to incises half the original length, Zion's call to the Faithful to come, see, and join in the lamentation acquires growing urgency.) The half-cadential punctuation at midpoint is somewhat complicated by the modulatory process. The half cadence in m. 33 suggests a move to the relative (G) major, but by the first beat of m. 34, where text and music of the first half sentence truly end (mm. 30–34 are a textual and motivic variation of mm. 17–26, just as mm. 34–38 will be a textual and motivic variation of mm. 26–30), the listener is no longer sure whether the sentence will lead to G major, to B minor, or back to E minor. Doubt is resolved when the second half sentence (mm. 34–38) ends in an unambiguous full cadence in G (with the prime in the soprano this time). What makes this tonal outcome inevitable is the entrance of the third protagonist: superimposed on the second vocal phrase is the first distich of the monophonic chorale, its first verse coinciding with the "antecedent" and its second with the "consequent"; the melody is unambiguously in G.

The third protagonist's entry has not only tonal but also formal consequences, both for the music already heard and for what is still to come. Up to this point the music fits the A-section norm of varied da capo form, diverging from that form with only one "extra" nonmodulating setting of the text between the ritornello and the normal modulating vocal phrase, which was needed to allow the A text to be heard clearly at the outset, without interference from the chorale. The formal schema of the chorale melody in its entirety is aab; with the end of the second vocal phrase the first "a" has been presented, leaving the listener with the expectation that the A section of the da capo is not yet finished and that some form of repetition is to come—certainly a repetition of the chorale's "a" phrase, and probably also a repetition of the accompanying music.

And, indeed, the fourth phrase of the chorus (mm. 38–57) does recycle the previous music (chapter appendix, pp. 72–78). A brief instrumental incise, uniting both orchestras in unison and ending with a half cadence, modulates back to E minor (mm. 38–42); this is a return to mm. 23–26, which concluded the first incise of the first vocal phrase. The next two measures (mm. 42–43) recapitulate the beginning of the second incise (mm. 26–27); here Zion and the Faithful get a new text, but whereas the second incise of the first phrase had had two verses, this text consists of only one. As a result, the remaining measures of the second incise (mm. 28–29) do not need to be repeated. Instead, mm. 42–43 are followed (mm. 44–52) without cadential articulation by a recapitulation of the complete second vocal phrase (mm. 30–38), in which the newly introduced text is accompanied by a new distich of the chorale. After the full cadence in m. 52 the phrase is rounded off by an instrumental appendix (mm. 52–57), presented by both orchestras in unison, which is based on the main motivic material of the opening ritornello—the only portion of the phrase that is not a recapitulation. The appendix stabilizes the hard-won G major as a tonic at the end of the aria's A section, accomplishing this task simply by prolonging the final tonic chord of the full cadence in m. 52 over the tonic pedal. The appendix should not be mistaken for an independent ritornello; not only would that be out of place in a varied da capo but it lacks the cadential articulation, whether internal or closing, that an independent phrase such as a ritornello would require.

Note how, apart from the final appendix, the logic of these events is driven by the chorale cantus firmus. The need to repeat the chorale's "a" phrase suggests that mm. 30–38 should be repeated, and this indeed accounts for mm. 44–52. This passage must, however, be preceded by a return from G major to E minor, hence it needs something that functions tonally like mm. 38–42, though not always with the same motivic content. Initially the words of Zion were carefully correlated with those of the chorale: Zion's telling the Faithful that the Bridegroom they should see is "als wie ein Lamm" (like a lamb) provokes the chorale gloss "O Lamm Gottes, unschuldig am Stamm des Kreuzes geschlachtet" (o innocent Lamb of God, slaughtered on the cross). Since the chorale melody is repeated with a new text, it makes sense that Zion now be given a new text and that she present it first, so that the chorale's new text can again provide a gloss; and, indeed, Zion's call to see "Geduld" (patience) is perfectly calculated to be glossed by the chorale's "allzeit erfunden geduldig" (always found patient). Bach had to compose the measures preceding the repetition of the chorale phrase in mm. 42–43 to allow Zion's text to precede that of the chorale. The only thing that may not be immediately clear is why Bach, or Picander, decided that only one verse of the Zion-Faithful's text would do where previously they had used two. However, had they upon repetition again used two verses, Bach would have set them to the music used before for the corresponding two verses in mm. 26–30. As only one verse is called for, it is understandable that he only recycles mm. 26–27 and that these measures are followed directly by a repetition of mm. 30–38. In skipping mm. 28–29 the cadential articulation at m. 30 disappears and hence mm. 38–57 present a single phrase rather than two; indeed, this may be the reason for the single line of text here rather than two. Recycling mm. 26–27 in mm. 42–43, finally, explains the motivic content of the retransition in mm. 38–42: as mm. 42–43 correspond to mm. 26–27, it made sense also to recapitulate the preceding passage to prepare them; hence mm. 38–42 correspond motivically to mm. 23–26, although they are now left textless, because their only function is to provide a tonal retransition.

In short, *all* of Bach's compositional decisions thus far can be understood in terms of the norms governing a varied da capo A section modified to accommodate a chorale cantus firmus. It would be reasonable now to expect Bach to follow ordinary varied da capo to set the B text as a modulating phrase, followed by a recapitulated second phrase (the first phrase of the chorus), either as a retransition back to the home key or in the tonic key throughout, and a recapitulation of the opening ritornello. He would need somehow to combine all of this, or more likely just the B section, with the "b" phrase of the chorale, as recapitulating its "a" phrases is obviously out of the question. Also to be expected is that something will not happen: that the extra verse added to the A text to accommodate the repetition of the "a" phrase of the chorale will not reappear.

The fifth phrase of the chorus (mm. 57–67) does indeed set a new text, the first line of the B text combined with the first line of the three-line "b" part of the chorale, and it does modulate (chapter appendix, pp. 78–81). The modulation is up the circle of fifths from G major (m. 57^2), through D major (m. 58^3), A minor (m. 60), and E minor (m. 61^3), to B (m. 63^3), but all of the cadences that mark its progress are weakened by the third in the soprano; the only full perfect cadence occurs at the end of the phrase, and it confirms the arrival in B minor. (The chorale by itself is in G major throughout.) Not only the tonal instability but also the novelty and triadic simplicity of the motivic content in the homophonic dialogue of the two choirs marks the beginning of the B section. Only the instrumental incise that closes the phrase and confirms its tonal goal (mm. 63^3–67) returns to previously heard material, namely the one moment of dialogue in the opening ritornello (mm. 14–17).

The sixth phrase (mm. 67–72) sets the same line of the B text combined with the next line of the chorale and is an abbreviated variant of the preceding phrase (chapter appendix, pp. 81–82). The modulation resumes, leading now from B minor (m. 67^2) to A minor and marked by a half cadence at the spot where the setting of the text ends (m. 70) and a full one at the end of the concluding instrumental incise (m. 72). Motivically, too, the vocal and instrumental portions of both phrases correspond (mm. 67^2–70 return to the material of mm. 57^2–63^3, and mm. 70–72 to mm. 63^3–67).

Not only musically but also textually the two phrases belong together, form a single unit: both set the same line of the Zion-Faithful text. This is, as usual, first presented on its own and then glossed by the chorale; Zion's call that the Faithful see "unsre Schuld" (our guilt) is answered by the chorale's "All Sünd hast du getragen, sonst müßten wir verzagen" (You have borne all sin, otherwise we should despair). The second phrase can be so much shorter than the first because this second time around there is no need to delay the chorale verse; the text to be glossed has already been heard before on its own.

So far the B section, too, can be understood according to the norms governing such sections in a varied da capo form modified to accommodate a chorale cantus firmus. It is what happens next that, for the first time in the chorus, seriously confounds the listener's expectations.

All of the remaining music (mm. 72–90) forms a single phrase, closed with a full cadence at the end and punctuated with a half cadence in the middle (m. 82; chapter appendix, p. 86). Tonally the first part of the phrase makes a retransition from A back to E minor; the second remains in the recovered home key. Motivically the two parts come back, respectively, to the content of the antecedent and the consequent of the opening ritornello. Mm. 72–82 follow the motivic events of mm. 1–9 very closely, expanding them somewhat to accommodate not just the retransition but, more important, one more verse of the chorale; this, we now know, requires that the text it glosses first be presented on its own and then repeated. Once the chorale has ended, the choirs can pick up the motivic material that closed the antecedent of the ritornello (mm. 79–82 are closely related to mm. 6–9). Mm. 82–90, in turn, repeat the musical content of mm. 9–17 almost literally. Note in particular the reappearance of the single feature most responsible for the antecedent-consequent character of the ritornello's structure, the fact that each half of the phrase opens with four measures of the same motivic-contrapuntal material—the two-part melodic double counterpoint imitated after a measure and a half a fifth higher and presented over an initially stationary bass.

The music alone might lead a listener to conclude that Bach had decided to close the chorus with a phrase making a tonal retransition before returning to the material of the first vocal phrase—a common way to begin the last section of the varied da capo form, the A'—and to leave it at that, without the closing ritornello. This would be highly unusual. However, closer attention reveals that the final phrase of the chorus recapitulates not the first vocal phrase, which closely resembles the opening ritornello, but the ritornello itself: the consequent of the first vocal phrase was much abbreviated compared to that of the ritornello, and it is the ritornello's consequent that Bach chooses to use here. In other words, the final phrase telescopes the recapitulation of both the opening vocal phrase and the ritornello into one phrase. Musically mm. 72–90 accomplish everything that the recapitulation of a varied da capo should, except that they do it all at once instead of successively.

But this is reckoning without the text, so we know that this cannot be the whole story. If mm. 72–90 were really the da capo, they would have to be set to the A text. But two verses of Zion's B text and one verse of the chorale remain to be set before that textual recapitulation can begin. These remaining verses of the central section are set to the phrase's antecedent; only the consequent takes up the A text again. Bach here accomplishes double telescoping: the antecedent conflates the ending of the B section text with the musical beginning of the A' section, and the consequent conflates the recapitulations of the text of the vocal phrase with the music of the ritornello.

And there is one more conflation. Picander had assigned the last two verses of the B text to Zion. Bach reassigns them, as well as the repeated A text, to both Zion and the Faithful. In m. 72 the first presentation of the B text ("sehet ihn aus Lieb und Huld Holz zum Kreuze selber tragen" [see him, out of love and grace, himself bear the wood of the cross]) is carried by the first choir only, whereas the second takes up just the opening exhortation: "Sehet" (see). Until now it had been Zion's role to exhort the Faithful; she initiated her dialogue with them (in m. 26) with this same "sehet." Already in m. 73 the second presentation of the text is shared by both choirs; by m. 75 the two ensembles have blended into one to accompany the chorale's gloss "Erbarm dich unser, o Jesu!" (have mercy on us, o Jesus!). The A text is thereupon also carried by the two choirs together, except at the end (mm. 87–90), where the dialogue for a moment forces the choirs to revert to their separate roles. Even there, though, the Zion's final "als wie ein Lamm!" is also picked up by the Faithful. In the last phrase Zion and the Faithful preserve their separate identities but speak a common text together.

In short, the opening chorus is a varied da capo, but one with a most extraordinary ending, which conflates in a single phrase what normally is presented in successive ones—the end of the B section and beginning of the A' section, as well as recapitulations of the first vocal phrase and the ritornello— and for good measure also blends the texts of the two protagonists into one. The effect is one not of impatient abbreviation or acceleration but, rather, of synthesizing culmination. Although the da capo lasts only nineteen measures, whereas the initial A section had fifty-seven, there is no sense of imbalance, no sense that the end does not match the expansive beginning, no sense of something missing. And, indeed, there is nothing missing, not even the final ritornello.

Bach's sophistication in treating the da capo form here goes far beyond anything his contemporaries, Handel included, could conceive. Formal sophistication, however, is not the point—or, in any case, it cannot have been the whole of Bach's point. But what was his point? Why did he construct this ending, when he had more conventional ways at his disposal to bring the chorus to a close? Surely not because of a protoromantic passion for blurring clearly articulated outlines, a New Critical love of ambiguity, a deconstructionist penchant for form that makes and unmakes itself; let us not be tempted here by irrelevancies. Bach's anachronism is more profound than that. To see clearly what Bach docs is also to begin to see why he does it. What he does is to make simultaneous what normally is (and earlier had been in the chorus), successive, and to abolish the succession of past, present, and future for the simultaneity of the present—in short, to abolish the flow of time in favor of the eternal Now.

APPENDIX TO CHAPTER 1
St. Matthew Passion, opening chorus, full score

61

65

helft mir kla - gen, kommt, ihr Töch - ter, helft mir kla - - - - - - - -

_____ ihr Töch - ter, helft mir kla - - - - - - - - - -

Töch - ter, helft mir kla - - - - - - - - gen, helft mir kla - gen, kommt, ihr Töch - ter,

Töch - ter, helft mir kla - gen, kommt, _____ ihr Töch - ter, helft mir kla - - - - - - -

66

68

70

am Stamm des Kreu - zes ge-schlach - - tet,

- gen, se - het den Bräu - ti - gam, seht ihn als wie ein Lamm, se - het den Bräu - ti-

- gen, se - het den Bräu - ti - gam, seht ihn als wie ein Lamm, se - het den Bräu - ti-

kla - gen, se - het den Bräu - ti - gam, seht ihn als wie ein Lamm, se - het den Bräu - ti-

- gen, se - het den Bräu - ti - gam, seht ihn als wie ein Lamm, se - het den Bräu - ti-

Wen?

Wie?

Wen?

Wen?

Wie?

Wen?

gam, seht ihn als wie ein Lamm!

gam, seht ihn als wie ein Lamm!

gam, seht ihn als wie ein Lamm!

gam, seht ihn als wie ein Lamm!

Wie?

Wie?

73

74

duld, se - het, seht die Ge - duld, se - het, seht die Ge-duld,

duld, se - het, seht die Ge-duld, se - het, seht die Ge-duld,

duld, se - het, seht die Ge-duld, se - het, seht die Ge-duld,

duld, se - het, seht die Ge-duld, se - het, seht die Ge-duld,

Was?

Was?

Was?

Was?

76

78

I 73

se - het ihn____ aus Lieb und Huld Holz zum Kreu - ze sel - ber tra -

Huld Holz zum Kreu - ze sel - ber tra - - - gen, se - - het ihn____ aus

Lieb und Huld____ Holz zum Kreu - ze sel - ber tra - - - gen, se - het ihn____ aus Lieb und

se - het ihn____ aus Lieb und Huld____ Holz zum Kreu - ze sel - ber tra -

7♮   6♮   4   8   6   7   7♯   7♮   5   6   6
♯   4   2   3   ♯   7   2   5
                                         ♯

II Fl. I, II

se - het ihn____ aus Lieb und Huld Holz zum Kreu - ze sel - ber tra -

se - - het ihn____ aus

se - het ihn____ aus Lieb und

se - het ihn____ aus Lieb und Huld____ Holz zum Kreu - ze sel - ber tra -

7♮   6♮   4   8   6   7   7♯   7♮   5   6   6
♯   4   2   3   ♯   7   2   5
                                         ♯

83

84

su!

tra - - - - - - -

tra - - - - - - -

sel - ber tra - - - - -

- gen, Holz zum Kreu - ze sel - ber tra - - - - -

2   A Crystal Flying Like a Bullet

A reader of Bach's two sets of preludes and fugues *The Well-Tempered Keyboard (WTC)* will be struck by the emphatic gestures with which the composer often announces the approaching end of a fugue. In most of these fugues something happens a few measures before the end that alerts the listener to expect closure. Take the very first, the C-Major, fugue of the first set (Example 3). For the greater part of its duration it is impossible to predict when or how soon the fugue will come to an end. Then quite suddenly, in m. 23, it becomes apparent that Bach is wrapping things up. Indeed, the final cadence comes at the beginning of the next measure; the remaining four measures merely prolong the final tonic chord over the tonic pedal point. The ending, impossible to predict for most of the duration of the discourse, yet comes not abruptly but is, rather, emphatically announced five measures ahead.

To understand how this effect is achieved, and, more important, why it is sought, it is necessary to understand how a fugue works.[1] Like every fugue in the two sets, the C-Major Fugue begins by presenting its melodic subject successively once in each voice, either on the first or on the fifth scale step of the tonic key (mm. 1–7[1]). In this case, though by no means always, the subject is constructed in such a way that the statement on the fifth scale step will reproduce the exact intervals of the original, first-scale-step, statement without any hint of a key change; this enables a so-called real answer. (In the case of a tonal answer the intervals of the fifth-scale-step presentation have to be adjusted to ensure that the key remains unchanged. Regardless of which method is used, what matters is that the subject be presented on both the first and fifth scale steps in the same key. Fugues more complex than this one may, of course, also introduce countersubjects and,

EXAMPLE 3. Bach, *WTC* I, Fugue No. 1 in C Major; D = Demonstration

EXAMPLE 3 *(continued)*

later on, additional subjects.) What follows, in this and every fugue, is Bach's demonstrations of what can be done with the subject contrapuntally.

In the C-Major Fugue there are seven such demonstrations, each designed to show how the subject can be combined with itself in imitation (this is known as a stretto fugue). Most of these demonstrations involve the subject's statement on the first scale step and an answer on the fifth scale step. In this fugue the subject can be so imitated at the distance of one beat, with the answer either above the statement (Demonstration 1, mm. 10³–12², bass and alto, marked D1 in Example 3) or below (Demonstration 2 [D2], mm. 7¹–8⁴, soprano and tenor), that is, in invertible counterpoint.[2] Imitation is also possible in minor (Demonstration 3 [D3], mm. 19^1–20^4, tenor and alto), but then the real answer introduces a sharp sixth scale step that conflicts intolerably with the flat sixth scale step toward the end of the statement and hence necessitates at least one chromatic adjustment. Bach chose to sharpen the offending note in the statement. This imitation, too, might be inverted, but Bach makes no use of this possibility. What works better in minor, requiring no chromatic adjustments, is imitation at a fifth below and at the distance of two beats (Demonstration 4a [D4a], mm. 17^1–19^1, tenor and bass). Again, this imitation might be inverted, and, again, Bach makes no use of the possibility. Instead, he does something much fancier (Demonstration 4b [D4b], mm. 16^2–19^1, soprano and alto, tenor and bass). Rather than use Demonstration 4a alone he combines it with Demonstration 2 to produce four-part imitation. He achieves this by following Demonstration 2 in C major at the distance of three beats by Demonstration 4a below in D minor. This causes fairly obvious parallel octaves between the first two notes of the bass and the alto, but Bach mitigated the problem somewhat (though only somewhat!) by eliminating the subject's opening rest in the bass and inserting the first note one eighth beat earlier.

Not all demonstrations have to involve the subject's statement on the first scale step and an answer on the fifth. It is also possible to imitate the subject at a lower octave after three beats (Demonstration 5a [D5a], mm. 14^2–16^3, tenor and bass). This imitation creates parallel octaves at the end, a problem Bach solved by abandoning the last two beats of the upper voice.[3] Rather than presenting Demonstration 5a alone, Bach combined it, again, with Demonstration 2, transforming D2's answer into the upper voice of D5a and thus creating three-part imitation (Demonstration 5b [D5b], mm. 14^1–16^3, alto, tenor, and bass). It is also possible to imitate the subject at the distance of two beats a fourth higher, at the first and fourth scale steps, respectively (Demonstration 6 [D6], mm. 24^1–26^1, tenor and alto). This combination, too, can be inverted, and Bach does so not as a literal inversion but transformed into the minor mode, at the fifth and first scale steps, as he had done earlier in Demonstration 4a. In his final demonstration Bach shows how the subject can also be imitated at the distance of three beats a minor sixth lower, that is, at the first and third scale steps, respectively (Demonstration 7 [D7], mm. 20^4–23^1, soprano and tenor); in this one case the answer is not "real" but sticks to the diatonic steps of the scale with the seventh step lowered.

Observe how Bach arranged the seven contrapuntal demonstrations into a series to make the fugue. The customary exposition of the subject (mm. 1^1–7^1) is immediately followed by Demonstration 2 (mm. 7^1–8^4, soprano and tenor). After a gap of a measure and a half (mm. 9^1–10^2), Demonstration 1 occurs (mm. 10^3–12^2, bass and alto), transposed up a fifth (and with the penultimate note of the answer sharpened), followed by another gap of a measure and a half (mm. 12^3–13^4). The next four demonstrations succeed one another without any more gaps: Demonstration 5b (mm. 14^1–16^3, alto, tenor, and bass); Demonstration 4b (mm. 16^2–19^1, soprano and alto, tenor and bass, with the first and last leading tones in the tenor sharpened); Demonstration 3 in the relative minor (mm. 19^1–20^4, tenor and alto, with the first third scale step and both sixth scale steps in the tenor sharpened); and Demonstration 7 (mm. 20^4–23^1, soprano and tenor, with the leading tone in the tenor consistently lowered) transposed up a fifth. Another gap (mm. 23^{2-4}) precedes the last Demonstration 6 (mm. 24^1–26^1, tenor and alto), which is followed by the final and demonstration-free measures (mm. 26^2–27^4). It should be noted that the first two gaps, while free of contrapuntal demonstrations, are replete with single statements of the subject; the first statement is at the fifth scale step (mm. 9^1–10^2, alto), the second at the fifth scale step of the relative minor (mm. 12^1–13^3, tenor, with all the leading tones sharpened), and this leaves only one beat at the end (m. 13^4) that is not filled with thematic substance. This one beat, and the three beats in m. 23, are the only nonthematic beats of the fugue before the last two measures.

It is striking how few transpositions Bach chose to use. Most of the demonstrations appear untransposed in C major or its relative A minor. Demonstrations 1 and 7 are the only ones to be transposed, and this only minimally, by a fifth up. A trek through many different keys is clearly not Bach's priority here. There is a ghost of a weak cadence on G in the middle of m. 10, but Bach begins to abandon the tonic key only after that cadence, with the first transposed demonstration (Demonstration 1) in m. 10^3–12^2. The modulation has an audible goal once the subject appears singly at the fifth scale step of the relative minor in mm. 12^1–13^3; that goal is confirmed by the subsequent cadence in A minor in m. 14^1, the first strong cadence in the piece. (It is now clear why the penultimate note of the answer in Demonstration 1, g', and all the leading tones in the following single thematic statement, all Gs, were sharpened: namely to give the modulation a sense of direction.) Bach evidently does not think that moving to the relative minor is much of a modulation, however, for he proceeds straight on with another demonstration in C major (Demonstration 5b). Only with the appearance of Demonstration 4b in mm. 16^2–19^1 is there a hint that the tonic key will be abandoned again—and not because of transposition (there is none) but because the complex structure of this demonstration combines an imitation in C major with one in D minor, thus initiating a motion toward the latter key that is confirmed two beats later (m. 19^3) by a cadence with a raised third; this cadence is weaker than the one in m. 14 because it occurs in the middle of the measure, but stronger than the one in m. 10 because it is provided with a proper bass and a suspension in the soprano. (Again, it is now clear that Bach sharpened the first and last leading tones in the tenor of the imitation in D minor to give the modulation a sense of direction.) The D minor offers only a momentary foothold, however, and the tonal motion continues with Demonstration 3 in mm. 19^1–20^4. This demonstration interlocks with the preceding one, beginning two beats before the cadence, which further weakens the cadence and explains why the first occurrence of the tenor's third scale step had to be sharpened. Sharpened sixth scale steps in the tenor, both f', further suggest that the motion is toward G major. Indeed, Demonstration 7, which follows in mm. 20^4–23^1, is transposed up a fifth so that it may project G; however, the consistently lowered leading tone in the tenor, f'♮, makes it clear that this G, too, is not the final goal but rather the dominant chord preparing a return to the home key. This is confirmed by the three nonthematic beats that follow; these end in m. 24 with a cadence in C major that, because of its broader soprano suspension and bass motion, is even stronger than the one in m. 14. This is also the final cadence of the piece. Like the final nonthematic measures, Demonstration 6, which follows in mm. 24^1–26^1, merely stabilizes the tonic key over the tonic pedal point in a customary way—that is (recall that this is an imitation on the first and fourth scale steps), by giving it a subdominant coloration.

The tonal plan is simple: areas of tonal stasis in the tonic key at the beginning (mm. 1^1–10^2) and the end (mm. 24^1–27^4) frame two areas of tonal motion, the first one moving from the tonic to the relative minor (mm. 10^3–14^1), the second from the tonic through the secondary dominant and dominant back to the tonic (mm. 14^1–24^1). Cadences mark the goals of tonal motion, the strongest one being in the tonic key at the end (m. 24^1) and the second strongest in the relative minor in the middle (m. 14^1). A weak cadence divides the second area of tonal motion (m. 19^3), and a yet weaker one (hardly a cadence at all) similarly articulates the first area (m. 10^3). Thus the main tonal signposts are: I (m. 1^1)—[V (m. 10^3)]—vi (m. 14^1)—[(V) (m. 19^3)—V (m. 21^3)]—I (m. 24^1). (I have placed the subordinate signposts in square brackets.) Tonally the piece is a composed-out cadence in C.

Thematic events seen in conjunction with the tonal plan reveal the fugue's overall form: exposition (mm. 1^1–7^1) and coda (mm. 24^1–27^4), both in the tonic key, frame two sets of demonstrations, one (mm. 7^1–14^1) beginning in the tonic key and ending in the relative minor, the other (mm. 14^1–24^1) beginning and ending in the tonic. The overall proportions are elegantly symmetrical, without beat-counting pedantry: six measures at the beginning (exposition) are answered by four measures at the end (coda); inside this frame are two sets of demonstrations, of seven and ten measures, respectively, each set articulated more or less in the middle.

The fugue as read here is the product of three distinct operations. First, it was necessary to invent the subject and figure out what could be done with it contrapuntally; that is, it was necessary to produce the essential components of the exposition and set of demonstrations. Second, it was necessary to decide on a logical tonal framework or plan for the piece. And third, it was necessary to fit the exposition and the demonstrations into this framework, an operation that could require transposing some of the demonstrations and chromatically inflecting some notes within them. (It is clear that the two transposed demonstrations in the C-Major Fugue, as well as all of the chromatic alterations not dictated by imperfections within the demonstrations themselves, were introduced to accommodate the overall tonal plan of the composition: otherwise there would be no need to transpose or inflect.) The first and second operations can be performed in any order: neither presupposes the other. The third operation, obviously, must follow the other two. All three operations are essential. Without them there would be no fugue. With them we get something reasonably close to a fugue, but several additional, less essential, operations are needed to complete the work: counterpoints can be added in voices not occupied by the subject; gaps between the demonstrations, if there are any, need to be filled; cadences need to be composed and ornamented; the whole needs to be performed.

Although each of the first two operations is essential, and although neither is the prerequisite for the other, they do not have equal weight in the process of composition, nor are they equally important to the aural experience and understanding of a fugue. Whereas a fairly basic level of musical literacy suffices for devising interesting and elegant tonal plans, inventing subjects capable of interesting and varied contrapuntal treatments requires an incomparably higher level of skill and imagination. And what is true for the composer is also true for anyone wishing to understand the work. For both performer and listener, the focus of interest in a fugue is the subject and what is being done with it contrapuntally. Performers and listeners tend to take a logical tonal plan for granted. Indeed, it hardly registers at all; given the temporal nature of music, the demonstrations have to appear successively, and so the order might as well be logical and shapely. Beyond that, the order is not of much interest. What matters are the subject and the demonstrations.

It is something of a bonus that we know how Bach himself viewed the matter, how he listened, and that for Bach the fun of a fugue lay in the contrapuntal treatment of the subject, not in its tonal outline or anything else. Bach's son and most significant pupil, Carl Philipp Emanuel, conveys this in a celebrated passage from a 1774 letter to Johann Nikolaus Forkel, his father's first biographer: "When he listened to a rich and many-voiced fugue, he could soon say, after the first entries of the subjects, what contrapuntal devices it would be possible to apply, and which of them the composer by rights ought to apply, and on such occasions, when I was standing next to him, and he had voiced his surmises to me, he would joyfully nudge me when his expectations were fulfilled." Earlier, in the 1750 obituary that C. P. E. Bach cowrote with another pupil, Johann Friedrich Agricola, they state: "He needed only to have heard any theme to be aware—it seemed in the same instant—of almost every intricacy that artistry could produce in the treatment of it." And in another letter to Forkel, dated 13 January 1775, C. P. E. Bach confirms the importance his father accorded to the first operation: "As for the invention of ideas, he required this [of his students] from the very beginning, and anyone who had none he advised to stay away from composition altogether."[4]

In short, what truly matters in a fugue is the invention of the subject and its contrapuntal treatment in a series of demonstrations. The second and third operations—devising a tonal plan and fitting the demonstrations to that plan—are of secondary importance. The crucial difference between the results of operation one, on the one hand, and the results of operations two and three, on the other, is that the latter are essentially temporal, while the former are not. In a tonal plan, temporality is of the essence: the temporal order in which stable and unstable tonal areas, keys, and chords follow one another matters and cannot be disregarded. This is not true of the demonstrations. They have to be presented in some temporal order, of course, but there is nothing essential or necessary about the particular order, apart from the tonal plan. They are a temporally unordered set.

In describing the demonstrations of the C-Major Fugue, I introduced them one by one in a specific order chosen from many that would have been equally serviceable. Bach tends to begin with simpler demonstrations and proceed gradually to more complex ones, but this is by no means always the case. The most complex demonstration in the C-Major Fugue, the four-part Demonstration 4b, is followed by several simpler ones. Or take Demonstrations 1 and 2. Presenting them side by side makes explicit the invertibility of imitations after one beat at the upper fifth or lower fourth. Yet there is nothing in the nature of these two demonstrations to have compelled Bach to introduce them in this rather than the reverse order. Granted, the order of the demonstrations is not completely arbitrary. Bach is, after all, a master craftsman. Since he must present the demonstrations in some order, he chooses more often than not a succession that fits the tonal plan. It makes sense that the most complex demonstration in the C-Major Fugue is correlated with the approach to the secondary dominant, tonally furthest from the home key. Similarly, it makes sense to have placed the only demonstration harmonically exploiting the subdominant in the coda, where it serves to stabilize the final tonic. Even so, compositionally nothing requires this order, nor does our understanding of the individual demonstrations depend on the order of presentation or on their placement.

Wagner, in a remark quoted in Cosima Wagner's diary entry for 15 January 1872, captured the complex temporality of a Bach fugue in a perfect image: "Such a Bach fugue is a crystal flying like a bullet, until it freezes on a pedal point."[5] The fugue is a genre that combines the atemporal and temporal layers, but it is the atemporal layer that focuses the attention of composer, performer, and listener. The temporal layer is not completely unimportant: Bach's temporal ordering of events is masterful, and his pacing subtle; he pays attention to both layers, as well as to how they are combined. But the two layers are not equal in importance.

By now it should be clear why Bach sought to keep the ending of the C-Major Fugue unpredictable until the last five measures, and how he achieved this effect. Because the nature of the genre is essentially atemporal, because one never knows in advance how many demonstrations there will be (as we have seen, Bach did not use all of the contrapuntal devices that would have been possible) or in which order they will be introduced, the end is in danger of seeming arbitrary and abrupt. Hence the need for emphatic gestures to announce that the end is imminent. In the C-Major Fugue this effect depends on relentless thematic saturation; even in the exposition, statements of the subject follow one another without a break, the last note of one always coinciding with the opening eighth-note rest of the next. (This is by no means normal practice; compare the very next fugue, in which two non-thematic measures precede the bass entry of the subject in the exposition.) The first nonthematic beat of the work occurs just before the first important cadence (m. 13^4). When Bach has an opportunity for another such beat before the next cadence (m. 19^2), he deliberately avoids it and instead begins the next demonstration prematurely. Thus the three nonthematic beats in m. 23, just before the final cadence, are striking because up to that point they are the longest stretch without the subject and hence sufficient to signal the approach of the end. The strong cadence and following pedal point do the rest. Needless to say, the specific form this effect takes varies from fugue to fugue. What matters is that the effect is sought, not how it is achieved.

—

Given that music, even more so than literature and quite unlike painting, is often thought of as the quintessentially temporal art, there is something peculiar in Bach's evident desire to neutralize time—to make it relatively unimportant, as in the C-Major Fugue, or to abolish it altogether, as in the St. Matthew Passion's opening chorus.

The desire is clearly neither limited to these two pieces nor exceptional in Bach's oeuvre. The da capo aria, the single most pervasive vocal genre of the era, allows a composer to ignore or neutralize time; at the very least it allows time's flow to be bent into a circle. As for the fugue, that genre is as central to Bach's conception of instrumental music as it is to posterity's image of Bach. What Georg Nikolaus Nissen claimed about Mozart—that in his last years he had *The Well-Tempered Keyboard* "always at his piano" (immer auf seinem Claviere)—is also true, whether literally or metaphorically, of most of the significant composers since that time.[6] More than any other of his supreme achievements, more than the St. Matthew Passion, the B-Minor Mass, or the Goldberg Variations, the *WTC* represents the essential musician's Bach.

The relative lack of interest in linear flow of time is not limited to the fugue. It is generally as characteristic of Bach's thinking in his instrumental music—from the retrospective contrapuntal genres to the most up-to-date Italianate genre of the concerto—as in his vocal music. Here the constructive principle of the ritornello appears in the da capo aria and often in choral movements as well. Consider, for instance, the opening chorus of the St. Matthew Passion or the opening Kyrie of the B-Minor Mass. In this movement, as Tovey has persuasively demonstrated, the initial instrumental ritornello (mm. 5–30) reappears beneath the vocal fugue in the dominant minor (mm. 48–72), and then again at the end in the tonic (mm. 102–end). Tovey comments: "The first Kyrie of the B Minor Mass is so vast that it seems as if nothing could control its bulk; yet the listener needs no analysis to confirm his instinctive impression that it reaches its last note with an astronomical punctuality."[7] True, but how different from the situation in a classic concerto, where the formal disposition is known in advance and hence the end can be accurately anticipated almost from the beginning. In the Kyrie, on the other hand, the conclusion can be anticipated only once the final ritornello is under way (and only assuming that the ritornello has been recognized as such). In other words, as in the fugue, Bach announces the final closure a little in advance because the lack of a predictable temporal disposition makes such an announcement necessary.

It is the main virtue of Laurence Dreyfus's illuminating book *Bach and the Patterns of Invention* to have demonstrated Bach's relative lack of interest in the linear flow of time on a range of instrumental genres favored by the composer.[8] Whether composing a two-part invention, a fugue, or a concerto movement, what mattered to Bach first and foremost, Dreyfus repeatedly and persuasively shows, was to find melodic-contrapuntal-harmonic material capable of interesting transformations and to determine what these transformations would be. The "invention" of a piece, in the terminology Dreyfus borrows from rhetoric, was the sum total of the material and its transformations. Since all transformations could not be presented at once in sounding music, they had somehow to be ordered in time. But this temporal "disposition" was a matter of relative indifference: Bach found a suitable order in full awareness that other arrangements might do equally well. The central interest, for composer, performer, and listener alike, lay not in disposition but in invention. (And, I might add, it was invention that required the most talent, skill, and ingenuity; disposition was a fairly easy matter by comparison.)

This primacy of invention over disposition certainly obtains in the fugue. Moreover, as Dreyfus shows, it obtains in other instrumental genres as well—even in the concerto, where what truly matters is neither the modulating solo section separating individual appearances of the tonally closed ritornello nor a predictable disposition of events (there is no standard tonal plan and no normal number of the ritornello and solo sections) but rather the "inventive treatment of the ritornello," the sum total of its transformations over the course of the movement.[9] The specific individual transformations of the ritornello, like the specific individual contrapuntal devices of the fugue, need to be disposed in a temporal sequence: they cannot be presented all at once. But the actual order in which they are presented is relatively unimportant; they are not there to articulate the linear flow of time. The ritornello transformations are an essentially unordered set, articulating the timeless contemplation of various aspects of a single thought. Similarly, in the da capo aria, the ritornello repetitions mark not the passage of time but, on the contrary, the timelessness of the contemplative reinterpretation of the central idea.[10] And indeed, whether in the St. Matthew Passion or in an opera, the flow of time in which dramatic situations change stops for the duration of the aria to allow the contemplation of one dramatic situation.

There is another area where Bach's predilection for the circular shape of time is much in evidence. As many critics have observed, Bach liked to collect his pieces into cycles. Martin Geck recently commented:

> To be sure, an individual work already says everything there is to be said, but it does so within the framework of its limited horizon. Series of works or cycles offer the possibility of powerfully extending this horizon, of pouring one thought into different forms of expression and thereby treating it exhaustively in the emphatic sense of the word. . . . In the *Inventions* and *Sinfonias*, the *Well-Tempered Keyboard*, the *Sei Solo* for violin, the four parts of the *Keyboard Practice*, and finally in the *Art of Fugue*—but also in the definitive shape of the Mass in B minor—one can trace the will to reveal the universal aspect of music in cycles that are not exhausted but exhaustive.[11]

Geck's understanding of a cycle is similar to Dreyfus's understanding of a single work: both forms allow thorough, though never complete, exploration of the possibilities hidden in an idea. The results of such "research" have to be presented successively, and a logical order for their presentation has to be chosen, but only rarely does the order itself matter or appear to be the only possible one. On some occasions the order takes the shape of the circle. There is a good reason for choosing this shape rather than another: the circle allows both infinity and closure. A circular cycle receives closure without losing its potential infinity.

Bach's series of preludes and fugues might have been ordered in a variety of logical ways—by ascending semitone, to be sure, but also by ascending fifths. Moreover, the series could be continued forever: Bach did not stop at twenty-four, and he might have gone beyond forty-eight, too. Among the advantages offered by a "good temperament" is not only that it makes all twenty-four keys acceptable to the ear but also that it allows closing the potentially infinite series by bending infinity into a circle: whether ascending by semitone or by fifths, in twelve steps one is bound to end up where one had begun.

The Goldberg Variations resemble the *WTC* in this respect. Here too potential infinity is avoided by means of the circle. "'Infinity,'" comments Geck, "is an association well-suited to a series of variations: Hoffmann/ Kreisler wants to continue composing the Goldberg Variations."[12] The reference is to E. T. A. Hoffmann's 1810 story *Johannes Kreislers, des Kapellmeisters, musikalische Leiden*, in which the hero, having just played through the *Aria with Sundry Variations*, cannot stop with No. 30, but plays on. Remember that Bach organized the thirty variations into groups of three, with the last one in each group a canon; beginning with a canon at the unison in No. 3, the canons continue at the second in No. 6, at the third in No. 9, and so on to the canon at the ninth in No. 27 (the last variation, No. 30, is not a canon but a *quodlibet*). Had Bach arrested the series of canons at the seventh or the octave, the end of the series would have resembled the way the *Well-Tempered Keyboard* closes, where the octave reduplicates the unison. But when Bach oversteps the limits of the octave, he suggests that the series could go on forever. With the return of the initial Aria at the end of the cycle, the potentially infinite series turns into a circle. It is the only way to arrest the uncontrolled growth.

Bach's fascination with canons belongs in this context, too. Canons often evoke the idea of infinity (the eternally resounding *canon infinitus*) and nonlinear time. About one such endless canon, the *Trias harmonica,* BWV 1072, Christoph Wolff has observed: "[T]he canon addresses the phenomenon of progressive and regressive time in that it can be performed forward and backward."[13]

What matters to Bach in most of his music, whether vocal or instrumental, is not the linear flow of time from past to future, beginning to end. Rather, time is either made to follow a circular route or neutralized altogether. But why does Bach prefer this shape of time rather than the other, why the circle rather than the straight line? It is time to circle back to the Passion.

3   There Is No Time Like God's Time

mit dir will ich endlich schweben
voller Freud
ohne Zeit
dort im andern Leben.
—PAUL GERHARD, "Fröhlich soll mein Herze springen"
   in Bach, Christmas Oratorio, BWV 248, No. 33

Time present and time past
Are both perhaps present in time future,
And time future contained in time past.
If all time is eternally present
All time is unredeemable.
—T. S. ELIOT, "Burnt Norton," Four Quartets

Why this powerful gesture that abolishes time in the opening chorus before the story of the Passion even gets underway?

We know that in his representation of the story Bach did not limit himself, as he might have, to setting the text of the Gospel but combined that
text with two other textual strands—traditional chorales and Picander's free
poetry. The Gospel text, which mixes diegetic and mimetic modes, the voice
of the story's narrator (St. Matthew, the Evangelist), and the voices of its
various personages (such as Jesus, Pilatus, and others), is a straightforward
narrative representing events that took place in a distant but nevertheless
historically and geographically identifiable—and real—location and time.
At no point is it unclear who is speaking. The identity of the speakers in the
other two textual strands is less transparent.

The chorales are selected from the traditional repertory of hymns regularly sung in Lutheran churches by congregations. It would be reasonable
therefore to assume that they represent the congregation, St. Thomas's congregation of Bach's time but also, more broadly, the Lutheran community
as it had developed between the early sixteenth and early eighteenth centuries. The chorales are the collective voice of the several generations of
Lutheran faithful up to and including Bach's own congregation, and thus
they represent the objective, authoritative utterance of the church. Appropriately, they are always sung by both choirs in unison. By contrast, the

anonymous speakers of Picander's recitatives and arias are individuals, and their da capo arias, with or without introductory recitatives, are always sung by single voices from one or the other of the two choirs, even though duets, or even larger ensembles, would not be inconceivable. The contrast with the chorales, as well as what they say, permits the conclusion that these voices stand for individual members of the congregation listening to the Gospel story. The voices are always individual reactions to what has just happened in the narrative, just as the chorales are always collective reactions. Thus the first independent chorale is a reaction to Jesus's announcement to the disciples of his impending crucifixion: "Herzliebster Jesu, was hast du ver-brochen, daß man ein solch scharf Urteil hat gesprochen?" (Dearest Jesus, what wrong have you done, that you should have received such a harsh sentence?). It is not the disciples speaking here: as far as they know, no verdict has yet been passed. It is, rather, the collective voice of those who already know the outcome of the story. Similarly, after Jesus has scolded the disciples for objecting to a woman's pouring precious ointment on his head ("Daß sie dies Wasser hat auf meinen Leib gegossen, hat sie getan, daß man mich begraben wird" [For in that she hath poured this ointment on my body, she did it for my burial]), the Passion's first recitative comments: "Du lieber Heiland du, wenn deine Jünger töricht streiten, . . . so lasse mir inzwischen zu, von meiner Augen Tränenflüssen ein Wasser auf dein Haupt zu gießen!" (You dear Savior, while your disciples foolishly squabble, . . . let me pour on your head an ointment of the streams of tears from my eyes). Again, the speaker here is not a participant in the story but rather someone hearing the story.

Bach maintains this division of function throughout, assigning the chorale settings to collective reflections on the just-presented events of the Gospel narrative, and the anonymous recitatives and arias to individual reflections.[1] But at six strategic moments in the Passion, Picander names his speakers. Who are these figures and what is their role? Who, in particular, is the Daughter Zion, the active, exhorting partner in the dialogue with the Faithful?

The topography of the Passion is organized around three hills: Mount Zion in Jerusalem, the Mount of Olives to the east of the city, and Golgotha to the west.[2] The summit of the Mount of Olives, where Jesus went to pray after the Last Supper and before his arrest (the garden of Gethsemane was located at the base of the Mount of Olives), was a traditional place of prayer (2 Samuel 15.30 and 32: "And David went up by the ascent of mount Olivet. . . . And . . . when David was come to the top of the mount, where he worshipped God."). For Christians the summit of Golgotha, where Jesus was crucified, became the center of the world, the place where Adam was created and buried, and where the history of salvation culminated in Jesus's blood being shed on Adam's skull, redeeming the fallen humanity. For Jews a similarly central position was Mount Zion, the seat of the Temple, that is, the central seat of worship, God's dwelling place and His eschatological mountain, the promise of peace on earth (Isaiah 2.2–4: "And it shall come to pass in the last days, that the mountain of the Lord's house shall be established in the top of the mountains, and shall be exalted above the hills; and all nations shall flow unto it. . . . for out of Zion shall go forth the law. . . . and they shall beat their swords into plowshares").

Since Zion stands for the Temple of Jerusalem, it is more than likely that for Picander and his audience the Daughter Zion was, proximately, a daughter of Jerusalem, a witness of the crucifixion, and, more generally, a daughter of the church—representing the individual member of the congregation—in dialogue with the Faithful, representing the congregation as a whole. That Daughter Zion is one of the Faithful is also suggested by the way she addresses them at the outset: "Kommt, ihr Töchter" (Come, you daughters). They are all daughters, presumably the "daughters of Jerusalem" who witness and lament Jesus on his way of the cross (as reported in Luke 23.27–31), but also, and more profoundly, daughters of the church. That the Daughter and the Faithful belong together is also suggested in No. 60 ("Sehet, Jesus hat die Hand"). When the Daughter tells the Faithful, "Sehet, Jesus hat die Hand, uns zu fassen, ausgespannt" (See, Jesus has stretched out his hand to grasp us), her very "uns" (us) grasps both them and herself. Similarly, in No. 67 ("Nun ist der Herr zur Ruh gebracht") Zion talks of "unsre Sünden" (our sins) rather than just of her own. To think of Zion as one of the Faithful is another explanation, in addition to the need for a suitably monumental opening and closing, for why Bach sets her words to more than one voice not only in No. 1 but also in Nos. 27a–b ("So ist mein Jesus nun gefangen"–"Sind Blitze, sind Donner in Wolken verschwunden") and 67–68 ("Nun ist der Herr zur Ruh gebracht"–"Wir setzen uns mit Tränen nieder"): quite likely it did not make much difference to Bach whether she is thought of as an individual or as a collective personage. This would also explain why Picander did not hesitate to bring Zion and her companions together and have them sing the same text at the end of each of his two Parts, in Nos. 27b and 68—and why Bach should anticipate this at the end of the opening chorus.

The Faithful provide another clue in No. 30 ("Ach, nun ist mein Jesus hin") when they address Zion with the words of the Song of Solomon 6.1, "Wo ist denn dein Freund hingegangen, o du Schönste unter den Weibern?

Wo hat sich dein Freund hingewandt? So wollen wir mit dir ihn suchen."
(Whither is thy beloved gone, O thou fairest among women? whither is
thy beloved turned aside? that we may seek him with thee.) This suggests
that Picander's dialogue is modeled on the dialogue of the maiden and the
chorus of her companions in the Song of Solomon. Note that the companions there are repeatedly referred to as "daughters of Jerusalem" (Song of
Solomon 1.5, 2.7, 3.5, 5.8, 16, 8.4) or "daughters of Zion" (Song of Solomon
3.11). In the traditional Christian allegorical reading of the Song, the enamored maiden stood alternatively for Christ's bride, for the church (as in
Revelation 21.2, 9), and for the individual soul. Further strengthening the
allegorical link between the daughters of Jerusalem from the Song and those
from Luke who witnessed the way of the cross is the traditional Christian
interpretation of the Song as a prefiguration of the Passion. Elke Axmacher
argues persuasively that the opening chorus alludes to the Song of Solomon,
specifically to 3.11 ("Go forth, O ye daughters of Zion, and behold king
Solomon with the crown wherewith his mother crowned him in the day of
his espousals, and in the day of the gladness of his heart"); she shows that
in the usual allegorical interpretation of this verse Solomon stands for Jesus,
his crown for the crown of thorns, his mother for the Jewish synagogue,
and his wedding day for the Passion, the day when he paid for his Bride with
his blood; note that already in the opening chorus Christ is called the
"Bräutigam" (Bridegroom).[3]

According to this reading, Zion's function is fundamentally no different
from that of the anonymous individual faithful of the arias, just as the function of the Faithful is no different from that of the protagonists of the chorales;
presumably their anonymity is dropped only because the two enter into a
dialogue. Not all the arias are Zion's arias, and not all the chorales are the
Faithful's chorales, but both Zion and the Faithful belong with the other
anonymous protagonists of the arias and chorales, respectively.

With two exceptions (Nos. 1 and 29), the protagonists both of the chorales
and of the free poems, whether anonymous or named, perform a single function in the work: they are not participants in the Gospel story; rather, they
listen to it like any member of Bach's audience, or as you and I do, and they
always react to, and reflect and meditate upon, the just-presented event. With
the exception of Nos. 1 and 30 ("Ach, nun ist mein Jesus hin"), which open
Parts 1 and 2, respectively, all of Picander's arias or recitative-aria pairs are
preceded in the libretto by a reference to the particular event that occasions
them. Thus the first recitative-aria pair is preceded by the inscription "Als
das Weib Jesum gesalbet hatte" (When the woman had anointed Jesus), the
second aria by "Als Judas die 30 Silberlinge genommen" (When Judas had

taken the thirty pieces of silver), and so on. (With the exception of No. 29 ["O Mensch, bewein dein Sünde groß"], the chorales could have been similarly identified had the libretto included the chorale texts.) In fact, the dramaturgy of the Passion closely resembles that of the contemporary *opera seria* in its practice of punctuating the action, set as simple recitative, with reflective and musically fully developed numbers, mostly arias, in which the action halts to allow the passion aroused by the most recent event to be expressed. However, whereas in an opera the job of passionate reflection is left to the protagonists of the drama, in the Passion the reflection comes from outside.

The effect of this operatic dramaturgy is that it periodically arrests and neutralizes time. In the Passion, as in an opera, dramatic time, the time of the represented events, stops every now and then to make room for a timeless moment of contemplation before resuming. The musical forms usually employed at these moments are designed to support this time-arresting effect. Like language, music takes time. It cannot actually be made timeless, but it can suggest timelessness by bending the linear flow of time from past to future into a circular shape—by making the ending approximate the beginning, rather than being radically different from it. Among the forms capable of capturing a timeless moment of contemplation, the da capo aria is the single most common one. As we have already seen, the varied da capo aria has a circular form; the literal da capo even manages to incorporate the smaller circles of its A sections in the larger circle of the whole. The strophic form of the chorale, repeating the same melody with each stanza, is an even simpler way of producing circularity. To be sure, in most cases this effect remains latent in the Passion, since only one stanza is sung at any one time. But Bach compensates for this by using the same chorale at several different points in the unfolding story. Thus Nos. 15, 17, 54, and 62 present different stanzas of Paul Gerhardt's "O Haupt voll Blut und Wunden"; similarly, Nos. 3, 19, and 46 are stanzas of Johann Heermann's "Herzliebster Jesu, was hast du verbrochen," and Nos. 10 and 37 come from Paul Gerhardt's "O Welt, sieh hier dein Leben."

But in *opera seria* time wins over timelessness. Since the personages who engage in passionate reflection are the same who engage in the action, time never stands still for more than a moment. Reflection over, action must resume; the moments of reflection are experienced as interruptions of the underlying, and more fundamental, flow of time. Opera encompasses no second, alternative, ontological world order; hence there can be no alternative order of time either. There is only the time of the protagonists, which can be interrupted but then resumes. In the Passion, by contrast, timelessness wins because it is more fundamental than time. The acting and reflecting personages are not just distinct from one another but belong to altogether different ontological levels. The individual and collective faithful who contemplate the story of the last days of Jesus's earthly existence, whether named or anonymous, do not take part in the story; they are not even in Jerusalem at the time of the crucifixion. The represented world of the Passion splits time into three ontologically distinct strands: the time of Jesus's martyrdom narrated by the Evangelist, the time of the Evangelist's narration, and the time when this narration is contemplated by the individual and collective faithful. These three represented temporalities are, however, neither parallel nor equivalent. The time of the story is always structurally embedded within, and dependent upon, the time of the storytelling: the latter forms the framework within which the former may appear. But in the Russian doll–like world represented in the Passion, the moments of contemplation form an even more fundamental frame for both narrator and story.

It is perhaps easiest to see the hierarchy of ontological levels, or frames, by considering the order in which this particular onion might best be peeled. A Passion setting without the outermost layer of contemplation, representing only the narrator and his story, is conceivable—and, indeed, there were many such settings before Bach's time. It is even possible to have the story without the narrator; in that case the story would be represented in the dramatic, rather than the diegetic, mode. What is not possible is to have only the layer of contemplation, or only the two outer layers, that of the contemplating faithful and that of the narrator. The story must be there, whether or not it is narrated and contemplated. For us, the listeners, what matters most is the story—that is the center of our attention. Structurally, or ontologically, however, the frame is more important. We may not care about the narrator, but the narrator makes the story visible. The time of the storytelling is ontologically prior, more fundamental, than the time of the story told. In the triplicate world of Bach's Passion, the structurally most important layer is the outermost frame, that of the contemplating faithful. (Moments of contemplation also form the musically most substantial layer in the Passion.) Even more primordial than the temporality of storytelling, the temporality of contemplation is, like the temporality of most of the Passion's music, of the da capos arias and chorales in which it is embodied, one of arrested flow of time. In the Passion, time (or, strictly speaking, the two temporalities of story and of storytelling) is nested within timeless eternity (the temporality of contemplation).

That the moments of contemplation are not merely operatic interruptions of narrative flow but form the outermost frame within which the nar-

rator and his story appear is nowhere more explicit than at the very beginning, in the opening chorus. "Kommt, ihr Töchter, helft mir klagen" (Come,
daughters, help me lament), Zion urges her companions, even though nothing has happened yet to justify lamentation and reflection. To say what she
does, she must know the story already—it must already have come to pass.
And to that story lamentation is indeed the fitting response. When, in the
final chorus, the Daughter and the Faithful together intone, "Wir setzen uns
mit Tränen nieder" (We sit down in tears), they are responding to the most
recent event of the story, the burial, but their tears are also those Zion called
for at the outset. (Remember that Bach and Picander create this opening anticipation of the conclusion by giving Zion and the Faithful a shared text both
in the last portion of No. 1 and in the last number of the Passion.) In the
world of the story, time passed—there was a beginning and, especially, an
ending. In the timeless world of contemplation, beginning and end are one.

Besides the opening chorus, only one other musical number departs from
the norm in not offering a reflection on the immediately preceding event.
This is the chorale fantasia No. 29 ("O Mensch, bewein dein Sünde groß").
Although it was written to open the second version of the St. John Passion,
Bach eventually used it to close Part 1 of the revised 1736 version of the St.
Matthew Passion. Bach's original ending for Part 1 was No. 29a, a simple
harmonization of a stanza from Christian Keymann's chorale "Meinen Jesum laß ich nicht" that functioned like any other chorale collectively
reflecting on what has just happened. Originally the Evangelist ended his
account of Jesus's arrest with a straightforward report on the behavior of
the disciples: "Then all the disciples forsook him, and fled." This is not how
the congregation hopes to behave: "Meinen Jesum laß ich nicht" (I shall
not forsake my Jesus). The new chorale fantasia, on the other hand, functions more like the opening chorus (which is what it initially was, of course)
and offers a collective reflection not on the immediately preceding event but
on the significance of Christ's sacrifice for the fallen humanity: "O Mensch,
bewein dein Sünde groß, darum Christus seins Vaters Schoß äußert und kam
auf Erden" (O man, weep over your grave sin for which Christ broke out
of his father's womb and came to earth).

With this substitution Bach may have renounced choral contemplation
of the immediately preceding event, that of the fleeing disciples, but he made
sure to provide reflection for the larger event of Jesus's arrest. Zion refers
to the arrest when at the beginning of Part 2 she reflects on "mein Lamm
in Tigerklauen" (my lamb in tiger's clutches) and asks, "wo ist mein Jesus
hin?" (where is my Jesus?). Bach probably decided on the substitution to
give Part 1 a musically more substantial closure. But in making it, he also

strengthened the dramaturgical effect of a timeless frame enclosing the temporal narrative. Like the opening chorus, the fantasia too issues a call to lamentation, linking itself through a chain of tears with both the beginning and the end of the Passion, a chain that leads from "Kommt, ihr Töchter, helft mir klagen" and "O Mensch, bewein" to "Wir setzen uns mit Tränen nieder."[4]

The fact that, unlike in opera, those who contemplate the story in a Passion do not participate in it has a time-attenuating effect in yet another sense. As we have seen, the represented individual and collective faithful who reflect on the story exist in an ontological order different from that of the personages of the story. Their time is different from Jesus's time, but they too, no less than Jesus, are part of the world being represented, and this further attenuates the temporal distance between the contemplators and the personages. The distance is not obliterated altogether: we know that the contemplators are not literally bystanders; they, no less than we, contemplate a representation of action rather than an actually occurring action. But even as this ontological distance is maintained, it is attenuated, for the contemplators are presented within the same representation as that within which the personages are presented. Both the situation and the effect are similar to what happens in paintings that show the Madonna and worshipping donors or faithful. We know that the Madonna, the Child, the saints, and the angels in Titian's *Madonna of Ca' Pesaro* (in S. Maria Gloriosa dei Frari in Venice) do not belong to the world of the proud Pesaro family who contemplate them. But when the two distinct worlds are brought together in a single representation, the distinction to some extent blurs and the distance diminishes. The same effect is produced in countless other representations of this sort, including Caravaggio's *Madonna of the Pilgrims* (in Sant'Agostino in Rome).

In the opening chorus of the St. Matthew Passion the distance between personages and contemplators is even further attenuated because here the contemplators (the Daughter and the Faithful) are also bystanders (the "daughters of Jerusalem" from Luke 23.27–31). In Axmacher's subtle reading, the representation hesitates between the historical (where the "daughters" come from Luke 23.27) and the allegorical (where they come from the Song of Solomon 3.11).[5]

More important, Picander and Bach help to attenuate the distance between Jesus's time and the time of the faithful by emphasizing "seeing" over "hearing" the story. "Sehet" (see), Zion repeatedly urges, and Bach makes this "sehet" the pivotal moment of his setting. In Picander's poem "sehet" is spoken only by Zion. In Bach's setting, however, the word is once, and once only, picked up by the Faithful (see chapter 1 appendix). This coincides with the crucial moment in m. 72 when the regular da capo form collapses, the successive becomes simultaneous, and the two protagonists start sharing the same text. Yet the second choir does not start doubling the first chorus until m. 73. Its separate "sehet" one measure earlier is not a musical doubling of Zion's "sehet" but rather echoes the time she first uttered this word, in m. 26. Without a painter's intervention a story that has already taken place cannot be seen; it can only be narrated and heard. Bach's insistence on seeing rather than hearing is, again, reminiscent of the Titian and Caravaggio paintings in which representatives of two distinct worlds exchange glances and, in "seeing" one another, are linked across the ontological divide. It is this sort of a glance, this pivotal "sehet" in m. 72 at the very moment when normal musical time flow is transfigured into eternity, that opens our understanding of the contemplators' role in the Passion: the "sehet" that converts time into eternity is the "sehet" of hermeneutics.

The creator who embraces in a single representation both the personages and the contemplators, both the story and its audience, does so to tell the real audience how to perceive the story. The contemplators are there to teach by example. Zion and her companions, as well as the anonymous individual and collective faithful, are there to show the congregation of St. Thomas's, and all future audiences of the Passion, how to "see" and what to make of the represented story. The Passion not only frames the sermon (which was read between the two Parts), it actually is a sermon—or, rather, it is both the Gospel reading to be interpreted and the sermon interpreting it.[6] The crowning component of this kind of hermeneutic exercise is *applicatio*, applying interpreted meaning to the particular situation of the audience and thus reflecting on the text's use or value for us.

—

Zion and the rest are there to tell us what to do, feel, and think. So what is it they are telling us?

They begin, in No. 1, by telling us that Jesus sacrificed himself to redeem our sins, and by asking us to "see" this—to see both what could be seen if we were eyewitnesses ("den Bräutigam" [the bridegroom], "als wie ein Lamm" [like a lamb], "Holz zum Kreuze selber tragen!" [himself bearing the wood of the cross!]) and to see the invisible ("die Geduld" [patience], "unsre Schuld" [our guilt], and how Jesus did what he did "aus Lieb und Huld" [out of love and grace]). The same general message is repeated at the end of Part 1 by the chorale fantasia No. 29 ("O Mensch, bewein dein Sünde groß") and at the end of Part 2 by recitative No. 67 ("Nun ist der Herr zur

Ruh gebracht"), which precedes the final chorus: the timeless frame that encloses the temporal narrative is the ideal place explicitly to spell out the Passion's central teaching.

The story of the Passion is so familiar that it is easy to forget just how incomprehensible it really is. It is only by reflecting on it that we can begin to realize how little we actually understand, and how much we need interpretive explanation of its teaching. Today its teaching has become opaque even to most Christians. As Hans Blumenberg has reminded us, "It is perhaps too little regarded that contemporary listeners of Bach's St. Matthew Passion [Blumenberg refers here to our contemporaries, not Bach's] are not only more or less 'nonbelievers' who have lost the capacity to grasp the 'dogmatic' of the suffering and dying One but, more important, 'the unenlightened,' who neither can nor wish to admit that they are 'sinners' and in need of redemption, whether this or some other kind."[7] In this respect we all require the help of theologians and historians of Christian doctrine.[8] Assuming that one is not treating the Passion merely as an object of aesthetic delectation (which, given its subject, would be an attitude of refined barbarism), the central question raised by the work—indeed, the central question raised by Christianity—is why Jesus's self-sacrifice was necessary. (It is a question that seems to have troubled Jesus himself in his prayer on the Mount of Olives: "O my Father, if it be possible, let this cup pass from me" [Matthew 26.39].) Although the Nicean Creed would have us believe that Jesus came from heaven "propter nos" (because of us), or "propter nostram salutem" (on account of our salvation), and was crucified "pro nobis" (for us), it did not address the question of why the sacrifice was necessary. This task, as Jaroslav Pelikan has explained, was assumed by Anselm of Canterbury (ca. 1033–1109).[9]

Anselm taught that God was not only merciful but also just, and that, were God's justice to be satisfied, man's sins could not simply be forgiven. The possibility of forgiveness required some form of satisfaction ("redemption" in the sense in which a loan may be redeemed). But man by himself was incapable of rendering God complete satisfaction, since this required that God be given something the sinner owned but did not owe, something greater than any debt owed and more valuable than everything that is not God. Man did not possess anything like this, but the life of God's son fulfilled the requirements. Christ's dual nature, at once divine and human, enabled satisfaction because whereas only a human being could render satisfaction for the human fall, and only a human could suffer and die, only God could grant sufficient repayment. When sinless Christ was punished on sinful man's behalf, sacrificed in payment for man's sins, his suffering had a redemptive value precisely because it was both undeserved and freely willed. This is how the cross redeemed mankind and how we were forgiven; this is how the requirements of both divine mercy and divine justice were met. The cause of the Passion was in our sins (in this sense Christ suffered and died "propter nos"); its purpose was our salvation, or reconciliation with God, brought about by the redemption of sins (in this sense Christ suffered and died "pro nobis").

Anselm's teaching was adopted by the Reformation and became the cornerstone of Lutheran orthodoxy. For the Reformers, unlike the Roman Catholic church, full redemption of sinners was achieved once sinless Christ had died on the cross; nothing else—whether the sacrifice of the Mass, the sacrament of penance, or individual good works—was needed or could add to that full redemption. In a Passion sermon of 1544 Luther insisted: "You should know and believe . . . that Christ suffered thus because of your sins, that God charged Christ with these sins and that Christ most obediently assumed them and paid for them, so that when you recognize that you are a sinner and have angered God you nevertheless do not despair, but are comforted by this suffering and compensation of our Lord Christ."[10] The effect of the Passion is to make us feel penitent but above all consoled and joyful. If our sins were its cause, our salvation is its purpose.

As Axmacher has demonstrated in detail, Picander in adapting Müller's sermons chose to diminish the theological content of his models, eliminating all references to God's wrath as the reason for the sacrifice, playing down God's active role in the story, stressing Jesus's humanity over his divinity, and concentrating on the loving, compassionate heart of the individual believer. Picander's text, Axmacher concludes, marks the Pietistically colored transition from strict Orthodoxy to the undogmatic positions of Lutheran Enlightenment. It is thus thanks to Picander that the Passion participates in the gradual trend away from the Anselmic-Lutheran doctrine of atonement which set in after 1700.[11] Characteristic of this trend is a shift in religious emphasis from God to Jesus, and from punishment to suffering, focusing less now on faith in God's redemptive actions and more on the mutual love between Jesus and humanity. Pietism, with its accent on feeling, mediates the process whereby the God-centered Orthodox vision gradually gives way to the anthropocentric vision of Lutheran Enlightenment.

If, therefore, we moderns are inclined to see in the Passion only a story of appalling injustice inflicted on an obviously good and innocent man, Picander and Bach are themselves partly to blame. (They can also be held partly responsible for a nineteenth-century revival of the Passion in the spirit of Friedrich Schleiermacher's theology, according to which religion was not thought or action but feeling transmitted by artful words and music.)[12] It is only in this context that the great twentieth-century Lutheran theologian Karl Barth's otherwise surprising criticism of Bach's Passion can be understood:

> It is a single sea of clouds, wonderfully undulating, to be sure, but in almost uninterrupted minor and consisting of sighs, laments and accusations, cries of terror, pity, compassion: a funeral ode that concludes in an outright dirge ("Ruhe sanft!"), that is neither defined nor determined by the Easter message, and in which Jesus the Victor remains entirely mute. How long before the Church realizes this, and how long before the untold thousands who may know only this one version of the Gospel's Passion story are told that what we have here is an abstraction, and that it is certainly *not* the Passion of *Jesus Christ?*[13]

The theologian's annoyance is actually easy to understand: in 1920 a Swedish archbishop, Nathan Söderblom, called Bach's Passion "the fifth Gospel."[14] For Barth, however, "the incomparable one" (der Unvergleichliche) was not Bach but Mozart, because in his view it is Mozart's music that embodies the love of life and fundamental optimism that link the Enlightenment of the eighteenth century with the essential message of Christianity.[15] This view makes some sense: after all, the Gospels do bring—they are—good tidings, and Bach's dissonant, chromatic counterpoint, relentlessly maintained literally from beginning to end, threatens to drown those tidings in a flood of tears. In the contest between the celestial, serene G major of the chorale and the earthy, tortured E minor of the aria of the opening chorus, the minor certainly prevails.

All the same, Barth is not quite fair: Bach can hardly be blamed for choosing not to emphasize the message of Easter Sunday in music written for Good Friday.[16] Moreover, Blumenberg's opposing view of the matter has merit too: "Only suffering and death [as opposed to the nativity, resurrection, and ascension] are common to all the Evangelists and have—thanks to the affinity that the first theologian, Paul, and his followers, Augustine and Luther, felt for the Cross—become the center of Christian thought. Bach is great because he assimilated this centering and set it to music."[17]

Although the transition away from the Anselmic-Lutheran vision left unmistakable traces in Bach's Passions, the process was by no means completed there. In Axmacher's opinion the text of the St. Matthew Passion remains rooted in Lutheran Orthodoxy and is only marginally touched by Enlightenment forces.[18] Pelikan, too, claims that the St. Matthew Passion still centers on the Anselmic doctrine, not least thanks to the chorale texts. Recall the chorale of the opening chorus: "O Lamm Gottes, unschuldig am

Stamm des Kreuzes geschlachtet. . . . All Sünd hast du getragen, sonst müßten wir verzagen" (O innocent Lamb of God, slaughtered on the cross. . . . You have borne all sin, otherwise we should despair). And the chorale at the end of Part 1: "Er für uns geopfert würd, trüg unsrer Sünden schwere Bürd" (He would be sacrificed for us, would carry the heavy load of our sins). Recall, finally, the last recitative of the Passion: "Habt lebenslang vor euer Leiden tausend Dank, daß ihr mein Seelenheil so wert geacht'" (Have lifelong thousand thanks for your suffering, for having considered the salvation of my soul to be worth so much). Our response to Christ's Passion is simultaneously sorrow at His suffering ("Wir setzen uns mit Tränen nieder") and consolation at our reconciliation with God. In the words of the final chorus: "Euer Grab und Leichenstein soll dem ängstlichen Gewissen ein bequemes Ruhekissen . . . sein" (Your grave and tombstone shall for the anxious conscience a comfortable pillow prove).

—

As we see, the hermeneutic *applicatio* is central to Bach's St. Matthew Passion: the events of the interpreted story happened "because of us" and "for us"; *propter nos* and *pro nobis* are indispensable components of the doctrine promulgated in the Credo. What is striking about Zion and the rest of the contemplators, however, is the relentlessness with which they encourage us to take an imaginatively active stance, to do the impossible and enter the world of the story as participants.

In the anointment scene in Bethany, where Jesus defends a woman against having used ointment wastefully, the alto responds in the recitative No. 5 ("Du lieber Heiland du") by offering to "pour on your head an ointment of the streams of tears from my eyes" (von meiner Augen Tränenflüssen ein Wasser auf dein Haupt zu gießen). The ensuing aria amplifies this: "daß die Tropfen meiner Zähren angenehme Spezerei, treuer Jesu, dir gebären" (May the drops of my tears be as pleasant spices for you, dear Jesus). Tears, no less than glances, establish direct eye contact across the ontological gap between the believer and Jesus.

During the Last Supper, after Jesus has told his twelve disciples that one of them will betray him and they all ask, "Herr, bin ichs?" (Lord, is it I?), the chorale (No. 10) answers: "Ich bins" (It is I). The disciples' troubled self-questioning—subject of so many pictorial representations—is answered in the affirmative by the eavesdropping faithful of the chorale, aware of their own fallen state and weakness and thereby representing the disciples. Here again we experience the ontological gap bridged. Shortly afterward, when Jesus gives the disciples bread and wine as his body and "blood of the new testament, which is shed for many for the remission of sins," announcing that this is the last time he will drink wine on earth, the soprano becomes one with the disciples in the recitative (No. 12): "Wiewohl mein Herz in Tränen schwimmt, daß Jesus von mir Abschied nimmt, so macht mich doch sein Testament erfreut" (Although my heart swims in tears because Jesus takes leave of me, still his testament makes me glad).

At the beginning of the Mount of Olives scene Jesus, comparing himself and the disciples to a shepherd with his sheep, tells the disciples that this night "the sheep of the flock shall be scattered abroad" but that after the resurrection he will go before them into Galilee. In response, the faithful of the chorale (No. 15) again identify with the disciples: "Erkenne mich, mein Hüter, mein Hirte, nimm mich an!" (Recognize me, my guardian, my shepherd, receive me!). And yet again, when Peter and the disciples tell Jesus that they will not deny him, the chorale (No. 17) speaks as one with them: "Ich will hier bei dir stehen; verachte mich doch nicht! Von dir will ich nicht gehen, wenn dir dein Herze bricht" (I want to stand by you here; do not despise me! I do not want to leave you when your heart breaks). Soon after Jesus, going to pray, tells Peter and the two sons of Zebedee: "My soul is exceedingly sorrowful, even unto death: tarry ye here and watch with me." The tenor's recitative (No. 19, "O Schmerz! hier zittert das gequälte Herz") answers for the disciples, "Ach könnte meine Liebe dir, mein Heil, dein Zittern und dein Zagen vermindern oder helfen tragen, wie gerne blieb ich hier!" (Ah! if my love could diminish or help you bear, my Savior, your trembling and your quailing, how gladly would I remain here!), and the aria (No. 20) continues in the same vein: "Ich will bei meinem Jesu wachen" (I want to keep watch beside my Jesus). When Jesus is arrested, the Faithful who accompany Zion's aria (No. 27a, "So ist mein Jesus nun gefangen") behave as if they were the protesting disciples: "Laßt ihn, haltet, bindet nicht!" (Leave him, stop, do not bind!). Note that the Evangelist has yet to mention their protest. Picander's libretto makes it clear that the Faithful are not literally the disciples but that they identify with the disciples so completely as to anticipate their angry protest. In the chorus that follows (No. 27b, "Sind Blitze, sind Donner in Wolken verschwunden") Zion and the Faithful join forces in what is perhaps the most terrifying outburst of collective rage in all of music.

During Jesus's interrogation by the high priests, when Peter, having thrice denied his master, "ging heraus und weinete bitterlich" (went out and wept bitterly), the alto identifies completely with him in his aria (No. 39): "Erbarme dich, mein Gott, um meiner Zähren willen! Schaue hier, Herz und Auge weint vor dir bitterlich" (Have mercy, my God, on account of my tears. Look here, heart and eye weep bitterly before you). And yet the alto is not impersonating Peter: the disciple himself spoke a moment earlier, and his was a bass voice. Rather, the anonymous believer is imaginatively bridging the gap between herself and Peter. The immediately ensuing chorale (No. 40) similarly speaks for the apostle: "Bin ich gleich von dir gewichen, stell ich mich doch wieder ein" (If I have just abandoned you, yet I come back). In the episode of Judas's repentance, which follows, the bass in his aria (No. 42) completely identifies with Judas, speaking as if he were Judas: "Gebt mir meinen Jesum wieder!" (Give me back my Jesus!). The distinction between the personage and the anonymous believer may seem more problematic here, as both are presented by basses. But the aria is sung by the bass of the second choir, whereas Judas's part was probably sung by the bass of the first choir. In any case the distinction between personages and contemplators has been firmly established by this time, so there is no danger of confusion.

Thus in the scene with Jesus before Pilate, when the governor asks the people, "Was hat er denn Übels getan?" (What evil has he done?), a believer answers in the soprano recitative (No. 48) as if she were one of the people: "Er hat uns allen wohlgetan" (He has done us all good). Again "as if" applies here. There is no danger that the soprano will be taken literally for one of the people. Rather, she is someone who listens to the story and in imagination identifies with its personages. The same occurs in the flagellation scene, when a believer imagines herself into the story and screams at Jesus's tormentors in the alto recitative (No. 51, "Erbarm es Gott"): "Ihr Henker, halt ein!" (Tormentors, stop!). Such a voice, no less than a glance, can carry across the divide separating contemplators from personages. Once the burial has taken place, the Daughter Zion and the Faithful together in the final chorus (No. 68) imagine themselves like "Mary Magdalene, and the other Mary, sitting over against the sepulchre": "Wir setzen uns mit Tränen nieder und rufen dir im Grabe zu: Ruhe sanfte, sanfte ruh!" (We sit down in tears and call to you in the grave: rest gently, rest in peace!).

Obviously, not all contemplation takes this imaginatively active form. On a number of occasions the faithful simply interpret the contemplated scene, without attempting to enter it. Sometimes they are touchingly naive and didactic, as when the tenor in recitative No. 34 explains in a Sunday-school manner why "Jesus schwieg stille" (Jesus held his peace) in the face of false witnesses: "Mein Jesus schweigt zu falschen Lügen stille, um uns damit zu zeigen, daß sein Erbarmens voller Wille vor uns zum Leiden sei geneigt, und daß wir in dergleichen Pein ihm sollen ähnlich sein und in Verfolgung stille schweigen" (My Jesus holds his peace in front of false lies, thereby to show us that his merciful will was inclined to suffer before us, and that in similar distress we should be like him and hold our peace in persecution).[19] In the overwhelming number of cases assembled here, however, the contemplators are not satisfied with such calm reasoning and instead cross over the onto-logical divide to participate in the story. They do not want merely to un-derstand what happened and why; they want to feel what it was like to be there. The temporal distance between them and the personages of the story cannot be obliterated, but in imagination they can bridge it. And since the contemplators' role is to teach us, the audience, by example, to show us the proper hermeneutic behavior, it follows that one of Bach's aims in this ser-mon is to attenuate the temporal distance between our world and the world of the story. This is not because he does not know how much time has passed since those distant events but rather because, being aware of how much time has passed, he wishes to neutralize it, to convince us that it is not important.

The privatization of faith so characteristic of Protestantism—the con-ception of religion as a private matter between the individual and God, and as a matter not in need of mediation by professional clergy—demanded that every believer internalize the message of the Gospels. To a Protestant, the story itself, or even the story as interpreted by the Church, is not enough; the story must be individually internalized, and that requires that the time of the story become the individual's time. Bach deploys an array of artistic means, both musical and dramaturgical, with the sole purpose of thwarting time and allowing the listener to hear the story as occurring in the present. If the injunction of "Sehet" is to be obeyed, time has to be rendered impo-tent, its flow either stopped or bent into a circle.

Not only the opening chorus but the Passion as a whole is marked by this wish to neutralize time and render insignificant its relentless flow from past to future. Bach accomplishes this to some extent with musical and dra-maturgical means drawn from *opera seria,* where action is periodically inter-rupted by passionate reflection embodied in circularly shaped da capo arias. He further draws on dramaturgical means proper to the epic-dramatic, or-atorical genre that is the Passion, which allows a composer to frame and em-bed the time of the story within the timelessness of contemplation, and to blur the temporal distance between personages and contemplators—that is, by implication, between Jesus and us.[20]

The desire to bridge the time gap between now and then is built into any act of interpretive contemplation and must be particularly pronounced when what is contemplated is an action undertaken *propter nos* and *pro nobis.* But it is not the only reason that Bach tried to neutralize the linear time flow in his music. What concerned him was not only the act of contemplation but also the specific character of the contemplated object. What is characteristic of Bach's Passion—complex temporality embedding linear flow of time within the framework of eternity—is also present in the personal story of Jesus, the explicit subject of the Passion, and in the story of humanity, the implied context of Jesus's story (the context within which the represented sacrifice makes sense, and the reverse, the context that makes sense thanks to the sacrifice).

To the extent that Jesus was a man, his life story, like that of any human being, had its irreversible temporal shape suspended between birth and death. But whatever Jesus himself may have thought about his nature, and whatever his earliest followers may have thought or whatever we may think today, for Christians as of the last decade of the first century—the time of St. John's Gospel—and surely for Bach and his congregation, Jesus was not only man but also God. His birth was God's incarnation, the enfleshment of the Logos ("And the Word was made flesh, and dwelt among us," as St. John's Gospel famously affirms [1.14]), and his death, followed by resurrection, was the return to whence he had come. As a man, he was temporal; his earthly existence had a beginning (he "was made flesh") and an end ("It is finished," were his last words, St. John reports [19.30]). But "before and after," as God, he was eternal: "The same [the Word] was in the beginning with God," says St. John (1.2). He "was" (not "was made," as in when he "was made flesh"), and was "in the beginning," the beginning of which Genesis 1.1 says that "In the beginning God created the heaven and the earth." Hence he was eternal.

The history of humanity exhibits a similar structure of linear temporality embedded within the envelope of eternity. Like every individual human life story, that of mankind too has linear irreversibility punctuated by the central events of creation, fall, redemption (the stages already traversed), and the expected resurrection of the dead at the end of earthly time; in the last words of the Credo: "Et exspecto resurrectionem mortuorum. Et vitam venturi saeculi" (And I await the resurrection of the dead. And the life of the age to come). The linear time of human earthly history is not infinite; it had a beginning and will come to an end. "Before" and "after" there is God's infinite time—"cujus regni non erit finis" (whose [Christ's] kingdom shall have no end), the Credo affirms—there is eternity.

Like the universe of Plato, the universe of Christians is split into two—the temporal, mutable here and now, this world in which we humans are born, dwell, and die, and the atemporal, immutable, transcendent beyond of God. But these two realms do not simply exist side by side. Rather, this world is enveloped in the transcendent one, is dependent on it, and owes its existence to it: "All things were made by him; and without him was not any thing made that was made," says St. John (1.3). It is this fundamental structure of irreversible time embedded in eternity, of man's time suspended in God's time, that Bach replicates in the St. Matthew Passion. And in adhering to this structure, Bach seems closer to Dante than to us moderns.

The *Divine Comedy*, Hegel wrote in the *Aesthetics*,

> has for its subject matter the eternal action, the absolute end and aim, the love of God in its imperishable activity and unalterable sphere . . . ; into this changeless existent it plunges the living world of human action and suffering and, more particularly, the deeds and fates of individuals. . . . There stands there . . . everything otherwise most fleeting and transient in the living world, fathomed objectively in its inmost being, judged in its worth or worthlessness by the supreme Concept, i.e. by God. For as individuals *were* in their passions and sufferings, in their intentions and their accomplishments, so now here they are presented for ever, solidified into images of bronze. . . . The figures of the real world . . . *have* moved and now in their being and action are frozen and are eternal themselves in the arms of eternal justice.[21]

Erich Auerbach considered this to be "one of the most beautiful passages ever written on Dante" and glossed it extensively in his own luminous essay in *Mimesis*.[22] The "all-inclusive subject" of Comedy, Auerbach wrote,

> is the *status animarum post mortem*. Reflecting God's definitive judgment, this *status* must needs represent a perfectly harmonious whole . . . ; indeed it must needs express the unity of God's universal order in a purer and more immediate form than this earthly sphere . . . , for the beyond . . . is not . . . evolution, potentiality, and provisionality, but God's design in active fulfillment. The unified order of the beyond . . . can be most immediately grasped as a moral system in its distribution of souls among the three realms. . . . For it is precisely the absolute realization of a particular earthly personality in the place definitively assigned to it, which constitutes the Divine Judgment.

The earthly, transient, temporal realm, Auerbach concluded, is "merely figural, potential, and requiring fulfillment" in the changeless, eternal beyond.[23] Bach's worldview is still based on this structure of the linear time of humanity embedded within the hierarchically more fundamental eternity of God.

⸻

"Gottes Zeit ist die allerbeste Zeit" (God's time is the very best time) proclaims an early cantata (BWV 106).[24] God's time is not just ontologically more important—prior in some sense, one without which there would be no time of the created world—but it is also better, "the very best," even. Why this preference for eternity?

Irreversibility, the essential feature of human time, is not without its attractions: irreversible time brings change and hence, for those who do not like their present situation, hope. As Tomasi di Lampedusa's Prince thought, "Finché c'è morte c'è speranza" (As long as there is death, there is hope).[25] We, too, occasionally see it in this light. Blumenberg writes:

> People have not always inquired about immortality and apparently will not always be inquiring about it in the future; from its entry into the biblical text after the Babylonian exile all the way to Kant's postulate of immortality, it was a position that . . . every new system had to occupy. It is only the actual lengthening of lifetimes and the less unpleasant ways in which this additional time is spent that have caused the interest in immortality to flag and its systematic position to disappear. It appears that even contemporary Christianity, around the world, scarcely mentions immortality in its rhetoric any longer, and thus unintentionally has abandoned a principal element of its historical identity.[26]

Perhaps. But the norm remained fear inspired by time's irreversibility : time devours everything we love and then it devours us too. God's time, time without irreversibility, is the very best because it allows permanence and thus holds death at bay. In Bach's cantata the words of Revelation 22.20 ("Ja, komm, Herr Jesu!" [Even so, come, Lord Jesus]) overcome those of Sirach (Ecclesiasticus) 14.17 ("Es ist der alte Bund, [Mensch] du mußt sterben!" [for the decree from old is, you must die!]), as belief in the inevitability of death facing humanity in its fallen state gives way to the hope of life everlasting bought back for us by Jesus's redeeming sacrifice, and fear of the ending gives way to longing for the Redeemer's second coming and the end of earthly time. In man's time all is vanity because sooner or later everything passes into oblivion. Our only hope of permanence is the promise that we may be translated into God's time. *Dei tempus optimum* because it allows the faithful to say: "Et exspecto resurrectionem mortuorum. Et vitam venturi saeculi."

It is because God's eternity is better than the irreversible time of humanity that Bach, like so many of his predecessors, celebrates it in his music, too. He reveals his preference for God's time when he privileges invention over disposition, atemporal exploration of possibilities hidden in an idea over the specific temporal order of the results of such research. Bach's mental capacities were so extraordinary that, had he addressed his music to God only, he might have dispensed with temporal disposition altogether: Bach's

God, like Leibniz's, could surely have heard all the transformations of material at once, and so, it almost seems, could Bach himself.[27] It is for the benefit of lesser mortals that the temporal arrangement of the transformations was introduced.

But the preference for God's time shows at an even more fundamental level. Mozart, Beethoven, Schubert, Schumann, Chopin, Wagner, Brahms, Debussy—the list might continue. All of these composers, whether actually or only figuratively, kept the *Well-Tempered Keyboard* on hand. It could not have been just for instruction on how to construct fugues; the sets contain the classic exempla of the genre, but the genre itself, for all its learned prestige and its nimbus of antiquity, interested posterity only intermittently. No, the reason the *WTC* remained a staple for subsequent composers is their recognition that Bach, to use Beethoven's characterization of 1801, is the *Urvater der Harmonie* ("progenitor of harmony")—not a "brook *[Bach]* but an ocean," as he famously punned on a later occasion, in July 1825, "because of his infinite and inexhaustible wealth of combinations and harmonies."[28] (We shall never know whether Goethe intended a similar pun when, in a letter of 28 March 1829, he reacted from Weimar to Zelter's reports of Mendelssohn's performances of the St. Matthew Passion in Berlin: "It is as if from a distance I heard the roaring of the sea" [Es ist mir als wenn ich von ferne das Meer brausen hörte].)[29]

By 1825 the understanding of harmony seems already to have been reduced to its narrow, modern sense of a musician's craft, the ability to combine different tones into chords and move from one chord to the next in a grammatically correct fashion. The expression of 1801, however, is notable for its implied divinization of Bach as harmony's creator and suggests that something of the premodern sense of the term still lingered. "Speaking universally . . . music is nothing but harmony," Gioseffo Zarlino had declared in 1558 in his *Le Istitutioni harmoniche*, a treatise that provided the rules of *prima prattica* with their definitive codification, and explained that harmony was the "concord of discords, meaning a concord of diverse things that can be joined together."[30] Harmony in this broader sense not only included the craft of making acceptable chords and chord progressions but embraced all consonant relations both between tones and between simultaneously moving melodic lines. The rules of harmony, like the theorems of mathematics, were timeless, immutable, eternal—although, again like the rules of geometry or algebra, they had to be discovered by successive generations. Moreover, the reach of the term harmony extended far beyond the world of sound: the "concord of diverse things" obtained as well in the human microcosm (the Boethian *musica humana*) and the larger cosmos (*mu-*

sica mundana). The audible harmony of musicians (*musica instrumentalis*) therefore reflected the intelligible harmony of the universe created by God. This is why the medium of music was so well suited for praising God. It is no accident that the only art that angels practiced in heaven was music.

There are three layers to the harmony that constitutes the essence of music. In its narrowest sense—the only meaning still fully surviving today—harmony is the craft of constructing chords and chord progressions. In a somewhat broader, still musical-technical, sense harmony also included counterpoint, the craft of combining diverse simultaneous melodic lines. In its broadest sense the audible harmony produced by musicians participated in the intelligible harmony of creation.

All three conceptions were very much alive for Bach. His few surviving remarks on the aims of his music making are remarkably consistent. Here, for instance, is how he reworded for his students a passage from Friedrich Erhardt Niedt's treatise on thorough bass, which controls the construction of chords and chord progressions:

> The thorough bass is the most perfect foundation of music, being played with both hands in such manner that the left hand plays the notes written down while the right adds consonances and dissonances, in order to make a well-sounding harmony to the Glory of God and the permissible delectation of the spirit; and the aim and final reason, as of all music, so of the thorough bass should be none else but the Glory of God and the recreation of the mind. Where this is not observed, there will be no real music but only a devilish hubbub.[31]

Here is Bach's belief in a nutshell: music is the craft of making "a well-sounding harmony" for "the Glory of God and the permissible delectation of the spirit." Bach does not explicitly say that well-sounding harmony is analogous to the harmonious nature of the creation and therefore suitable for glorifying God, but this can legitimately be surmised, being an essential component of Bach's intellectual tradition.

From scattered remarks left by those who knew Bach—his musician sons, students, and critics—we can flesh out this idea. When, like Beethoven, they saw Bach as the progenitor of harmony, it was with at least the first two and perhaps all three layers of the meaning of harmony (of chord progressions, simultaneous lines, and creation) alive in the term. In particular, they believed that well-sounding harmony controlled by thorough bass is not simply a matter of connecting correctly constructed chords by means of approved bass progressions but also involves correct voice leading in the texture—that is, that counterpoint is a component of harmony.

This vision of Bach as master of harmony in its broader senses was held in the composer's lifetime, too, and comes across clearly in the famous Scheibe-Birnbaum controversy of 1737–38. It is characteristic of Bach's critic, Johann Adolph Scheibe, that he simultaneously objects to the composer's Bach's preferring polyphonic texture, in which every voice is melodically significant, to a monophonic one, both fashionable and simpler, in which a single melody is supported by a melodically insignificant accompaniment (in Bach's music, he says reproachfully, "all the voices must work with each other and be of equal difficulty, and none of them can be recognized as the principal voice") *and* opted for the narrowest understanding of the term harmony as separate from, and opposed to, melody and hence synonymous with accompaniment. In Bach's music, he writes, "Every ornament, every little grace, and everything that one thinks of as belonging to the method of playing, he expresses completely in notes; and this not only takes away from his pieces the beauty of harmony but completely covers the melody throughout."[32] For his part, Johann Abraham Birnbaum, the composer's defender—and probably also his mouthpiece—objected to Scheibe's preference for homophonic texture while embracing the older, broader notion of harmony:

> Now, the idea that the melody must always be in the upper voice and that the constant collaboration of the other voices is a fault is one for which I have been able to find no sufficient grounds. Rather is it the exact opposite which flows from the very nature of music. For music consists of harmony, and harmony becomes far more complete if all the voices collaborate to form it. Accordingly, this is not a failing but rather a musical perfection . . . characteristic of the Italian taste, nowadays everywhere so highly admired, especially in church works. The author need only look into the works of *Praenestinus* [Palestrina], among the old composers, or Lotti and others among the more modern ones, and he will find not only that all the voices are continuously at work but also that each one has a melody of its own which harmonizes quite well with the others.[33]

Bach's sons and students confirm this understanding of music. In their jointly penned 1750 Bach obituary, Carl Philipp Emanuel Bach and the Bach student Johann Friedrich Agricola clearly include counterpoint as a component of harmony:

> If ever a composer showed polyphony in its greatest strength, it was certainly our late lamented Bach. If ever a musician employed the most hidden secrets of harmony with the most skilled artistry, it was certainly our Bach. No one ever showed so many ingenious and unusual ideas as he in elaborate pieces such as ordinarily seem dry exercises in craftsmanship. He needed only to have heard any theme

to be aware—it seemed in the same instant—of almost every intricacy that artistry could produce in the treatment of it.[34]

In a similar vein Friedrich Wilhelm Marpurg wrote of Bach in the Preface to the 1752 edition of *The Art of Fugue:* "No one has surpassed him in thorough knowledge of the theory and practice of harmony."[35] And in the dedication of his *Treatise on the Fugue,* Part 2 (1754), addressed to Bach's two oldest and musically most distinguished sons, Wilhelm Friedemann and Carl Philipp Emanuel, he elaborated: "At the very time when the world was beginning to degenerate in another direction, when light melody making was gaining the upper hand and people were becoming tired of difficult harmonies, the late Capellmeister was the one who knew how to keep to the golden mean, and taught us how to combine an agreeable and flowing melody with the richest harmonies." All of these musicians were active in Berlin at some point during the second half of the eighteenth century (C. P. E. Bach as court harpsichordist, Agricola as leader of the court orchestra, and Marpurg as administrator in the royal lottery), and it is clear that there, at least, Bach the father was remembered primarily as the progenitor of harmony. The same sentiment was still evident in 1796, when Johann Friedrich Reichardt, until recently the court conductor in Berlin, declared: "Never did a composer, not even the best and deepest of the Italians, exhaust all the possibilities of our harmony as did this great artist."[36]

For all of these musicians, harmony included the most learned contrapuntal genres of fugue and canon, but these were not essential. What mattered primarily was correct polyphonic voice leading, by means of which every component of every chord was also a component of a melodic line, thus keeping linear and vertical dimensions of the texture in balance. This idea was expressed with particular clarity in 1774 by another Bach student active in Berlin, Johann Philipp Kirnberger, *Kapellmeister* to the King's sister, Princess Anna Amalie: "There is perhaps in the whole science of writing nothing more difficult than this: not only to give each of the four voices its own flowing melody, but also to keep a uniform character in all, so that out of their union a single and perfect whole may arise. In this the late Capellmeister Bach in Leipzig perhaps excelled all the composers in the world."[37] Kirnberger's treatise *Die Kunst des reinen Satzes in der Musik,* of which Part 1 appeared in 1774 and Part 2 in three installments in 1776, 1777, and 1779, centered on this most difficult thing, the "pure texture" (*reiner Satz*) epitomized in Bach's four-part chorale harmonizations, the collections of which were published by Birnstiel in Berlin in 1765 and 1769, and by Breitkopf in Leipzig in 1784.[38] C. P. E. Bach himself spelled out the significance of the publication in his foreword to the 1765 Birnstiel edition, speaking of "the quite special arrangement of the harmony and the natural flow of the inner voices and the bass, which are what above all distinguish these chorales," and adding: "And who nowadays denies the advantage of that instruction in writing by which the beginning is made with chorales instead of stiff and pedantic counterpoint?"[39] Reichardt wrote similarly in support of the later Breitkopf publication: "If any work has ever deserved serious support by German friends of art, it is this one. The contents: chorales—greatest work of German art; the creator of harmony: Johann Sebastian Bach—greatest harmonist of all times and nations; the editor: Johann Philipp Kirnberger—most discerning artistic adjudicator of our time."

More so than anyone else, Kirnberger was able to give concrete theoretical substance to the commonplace of Bach as the supreme harmonist. He not only located the core of Bach's practice in the chorale harmonizations but also defined the rules governing them. Pointing out that after removing all the "nonharmonic tones" (harmoniefremde Töne; that is, passing tones and suspensions) the harmonic skeleton would, given the invertibility of chords, consist of only two classes of chords (namely, three kinds of triads and four kinds of seventh chords), he showed that a few simple rules governed the progressions from one chord to the next. Moreover, any work of Bach could be reduced to its underlying skeleton in this manner, as Kirnberger famously demonstrated when he progressively reduced the final fugue in *WTC* I (BWV 869) first to its underlying four-part thoroughbass structure, then to a bass line with all the consonant and dissonant chords, and, finally, to a bass line with only essential harmonies.[40]

Bach's understanding of himself as primarily a harmonist, as well as his understanding that the essential components of harmony included melodic voice leading of the inner parts (not just of soprano and bass)— and that sophisticated contrapuntal techniques were optional—was transmitted to posterity by the Berlin circle. C. P. E. Bach, in particular, bequeathed the notion to his father's first biographer, Johann Nikolaus Forkel. In a letter of 13 January 1775 Bach told Forkel:

> In composition he started his pupils right in with what was practical, and omitted all the *dry species* of counterpoint that are given in Fux and others. His pupils had to begin their studies by learning pure four-part thorough bass. From this he went to chorales. . . . The realization of a thorough bass and the introduction to chorales are without doubt the best method of studying composition, as far as harmony is concerned.[41]

Forkel's 1802 biography clearly reflects C. P. E. Bach's influence:

> In such an interweaving of various melodies which are all so singing
> that each may, and really does, appear in its turn as the upper part,
> Johann Sebastian Bach's harmony consists, in all the works which he
> composed from about the year 1720, or the 35th year of his age, till his
> death. In this he excels all the composers in the world (see Kirnberger's
> *Kunst des reinen Satzes*, p. 157).

Elsewhere in the book he wrote: "There are persons who are of opinion that
Bach perfected harmony only. But if we have the right conception of harmony . . . we cannot even imagine it without melody." Bach's composition
students, Forkel went on to tell his readers, had

> to pay constant attention to the consistency of each single part in
> and of itself, as well as to its relation to the parts connected and con-
> current with it. . . . This high degree of exactness in the management
> of every single part is precisely what makes Bach's harmony a mani-
> fold melody. . . . He considered his parts as if they were persons who
> conversed together like a select company.

Ultimately Forkel confirmed that "whoever desires to become acquainted
with Bach's method of teaching composition in its whole extent finds it
sufficiently explained in Kirnberger's 'Art of Pure Composition' [*Kunst des
reinen Satzes*]."

Aspects of the Bach understanding that was peculiar to Berlin, along with
the Bach cult generally, were undoubtedly transmitted to Vienna by Baron
Gottfried van Swieten, who had come across Bach's music during his time
as the imperial *chargé d'affaires* in Berlin from 1770 to 1777. After his return to Vienna, now as Imperial Court Librarian, he began to organize the
private concerts in which Mozart first became aware of Bach.[42] Nor did Kirnberger, who had given the Berlin conception of Bach its most elaborate theoretical codification, remain unknown in Vienna: *Kunst des reinen Satzes*,
previously published in individual parts, received its first complete edition
in Vienna in 1793.[43]

When Beethoven called Bach the *Urvater der Harmonie* he undoubtedly chose his words judiciously. We see reflected in them a tradition of
understanding what centrally mattered in Bach's music that can be traced
back to the composer himself. As Zelter, yet another link in the Berlin Bach
tradition, soberly and correctly reported to Goethe in a letter of 9 June 1827,
"Bach is considered the greatest harmonist, and rightly so" (Bach gilt für
den größten Harmonisten und das mit Recht).[44] It is emblematic of posterity's reception of the *Well-Tempered Keyboard* that Chopin's twenty-four

Préludes, Op. 28 (1836–1839), surely the most artistically significant among the direct emulations of the Bach sets, do not contain a single fugue. The fundamental lesson taught by the *WTC* was not about higher contrapuntal techniques but about harmony in the broader sense, which included voice leading: all the voices did not always have to be equal, but melodic integrity had to be preserved in all of them, even when they receded into the background. Monteverdi, in his ending to *Orfeo,* taught the same lesson: that the *prima prattica* was superior to the *seconda prattica;* that obbligato texture, in which all voices are melodically and motivically significant and which embodies the harmony of God's creation, is superior to the monodic texture of melody with accompaniment, which the enlightened opinion, in Bach's time no less than in Monteverdi's, thought best able to capture and express man's subjectivity.

Monteverdi's lesson is consistent with what Bach himself thought was essential in music. What is less clear is whether Bach's successors also took seriously the third layer in the meaning of harmony—that music's sounding harmony reflects the intelligible harmony of God's creation. Bach no doubt did take it seriously, since it was this layer that would have accounted for music's ability not only to entertain the mind but also to praise God. It is this centrality of harmony in Bach's conception of music which, in addition to and above all else, testifies to his preference for God's time, his belief that God's eternity is preferable to all-devouring, irreversible human time. The rules of harmony require time to be discovered, and their application in an actually existing piece of music requires time, too, but they possess the permanence that transcends any purely human construct. Thus the exploration of musical harmony is one way to contemplate what truly endures.

—

For Bach the name of what most truly endures was "God." Hence music—harmony—could serve as a metaphor for God. After Bach's time, and certainly for us, the matter is more complicated and requires case-by-case consideration. The Enlightenment accelerated the process whereby, for the educated European elites at least, God himself increasingly became a metaphor. When toward the end of the century Kant revealed what a "religion within the limits of reason alone" would be like, it turned out that much of what was specific to the Judeo-Christian tradition, including the personal God, the Fall, Redemption, and Christ himself, would need to be discarded. What remained was God as a "regulative idea of reason"—a symbol beyond the outer limits of cognition but useful in giving direction to our will; a sign of the perfection which, though strictly speaking unknow-

able and unimaginable, as well as unattainable here on earth, might nevertheless offer us guidance and direction, a practical orientation when faced
with choices; a goal not to be reached but worth aspiring to. But Kant's God,
unlike Bach's, is no longer the source of moral law; quite the contrary. The
root of the moral law is our autonomy, and God's existence, together with
these other "ideas of reason," the reality of freedom and the immortality
of the soul, becomes dependent on morality—becomes something that the
experience of our morality allows us to believe in, to postulate: the "upright
man may well say: I *will* that there is a God, that my existence in this world
be also the existence in a pure world of the understanding beyond natural
connections, and finally that my duration is endless."[45] If God, immortality, and freedom did not exist, they would have to be invented.

Goethe's memorable reaction to the experience of hearing Bach's music,
including probably something from the *WTC*, played to him on the organ
by the *Badinspektor* Johann Heinrich Friedrich Schütz at Bad Berka in December 1818, an experience he recalled years later in a letter to Zelter, is in-
dicative of the spiritual difference a mere century (but what a century!) can
make: "It is as if the eternal harmony were conversing within itself, as it
may have done in the bosom of God just before the Creation of the world.
So likewise did it move in my inmost soul, and it seemed as if I neither possessed nor needed ears, not any other sense—least of all eyes."[46] Thanks to
"the eternal harmony," the sensible music, one for which one does need ears,
is surpassed here in a vision of intelligible permanent order, "God just before the Creation," before time. These are all terms Bach would understand
and approve of. And yet, a subtle but fundamental shift has taken place, for
Goethe's God is more like Kant's than like Bach's. Judeo-Christian mythology has joined the Greco-Roman as another department of the cultural an-
tiquarian market to be explored when constructing the modern Faustian
myth. The ultimate reality, "the indescribable" (das Unbeschreibliche; *Faust*,
12108) is unattainable here in this world in which "everything" is "transient" (Alles Vergängliche; 12104). All we have are our transitory myths,
our stories, every one of them "only a metaphor" (nur ein Gleichnis; 12105).
The phenomena of sensuous perception, all that we can know in this world,
may at best serve as symbols, as vehicles transporting us to the outer limits of our knowledge, and beyond these limits we vaguely expect the presence of the indescribable, unconditional noumenon. "We have our life in a
colorful reflection," says Faust (Am farbigen Abglanz haben wir das Leben;
4727). Or, as Goethe put it more prosaically in 1825 (and as Caspar David
Friedrich attempted to demonstrate in practically all of his paintings), "the
true, which is identical with the divine, can never be known by us directly;

we see it only in a reflection, example, symbol, in single and related phenomena. We are aware of it as of an incomprehensible life and cannot give
up the wish to comprehend it anyway" (Das Wahre mit dem Göttlichen iden-
tisch, läßt sich niemals von uns direkt erkennen, wir schauen es nur im
Abglanz, im Beispiel, Symbol, in einzelnen und verwandten Erscheinungen;
wir werden es gewahr als unbegreifliches Leben und können dem Wunsch
nicht entsagen, es dennoch zu begreifen).[47]

The only thing we can really know about the transcendent realm is that
it is not like this world—not finite, not temporal, not imperfect. Music centered on "the eternal harmony"—abstract and, unlike architecture, which
is equally abstract, nonfunctional and autonomous—is indeed our best sensuous image of the intelligible but indescribable perfection beyond the limits of knowledge. It is our best "proof" of the possibility of its existence, the
best justification of our hope in it. Hence the ease with which those who
thought seriously about music after Kant reached for religious language.
Recall E. T. A. Hoffmann's claim of 1814:

> Sound audibly expresses an awareness of the highest and holiest, of the
> spiritual power which enkindles the spark of life in the whole of nature,
> and so music and singing become an expression of the total plenitude of
> existence—a paean to the Creator! By virtue of its essential character,
> therefore, music is a form of religious worship . . . and its origin is to be
> sought and found only in religion, in the church.[48]

Recall, too, how, according to Anton Schindler's admittedly unreliable
testimony of 1840, Beethoven, on his visits to van Swieten's home in his
early years in Vienna, was frequently obliged to finish the evening by playing "half a dozen Fugues by Bach, 'by way of final prayer.'"[49] Reliable or
not, the anecdote aptly captures the sense of the *WTC* as a collection of daily
prayers appropriate for the post-Christian, rational, Kantian religiosity. If
Bach could still see in harmony a metaphor for God, Goethe was already
speaking from the other historical shore—from the world in which metaphors are all we have. In this new world, our world, it is God who has become the metaphor for harmony.

Jean-Jacques contra Augustinum

A Little Treatise on Moral-Political Theology

> the golden house of *is*
> Collapses, and the word *becoming* ascends.
> —CZESŁAW MIŁOSZ, *A Treatise on Poetry*

AUGUSTINE

In a private notebook of 1967 Nicola Chiaromonte wrote: "Any profound consideration of our time should begin by recognizing a fact: until *yesterday*—and this yesterday may be dated from the French Revolution or from the Russian one, from the first world war or from the second, it makes no great difference to the aims of the consideration—until *yesterday*, then, we still lived in a Christian age. Today, no longer."[1] God's slow, still uncompleted but seemingly inexorable dying, his transformation from a living presence and active force into a metaphor, has often been identified, by Nietzsche and countless others before and after him, as a central feature of the transition from premodern to modern Europe. Did it—does it—in fact happen, and if so, why? How can a God die, and what does such a death mean?

A nonbeliever will suspect that at some point God's job was done—his function no longer needed, or perhaps taken on by someone else. Indeed, most likely what we call the death of God involves not God alone but also man. The phrase names complex and correlated transformations in our understanding of God and of ourselves.

A Christian is not merely fallible; he (and she) is fallen. The anthropology of the story of creation and fall in Genesis 2.4–3.24 is breathtaking in its profundity and concentration. Two features are central to the human condition. First, unlike God and like all other living beings on earth, we are created and mortal, that is, finite—driven from the garden of Eden so that we might not eat of the tree of life and live forever. Second, like God (in whose image, according to the alternative account in Genesis 1.26–27, we have been created, male and female) and unlike all other living beings on earth, we know the difference between good and evil (having eaten of the tree of knowledge) and are thus capable of choosing between doing one or the other. Knowledge and capacity conjoined make us morally responsible; one could not be held morally responsible if one did not know the difference between good and evil or was unable to choose between them.

In principle, mortality and moral responsibility might have remained unrelated; neither necessarily implies or causes the other. Just as beings exist who are mortal and irresponsible, it is possible to imagine one who is immortal and responsible. It would even be possible to read the biblical story of the fall in this way. The story suggests a relationship between mortality and responsibility, but the nature of this relationship is much less clear than the centuries of Christian interpretation have accustomed us to believe. In the biblical story, mortality results from our coming to know good and evil: according to Genesis 2.17, the Lord, in forbidding Adam to eat from the tree of knowledge, told him that "in the day that thou eatest thereof thou shalt surely die." He does not explain why the two should be causally connected like this, but the serpent suggests an answer. When tempting Eve with the fruit, he first denied that the knowledge would result in death: "Ye shall not surely die." Immediately following this lie he added the intriguing insinuation: "For God does know that in the day ye eat thereof, then your eyes shall be opened, and ye shall be as gods, knowing good and evil" (Genesis 3.4–5). [2] The serpent's insinuation, it turns out, was not a lie; the Lord himself confirmed it once Adam and Eve had eaten the fruit and their eyes had been opened, when he said (to some unspecified heavenly beings, presumably angels): "Behold, the man is become as one of us, to know good and evil: and now, lest he put forth his hand, and take also of the tree of life, and eat, and live for ever: Therefore the Lord God sent him forth from the garden of Eden" (Genesis 3.22–23). It appears, then, that death must result from knowledge, because we would otherwise be altogether like gods and no different from angels. But this is hardly a reason. It is, rather, a narrative designed to show that humans, while like gods in being morally responsible, are unlike them in being mortal. Although the Genesis story seems to say that we are mortal *because* we are responsible, on closer inspection it may merely be saying that we are mortal *and* responsible—different from angels in the first regard and from animals in the second.

This is not how most Jews, or most Christians from St. Paul on, chose to read the story of the fall. Paul's reading of the story in the light of his understanding of what Jesus's death on the cross meant has shaped Christian teaching more decisively than any other (his *Epistles*, written during the 50s, are the earliest of the New Testament texts); St. Augustine's subsequent codification of the doctrine of original sin (I will rely here primarily on *De civitate Dei,* written 413–26) would be unthinkable without Paul.[3] Paul accepted literally that human mortality resulted from our parents' eating the forbidden fruit, and his explanation for why the two, mortality and the eating, were causally connected differed from that of the serpent by stressing that it was "one man's [Adam's] disobedience" (Romans 5.19). Not to obey God, not to render him what was due, was sin—Adam's sin and his fall. (This would seem to lead to the conclusion that to obey God is synonymous with doing good and to disobey him synonymous with doing evil.) Death was the punishment: "by one man's offence death reigned by one" (Romans 5.17), and "For the wages of sin *is* death" (Romans 6.23). We humans inherit from our first parents both the sin and the punishment. The later, Augustinian, idea of sin and death transmitted from one generation to the next by means of sexual propagation (like syphilis in an Ibsen drama) may be debatable, but it cannot be denied that, like Adam, human beings can be disobedient and, in fact, are so—at least occasionally. Paul, in any case, took this sensible position: "By one man sin entered into the world, and death by sin; and so death passed upon all men, for that all have sinned," he wrote in the *Epistle to the Romans* (5.12). Even if the causal relationship between death and human capacity for evil is true only in a figurative sense, there is no doubt that for Paul our freedom and our finitude are necessarily and systematically connected through the mechanism of man's disobedience and God's punishment.

Sin (disobeying God, and choosing and doing evil) and death are thus the interconnected marks of imperfect human nature. It is this imperfection that makes us crave that our nature be transformed into a different, perfect one, makes us crave salvation, reconciliation with God that would free us in some sense (exactly what sense has been the subject of centuries of theological speculation) from sin and death and allow us to attain everlasting life—if not in this world and time, then at the end of the world and time, when we could expect, in the words of the creed, "the resurrection of the dead and the life of the age to come." Paul anticipated the creed's expectation in his First Epistle to the Corinthians (15.52–53): "the trumpet shall sound, and the dead shall be raised incorruptible, and we shall be changed. For this corruptible must put on incorruption, and this mortal *must* put on immortality." The gospel—good tidings—was just that, a promise of salvation, reconciliation with God, radical transformation of human nature so as to liberate us from sin and death.

This promise was based on Paul's radical reinterpretation of the catastrophe of Jesus's ignominious death on the cross in the year 30. During the few years of his ministry, ca. 28–30, Jesus considered himself, and was understood by his disciples, to be an eschatological prophet of the imminent coming of God's kingdom—that is, God's presence among men and women, which would require that humans act charitably (with mercy and justice) toward one another.[4] Shortly after the crucifixion, the disciples and their Aramaic-speaking Jewish followers, led by Simon (also called Cephas or Peter), enriched this understanding and turned the catastrophe into a triumph by claiming that Jesus had been rescued from death ("resurrected") and that at the end of time, now fast approaching, Jesus would be the "messiah" (anointed one; *christos*, in Greek), a deputy with powers to act in God's name as the apocalyptic judge. With this claim Christianity was born. (Note that neither Paul, writing in the 50s, nor the authors of the three synoptic Gospels, writing in the 70s and 80s, considered Jesus to be God; this identification occurred only in the last decade of the first century among the Greek-speaking Gentile converts, as documented in the Gospel of St. John.) When Christ's second coming took longer than expected, the Hellenized Jews of Palestine and the Diaspora, led by Paul, began claiming that the prophet already reigned as the messiah in heaven, where he, the Savior, atoned for humanity's sins and reconciled man with God. (That the gospel was for all of humanity, and not just for the Jews, was one of Paul's distinctive claims; he was the apostle for the gentiles. "There is neither Jew nor Greek, there is neither bond nor free, there is neither male nor female: for ye are all one in Christ Jesus," he wrote to the Galatians [3.28].)[5]

Whereas a millennium passed before Christians had a coherent and authoritative explanation of how salvation came about (provided in Anselm's *Cur Deus homo?* of 1099), the fact of its being accomplished was something Paul claimed from early on. Strictly speaking, the claim was not for salvation's being accomplished outright but for its having been initiated by the coming of Christ, the crucified and raised Jesus, with the promise that the process of salvation would be completed with the messiah's return at the end of time. In Paul's view, Adam was "the figure of him that was to come" (Romans 5.14).[6] The second Adam was "our Lord Jesus Christ, who gave himself for our sins, that he might deliver us from this present evil world" (Galatians 1.3–4), and his obedience somehow made up for the first Adam's disobedience, undoing its results and triumphing over sin and death. (Anselm's doctrine of atonement subsequently showed how this sacrifice resolved the paradox of divine justice and mercy, the contradiction between God's merciful choice to save us and his need to uphold justice, which would be violated if he simply pardoned us without requiring satisfaction for our sins.) "For as by one man's disobedience many were made sinners, so by the obedience of one shall many be made righteous," we read in the Epistle to the Romans

(5.19). And again: "For since by man *came* death, by man *came* also the resurrection of the dead. For as in Adam all die, even so in Christ shall all be made alive" (I Corinthians 15.21–22). The same contrast would be echoed by Augustine (*The City of God*, 21.15): "For as by the sin of one man we have fallen into a misery so deplorable, so by the righteousness of one Man, who also is God, shall we come to a blessedness inconceivably exalted."

Christ's taking humanity's sins upon himself and expiating them was a prerequisite of redemption, but it certainly did not ensure the salvation of every individual. What, then, determined one's final eschatological destiny—salvation or its opposite, damnation? Here Christians faced a paradox perhaps even greater than that of divine mercy and justice, namely the paradox of divine grace and human freedom; this paradox could easily be seen as the central force driving the doctrine's development through the centuries, a paradox whose very intractability assured the intellectual fertility of the tradition. God was omnipotent, but man was endowed (by him) with free will. To assert that my salvation or damnation depends on my own moral choices and actions (on my "works," in Pauline language) was to uphold the importance and dignity of human freedom and moral responsibility, as well as God's justice, but at the same time to limit what could not be limited, God's omnipotence—to claim, in effect, that God owes me salvation because I have been good.[7] To assert that my ultimate destiny depends on God alone, on his saving grace, and not on what I choose and do, was to uphold God's omnipotence but to render human freedom and responsibility worthless and meaningless and thus a gift of dubious value. It also imposes the task of reconciling the idea of unmerited salvation (or, especially, damnation) with that of justice, a task so difficult that most people would sooner or later have to invoke God's inscrutability. (Unmerited damnation was a particular stumbling block, since unmerited salvation, although not perhaps just, at least credited God with mercy.) One could of course claim that no such thing as unmerited damnation exists, that, given humanity's corrupt nature, damnation is the default fate, so to speak, and requires no special explanation; it was salvation that was truly unmerited, a gift of mercy. The former position, commonly labeled Pelagianism (after an Augustine contemporary and adversary, Pelagius, who advocated it), did not deny grace altogether but considered it helpful rather than necessary, stressing instead the centrality of free will: we owe the ability to do good to God's grace, but choice and action are our own, as is the potential merit. Augustine defended God's unconditional omnipotence, a position that implied the doctrine of predestination: whether I shall be saved or damned, whether I shall receive grace or not, has nothing to do with merit but is predetermined by God's inexplicable and inscrutable decision.

Augustine could find plenty of support for his views in Paul's letters.[8] Paul never tired of telling his readers that their salvation was not a matter of good works done in obedience to Mosaic law but solely a matter of faith in Christ—that is, of trust in God's mercy, in his desire for human salvation—and that this is evident from his having sent the redeemer. "A man is not justified by the works of the law, but by the faith of Jesus Christ," he wrote to the Galatians (2.16), adding significantly (2. 21): "for if righteousness *come* by the law, then Christ is dead in vain." In other words, there would have been no point to Christ's sacrifice if we could justify ourselves by our own efforts. Paul wrote in a similar vein to the Romans (3.28): "Therefore we conclude that a man is justified by faith without the deeds of the law." Even then there must have been those who were troubled by the predestinarian implications of Paul's message in Romans 9.18–19: "Therefore hath he mercy on whom he will *have mercy,* and whom he will he hardeneth. Thou wilt say then unto me, Why doth he yet find fault? For who hath resisted his will?" Like Augustine, Paul did not so much resolve this problem as bow his head before an inscrutable mystery (9.20): "Nay but, O man, who art thou that repliest against God? Shall the thing formed say to him that formed *it,* Why hast though made me thus?" A little later, he came even closer to spelling out the doctrine of predestination (9.22–23): "*What* if God, willing to shew *his* wrath, and to make his power known, endured with much long-suffering the vessels of wrath fitted to destruction: And that he might make known the riches of his glory on the vessels of mercy, which he had afore prepared unto glory?"

To be sure, Paul offers support, too, to those who maintained the importance of human merit, as in Romans 2.6–10: "Who [God] will render to every man according to his deeds. . . . Tribulation and anguish, upon every soul of man that doeth evil . . . ; But glory, honour, and peace, to every man that worketh good." The church, in any case, attempted to steer a middle course between the extremes of Pelagianism and Augustinianism, wanting to acknowledge both the grace of God and man's free will and pointing out that both had a common creator. Even after Pelagianism was condemned as heresy in 431, the church did not therefore accept the doctrine of predestination. The middle course (or, if you will, the fudge) often took the form of what later came to be called Semi-Pelagianism (not a term of praise, of course, given that Pelagius was declared a heretic; Semi-Augustinianism would have been just as accurate): the church deemed grace to be indispensable and necessary to salvation and, rejecting predestination, affirmed free will and its corollary, moral responsibility.[9] Both grace and merit, faith and works, were necessary for salvation. Grace was there to incline, not to coerce, free will. Its inspiration could be freely rejected or freely accepted. Thus individual will remained free even (or, perhaps, especially) when influenced or shaped by grace, since the choice between good and evil was the individual's choice. The intellectual underpinning of the church's efforts to harmonize grace and free will was perfectly captured by Bernard of Clairvaux: "Take away free will, and there is nothing that needs to be saved; take away grace, and there is no way to save it."[10] This harmonization was unacceptable to Luther, who reasserted the radical doctrine of Paul and Augustine, the doctrine of justification by faith alone: at bottom, the disagreement between Protestants and Catholics was the quarrel between strict Augustinians and Semi-Pelagians, or rather Semi-Augustinians. (Within Catholicism itself, strict Augustinianism was propagated in seventeenth-century France by the spiritual movement of Jansenists centered around the convent of Port-Royal, a movement that, thanks to Pascal and Racine, indelibly stamped the country's highest cultural achievements of the period and confronted the Roman Church with the unenviable task of having to suppress dangerously heterodox teaching without explicitly condemning Augustine himself.)

Yet even Christians such as Paul, Augustine, and Luther, who emphasized God's omnipotence over man's freedom and hence based their hope of salvation on their faith in Christ rather than on works, did not consider themselves authorized to engage in evildoing while awaiting God's predestined verdict. ("What then? shall we sin, because we are not under the law, but under grace?" asks Paul [Romans 6.15], only to answer, quickly and predictably, "God forbid.") How one lived one's life on earth was to be guided by Jesus's example and teaching—in particular by the two great commandments reported in Mark 12.29–31 (as well as Matthew 22.37–39), the second already given by the Lord to Moses (according to Leviticus 19.18): "Thou shalt love the Lord thy God with all thy heart, and with all thy soul, and with all thy mind, and with all thy strength . . . thou shalt love thy neighbour as thyself." Paul confirmed (Romans 13.8–10) that all law and all commandments were contained in the second one, summarizing his view as follows (10): "Love worketh no ill to his neighbour: therefore love *is* the fulfilling of the law." Luther cleverly argued that with regard to human conduct in this world, his position in fact had one clear advantage over that of Catholics: not needing to worry about earning salvation by merit relieved one of mortal anxiety (Am I being good enough?) as well as possible bad faith (Am I doing good works for my benefit rather than my neighbor's?).

Two great commandments are at the heart of Augustine's vision of the contrast between what he called the two cities[11]—"There are no more than two kinds of human society, which we may justly call two cities" (*The City of God*, 14.1)—the heavenly and the earthly one, "one composed of the good, the other of the wicked" (12.1). The two "are in this present world commingled" (11.1) but will be permanently separated at the end of time: "The one is predestined to reign eternally with God, and the other to suffer eternal punishment with the devil" (15.1), although, strictly speaking, the latter one "shall not be everlasting (for it will no longer be a city when it has been committed to the extreme penalty)" (15.4). Which community you belong to depends on the direction of your will—on which kind of desire or "love" you choose and follow. "The right will is . . . well-directed love, and the wrong will is ill-directed love" (14.7). But what is well-directed love? Because human reason is fallible, man needs "a divine Master, whom he may obey without misgiving, and who may at the same time give him such help as to preserve his own freedom. . . . But this divine Master inculcates two precepts—the love of God and the love of our neighbour" (19.14). Well-directed love, then, is guided by Jesus's two commandments. "He who resolves to love God, and to love his neighbour as himself, . . . is on account of this love said to be of a good will; and this is in Scripture more commonly called charity" (14.7). To become a member of the earthly city, on the other hand, you do not need to be an all-out evildoer, the kind of person who takes pleasure in distinterestedly harming another. It suffices that your love is directed toward yourself instead of toward God and your neighbor. "Accordingly, two cities have been formed by two loves: the earthly by the love of self, even to the contempt of God; the heavenly by the love of God, even to the contempt of self" (14.28).

This is not to say that love of self is forbidden. On the contrary, Augustine expressly includes the self among the objects Jesus's two commandments instruct us to love: "In these precepts [the two commandments] a man finds three things he has to love—God, himself, and his neighbour" (19.14). But there is a clear hierarchy among the three love-worthy objects, such that the self is subsumed in and transcended by the neighbor, who is in turn subsumed in and transcended by God. A love is well-directed when it moves from a less important object to the more important one, without thereby abandoning the former; it is ill-directed when it gets arrested at any of the lesser objects. Thus self-love, lest it become a merely selfish cupidity, should be subsumed in the disinterested love of one's neighbor, transcended by charity, so that one lives "in well-ordered concord with all men, as far as in him lies," which happens when he "in the first place, injure no one, and, in the second, do good to every one he can reach" (19.14). One might think that this is as good a formulation of what it means to lead a morally worthy life as we are ever likely to get, but no: to stop at love of neighbor would be a kind of idolatry, setting up a lesser good in place of the supreme one. The steps in Augustine's argument leading to this conclusion are clear. Real and stable human happiness can be achieved only once the individual is no longer agitated by a potentially infinite chain of desires, and that can happen only when the chain of desires reaches the ultimate, eternally unchangeable good. "The blessedness which an intelligent being desires as its legitimate object results from a combination of these two things, namely, that it uninterruptedly enjoy the unchangeable good, which is God; and that it be delivered from all dubiety, and know certainly that it shall eternally abide in the same enjoyment" (11.13). No created object, being mutable, could serve as such an ultimate good, not even an object as relatively exalted in the hierarchy of beings as another human. The only possible candidate for this role is the unchangeable Creator: "There is no unchangeable good but the one, true, blessed God; . . . the things which He made are indeed good because from Him, yet mutable because made not out of Him, but out of nothing. . . . They are not the supreme good, for God is a greater good" (12.1). Therefore, "he who inordinately loves the good which any nature possesses, even though he obtain it, himself becomes evil in the good, and wretched because deprived of a greater good" (12.8). This is why it is not enough to love one's neighbor.

A true, concordant community is, moreover, only possible when all its members are bound together by desiring something in common—and when this something can be desired in a noncompetitive fashion, so that my obtaining it does not mean that you will have less or none. For Augustine, it seems, God is the only conceivable object of this sort. The community of the charitable is ultimately held together by what they all love in common: "And those who have this good [God] in common, have, both with Him to whom they draw near, and with one another, a holy fellowship, and form one city of God" (12.9). The earthly city, by contrast, "has its good in this world. . . . But as this is not a good which can discharge its devotees of all distresses, this city is often divided against itself by litigations, wars, quarrels, and such victories as are either life-destroying or short-lived" (15.4). At its best, "the earthly city, which does not live by faith, seeks an earthly peace, and the end it proposes, in the well-ordered concord of civic obedience and rule, is the combination of men's wills to attain the things which are helpful to this life" (19.17). Augustine does not expect that the city of God could ever be fully realized on earth. Consequently, the proper politics of its members is the politics of conservative accommodation to the earthly city: "So long as it [the heavenly city] lives like a captive and a stranger in the earthly city, . . . it makes no scruple to obey the laws of the earthly city, whereby the things necessary for the maintenance of this mortal life are administered" (19.17). The maintenance of this mortal life is, however, very much subordinate to what truly matters—the achievement of salvation. Politics is not the arena where human beings can ever fully realize themselves.

Everyday experience suggests that, regardless of what it does for an individual's prospects for otherworldly salvation, consistently doing good works does not shield anyone from suffering and death in this world; conversely, of course, evildoing does not guarantee earthly torments for the perpetrator. Like unmerited damnation in the afterlife, unmerited suffering in this one proved a difficult problem for religious thinkers and was subject to diametrically opposed interpretations by Pelagians and Augustinians.[12] Death was actually less of a problem: for Augustine, there was no such thing as an unmerited death (we are all sinners); and Pelagians could argue, not unreasonably (as Pelagius's follower Julian of Eclanum did) that death, in being a consoling promise that our sufferings will not last forever, as well as transition to the life of the age to come, is actually an example of God's mercy. But unmerited suffering—in particular, the suffering of infants and very young children—was something of a stumbling block. Again the Pelagian position creates difficulties. Augustine believed that the suffering of infants was nothing less than proof of original sin: since a just God would not allow innocents to suffer, and since they evidently do suffer, they must be infected with the sin of their parents. The doctrine of original sin allowed Augustine to confront the suffering of infants without endangering our faith in God's omnipotence and justice. The Pelagians, however, found the doctrine unacceptable and offensive to divine justice. (How can I be held responsible for my ancestors' choices and actions?) They chose, therefore, to separate natural and moral evils: suffering could be a natural fact (caused by such factors as disease or natural disaster) rather than a sign of moral evil and guilt. Eventually the church, too, found it possible to distinguish moral evil, *malum culpae,* or suffering caused by men, from natural evil, *malum poenae,* suffering not caused by men. This did not, however, solve the problem of unmerited suffering, whether caused naturally or by the evil of others. Even though God might have good reasons not to limit human freedom, even the freedom of evildoers, how can an omnipotent and just God allow unmerited suffering, no matter what its cause, and especially when it has natural causes.

It is important to distinguish between the respective merits and difficulties of each of these three positions, Augustinianism, Pelagianism, and Semi-

Pelagianism. Each of these positions confronts the central problem of evil (*unde malum?*)—a bundle of problems, really, of which two prove to be particularly intractable: How to explain unmerited damnation? and How to explain unmerited suffering? (Unmerited salvation and unmerited bliss have troubled thinkers much less.) The difficulty lies in arriving at answers that would accommodate the assumption of the existence of an omnipotent and just God in tandem with the idea that human will is free.

The Augustinian position on unmerited damnation and suffering has the advantage of being intellectually more coherent than the others. Strictly speaking, unmerited damnation and suffering do not exist: human nature after the fall is corrupt and deserves whatever punishment it gets. If God in his mercy chooses to save us, or to preserve us from suffering, this, like any pardon extended to a criminal, is not incompatible with justice. This safeguards both God's omnipotence and his justice. As for human will, it is free under grace (although, again, given Augustine's claim that the gift of grace is irresistible, strict Augustinians will find it hard to defend the belief in the freedom of will). The coherence of the Augustinian position depends on the doctrine of original sin: the whole picture makes sense only if it is assumed that human nature is fatally flawed, that without grace we can only will evil.

Pelagians, in claiming that our eschatological destiny is in our own hands, cannot easily accommodate the notion of divine omnipotence, nor can they explain why divine justice allows unmerited suffering. As for the doctrine of original sin, they do not need it: far from being corrupt, human nature is inherently good, and Pelagians believe that human beings are capable of choosing good without supernatural help.

Semi-Pelagians, finally, want to have it both ways, which, given the complexity of the human condition, may be wise but makes it difficult to maintain intellectual coherence. The Catholic position is perhaps best understood as Augustinianism with a human face—Augustinianism, that is, that makes some allowance for merit or demerit as a factor in individual salvation or damnation, whereby divine justice becomes easier to comprehend. To the extent that it does so, however, it questions divine omnipotence.

Common to all the participants in this debate is belief in the existence of an omnipotent and just God, as well as the assumption that there is some freedom of the will, though not all positions can coherently accommodate all the assumptions. Where the positions differ most deeply is in their understanding of human nature: fallen humans are either fundamentally evil and in need of supernatural assistance if they are to choose and do good; or they are fundamentally good and capable of choosing and doing good on their own.

At the very least, all Christians, whether Catholic or Protestant, considered themselves to be part of a fundamentally good world created by an omnipotent and just (as well as benevolent and merciful) God. They considered themselves to be rational and free—that is, to know the difference between good and evil and be able to choose between them—but marked by the imperfections of sin and mortality as the result of Adam's fall at the tree of disobedience, and hence in need of salvation to remove these imperfections. They had faith that Christ on the tree of the cross had, by paying for the fall, initiated the salvation process; and they hoped that the Messiah's second coming at the end of time would complete the process of redemption. They also knew that, as a result of the fall, they needed the supernatural assistance of God's grace if they were to choose and do good on earth and in time, and if they were eventually to be saved in the beyond. What they could not agree on was whether faith alone was sufficient for an individual's salvation—as the Augustinian Protestants claimed, who emphasized God's omnipotence at the expense of human freedom (and at a large cost for human ability to comprehend God's justice), or whether faith had to be combined with good works of neighborly love—as the Semi-Pelagian (or Semi-Augustinian) Catholics thought, who wanted to maintain a balance between divine grace, on the one hand, and human freedom and moral responsibility on the other.

Excluded from Christian belief was the option offered by the excommunicated Pelagius, who emphasized human free will and responsibility at the expense of God's omnipotence (and implicitly at the expense of his justice) and played down the need for supernatural help, stressing instead autonomous human capacity to choose and do good, as well as to gain salvation. But such exclusions are rarely forever. One way to understand the process that marked the transition from the Christian to the post-Christian world is to recognize therein a revision of some of the central Augustinian positions. Modernity, in particular, might be seen first as a revival of Pelagianism (usually under different names, of course);[13] and, second, as a decision to abandon (or bracket) the hope of the heavenly city and instead turn seriously to the task of properly ordering the earthly one. Jean-Jacques Rousseau played a central role in this story. If the Christian era was primarily the age of Augustine, the modern age could be considered primarily the age of Rousseau.

THE BIRTH OF AUTONOMY

In the Judeo-Christian worldview the place reserved for humans in the hierarchy of God's creation was at the very top of earthly beings, right below the heavenly ones. Placing humans above other animals rested on the reasoning that they are the only earthly creatures with the moral status otherwise reserved only for angels—a kind of creature, in other words, whose actions can be characterized as good or evil and praised or blamed on this account. Human standing depended on being morally responsible, and moral status in turn depended on the endowment of reason (allowing humans to distinguish good and evil) and free will (allowing humans in any situation to choose what they will do). The most persuasive version of theodicy in the Christian tradition rested on the assumption that evil was not a sign of God's cruelty but rather the result of human free will, and that evil was a price worth paying for an endowment upon which depended the dignified standing of humans above all other earthly creatures. This is why the Augustinian doctrine of free will played such a central role in Christian anthropology. The doctrine was flawed, however. By the seventeenth century at the latest, some thinkers began to realize that free will did not suffice to explain moral responsibility.[14]

Thinkers like Hobbes and Locke saw essentially two problems. First, for me to be morally responsible, that is, for my action to be subject to praise or blame in terms of good or evil, the action must be mine alone, which means that my will to act in this way rather than another must be free from external cause or determination. This applies even when one takes human actions to be not mechanically caused but motivated by reasons: here, too, my reason for acting one way rather than another must be free from external determination, otherwise I cannot be held responsible for the action. But by that definition, morally responsible human action would be the one thing in the world outside the rules of mechanical causality. For one of the unshakable assumptions of modern science—at least until the arrival of quantum mechanics suggested that the interaction of elementary particles might depend on chance rather than causality—was that everything in nature is mechanically determined. Consequently it was necessary either to give up the notions of free will and responsibility (this is what Hobbes and other determinists chose to do) or to accept some form of intellectually uncomfortable dualism whereby humans, otherwise subject to the same natural laws as everything else, additionally participated as agents in some sort of supernatural order. This, however, was by far the lesser of the two problems. The Christian response to this dilemma is that humanity's participation in two different orders of reality, natural and supernatural, is precisely what the Christian worldview proclaims.

The real problem lies elsewhere. The theory that human actions result from decisions made by undetermined free will makes these actions appear arbitrary, a matter of chance rather than choice. Arbitrary actions, however, cannot be subject to moral responsibility. Since morality involves following a system of norms or standards, an action can be judged praiseworthy only when it was rationally chosen according to a criterion consistent with these norms rather than having been stumbled upon arbitrarily or accidentally: we cannot impute responsibility to an irrational agent. By contrast, a responsible agent has reasons for the actions he chooses; his actions need to be consistent with, and hence determined by, a preexistent system of norms. Thus the theory of undetermined free will seems to lead to an aporia: on the one hand, an agent is morally responsible only if his actions, as well as his reasons for choosing those actions, are independent of external determination; on the other hand, his actions cannot result from arbitrary decisions but must follow from rational choices determined by a preexistent system of moral norms.

The historical importance of Rousseau rests primarily on his being the first explicitly to show a way out of this dilemma (not being a systematic thinker, he left it to later academic philosophers, Kant and Hegel in particular, to work his ideas out fully). Since moral responsibility could not depend on the traditional concept of human will free from outside determination, it was necessary to supplement the notion of free will with a new concept of freedom as autonomy. Here the will is seen as determined by itself. The solution depended on distinguishing between an action determined by causes and one motivated by reasons. An agent is responsible for his action when that action is both causally undetermined (this keeps in place traditional theory's claim that free will was a necessary condition of responsibility) as well as motivated (or determined) by reasons (this resolves the problem that free will alone was not sufficient); further, these reasons had to be the agent's own, whereby a new theory of freedom as autonomy, or self-determination of the will, supplemented the traditional conception of free will.

Given that the agent's choice of action must be determined by a preexistent system of moral norms, do these norms have to be the agent's own? Or could they have been authored by someone else—his God, say, or his society—so long as it was his choice whether to follow them or not? The short answer is that whereas the norms must be the agent's, they may originally have been formulated by someone else. Rationality dictates that the reasons for my action must be mine: I cannot be *forced* to accept someone else's reasons (torturers could force me to proclaim that two plus two equals five, but they could not force me to believe that), I can only be *convinced* by my or someone else's arguments; it is by accepting them that I make them my own. Reason recognizes its norms as valid for all rational creatures; if I am a rational creature, such norms are simultaneously universal and mine. In this sense, even if someone else came up with them before I did (just as someone else realized before I did that two plus two equals four), the norms of reason are self-legislated.

Thus Rousseau supplemented the traditional concept of freedom—as one in which the will is not causally determined—with the modern concept of freedom as autonomy or rational self-determination of the will. (Henceforth I shall use the term "freedom" to refer to the traditional concept and "autonomy" to refer to the modern one.) With the invention of autonomy, modern self-understanding gained something so central and fundamental that Kant (who gave the notion of autonomy its fully systematic and most influential form) was moved to call Rousseau a second Newton (and to hang Rousseau's portrait over his desk as the only picture in his house)—that is, someone who set the study of the moral realm on foundations as strong and modern as those Newton set up for the natural world.[15] With this fundamental discovery Rousseau was able to rewrite the story of the human fall and offer a new vision of the prospects for individual and collective salvation.

Although the notion of freedom is fully comprehensible with reference to a single individual, the notion of autonomy makes no sense without reference to others, to a community. Freedom, we might say, is inherently individualist; autonomy, on the other hand, is communitarian. The function of autonomy is to impose limits on potentially infinite human desire and establish norms for the agent's conduct that tell him what he should and should not do. With God's legislation thus replaced by self-legislation, limits of that kind can be defined only with reference to other humans. The agent will know what not to do by reflecting on what Rousseau dubbed "that noble maxim of rational justice 'Do unto others as you would have them do unto you.'"[16] Similarly, his decisions on what to do will be influenced solely by matching his individual capacities with the opportunities offered by the institutions and practices of his society (one can become a musicologist only when one is a member of a society where the practice of musicology and such institutions as universities, academic presses, and so forth are known). An autonomous individual chooses his values freely, but this does not mean that he conjures them out of thin air by assuming the place formerly occupied by God. An autonomous individual's identity and coherent self can emerge only against the background of a shared culture.

Moreover, autonomy can only supplement freedom, it cannot replace it. Although freedom may be conceivable without autonomy (one can imagine someone whose will is free of causal determination but who leaves it without rational guidance), the reverse is not the case: freedom is a prerequisite of autonomy; the will can only be determined by reason if it is at least occasionally free of causal determination. It follows that the modern moral-political outlook must combine both freedom and autonomy. Admittedly, they make for an unstable compound, and in different proportions they produce both different versions of the modern view of man and the tensions between those different versions that are so characteristic of the modern age.

Schematically speaking, a moral outlook that maximizes freedom and minimizes autonomy leads, when pushed to the extreme, to a pathology of "absolute freedom"—the position of someone who leads an empty, meaningless existence because he is so enamored of freedom that he refuses to commit to the cultivation of specific practices or institutions, any of which would inevitably impose limits on his freedom.[17] Such a "person" runs the risk of incoherence, inability to achieve a clearly delineated self. At the opposite end of the spectrum an outlook that maximizes autonomy and minimizes freedom leads, when pushed to the extreme, to the pathology of a morality so rigorous and rigid that it leaves no room for contingency, for learning from experience, for evolution, or for change. The risk in this case is that of inauthenticity—of a self not one's own but rather wholly defined by others.

In the political realm, the position that emphasizes freedom is commonly called "liberalism," while the one that emphasizes autonomy is "democracy," and this is how I shall use these terms here (ignoring the many other, often contradictory, meanings they have accumulated over time). At least since the seventeenth century, sociopolitical thinkers began increasingly to recognize that the complex modern public sphere was not fully coextensive with the state, with its monopoly on the legitimate uses of coercion and violence; in addition to the state, the public sphere also contains civil society, encompassing all those areas of the community's life—most prominently, the market—that can largely regulate themselves without undue interventions from the state. Essential to liberalism (a tradition whose foundational text is John Locke's *Second Treatise of Government*, published in 1690) is the wish to minimize the role of the state and maximize that of civil society. By contrast, democrats (for whom the foundational text is Rousseau's *The Social Contract*, published in 1762), wish to enlarge the competence of the state as much as possible and minimize the independent civil-social realm.

Although liberals recognize that a responsible individual must be motivated by reasons, they do not see why society should want to impose limitations on the empirical desires of individuals or on their pursuit of happiness, unless these interfere with the desires and pursuits of others; in particular, they see nothing degrading in the unlimited production and consumption of material goods, which are suspect to Christians and Rousseauists alike. This liberal acceptance of unlimited desire is a fruit of the Reformation. Christians believe that God established proper limits and purposes on potentially unlimited human desire. But once the Reformation shattered the unity of the Western Christian church, God ceased to speak with one voice; disastrous conflicts resulting from quarrels among his interpreters eventually suggested that the most practical solution would be religious tolerance and the state's noninterference in church affairs—that is, separation of church and state. More important, liberals chose to follow the radical Protestantism of their Puritan predecessors in believing that what matters most for humans—salvation—does not depend on community (the church included) but involves only the individual's immediate relationship with God; similarly, they followed Christians in believing human individuality to possess dignity and moral significance independently of membership in a community. (Where liberals differed from Puritans was, of course, in their belief that not only otherworldly salvation but also secular, this-worldly visions of happiness are worth pursuing.) If God were no longer imposing unambiguous limits on human desire, individuals could pursue visions of happiness according to their own lights, and for that to be possible they had to be granted the space in which freely to script and enact their life stories.

The essence of the liberal position is concern for preserving free and inviolable space around individuals so that they can pursue their goals as they see fit, without unnecessary interference. The task of the legitimate government is to maintain order, prevent conflicts, and, when conflicts do arise, resolve them peacefully. The political community is not the essential locus of moral self-realization. Rather, it is a practical arrangement allowing individuals to pursue their moral self-realization without needless hindrance. The government derives legitimacy not from God (as in the case of the divine right claimed by Christian kings) but from purely human arrangements—such as consent, however defined and expressed, of the governed (as propounded by Locke and his American heirs), or simply traditional customs and practices of the community (as propounded by Hume, Burke, Chateaubriand, and other conservative liberals); the sovereignty of such government can never be absolute, since to take away from the individual all prepolitical freedom would contradict the very purpose for which the state was established and hence deprive the state of its legitimacy.

Democrats reject this individualism. Unlike Christians and liberals, they do not believe that any single individual is endowed with a moral status independently of membership in a community. Rather, they go back to the ancient Aristotelian tradition in which humans can achieve moral standing only in the context of a political community. In short, whereas for liberals the individual is prior and the community derived, for democrats it is the community that has priority, and individuality is realizable only in that context: it is this original (nonderived) entity—the "people"—that can and should impose legitimate limits on the potentially endless desires of its component individuals, thus endowing them with moral status and dignity. Democrats see no need for creating an inviolable space around each individual; hence they see no need for imposing limits on the state. The legitimacy of sovereignty derives neither from traditional arrangements nor from the consent of each governed individual but instead (as for Rousseau and his Jacobin heirs) from the will of the people as a whole, however expressed.

The modern political outlook, like the moral one, is a tense and unstable compromise between two extremes. All Western liberal democracies fall somewhere along the spectrum between the American model, which emphasizes the liberal component of the equation, and the French model, with its preference for the democratic component.[18] Alexander Herzen captured the contrast with admirable clarity in his letter to Chicherin:[19]

> Civic religion—the apotheosis of the State—is a purely Roman idea and in the modern world, principally French. It is consistent with a strong state, but is incompatible with a free people; through it you may get splendid soldiers, but you cannot have independent citizens. The United States of America, on the contrary, have, so far as it is possible, abolished the religious character of the police and the administration.

When the two components separate entirely, the extremes of liberalism and democracy result in characteristically modern political pathologies. Liberalism without democracy produces autocratic regimes that do not allow citizens any say in the operation of the state but leave civil society relatively undisturbed (one hopes that, increasingly, this will be the case in China after Mao). Democracy without liberalism produces totalitarian regimes where the state, claiming to express the will of the people (as articulated by the party elite and their leader), tries to obliterate any independently existing civil society in the name either of the future universal brotherhood of men (as in Stalin's Russia) or of primordial nationalist unity (as in Hitler's Germany). It is this inherent instability of the modern outlook that makes all talk of the "end of history" so implausible.

ROUSSEAU

Whatever one's opinion of Christian teaching, there is no denying that first, it attempts to provide answers to most of the central questions that are likely to occur to a self-reflective person wondering how to live his or her life; and second, its answers are not frivolous and deserve to be taken seriously. A Christian knows who he is and how he differs from other creatures—above all he knows that he is fallen and thus always capable of doing evil and likely to do it at least some of the time. He also knows what kind of person he should try to become and, conversely, whom he should not emulate; that is, he knows what good and evil actually are. His sense of ethics is governed by the commandment to love his neighbor as himself—to be guided by charity rather than concupiscence—and while he is as likely to encounter morally perplexing situations as anyone else, at least he can be reasonably sure that it is good to offer disinterested help to a suffering neighbor and evil to inflict suffering on another, whether out of self-interest or, worse, disinterestedly. If his political stance is less clearly defined, this is not an oversight but rather the consequence of a worldview that deliberately devalues the political realm. The ultimate purpose of his individual existence is the pursuit of salvation (and avoidance of damnation), and this eschatological drama is simply not played out on the political stage. Jesus's teaching that one should "render to Caesar the things that are Caesar's, and to God the things that are God's" (Mark 12.17; also Matthew 22.21 and Luke 20.25) suggests accommodation with the powers that be, so long as this is consistent with membership in a community of the charitable united by their love of God; this last is an important qualification: from Simon Peter's time until ours, it has on occasion led Christians into conflict with established state powers. What truly matters in this view, the question of salvation, is not dependent on politics.

The Christian worldview provides serious and compelling answers to the questions: Who am I? Who should I become, that is, what should my ethics and politics be? and What is the ultimate meaning of my existence? A successful, or at least viable, alternative to Christianity must provide answers at least equally serious and compelling. There are many ways to read a thinker as seminal and fertile as Rousseau, but one way—and the way I shall pursue here—is to see his work as the attempt to formulate a viable alternative to Christianity that answers these questions. No single thinker can be expected fully to represent the modern worldview. This outlook, like that of Christians, is woven of competing strands that coexist uneasily without allowing a completely satisfying or tidy compromise. If Augustine stresses the idea of God's omnipotence and man's dependence, Rousseau advocates the opposite, Pelagian, extreme, which emphasizes man's autonomy. In this respect Rousseau seems to be the representative face of modernity because, like Augustine, he represents what is most characteristic about the outlook of his age in the most radical and uncompromising fashion. In fact, Rousseau could be regarded as Augustine's secret opponent. (Is this why in his spiritual autobiography Rousseau copied the title, as well as some key episodes, from that of the great church doctor?) Rousseau attempted systematically to rewrite Christian teaching, complete with an alternative telling of the story of human fall (primarily in the *Discours sur l'origine et les fondements de l'inégalité*, published in 1755) and an alternative vision of the prospects for both individual and collective human salvation (discussed, respectively, in *Émile* and *Du contrat social*, both published in 1762).

"Everything is good as it leaves the hands of the Author of things; everything degenerates in the hands of man."[20] A master of arresting opening sentences, Rousseau begins *Emile* with an evocation of his own rewriting of Genesis in the *Discourse on Inequality*. Those who mock Rousseau for his naïve belief in the natural goodness of man and contrast this with the more tough-minded and realistic, darker Augustinian vision forget how similar Rousseau's understanding of the beginnings of human history is to that of the Judeo-Christian tradition. In both, the innate, natural, God-given goodness of man precedes the fall but does not survive it intact, and in both the fall is the work of man alone. The crucial difference between the two is that after the fall Augustine's man is incapable of getting back up on his own, instead requiring God's grace; Rousseau's man is able, though by no means certain, to repair the damage without supernatural help, by his own efforts.

Pelagianism stops being intellectually incoherent as soon as one gives up believing in the existence of an omnipotent and just God. Like his Christian predecessors, but unlike Hobbes and a great many of his enlightened, determinist contemporaries, Rousseau holds fast to belief in the freedom of the will but not in the Christian God. Not that he does not believe in God— on the contrary—but judging by the "Profession of Faith of the Savoyard Vicar" in Book IV of *Emile*, he is not much interested in divine omnipotence or justice, because he is not obsessed, as Christians are, by the question of salvation and damnation. He does believe in life after death, but he awaits it without trepidation, in full confidence that God will receive him as a loving father. His God is above all benevolent, a loving and good Creator whose presence permeates creation (which, consequently, is also good) and certain not to punish his creatures after death (though I am not entirely sure that this dispensation included Rousseau's real or imaginary persecutors— Voltaire, Diderot, Hume, and many others).[21] Without the need for divine redemption, Jesus is neither divine nor a redeemer; he is a supremely good man, a teacher and an example of charity martyred by his society—that is, someone like Rousseau himself, in his own estimation. Rousseau's religion is a strictly private affair, the existential need of a tormented heart in search of consolation. "I have suffered too much to live without faith," he told Voltaire.[22] Or, as he wrote to one of his friends: "I desire too much that there should be a God to be able to doubt it, and I die with the firm conviction that I shall find in His bosom the happiness and the peace I have not enjoyed in this world." But in Rousseau's view of man's condition and destiny God has no truly indispensable role to play. At most, he underwrites the goodness of his creation. Once it has been said that nature is good, however, no more need be said. To add that nature is good because she comes from the hands of a good creator sounds like a further explanation but is really no more than a redundant embellishment.

Moreover, nature's goodness, though Rousseau often proclaims it, on closer inspection turns out to be far from entirely straightforward. Strictly speaking, the notions of good and evil do not apply before the fall: natural man is neither good nor evil but, rather, innocent of such notions. Rousseau's nature is a morally neutral realm of necessity; when he proclaims it "good," he means to indicate that it is beneficial for humans to live in harmony with this necessity and harmful, as well as pointless, to oppose it.

As a preliminary approximation (and no more than an approximation), one might say that in Rousseau's view the position occupied in Christianity by God is now occupied by nature. To be sure, nature is not a person, and she does not actively intervene in human history to affect human salvation. But, like God, she would appear to be the ultimate reality—the realm of being and necessity. Replacing God with nature might initially seem to bypass the contradiction that has plagued theological speculation for so many centuries—the contradiction between God's omnipotence and human freedom. Giving up on God, however, does not solve the problem, for it remains in the contradiction between determinism and free will. But Rousseau is not a determinist, and this problem does not trouble him. He simply accepts as given the human potential capacities for freedom and rationality, even though they contradict the otherwise universal determinism of nature, and he concentrates on natural necessity and human freedom as the main protagonists of history.

Rousseau's history has the same three-stage outline as that offered by Christianity: it is the story of original harmony between man and ultimate reality—something infinitely larger and more powerful than man in which, having been created in its image, he nevertheless somehow participates; of this harmony's destruction through man's choices and actions, which have led to the fallen state in which humanity presently finds itself; and of the possibility that harmony may be restored in the future. The differences are as important, however, as these structural similarities. The place of ultimate reality is occupied now not by God but by nature: the fall consists in disobedience against nature; and salvation is understood as reconciliation with nature. These differences are of truly epochal significance. In Rousseau's world, man is no longer confronted with a transcendent realm representing a level of reality radically different from his own; instead, humanity and nature occupy one and the same level of reality. Because we are natural beings and a part of nature, our fall is a denial of ourselves, the result of disobedience toward our own nature. Further, because there is no transcendent realm—no outside—saving grace cannot come from outside. If we are to be saved, it can only be by our own efforts.

As he leaves the hands of his Author, man lives alone in happy harmony with nature, of which he is a part, much like other animals, and from whom he differs only in his capacities (so far more potential than actual) for freedom, self-consciousness, and self-improvement—what Rousseau calls "perfectibility." Like other animals, however, he is actually innocent in the sense of being unselfconscious, governed not by consciously established purposes but by a healthy and natural instinct of self-preservation, *amour de soi* (self-love), which prompts him to take care of his few authentic, natural, easily satisfied needs.

As in the Genesis story, the human capacities for free choice, self-consciousness, and self-improvement are the source of estrangement from paradise, and as in Genesis, the fall coincides with the birth of self-consciousness. (Recall the first thing that happened to Adam and Eve after they had eaten of the forbidden fruit: "And the eyes of them both were opened, and they knew that they *were* naked" [Genesis 3.7].) Evil is born of what is most characteristically human (a point overlooked by those who accuse Rousseau of a naïve trust in man's goodness), of what makes us different from other animals: our capacity to redouble our consciousness, to see ourselves imaginatively as if through the eyes of another. The name of this evil-generating mechanism is *amour-propre* (self-regard). This capacity is triggered when man, driven mainly by need resulting from natural disasters or shortages, gradually becomes social, settles, organizes into families and larger units, and establishes property. In nature, man was concerned with the fulfillment of his few simple and authentic bodily needs. In society, man loses his naïve and immediate relationships to himself and his world and begins to imagine how he and the world might appear to others. His needs multiply, intensify, and cease being authentic when he begins to desire what others desire—desiring not because he truly needs but because he wants to impress others, and through others himself. Self-esteem is now dependent on the esteem of others, and hence it is the esteem of others that he desires more than anything: "the savage lives within himself; social man lives always outside himself; he knows how to live only in the opinion of others, it is, so to speak, from their judgment alone that he derives the sense of his own existence."[23] (For Rousseau, human history—and misery—begins in earnest with the struggle for mutual recognition that Hegel later analyzed as the master-and-slave dialectic.)[24] To be sure, as Rousseau writes, "this yearning for distinction which keeps us almost always in a restless state is responsible for what is best and what is worst among men."[25] More important, perhaps, *amour-propre* can never be satisfied: we can never have enough esteem from others because however much we have, we want more—and ultimately we want "others to prefer us to themselves, which is impossible."[26] Hence socialized man cannot build human happiness on this desire as solitary natural man can build on the authentic desires in himself. Self-regard causes man to become divided, spiritually dependent on others, and alienated from nature—that is, from his own authentic self. And the dependence is not only spiritual, it is bodily, too, since endlessly multiplying needs require others for fulfillment and lead to infinitely escalating conflict, inequality, and selfish exploitation of others—eventually to a Hobbesian war of all against all and the resulting need to establish peace by means of a social contract instituting a political society under a system of positive law.

But bodily dependence is merely an effect: spiritual dependence is the cause. If evil is ever to be eradicated and man returned to the happy condition of harmony with his own nature, spiritual dependence must be addressed first (and so Rousseau does in *Emile*). Only healed, spiritually independent individuals will be able to replace the fraudulent social contracts on which their actual political societies are based, contracts that give the rich license to exploit the poor, with a just contract founding equal liberty under law for all (as Rousseau describes in *The Social Contract*). In neither case does Rousseau advocate simply forgetting human history and civilization or returning to man's point of departure, the condition of happy brutes. He knows that this would be impossible, perhaps even undesirable. Rather, he wants humanity civilized and social but freed from the ill effects of civilization and sociality, disalienated, returned to its true nature and reconciled with it. In other words, the whole point of his project is not to negate culture, but to reconcile culture with nature. His most perceptive readers, Kant above all, understood this point perfectly; this is evident in Kant's description of Rousseau's project in his 1786 essay on the "Conjectural Beginning of Human History": "In his *Émile*, his *Social Contract*, . . . he tries to solve this much harder problem: how culture was to move forward, in order to bring about such a development of the dispositions of mankind, considered as a *moral* species, as to end the conflict between the natural and the moral species."[27]

The moral status that raises humanity above nature rests on the human potential for autonomy—that is, not merely freedom from causal determination of the will but the will's capacity for rational self-determination. But the fallen condition in which we presently find ourselves is the result of our having exercised the very capacities on which autonomy depends—the capacities for freedom and rationality. Since it is impossible to return to the prelapsarian state, the only way forward is to exercise those two capacities in such a way as to bring about autonomy. Rousseau wants us—individually and collectively—to stop obeying others and begin to govern ourselves.

In his education of Emile, Rousseau aims at making him as self-sufficient and as spiritually independent of imagined and real others as possible. He is to learn how to accept natural necessity—including that of suffering, at least occasionally, and certainly that of dying—without excessive fear and without developing superstitious beliefs in supernatural protectors, helpers, and consolers. (Thus he learns to accept only those beliefs for which there is clear evidence, learns, in other words, to distinguish science from superstition.) And he learns how to forestall the development of self-regard; how to pay attention to his own authentic, healthy, and natural bodily needs; how to abstain from competing with others; and how to ignore the opinions of others. Above all, he learns how to esteem himself without caring whether or not others do. His relations with others are initially governed by only one commandment: harm no one.

Only after he is protected from fear, superstition, and self-regard, with the habits of intellectual and moral independence firmly in place, is Emile ready to benefit from, rather than be corrupted by, society and its culture. What causes his entrance into society (and, by extension, into the condition of moral responsibility) is the one natural inclination that both is an authentic need and precludes his being able to ignore others: namely, sexual desire. To arrest this desire at the stage where it is a purely natural bodily need is problematic, because once this need is satisfied he would have no further inducement to be interested in, or concerned for, the other. Because the satisfaction of this particular need depends on another person, sexual desire can easily lead to the birth of self-regard. The task is to steer it in such a way that it does not do so—that it becomes, instead, the foundation of a noncoercive and noncompetitive concern for others. Ideally, desire should be driven not only by the bodily but also—and especially—by the spiritual qualities of the other. This requires imagination, which can transform desire into something richer than mere appetite: love. With such transformation, desire can become the basis of an enduring reciprocal relationship of mutual respect and affection, one that acknowledges that the other is free—and hence not subject to coercion; and one's equal—and hence more than an instrument for the satisfaction of a personal need. At the level of a single relationship of this kind, therefore, it is possible to abolish "the conflict between the natural and the moral species." So far Emile's education has led him to the threshold of ethics remarkably similar to those of Augustine, who wanted each human being to live "in well-ordered concord with all men," that is, "in the first place, injure no one, and, in the second, do good to every one he can reach" (*The City of God*, 19.14). If Emile is to move beyond this threshold, however, the relationship with his beloved needs to be the model for his relationships with everyone in his life—a model, that is, for a noncoercive and noncompetitive concern for others.

In other words, the remaining task is to use this kind of reciprocal relationship, one that acknowledges the dignity, freedom, and equality of another, as the model for relationships between all citizens in a political society. Then, indeed, "the conflict between the natural and the moral species" may be resolved and humans can enter the third and last stage of their development. Humanity's current condition can only be corrected if necessity and freedom are reconciled. This is the task laid out in *The Social Contract*, which famously begins: "Man was born free, and he is everywhere in chains."[28] In the fraudulent contracts on which existing societies are based, systems of positive law operate that are designed to prevent war of all against all by means of peaceful but unjust resolution of conflicts over resources—unjust because designed for the benefit of the rich at the expense of the poor. Rousseau proposes to replace these systems with a just contract whereby every citizen will be free under law. To understand this proposal—to see why Rousseau intends something different from the liberals' compromise between individual desire for freedom of action and collective need for social peace and justice—it is important to keep in mind that Rousseau defined freedom not as freedom from all determination but as self-determination.

Liberals believe that limited individual autonomy (limited by the need of each individual to respect the autonomy of others) is as far as humans can go in the direction of self-determination. Rousseau and critics of liberalism inspired by him believe that this is not far enough. Liberal society is an arena of competing egoisms, in which the state is responsible for seeing that competition does not degenerate into violence. Beyond that there is nothing that binds individuals, nothing that might encourage noncoercive and noncompetitive concern for others. Rousseau's solution is democratic politics—the principle of autonomy applied not just to the individual but to the whole political community, the state.

Unlike Christians and liberals, Rousseau goes back to the ancient Aristotelian tradition that sees the polis—not the individual—as the true locus of moral self-realization. Under the social contract he proposes, everyone trades in individual prepolitical freedom for political freedom—that is, for the chance to participate in an autonomous community. The contract demands "the total alienation by each associate of himself and all his rights to the whole community." Since under it, "the conditions are the same for all, . . . it is in no one's interest to make the conditions onerous for others." Thus, "each individual, while uniting himself with the others, obeys no one but himself, and remains as free as before."[29] The political society thus created is not merely the sum of individuals, but a new entity, a single whole, a people (a nation, a republic), with a single will (the "general will"). Conversely, each adherent is transformed from an isolated individual in pursuit of private interests into a citizen committed to the furthering of the public good. "Each one of us puts into the community his person and all his powers under the supreme direction of the general will; and as a body, we incorporate every member as an indivisible part of the whole." Where liberals ask each individual to alienate a part of his freedom and invest their minimal sovereign with the power to protect public order, Rousseau proposes that individuals give up all of their freedom in exchange for participation in an autonomous and all-embracing state—that is, in exchange for becoming the sovereign themselves, not individually, of course, but as the people.

Should a citizen become deaf to the reasonable voice of the general will within himself and follow instead a private interest dictated by his enslaving passions, "he shall be forced to be free" (on le forcera d'être libre), as Rousseau famously put it.[30] A century later, Dostoyevsky savagely derided this sort of program in his novel *The Devils*, when the possessed revolutionary Shigalyov proudly declaims: "Starting with unlimited freedom, I arrive at unlimited despotism." Undeniably, Rousseau's contract has totalitarian implications.[31] I have briefly outlined why such implications are inescapable if democracy in its pure form, untempered by liberalism, were to be extended to its full capacity; in that case the general will embodied in the all-powerful state would destroy both individual freedom and any independent institutions of civil society that might mediate between the individual and the state. Rousseau sees no need to protect individuals and minorities from the decisions of the sovereign general will. (What is worse, the ancient polis, where a few thousand citizens participated directly in political deliberation and decision making, is largely unrecoverable under modern conditions, so in practice the general will can easily be usurped by the will of a ruling elite and a charismatic leader.) Rousseau's reputation as Robespierre's father and as the grandfather of the more recent totalitarian ideologies—whether of the left, with its hope to bring about universal brotherhood, or of the right, with its aim to recover the primordial unity of the nation—is at least partly deserved.

Nevertheless, this does not invalidate Rousseau's great discovery—the principle of autonomy. His mistake was not in claiming that humans can and should govern themselves but in possibly forgetting that freedom is a prerequisite of autonomy and in shifting the application of autonomy from the individual and civil society to the state alone. To be sure, he preached both individual and communal autonomy, and he was right to claim that autonomous individuals should aspire to autonomous political communities. But his belief that there need be no conflict between the two seems unfounded: given that incompatible moral systems are possible, a general will that decides against one such system is not simply subjugating private interests and passions. For the same reason, his belief in the moral priority of the community over the individual seems unjustified. He may have assumed that those adhering to the social contract had received Emile's education. Unfortunately, those who have not received this education and are still enslaved by their passions require terror to force them to be free. We do not know whether the utopia of fully autonomous individuals forming a fully autonomous community is realizable on earth, but if the experiments of the past century are anything to go by, the possibility seems remote. Mainstream and less radical moderns would do better to treat Rousseau's program as an ideal to be approximated but never reached, recognizing the necessity of a messy and uneasy compromise between liberalism and democracy and allowing civil society, as well as the state, the benefit of communal autonomy. In fact, given that the state backs its decisions with coercive powers, the liberal tradition has an edge over Rousseau in looking to the private sphere and civil society to serve as the spaces that allow noncoercive concern for others, mutual interdependence, and voluntary cooperation.

Rousseau created a self-image and a self-understanding that offered the moderns an intellectual and emotional alternative to Augustinian Christianity. Above all, he was the first modern to articulate clearly an outlook centered on the notion of human autonomy, and to provide a secular version of the grand narrative of the past fall and future salvation. In both these respects, Kant and Hegel were his successors.

THE CHRISTIAN AND MODERN OUTLOOKS COMPARED

In sum, then, both premodern Christians and post-Christian moderns see themselves as very special animals—animals with a moral status and hence in some mysterious way not completely subject to natural causation. This is no problem for Christians, since they take the existence of the supernatural realm for granted, but it is a source of endless metaphysical puzzling for the more naturalistically minded moderns—especially if they are honest enough (and faithful enough to experience) to find a thoroughgoing determinism unacceptable. Freedom is the only miracle the moderns recognize, but its existence sufficed to suggest to those like Rousseau and Kant that the realm of the spirit could not be completely reduced to that of nature. (The jury is still out on whether their incompatibilist views are correct or not.) However, the truly distinctive feature of the modern outlook is its conception of freedom, which is richer and deeper than previous views: although Christians know they are free (and thus capable of acting independently of natural causation), the moderns know that in addition to being free they are also autonomous (and thus capable of acting in accordance with self-established rational norms). Hence the moderns recognize what Christians did not: that freedom and rationality are systematically related to one another. Reason is the capacity that only humans have, the capacity to set goals and hence remake oneself—the capacity for what Rousseau dubbed "perfectibility."

A modern's answer to the question, Who am I? is thus similar to that of his predecessors, except that the modern additionally sees himself as autonomous. This difference affects every aspect of his outlook. When thinking about the question, Who should I become? or How should I live my life individually and collectively? he does not necessarily reject the answers given by the Christian tradition. But even in accepting traditional answers the moderns filter them through the prism of autonomy and thus transform them.

In thinking about their individual existence, Christians above all desire salvation in the afterlife, and in the meantime they wish to do good in this life. The moderns simultaneously adopt and transform these wishes. Let us consider, first, their ethics. We have seen that Augustine interpreted his divine Master's "two precepts"—"the love of God and the love of our neighbour"—to mean that man must love three objects, which ascend from himself to his neighbor and from there to God. Initially Jean-Jacques repeatedly instructs Emile that his first duty is to himself; as far as Emile's duty to his neighbor is concerned, his preceptor's recommendation is no different from Augustine's, who taught that one should "in the first place, injure no one, and, in the second, do good to every one he can reach." Yet even if their moral precepts are the same, there is a fundamental difference in the way Augustine and Rousseau reach and justify them. Augustine's are based on divine authority, on Jesus's explicit commandments. Rousseau derives and justifies his only with reference to human autonomy: not God but the rational will gives the moderns the norms by which they are to live.

From ethics we turn, second, to the question of happiness. The moderns want to be good, but they also want to be happy, and hence they wish to follow not only the precepts of morality but also those of prudence. Of course, a Christian wants to be happy, too, but he most desires eternal bliss hereafter; the nature of that happiness, insofar as it can be imagined—and imagined it was, repeatedly and ardently, by Augustine in the last part of the *City of God*, as well as by Dante and countless painters and composers—is the same one for all those who will be saved. A modern desires to be happy in this life (even when he expects another as well), and he wants his happiness custom-made to his own specifications. He expects to be able to form his own idea of the greatest possible well-being or satisfaction over the entire duration of his life, and he expects to pursue this end prudently and choose it over momentary satisfaction. Here, again, the ideal of autonomy accounts for the difference between Christian and modern visions of bliss. A Christian depends for the content and attainability of his ultimate happiness on God alone; a modern knows that he does not dispose of the other world, but on earth he defines the content of his happiness himself and hopes to attain it by his own efforts.

To a Christian, the modern emphasis on love of self, and on the individual's right to choose his own life-project freely, potentially conflicts with the duty to love one's neighbor and thus smacks of cupidity. The moral significance of Adam Smith's epochal discovery of the "invisible hand" (in *An Inquiry into the Nature and Causes of the Wealth of Nations*, 1776), which coordinates egoistically motivated actions of individual players in the marketplace so as to produce efficient, socially and economically desirable outcomes—a discovery that Mandeville had anticipated with his slogan "private vices, public benefits," the subtitle of his *The Fable of the Bees*, which appeared in its definitive form in 1729—consists in the demonstration that the love of self cannot be automatically equated with cupidity. On the contrary, choosing and following one's individual calling, far from being incompatible with "public benefits," is the best way to contribute to the common good and thus more fundamentally beneficial than any charity.

As a result of their heteronomy, their dependence on God, Christians do not see the pursuit of eternal bliss hereafter to be in conflict with the pursuit of moral goodness on earth: God is their harmonizing principle. For the moderns, by contrast, the two pursuits, of earthly happiness and of goodness, may, and often do, collide: they see morality as establishing limits to acceptable visions of individual happiness and are thus faced with the need to balance the demands of happiness with those of morality. The balance is inherently unstable: there is no formula to calibrate it perfectly once and for all. Those who choose to emphasize happiness at the expense of morality and go too far in this direction earn the name of libertines (as in the case of Don Giovanni). Those who choose the opposite direction may become stern, sententious moralists (as in the case of Sarastro). Most of us muddle through somewhere along the spectrum between these extremes (as in the case of Figaro and Susanna).

It is in their thinking about collective existence, that is, in their politics, that the moderns depart most from the Christian tradition. And here, too, the divergence is brought about by the ideal of autonomy. Christianity's greatest contribution to politics was the recognition that politics did not matter all that much. The ancient Aristotelian tradition claimed that only within the context of the polis was it possible for men fully to realize their moral potential. Jesus, by contrast, advised leaving politics to Caesar, since politics do not affect human salvation; it was in the prepolitical realm that humans achieved their full moral realization.

The politics of the moderns, given their ideal of autonomy and resulting understanding of happiness and morality, is a never-ending attempt to achieve a precarious, necessarily unstable synthesis of Aristotelian and Christian conceptions. A modern human, to be able to pursue an individual vision of earthly happiness, must value the prepolitical realm as much as a Christian does. At the same time, however, precisely because it is a matter of happiness on earth, not in heaven, a modern cannot afford to devalue politics altogether. On the contrary, he needs to insist on political institutions and practices that leave a free prepolitical sphere that allows (within certain legitimate limits) every individual to pursue happiness as he or she pleases. With that, Christian indifference to politics is transformed into the politics of liberalism. To be not merely happy but also moral, on the other hand, moderns need to live in a self-ruled community: unlike the individually defined content of happiness, the norms of morality are a matter not of individual decision but of collective discovery over many generations. These norms are continuously established and revised by a deliberating, self-correcting, multigenerational community of free and autonomous individuals. And for this to work, a modern needs to be a democrat and a liberal, a combination that is as unstable as the balance between happiness and morality. In this regard, those leaning toward the libertine extreme on the individual-existence spectrum will emphasize liberalism in their politics (and, if they lean too far, run the risk of supporting autocratic regimes); those inclined toward moralism will stress democracy (and, if radical and one-sided enough, risk embracing totalitarianism). Most moderns, one hopes, will opt for the liberal-democratic muddle between these extremes.

Finally, pressure from the ideal of autonomy has also transformed the grand Christian narrative of human destiny into something new. The modern narrative is similar to the Christian one in that it starts with harmony between man and an ultimate reality and proceeds from there through man's willful destruction of this harmony—resulting in his present fallen state of alienation from the ultimate reality—to the possibility of future salvation and restored harmony. But the modern narrative is different because for moderns the ultimate reality is nature, not God; hence their salvation, if it ever comes, is not the work of God but must be their own work (in the Christian story, the fall is the work of man, but the salvation is the work of God).

Moreover, the same human capacities—freedom and rationality—that are responsible for the fall are also our only hope of salvation. The desired end of history is not a return to the prelapsarian state of innocent unselfconsciousness before these capacities were exercised, which is impossible, but full development of individual and collective autonomy; harmony between man and nature would then be restored not because man has been absorbed back into nature but because nature will have become fully humanized. The two competing strands within the modern outlook envisage the process of restoration differently, however. For Locke and the liberal tradition that followed him, humanization of nature entails ever increasing control of, and hence independence from, nature. At the same time, the space in which individuals can independently pursue their separate visions of happiness will steadily increase. For Rousseau and the democratic critics of liberalism, this cannot suffice, since they believe that humans can achieve a very high degree of control over nature and still be enslaved by the desires and passions of *amour-propre*. In this view what needs to be humanized and controlled is not so much external nature as the nature within: we must master our desires and passions through moral-political self-legislation, and we must do this both as individuals and as a community. Overcoming alienation—that is, the reintegration of the isolated self into a larger whole—involves, in this tradition, integrating all free and autonomous individuals into a community of equals. Rousseau believed that man begins his adventure as a part of nature but ends it as a part of a polis, a citizen. Only thus can "the conflict between the natural and the moral species" be ended.

Moderns call the movement toward this desired end (regardless of whether this end takes the individualist or the communitarian form) progress—and in the modern outlook this idea takes the position that "salvation" had previously taken. The idea of progress was much worshipped in the nineteenth century—and since the catastrophes of the twentieth, which made it doubtful that what actually happens in history deserves this name, much derided. It is important to remember, however, that progress should be properly understood as a normative, not a descriptive, notion; one that names what should happen, not what actually does happen. Hence it is not a notion that can be falsified by reality, no matter how discouraging reality may be. Its function, in other words, is not to tell us what happens, let alone what must happen, but to provide us with a yardstick by which we can evaluate what has happened. It is hard to see how without such a yardstick humans could ever undertake collective action, could ever decide between doing this and doing that. It is equally hard to see what could take its place if the notion of progress were to be abandoned. Those who would claim that we have entered a postmodern era, and that this is a good thing, need to explain either how collective actions can be decided without the guidance of norms (without any normative "metanarratives") or which norms should replace the idea of progress.

It is clear, then, that the modern ideal of autonomy transformed every aspect of the traditional outlook. Even religion was not left untouched. Although it is not yet true that God and religion are dead, they too have been subtly affected and changed by modern self-understanding. First, hope for otherworldly salvation and faith in a transcendent God who is master of humanity's eschatological destiny—both inescapable for premodern Christians—were transformed by the moderns into something that was no more than an option. Second, even when they exercise this option, the moderns characteristically make their religion a matter of an autonomous choice. For our ancestors, to be converted was not a matter of choice, but of being swept off one's feet and turned around by the power and gift of grace. For us moderns it is, rather, a matter of *our* making "wagers" or taking "leaps of faith."

Even more important, God—even for moderns who choose to be

religious—is no longer the indispensable guide to appropriate conduct on earth. He may continue to dispense salvation and damnation in the hereafter, but he is not needed to define the moral and political norms to be followed on earth: these are collectively established and refined by autonomous human communities. Similarly, he may continue to determine the content of the bliss each individual saved soul will enjoy in heaven, but he does not dictate the content of earthly happiness: that each of us wants to define and shape individually.

By the same token, however, it is clear why religion is unlikely to disappear completely under modern conditions. Human autonomy is an adequate substitute for divine guidance on earthly conduct, but it cannot replace God's other functions. We cannot feel fully at home in a world where virtue often goes unrewarded and vice unpunished, and where those who suffer innocently cannot expect to be helped or their past misery redeemed or recompensed. Only faith can give us the world as it should be. The post-Christian world is a harsher place, and less of a home, than the world religion used to provide. This is why "wagers" and "leaps" are likely to retain their attractiveness.

Post-Christian homelessness is the source of yet another potential pathology characteristic of modernity: the pathology of utopianism. If it is true that only religion can give us a sense of being at home in the world, it is also true that religion offers this as a transcendental hope only. Religion does not promise a return of the earthly paradise but only a hope that we might find a home in the eschatological future of the beyond. The wish to bring such hopes back to earth, the belief that humans could ever be fully at home in this world, is, on the other hand, the essential feature of utopianism. And this invariably ends in coercion and disaster as, inspired by a vision of earthly paradise, the utopianists use force to create that home on earth, without noticing that they have transformed it into a prison ("on le forcera d'être libre").

At the beginning of the story traced in this Interlude lay the question of evil. The presence of evil, and of suffering and death, splits the human world by revealing the gap that separates what is from what ought to be. This gap drives history and constitutes the mainspring of human creative efforts to close it, as Goethe's Lord knew when he gave Faust the companion Mephistopheles. Such efforts are either practical—designed to close the gap, or at least make it narrower; or theoretical—designed to explain the evil in the past and present, and to offer hope of a better future. Whereas both Augustine and Rousseau understood evil (or at least moral evil) to be the result of wrong but free choices made by humans in the past, the former put his hope in divine love and mercy, thereby enveloping the linear time of human history in God's eternity, whence we emerged and to which we long to return; Rousseau, by contrast, put his tentative hope, such as it was, in humanity's own efforts to repair the self-inflicted damage, thus liberating the linear time of human history from a transcendent envelope.

The relationship between the outlook of premodern Christians and that of post-Christian moderns is the subject of an impressively learned "secularization debate"; principal installments in this debate were Karl Löwith's 1949 book *Meaning in History* and Hans Blumenberg's 1966 riposte in *The Legitimacy of the Modern Age*. "Philosophy of history," Löwith argued, is "a systematic interpretation of universal history in accordance with a principle by which historical events and successions are unified and directed toward an ultimate meaning." In this sense it is entirely dependent on "the theological concept of history as a history of fulfillment and salvation." It cannot be a science, "for how could one verify the belief in salvation on scientific grounds?" Rather, it represents a secularization of the eschatological pattern developed in the Judeo-Christian faith in salvation, which arose as an attempt to give meaning to evil and suffering. But the need for such meaning did not disappear with the loss of faith in a protective, caring God, and hence faith in historical progress, in the course of which evil would be gradually eliminated, replaced faith in divine Providence.[32] Blumenberg defended the "legitimacy" of modernity, that is, the originality and independence of such key modern notions as progress. Although he agreed that such notions may occupy the same space and answer the same questions and needs as religious ones, he nevertheless insisted that they were original to modernity, as opposed to having been derived from premodern notions. Providence and progress were alternative ways to address the problem of evil, and there was no reason to see either as derived from the other. In particular, Blumenberg stressed the infinity of progress over the finality of eschatology:

> The idea of infinite progress also has a safeguarding function for the actual individual and for each actual generation in history. If there were an immanent final goal of history, then those who believe they know it and claim to promote its attainment would be legitimized in using all the others who do not know it and cannot promote it as mere means. Infinite progress does makes each present relative to its future, but at the same time it renders every absolute claim untenable. This idea of progress corresponds more than anything else to the only regulative principle that can make history humanly bearable, which is that

all dealings must be so constituted that through them people do not become mere means. If eschatology or messianism were really the substantial point of departure of the modern historical consciousness, then that consciousness would be permanently and inescapably defined by teleological conceptions, by ideas of ends.[33]

I cannot here do justice to the subtlety and complexity of the arguments and positions taken on both sides. I can only suggest that the picture offered in this Interlude presents a view in which modernity inherited Christian notions and narrative lines (this is Löwith's viewpoint) at the same time that (as propounded by Blumenberg) it transformed them so radically as to make them into something truly new. The mainspring of this transformation is the new ideal of autonomy: this is the source of the originality and legitimacy of modernity.

THE EMANCIPATION OF TIME

The modern ideal of autonomy made God an optional choice with regard to our putative existence in the hereafter and made him entirely superfluous with regard to our earthly existence. This in turn fundamentally altered the relationship between the values attributed to time and those attributed to timeless eternity. It is no longer true for us, as it was for Bach, that "God's time" is better than human time. On the contrary, we tend to prefer human time to God's eternity.

While alive on earth, humans—premodern and modern alike—have no choice but to imagine and understand their existence as occurring in the medium of irreversible, linear time, which moves inexorably from past, through present, to future. This was certainly clear to Augustine, the first great theorist of time. In the famous discussion in Book 11 of the *Confessions* he suggested that, whatever the ontological status of time, the human mind cannot be aware of itself outside its dimensions:

> Clear now it is and plain, that neither things to come, nor things past, are. Nor do we properly say, there be three times, past, present, and to come; but perchance it might be properly said, there be three times: a present time of past things; a present time of present things; and a present time of future things. For indeed three such as these in our souls there be; and otherwhere do I not see them. The present time of past things is our memory; the present time of present things is our sight; the present time of future things our expectation. If thus we be permitted to speak, then see I three times; yea, and I confess there are three.[34]

This is just as clear to the moderns. Kant believed that time is the in-variant and necessary "form" or condition of any possible perception that the mind can have of itself—just as space is the necessary condition of any perception that the mind can possibly have of objects outside itself.[35]

But conditions that are inescapable for the embodied human mind on earth do not obtain in the beyond and certainly do not limit God. In *The City of God* Augustine suggested that God's paradoxical "temporality" was timeless eternity. Unlike ours, God's mind does not need time: "For He does not pass from this to that by transition of thought, but beholds all things with absolute unchangeableness; so that [all] of those things that emerge in time . . . are by Him comprehended in His stable and eternal presence" (11.21). Similarly, it made no sense to speculate about the time of God's rest before the creation (11.6):

> For if eternity and time are rightly distinguished by this, that time does not exist without some movement and transition, while in eternity there is no change, who does not see that there could have been no time had not some creature been made, which by some motion could give birth to change . . . and thus . . . time would begin? Since then, God, in whose eternity is no change at all, is the Creator and Ordainer of time, I do not see how He can be said to have created the world after spaces of time had elapsed. . . . The world was made, not in time, but simultaneously with time.

We cannot escape time while on earth, but just as eternity "preceded" time, so will it "follow" when time comes to an end; and in the beyond, the saved will somehow participate in God's eternity: "And this the prophetic narrative promises also to the men to whom it speaks . . . that they themselves, after those good works which God does in and by them, if they have managed by faith to get near to God in this life, shall enjoy in Him eternal rest" (11.8). And again: "the end or supreme good of this city [of God] is either peace in eternal life, or eternal life in peace" (19.11).

The preference for God's eternity and rest over human time and motion is unmistakable: for each individual and for humanity as a whole, the de-sired end is eternal rest and peace in God's heaven; the restless temporal strivings of life on earth are just a stage on the way toward this final goal— a stage to be endured since it leads to something infinitely better, rather than to be enjoyed for its own sake. Not so for the moderns. If salvation is no longer the unquestioned, exclusive, supreme good, and if, moreover, God is irrelevant to our earthly pursuits, the balance between time and eternity must be altered: time, motion, change can now be enjoyed rather than merely tolerated; they can be valued as much as or more than eternity and rest.

Modernity emancipates human time from the enveloping divine eternity, learns to appreciate it for its own sake, demotes eternity from its supreme position, and relegates it to the role of an option.

The moderns tend to value time above eternity for at least two reasons. First, they know that time is the medium in which the one existence they are certain of takes place; when it comes to eternity, they either do not worry about it at all or leave the worry to the private conscience of those who choose to be troubled by it. The second, closely related, reason has to do with God's withdrawal from earthly affairs into the beyond. If God is not the moral legislator, it follows that the moral and political norms guiding our actions, and the shapes under which we imagine our happiness, are no longer actions and shapes that were given humanity in advance, at Mount Sinai, say, or anywhere else. Rather, they have to be laboriously discovered over time, individually and collectively, by the only reliable method available to us, that of trial and error. Individual biographies and collective history are now the indispensable arenas where such discoveries are made. As temporal biography and history replace God's eternity, time, not eternity, is the dimension in which humans realize their highest aspirations for happiness and morality.

This is why in the modern era the novelistic subgenre of *Bildungsroman* — the story of how an individual finds out who he or she is and what shape of happiness should be pursued—becomes such a common product. (As Friedrich Schlegel famously proclaimed, "The French Revolution, Fichte's philosophy, and Goethe's *Meister* are the greatest tendencies of the age.")[36] This is also why philosophy of history becomes so important to the moderns and becomes their "eschatology," their view of where humanity is ultimately heading. Being a modern form of eschatology, it is less concerned with the city of God than with the city of man. Recall that the "supreme good" of the city of God is "eternal life in peace." The earthly city, on the other hand, "has its good in this world" (*The City of God*, 15.4). It too aims for peace, knowing full well that such peace can only be provisional, transient like all earthly things. Christians make use of this peace while on earth, but they do not make it their supreme good (19.17):

> The earthly city, which does not live by faith, seeks an earthly peace, and the end it proposes, in the well-ordered concord of civic obedience and rule, is the combination of men's wills to attain the things which are helpful to this life. The heavenly city, or rather the part of it which sojourns on earth and lives by faith, makes use of this peace only because it must, until this mortal condition which necessitates it shall pass away.

In Augustinian terms, the moderns are inclined to locate their "supreme good" in the peace of the earthly city, and to leave the city of God to whoever cares about such things. Kant, for example, postulates that the final goal of human history is the establishment of a perfectly just political constitution for each individual society and the establishment of perfectly just and stable relations among the political societies so constituted. Like everything else in the modern outlook, modern understanding of the ultimate destiny of humanity, while superficially similar to the Christian one, is powerfully inflected by the ideal of autonomy. A Christian knows humanity's ultimate destiny because of divine revelation. Kant cannot know it this way; he cannot claim to know how the story of humanity will end. But he can *postulate* an idea of such an end that contains the direction of human progress (given that this is a normative, not a descriptive, notion). He does just that in his 1784 essay on the "Idea for a Universal History from a Cosmopolitan Point of View," where he presents history in terms of the development of the natural capacities of the species.[37] Given humanity's unique natural capacity for what Rousseau called "perfectibility"—our rational ability to set out our own ends and thereby to reinvent ourselves as well as to bequeath our inventions to other members of the species for further modifications in an open-ended process—it makes sense to postulate as nature's end for humanity the creation of perfectly just, stable political conditions that would allow human capacities to be perpetuated and developed without hindrance: "The history of mankind can be seen, in the large, as the realization of nature's secret plan to bring forth a perfectly constituted state as the only condition in which the capacities of mankind can be fully developed, and also bring forth that external relation among states which is perfectly adequate to this end."[38]

The idea that gives direction to historical progress is not just normative but also hermeneutic, that is, it is a principle that allows one to make sense of what would otherwise be a mere chronicle of successive past events. Rousseau and, following him, Kant and Hegel, propose with increasing complexity and sophistication to understand the development of the human species in terms of gradually unfolding rationality and freedom, gradually growing awareness of what is involved in committing to freedom for oneself and one's political community and in acting consistently with this awareness.[39] Rousseau and those that came after do not claim that they know the future course of history or that the successive stages of past historical development were inevitable. They do claim to know which future direction would be desirable and to be able to make sense of the past as a story of progress, however halting, toward increasing freedom and rationality.

The logic underlying development from one stage to the next was best captured by Hegel, who gave it the name of dialectic; again, though, the general outlines of this idea were already perceived by Rousseau and Kant.[40] Whether as individuals or as communities, we never start from zero: we always inherit an already existing system of moral-political norms and practices. At each stage of development, be it individual or collective, contradictions may arise between the moral and political norms we profess and the way our individual and collective lives are actually organized; this includes, for instance, the contradiction between professing moral equality for all humans and at the same time owning slaves or depriving women of the right to vote. Once we become aware of such contradictions and perceive the irrationality of the status quo, we may want to resolve discrepancies by looking for more rational alternatives. If this search proves successful, we move to the next—both more rational and freer—stage of development. The past can be interpreted and evaluated only from the level of rationality and freedom today. This level may be surpassed in the future. Rational norms are not infallible, independent of specific cultural conditioning, or eternal. On the contrary, they are subject to continuous self-criticism and improvement. But this does not make them less rational, and at any rate, they are the best available to us at any stage of historical development, for we have no access to divine or rational standpoints beyond history. The inescapable historicity of reason does not undermine its authority but does force us to take time and change seriously.

The idea is not that history is naturally and inevitably determined to develop in the direction of ever increasing rationality and freedom and that, consequently, one can predict the future. Rather, the direction provides a norm that enables us to make sense of what actually happens in history. Rousseau, Kant, and Hegel should not be made responsible for the mistakes and crimes of Marx and his heirs. With them the fatal notion of historical determinism became entrenched, convinced as they were that a specific future was inevitable and hence its arrival should be hastened by all means available, terror included. Admittedly Hegel may have had more confidence in the inevitability of progress than is rational. But he too considered his dialectic to be not a key to the future but a hermeneutic device for interpreting the past.

In any case there is only a superficial resemblance between the "perpetual peace" that Kant believes to be the goal of human history and the "eternal life in peace" that is Augustine's "supreme good."[41] The essential difference is that Kant's goal is innerworldly; hence, unlike the otherworldly goal of Augustine, it neither postulates the eventual escape from time into eternity nor privileges rest over change. On the contrary, the whole point of establishing perfectly constituted states and peaceful relations among them is to create conditions in which humanity's rational capacities for self-improvement can be fully unleashed. The end of history is not the state of passive, atemporal contemplation of divine perfection but rather a state of active, open-ended development.

In their thinking about the moral realm (that is, the specifically human one), the moderns shifted the balance of their esteem decisively from eternity, rest, and immutability—previously privileged by the ancients and medieval Christians—toward time, motion, and change. The same shift occurred also in thinking about the realm of nature. (It is an open question, and one beyond my scope or competence, as to how exactly the two shifts are related: are they parallel but independent of each other, or is one the cause of the other, or are both the result of a single underlying cause or set of causes?)

There are, schematically speaking, at least two ways to interpret the early modern scientific revolution.[42] One is to stress the shift that occurred in the metaphysical foundations of science.[43] Premodern Aristotelian science took a teleological view of nature. In this view the concept of each thing is identical with its purpose, its essence, what it ought to be. This *telos* of the thing has a higher ontological status, and greater perfection, than what the thing actually is in the process of its becoming, since unlike the thing in its development, which is changeable and perishable, the purpose of the thing is immutable and eternal. Because of this higher ontological status, the purpose of the thing exerts a causal influence on the becoming thing, and it gives direction to the becoming—this is called the "final" causality. To understand the process of becoming is to show its purpose—the perfection toward which the thing is striving. It is clear that in this view of nature, being takes priority over becoming, essence over existence, immutability over change, and eternity over time. By contrast, the modern Galilean-Newtonian science takes a mechanistic view of nature. The moderns are nominalists. They treat concepts as mere names that bring diverse objects under a single umbrella for reasons of convenience, and they deny them more lofty ontological status. Particularly when dealing with nature they deny any reality to such notions as purpose, essence, or objectively existing norm, and hence they reject explanations that operate according to the final cause. Instead of explaining the continuous processes of change observable in nature as a phenomenon driven by final purposes, they prefer to explain change by capturing the relevant features of the present state of the thing (reduced to a mass moving in space and time) and discovering the mechanism of mathematically equivalent cause and effect that drives the process of change (this is called the "efficient" causality): "An explanation of anything is felt to be entirely adequate if it discovers some other mathematically equivalent event such as will enable the exact prediction of the former or the occurrence of the latter."[44] In this view there is no reason to privilege being over becoming or essence over existence: becoming—existence—is all there is. It is also clear that the disappearance of such notions as being or essence has broken the priority of eternity over time: time and change are no longer subservient to eternity and immutability.

Those who do not want to see science saddled with metaphysical commitments, and who see it instead in methodological terms, take a somewhat different view of the nature of modern science.[45] What is characteristic of modern science, such pragmatists think, is not any particular set of metaphysical assumptions but rather "its ability to reformulate the questions raised in the course of our lives in such a way that we may begin to answer them to our satisfaction . . . . What gives science its character is not an a priori conception of nature, but rather its approach to the problems that nature poses for human beings." Science, according to this view, is about "a search for a way of living" rather than "a search for absolutes."[46] To see science in these terms allows putting aside unanswerable questions (such as how to hold in one view both freedom and determinism) and to see a continuity rather than an unbridgeable gap between the natural and moral realms. Even if we allow the notion of purpose only in thinking about the moral realm, and conduct investigations into nature with regard to our actions' means rather than ends, inquiries in these areas will have much in common. In particular, both inquiries are guided by the search for a better way of living, and both, having given up belief in essence, are dynamic and open-ended. There being no such thing as human essence, each individual's vision of happiness and each community's set of moral and political norms is subject to continuous and never-ending revision and refinement, a process as open-ended as that of scientific inquiry into, and technological mastery over, nature. Pragmatic understanding of science leaves no room for the premodern privileging of rest, immutability, and eternity over motion, change, and time.

In the intellectual tradition shaped by Plato, Aristotle, and Christianity, the infinite superiority of eternity over time, and being over becoming, was obvious. Modernity—scientific as well as moral-political—is at bottom an attempt to set this picture aside and emancipate time. Ultimately this is the meaning of the death of God. Augustine raised two essential complaints about the temporality of humans' earthly existence. First, and obviously, what was wrong with such existence was that it came to an end: mortality. Second, and less obviously, time causes us to relate to everything, even ourselves, in a mediated fashion: the present forever slips from our grasp because we can capture experience only in memory or expectation. Modernity gave up on such complaints and simply embraced the contingent and mediated character of human existence—finitude in the broadest sense of the term.

FROM COSMOS TO HISTORY

The change in European humanity's self-understanding did not occur in a vacuum. Rather, intellectual changes were accompanied, and probably driven, by changes in social, economic, and political practices—above all, perhaps, by the transition from a relatively static, subsistence-oriented, agricultural economy to a dynamic, growth-oriented, mercantile-industrial economy. This unprecedented and accelerating growth—a new experience in history—suggested to Locke and his successors that production of material goods was not the lowly activity it had been considered in the Aristotelian tradition, an arena of mere preservation of life, a sphere where man was seen to be no different from other animals. Certainly this sphere had been thought infinitely less important than the political sphere, where free men could devote themselves along with their fellow citizens to the pursuit of rationality, the quality that distinguished humans from animals. But economic growth that brought improvement to humanity became invested with moral significance, transforming production into a sphere of moral self-realization.[47] This change of perception forms part of the background to the new valuation of time.

In a 1949 book, *The Myth of the Eternal Return*, Mircea Eliade argued that for much of the duration of the human adventure, societies from the most archaic to present-day European agrarian ones lived in "cosmos" rather than "history" and embraced a circular rather than linear conception of time.[48] In traditional societies a profane action or object in the incessant flow of real-world time could acquire meaning only if related to something other than itself—to something in the world of transcendent, eternal, sacred reality. As everything of value and importance was thought to have originally been revealed to humanity by gods, human actions acquired meaning only insofar as they repeated mythical models. The effect of thinking like this was to suspend profane time and activate sacred eternity: "In so far as an act (or an object) acquires a certain reality through the repetition of certain paradigmatic gestures, . . . there is an implicit abolition of profane time, of duration, of 'history.'"[49] Not every object, and not everything one did, was meaningful, of course; much of the experience was submerged in meaningless, profane time. But at essential periods, ritual lifted participants from the meaningless flow of "history" and raised them into the world of meaningful, unchanging, eternal "cosmos."

The time of history is irreversible, the future always different from the past. Traditionally, historical time was seen as devouring or destroying, bearing change and death. A major shift occurred when this sort of time began to be seen as the product of individual, free creativity and to be celebrated as the source of what is new and unprecedented. This is a relatively recent phenomenon, defining modernity by privileging its vision of infinite linear progress. Traditional societies did what they could to hold linear time at bay, abhorring the freedom and novelty of history and craving instead the immortality, repetitiveness, and permanence of nature. Their time was not linear and irreversible but cyclical, and marked by periodic returns and repetitions. The model for traditional time was the cycle of seasons, in which each year repeats the cosmogonic act and regenerates life in the eternal return to the moment of birth. Cyclical cosmic time, in annulling time's irreversibility and refusing history, allows the individual to escape from the meaninglessness of profane reality's incessant change.

An essential step on the way to modernity was the Hebrew discovery that irreversible history could be intrinsically valuable because it reveals God's successive interventions in the affairs of humanity. In Messianism, time was no longer periodically renewed. Rather, its regeneration was expected to occur only once. Christianity adopted this standpoint, seeing the entire course of human history—from the initial fall, through the incarnation, to final redemption—as irreversible. Messianism, on the other hand, only tolerated history; the ultimate expectation was that history would end and eternal order be restored. Messianism saw history as merely separating the two eternities. Moreover, traces of the archaic vision of eternal cyclical return survived even in Christianity's liturgical year, with its periodic repetitions of the Nativity, Passion, and Resurrection. Nominally Christian agrarian populations of Europe can continue to live by the cosmic cyclical rhythms of nature even as secular elites have long since embraced the irreversibility of history and the vision of infinite linear progress generated by free human creativity.

The political subtext of Eliade's theory is immaterial here. It is understandable that, at mid-twentieth century, European intellectuals like Eliade, who considered the modernist vision of historical progress (whether in its liberal or Marxist version) discredited, would search for traditionalist or even archaic escapes from the terrors of history; the paradigmatic case is that of later Heidegger. Of interest here is not Eliade's motivation but his reading of what constitutes the difference between modern and traditional societies. Similar readings have been developed independently of Eliade by more recent historians.

In a 1985 book, *The Disenchantment of the World: A Political History of Religion*, Marcel Gauchet argues that modern social order differs radically from all previous ones because of our attitude toward time and change. Gauchet's world history plots three stages: first, for dozens of millennia preceding the emergence of the state, were the primitive societies, whose politics were dominated by religion; then, with the rise of the state around 3000 B.C. in Mesopotamia and Egypt, there followed five millennia of religion dominated by politics; finally came modernity, where religion has been excluded from the political domain and relegated to the margins of private life. "Somewhere around 1700," writes Gauchet, "the deepest ever fracture in history occurred, namely, the establishment of human becoming in a logic and mode diametrically opposite to what it had been from time immemorial."[50] Where our ancestors tried to secure their identity by submitting to an inherited order and avoiding change, we moderns embrace change and favor individual creation, including self-creation.

Gauchet's understanding of primitive, prepolitical societies is strikingly similar to Eliade's. Gauchet, too, sees them as societies in which religion appears in its purest form and determines all social order. "The real kernel of religious attitudes and thought lies in accepting the *external as the originating source and the unchangeable as law.*" Whatever has meaning and value already happened in the mythical primordial past, when our world was established by beings—the gods, heroes, our ancestors—who are different in kind from us. Here the human role is to preserve and perpetuate this inheritance by repeating the founding events, by regularly coming back to them in ritual and thus regenerating the world. Temporal orientation is toward the past, and the shape of time is cyclical, governed by periodic returns. As Gauchet writes, "The essence of the religious act lies wholly in this antihistorical frame of mind."[51] European peasant societies preserved traces of this attitude until as recently as one hundred years ago.

In Gauchet's scheme the five millennia since the emergence of the state are something of a halfway stage between prehistory and modernity. The sacred past that legislates for the profane present is no longer beyond reach. Rulers act in the name of gods who can be entreated and whose will can be interpreted. Here we see a slow, imperceptible transition from a social order wholly received from the gods to one wholly willed by humans. In this sense the great world religions, Christianity above all, are less perfect religions than the archaic ones; they are stages along the way in which humans gradually took responsibility for themselves, and for their meanings and laws, away from the gods.

The end of this transition occurred in the eighteenth century, when modern social order appears—completely emancipated from dependency on the beyond and autonomous in its political power relationships, its economic and technological relationship with nature, and its intellectual understanding of the world. To us the world no longer seems unalterable; rather, it is something for us to make and remake. Our ancestors' passivity and static dependency has been replaced by dynamic self-sufficient activism. And thereby modern social order reverses the original temporal orientation toward the past:

> A society no longer externally determined is a society which must necessarily turn completely toward the future. The future is the obligatory temporal orientation, legitimacy converted into time, of a society containing its own ordering principle. The age of religion was also the reign of a certain legitimate temporality, basically that of the past where pure primeval religion was mixed up with the indivisible dictatorship of origins. . . . From now on, there is no legitimate obligation to renew what used to be, but rather one to create what does not yet exist and what ought to happen.[52]

Gauchet, like Eliade, saw this new attitude, which embraces change and abandons cyclical for linear time, to be definitive of modernity.

The change in the shape of time that came with modernity is also the subject of an important 1979 collection of essays by Reinhard Koselleck entitled *Futures Past: On the Semantics of Historical Time.*[53] In this book Koselleck, unlike Eliade and Gauchet, is not interested in the distant archaic past and contrasts modernity only with the immediately preceding stage, where his conclusions are reminiscent of Eliade's.[54] Between 1500 and 1800, Koselleck argues, a transformation occurred in how Europeans imagined the shape of historical time. In premodern European societies, the experience of history was based on repeatability. The future held nothing truly novel and was bound to return in a cyclical fashion to a state known from the past. Just as nature goes eternally through the annual cycle of seasons, political humanity was thought repeatedly to recycle a small number of possible constitutions. Modernity detached the future from the past. Modernity—*Neuzeit*—was to be truly a *neue Zeit.* Well before the French Revolution the eighteenth-century philosophy of progress, fueled by the new experiences of scientific, technological, and economic growth, considered a radically new future to be possible. This new future would be characterized by two features: first, novelty; and second, accelerating rate of speed. The Revolution helped disseminate this new way of experiencing and imagining historical time. Time's cycle had been straightened into an arrow, and the arrow was traveling ever faster.

In the first part of this book I presented Bach as the musician who aspired to capture the traditional Christian worldview in music that correspondingly subordinated linear temporality to visions of eternity. In the part that follows I will show how Mozart captures aspects of the modern outlook in music that liberates and celebrates linear time.

PART II

Mozart's Arrow

4 Mozart at Play

The concept of form involves the interrelated concepts of the whole and its parts. Only an object that is a whole and articulated into distinct parts can be said to possess form. Form is an intelligible relationship between parts and a whole, where all the parts, rather than being merely a heap of unrelated elements, contribute to the establishment of the object as a whole. It is not necessary but certainly most natural for the parts to be organized hierarchically: just as an object may enter into intelligible relationships with other objects by becoming a part of a larger whole, so may a part be articulated into its own parts and become a lesser whole in its own right. To understand the form of an object is to understand how it is divided into parts and how the parts are related to one another and to the whole—that is, what function each part has in the make-up of the whole.

One of my central claims in this book is that at some point between the early and late eighteenth century, between Bach and Mozart, musical form became primarily temporal and the attention of musicians—composers, performers, and listeners alike—shifted toward the temporal disposition of events.[1] By Mozart's time, the form of a musical work is temporal; that is, it consists of a number of phases or parts that succeed one another in a determined order. To understand such a form requires recognizing how the object is divided into successive phases and how the phases are related to one another and to the whole—that is, recognizing the function each phase has in the whole, in the transformation of a mere succession of unrelated elements into a configuration of intelligibly related phases.[2]

For successive phases to relate intelligibly, and a succession to become a configuration, earlier phases must not only precede but also in some way cause the appearance of later ones, and these for their part must not only succeed but also follow from the earlier ones—one-after-another must be-

179

come one-because-of-the-other. For this to happen, the phases must function as beginning, middle, or end. The beginning phase is the only one that does not require any earlier phase, but it does require and in some way must cause the appearance of another, later phase. The ending phase, conversely, does not require a subsequent one but it must require and in some way follow from an earlier one. And the middle phase requires and follows from an earlier phase as well as requiring and causing a later one. Relationships of causing or following, if they are present, may but do not have to obtain between immediately adjacent phases only. More complex and sophisticated temporal forms exhibit a large number of nonimmediate, long-range causative relationships between phases.

The concept of form is inextricably linked with that of matter or material. Form in an object is embodied or materialized; matter is formed. And matter is needed if a form is to be realized. The two fundamental functions of matter are those of articulating the whole into parts and integrating the parts into a whole. If it is true, as I claim here, that the guiding ambition of the classical instrumental composers was to create works in which individual phases do not merely succeed one another but are configured into wholes, the question arises: what were the material means with which they realized this ambition?

Current thinking about classical instrumental music privileges two factors—key and theme—as particularly important for the creation of forms.[3] In this view, late eighteenth-century musical logic primarily concerns a tonal plan based on opposition between stable and unstable tonal areas; of secondary importance is a superimposed thematic plan based on exposition, development, and recapitulation of themes. In the genre of the concerto, further, a third factor becomes operative and coordinated with the other two: that of opposition between the tutti and solo sections of a movement, opposition between the two "voices" conveying the musical discourse. Finally, yet one more factor fundamentally contributes to the creation of the classic instrumental forms, a factor commonly overlooked today but central in late eighteenth-century thinking, namely, the use of cadences to punctuate musical discourse. I do not claim that classic form is the product of punctuation alone but, rather, that it results from a complex interaction of all four factors—punctuation, voice, key, and theme. Punctuation, however, plays the central role in this interaction and provides an indispensable framework for understanding the roles played by the other three factors.

Cadence is a device to close a phase or the whole of a musical discourse. It symbolizes closure—not as an arbitrary signal but as the experience of reaching a goal. A stylistically competent listener, even if not musically literate and unable to recognize and name the cadence, feels closure. Diverse musical factors—harmonic, melodic and contrapuntal, and metric—collaborate to produce this experience.

Because the function of cadences is to provide a sense of closure, they are naturally considered among the factors articulating musical form. But cadences can serve also to integrate form. The sense of an ending, to borrow Frank Kermode's phrase,[4] is the single most important moment transforming a temporal succession of unrelated elements into a unified configuration of related phases. The ending is the essential function within the temporal form because with it the form gets its "point," its goal. All the implications of earlier phases are finally explicitly realized, and thus the phases, whose relationship to one another might until then have been unclear, are now integrated into the whole.

The sense of closure provided by cadences is a matter of degree: cadences can be stronger or weaker. Experience shows that the stronger the cadence, the longer the time span for which it may provide closure. This remarkable fact has far-reaching formal implications. A musical style that develops a hierarchy of cadences, in which the relative strength of cadences is clearly differentiated and graded, will acquire a capacity to organize its phases hierarchically. The strongest cadences will close the discourse as a whole; the weaker ones will close parts of the discourse; still weaker ones will close parts of the parts. This sort of hierarchical organization of phases is the hallmark of the classical style.

There is a venerable tradition of regarding cadences as the single most important factor in the creation of musical forms. It extends from the beginning of the more systematic thinking about musical form in the late sixteenth century (to say nothing of even more ancient precedents in chant theory) to the very end of the eighteenth century, and it underlies what Carl Dahlhaus aptly named the rhetorical concept of musical form.[5] Heinrich Christoph Koch, by far the most penetrating and representative theorist of musical form in Mozart's time, is still operating squarely within this tradition.[6] A modern reader of his three-volume *Versuch einer Anleitung zur Composition*, which appeared between 1782 and 1793, must be struck by how little interest Koch shows in such matters as a composition's tonal plan or thematic argument. Instead, Koch is guided by the rhetorical idea of musical composition, the vision of music as a discourse articulated like speech by means of stronger and weaker cadences into a hierarchy of parts:

Certain more or less noticeable resting points are generally necessary in speech and thus also in the products of those fine arts which attain their goal through speech, namely poetry and rhetoric, if the subject that they present is to be comprehensible. Such resting points are just as necessary in melody if it is to affect our feelings. . . . By means of these more or less noticeable resting points, the products of these fine arts can be broken up into larger and smaller sections. Speech, for example, breaks down into various sentences through the most noticeable of these resting points; through the less noticeable the sentence, in turn, breaks down into separate clauses and parts of speech. Just as in speech, the melody of a composition can be broken up into periods by means of analogous resting points, and these, again, into single phrases and melodic segments.[7]

Koch's thinking about musical form rests on the central notion of punctuation. Form, for him, is "punctuation form."

During the nineteenth century punctuation gradually lost its fundamental importance for the theory of musical form. Even Hugo Riemann's profound interest in it late in the century (interest that did not escape Nietzsche's attention)[8] could not stop this decline: the change of paradigms that guided the thinking about music after 1800 was irreversible.[9] Musicians stopped taking much notice of punctuation as the rhetorical concept of form was replaced by the notion of thematically and tonally driven musical logic—a change precipitated by the rapid disappearance of rhetoric from the intellectual horizon of educated Europeans and its replacement with philosophical aesthetics as the foundation of all theory and speculation about the arts. Once convention became suspect and romantics began to praise uniqueness above all else, it was inevitable that cadence, regarded as the most conventional of all musical phenomena, would give way to theme, considered the seat of compositional originality and individuality.

In thinking about classical form it is prudent, however, to recover what romanticism has obscured, and to consider punctuation seriously. This is not merely an act of courtesy toward our musical ancestors, paying attention to what they thought they were doing before imposing our own interpretations on their works. After all, there is no reason to believe that they were in a privileged position and understood their actions better than we could. We certainly have no such privileged access to our self-understanding; others may, and often in fact do, understand our actions better that we understand them ourselves. No, giving serious consideration to the rhetorical concept of form is simple economy of interpretative efforts: we should review the agent's own interpretation of what he is doing before expending efforts on our own interpretations; his just might turn out to be adequate, that is to say, more or differently illuminating than anything we can come up with ourselves.[10]

The piano concerto was, of course, not the only instrumental genre to which Mozart gave his best efforts. Surely the G-Minor piano quartet, the six string quartets dedicated to Haydn, the last four string quintets, and the last four symphonies are among his most significant creations. In no other genre, however, did he leave as many masterpieces as in that of the piano concerto: K271 (January 1777) was arguably his first masterpiece in any genre and, together with the 1779 Sinfonia concertante, unquestionably the most impressive work of his Salzburg years. Among the series of twelve concertos composed for the four successive Viennese concert seasons between late winter of 1784 and early winter of 1786, at least nine works, K. 453 to K. 503, must be considered masterworks. Moreover, given the close proximity of instrumental concerto and operatic aria—in both a soloist is cast against an orchestral framework—it is appropriate that the composer for whom opera was central would choose the concerto when presenting himself to the public as a performer and would lavish on it some of his best inspirations.

—

Harmonic, melodic-contrapuntal, and metric factors all go into making a cadence. An adequate description of cadences in a given repertory must consider the harmonic functions of the several chords of which they are composed, the melodic content of the structurally important voices (in the eighteenth century that was soprano and bass), and the metric placement of the chords within measures. Here it will be useful briefly to summarize the results of an earlier investigation, in which I applied the late eighteenth-century notion of punctuation form to the allegros of Mozart's piano concertos in great detail.[11]

Mozart wrote two kinds of cadence: full cadences (ending on the tonic triad) and half cadences (ending on the dominant chord). (Occasionally a full cadence is transformed into a deceptive one when the final tonic triad is replaced by an unexpected harmony.) In a fast movement the last chord of a Mozart cadence is always placed on the strongest—the first—beat of the measure. The penultimate harmony in the full cadence is, of course, always the dominant, either plain or, in the great majority of cases, embellished with a 6/4 suspension; preceding the dominant in the full cadence is either one of the subdominant-function chords, or one of the tonic-function chords. In a half cadence the chords that may precede the dominant are the same as the ones that precede the dominant in a full cadence. The final tonic and the penultimate dominant of the full cadence, as well as the final dominant of the half cadence, are always in root position. Finally, the last chord of a full cadence always has the prime not only in the bass but also in the soprano.

If Mozart was able to articulate highly complex hierarchical forms using only two cadences, it is because he knew how to calibrate the strength of a cadence. Recall that the stronger the cadence, the longer the time span for which it may provide closure. Both of the two basic cadences can be made stronger or weaker depending on the span that required closure. Strengthening is achieved by extending the duration of individual cadential chords. In the basic cadence each chord takes at least one beat of a quarter-note value, with the final chord taking an entire measure. All of these chords can be extended at will: extending the final tonic emphasizes the point of arrival; extending the dominant, whether penultimate or final, or the preceding chord, intensifies the expectation of arrival.

Extension of the final chord takes the form of an appendix. Extending any part of the cadence preceding the final chord results in internal extension or parenthetical insertion: either by extending the basic chords beyond their one-beat minimum or by inserting additional harmonies. The most impressive example of internal extension is, of course, that of the dominant-function chord with 6/4 suspension in the soloist's cadenza.

Just as extending the duration of chords strengthens the cadence, so contracting duration will weaken it. Contraction serves to connect more closely the phrase that is ending with the phrase that follows, so as to weaken the articulation between them. Since it is difficult to shorten the one quarter-note beat required for all but the final chord, contraction may affect only the final chord, which normally takes a whole measure.

In Mozart's music, contraction takes two forms: the link and elision. Two factors operate in normal articulation between two phrases. First, the final harmony of the first phrase falls on the first beat of the phrase's last measure, and the first melodic note of the second phrase falls on the first beat of the next measure, which is the first measure of the second phrase. Second, there is at least one beat and at most three beats of general rest in both the melody and the accompaniment at the end of the first phrase. A link consists of preserving the first factor and obliterating the second; this weakens the cadence. An elision weakens the cadence still further by obliterating both factors: the last harmony of the first phrase and the first melodic note of the second coincide on the same beat.

With two types of basic cadence (full and half), as well as various forms of extension (appendix, internal extension, and parenthesis) and contraction (link and elision) at his disposal, Mozart was able to project a discernible hierarchy of punctuation points and hence also a hierarchy of temporal phases closed by these points. Knowing his punctuation tools, we can now examine and compare the musical forms he fashions with them to discover his generic norms, what David Rosen calls Mozart's "standard operating procedure."[12]

In Koch's terminology, to be freely adapted here, the shortest independent temporal part of a composition—the part ending with the weakest, contracted cadence—is called a "phrase"; a series of phrases ending with a stronger kind of full cadence (either uncontracted, or extended, or both) is called a "period." Mozart's basic concerto allegro form contains three periods of this sort, here referred to as the first, second, and fourth periods; the first normally corresponds to the first tutti, the second to the first solo, and the fourth to the vestigial third tutti and third solo together. Each of these three periods has an identical internal form. The strongest cadence is, of course, a full cadence at the end. The second strongest cadence in each of the three periods is a half cadence with an appendix. This divides the period into two sections. Each of these sections consists of two phrases, the first of which is closed by the weakest—because often unextended and always contracted—full cadence. The function of the first phrase is to begin the period. That of the second is to divide the period into two halves, that is, to close its first section. At the same time, since the second phrase ends with a half cadence and not with a full one, its closure is felt to be incomplete and thus prepares the arrival of the second section. The third phrase marks the beginning of this second section, and the fourth phrase ends the period.

The second and fourth tuttis, unlike the first one, do not constitute complete independent periods. They consist, rather, of extra closing phrases joined to the preceding periods. The cadences ending these tuttis are invariably stronger than those of the preceding periods. In the basic form the second tutti consists of only one phrase, and the fourth tutti consists of two phrases, the first of which closes with a cadence contracted but also tremendously extended by the soloist's cadenza. These additional closing phrases have a clear function: the second tutti divides the composition into two halves by providing an ending for its first part; the fourth tutti, which is longer than the second and contains in the cadenza the largest cadential extension of the movement, ends both the second part and the composition as a whole. Without the second tutti the movement would not have two parts; without the fourth the two parts would not be symmetrical and the movement would not have an appropriate ending.

The soloist's cadenza provides the climax of the movement, the moment when, compounding the high tension of a long-suspended dominant 6/4 with the excitement of improvisatory acrobatics, the solo performer reviews the main events of the discourse now coming to an end. At the same time the cadenza ensures that the movement arrives at what has been the goal of all preceding events. The fact that the cadenza is improvised (whether actually or fictionally, no matter) compounds its climactic, revelatory character: until now the pianist, like an actor in a drama, played a part written for him by the composer; now he steps out of the prescribed role and speaks in his own name. For this one moment, the distance between player and personage being played disappears. Even when Mozart played the concertos himself (and he wrote many with himself in mind as soloist—in his Viennese maturity they were his main vehicle of self-presentation to the public as a player, and they contained his own greatest parts), most of the time he was playing the part of "Mozart," the way Molière might be playing the part of Orgon, Alceste, Harpagon, M. Jourdain, or Argan.[13] Only in the cadenza could "Mozart" take off the mask and reveal himself as Mozart. When the concertos are played by someone other than Mozart, as they inevitably must be, this point can be made even more clearly—which is why the wish to avoid stylistic incongruity on the part of those who improvise or write cadenzas seems to me profoundly misguided. What can be more thrilling than to hear Beethoven's personality unmistakably detach itself from the role the moment his cadenza for K. 466/i begins?

One phase of the concerto allegro remains to be considered: the second solo. For Koch this solo constituted a period in its own right, since its temporal dimension makes it comparable to the other three periods. But in most respects this is a highly irregular period. Unlike the other three, it may consist of as little as a single long phrase closing with a half cadence and an uncontracted appendix.

The basic concerto allegro form might be schematically represented as A1–A2–B–A3 (Table 1). The most striking feature of the form is the preoccupation with symmetry and balance that guides the division of the whole into two halves on every level. The composition consists of two parts, each of which contains two periods and an additional closing phrase or phrases. With the exception of the third, all periods consist of two sections, and each of these, in turn, of two phrases. The third period's irregularity strengthens rather than weakens the overall balance and symmetry, for by disrupting the order established in the first half of the composition, its restoration in the last period is all the more desirable and satisfying. Order that is never threatened can hardly be thematized and perceived. One half answering and balancing the other half, order imperiled but ultimately prevailing—this is what Mozart's sense of form requires.

One half answering and balancing the other, like two wings of a sym-

TABLE 1. The basic concerto allegro punctuation form

Part I

Period 1 (regular)
Period 2 (regular)
Closing phrase:
  ends with the uncontracted full cadence or appendix;
  ends Part I and divides the whole into two parts.

Part II

Period 3 (irregular): ends with the half cadence and uncontracted appendix.
Period 4 (regular)
Closing phrase 1:
  ends with the full cadence contracted and enormously extended by the cadenza.
Closing phrase 2:
  ends with the uncontracted full cadence or appendix;
  both closing phrases 1 and 2 end the whole.

metrical facade: this kind of form may safely be called "architectonic," as Jacques Handschin has done, provided we are not seduced by the metaphor into thinking that it is literally like architecture—that is, atemporal.[14] On the contrary, answering and balancing, establishing order, disrupting and then restoring it—all of this crucially depends on the temporal disposition of events, on linear shaping of time, and on orientation toward a final goal, with temporary, hierarchically subordinate goals met and passed along the way.

It is important to note that the concerto allegro form turns out to be a large-scale variant of the most pervasive pattern of the era, one Leonard G. Ratner has called the "two-reprise" form.[15] This pattern underlies much of the music written by Mozart and his contemporaries and is frequently found both on the level of a single phrase and of a whole movement. Central to this pattern is the ideal of bipartite, symmetrical balance, in which the second half answers the first and provides a resolution to its tensions and problems—it is, in short, an antecedent-consequent phrase writ large. Since a four-phrase period is the fundamental building block of the form, the pattern's most basic, minimal variant must consist of two such periods; further, the harmonic and thematic content of these two periods must be sufficiently similar to provide a sense of correspondence, and sufficiently different to justify the sense that the second does not merely repeat but answers and resolves the first. The simplest guise of this pattern fills the corresponding

TABLE 2. Distribution of ritornellos and solos in the concerto allegro

Part I	
Period 1	= Ritornello 1
Period 2	= Solo 1
Closing phrase	= Ritornello 2

Part II	
Period 3	= Solo 2
Period 4	= (Ritornello 3), Solo 3
Closing phrases	= Ritornello 4 (with embedded cadenza)

phrases of the two periods with corresponding thematic contents, moves away from the home key for the second half of the first period, and resolves the resulting harmonic tension in a second period that remains in the home key from beginning to end. A "sonata allegro without a development," as this is commonly called (where the first period is an "exposition," the second a "recapitulation"), can be expanded in various ways. Adding a "development" (our third period) between the two periods might seem to threaten the bipartite ideal but actually does not do so when the first period is repeated and the last one is not, as would be customary. The resulting "sonata allegro" has an A1–A1–B–A2 pattern that is very close to the one we have identified in the concerto allegro.

The concerto allegro results from crossing sonata allegro form with such inherited generic requirements of the concerto as the alternation of framing tutti ritornellos and solo episodes, whereby the resulting form is guided by the ideal of bipartite balance (Table 2). The transformation of a sonata into a concerto allegro could not be more logical. When the soloist is given the main substance of a movement, it follows that the first period of the sonata, the "exposition," becomes the first solo (period 2 in Table 1); the "development" then becomes the second solo (period 3), and the last period, the "recapitulation," becomes the third solo (period 4). Since in a concerto the tonally stable (nonmodulating) ritornellos traditionally provide a frame for the frequently unstable solos, the three solos of the concerto require framing by four ritornellos. Instead of repeating the first period of the sonata, the composer casts the opening first ritornello in the form of a full regular period (period 1); in obedience to the generic tradition in which ritornellos do not modulate, the structural modulation away from home key is reserved for the first solo only. By this point the composer will have used all of the components of sonata allegro form. But in a concerto the bipartite division is additionally clarified by a closing phrase at the end of Part 1 and two closing phrases at the end of the whole. It makes perfect sense that these are projected as ritornellos too: the second ritornello at the end of Part 1 and the final ritornello at the end of Part 2. There is, strictly speaking, no room for more than these three ritornellos (one each at the beginning, end of Part 1, and end of Part 2), no unoccupied phrase with a useful function to perform left. Therefore, the third ritornello, the one separating the second and third solos, survives in a vestigial form only: it does not get a separate phrase of its own but is usually marked briefly at the very beginning of the fourth period.

Order imperiled but ultimately prevailing: it is this sense of form that allows us in large measure to account for Karl Barth's profound observation that whereas "darkness, chaos, death, and hell do appear [in Mozart's music] . . . not for a moment are they allowed to prevail."[16] Barth continues his meditation:

> The Mozartean "center" is not like that of the great theologian Schleiermacher—a matter of balance, neutrality, and finally, indifference. What occurs in Mozart is rather a glorious upsetting of the balance, a *turning* in which the light rises and the shadows fall, though without disappearing, in which joy overtakes sorrow without extinguishing it, in which the Yea rings louder than the ever-present Nay. . . . We will never hear in Mozart an equilibrium of forces and a consequent uncertainty and doubt. . . . This feature is enough to mark Mozart's church music as truly sacred. . . . Mozart . . . always achieved this consoling turn.

In large measure responsible for both the "upsetting of the balance" and the final "consoling turn" is Mozart's sense of linear temporal form and temporal disposition: initial balance is the prerequisite for the upset of balance, and that must be followed by the consoling turn. I am tempted to extend Barth's meditation and observe that Mozart's fundamental optimism, his sense that, though shadows will not be forgotten, things will turn out all right in the end, is not necessarily or exclusively religious. It is, rather, a sense of life characteristic of pre-revolutionary—pre-Terror—Enlightenment (Kant's view of history comes to mind as another example of the same trust, which similarly escapes the charge of naïveté because it is tempered by the same awareness of the possibility of tragedy). This *Lebensgefühl* has been utterly absent from art for so long now that we cannot but hear in Mozart's music a voice from a very distant and alien past.

Yet Barth was right to suspect that the sense of life finding its embodiment in musical form had a religious dimension too. In a famous letter of 4 April 1787, addressed to his gravely ill father (Leopold died on 28 May), Mozart wrote:

> As death, when we come to consider it closely, is the true goal of our existence, I have formed during the last few years such close relations with this best and truest friend of mankind, that his image is not only no longer terrifying to me, but is indeed very soothing and consoling! And I thank my God for graciously granting me the opportunity (you know what I mean) of learning that death is the *key* which unlocks the door to our true happiness. I never lie down at night without reflecting that—young as I am—I may not live to see another day. Yet no one of all my acquaintances could say that in company I am morose or disgruntled. For this blessing I daily thank my Creator. [17]

Too urbane and civilized to be morose or disgruntled in company, the author of this letter was yet no stranger to life's shadows. And while he wrote to offer his father encouragement, there is no reason to doubt the sincerity of a faith that allowed him to consider death to be the true goal of our existence and the final consoling turn. Nor is there any reason to believe that this faith was formed only during Mozart's last years. Our most profound convictions are formed and reformed over an entire lifetime. The same conviction of 1787 is present, albeit inchoate and naïvely expressed, in a letter the fourteen-year-old wrote from Bologna to his mother in Salzburg on 29 September 1770:

> I am sincerely sorry to hear of the long illness which poor Jungfrau Martha has to bear with patience, and I hope that with God's help she will recover. But, if she does not, we must not be unduly distressed, for God's will is always best and He certainly knows best whether it is better for us to be in this world or in the next. She should console herself, however, with the thought that after the rain she may enjoy the sunshine.[18]

Like the cadence, the concerto allergro form may appear in its basic, extended, or contracted guise. The generic model reconstructed thus far was the normative blueprint underlying actual compositions. In considering a composition as a whole, it is important to keep in mind the functions performed by each of the essential blueprint phrases. Strictly speaking, each of these phrases is no more than a function slot, a place to be filled with one or more phrases capable of performing the given function. The extension of the basic form occurs when a slot is filled with more than one phrase. A contraction occurs when a slot is left empty or when two successive slots are joined into one.

Examples of contraction are rare. They are most likely to occur in the first period, since the formal gaps and ambiguities introduced there can be filled in and clarified in the second and fourth periods. Unlike contraction, extension of the form—function slots being filled with more than one phrase each—is fairly common. Given that all phrases in any one slot should be capable of performing the functions of that slot, it is not surprising that they all close with the same kind of cadence; thus all phrases in the second-phrase position in the regular period end with a half cadence, whereas all the phrases in the other positions end with a full cadence. All internal phrases in a single-phrase position close with cadences that have been contracted to increase the sense of continuity and prevent too many interruptions to the flow of the discourse.

I see Mozart's form not as a rigid mold but as a flexible recipe with a few indispensable ingredients and procedures that a creative cook can supplement in a variety of ways; better yet (better, since this comparison captures the essential linear temporality of the form), I see it as a *commedia dell'arte* scenario, which prescribes a few indispensable events and their order but leaves the artists at liberty to flesh out the plot with optional additional incidents in rule-governed improvisation. This vision of form—flexible recipe for making music rather than rigid mold to be filled with it—allows us to understand how Mozart's concertos can belong so unquestionably to a recognizable genre and yet exhibit such a high degree of individuality not just in material but also in form. It also allows us to appreciate the closeness of composition and improvisation in Mozart's creative thinking, and the essential rule-governed freedom of both.

"I hear Mozart . . . at play," says Karl Barth, and he continues: "Beautiful playing presupposes an intuitive, childlike awareness of the essence or center—as also the beginning and the end—of all things. It is from this center, from this beginning and end, that I hear Mozart create his music. I can hear those boundaries which he imposed upon himself because it was precisely this discipline that gave him joy."[19]

—

The harmonic content with which Mozart filled punctuation form, in concertos as in most other genres, is so predictable and schematic as hardly to warrant comment: in the first solo (or in the exposition of a sonata), the second phrase initiates the structural modulation away from the home key and prepares the arrival of the second key by means of a secondary dominant; the third phrase confirms the arrival of the second key. In the second solo (or the development)—harmonically most unstable and variable—further modulations eventually issue in a retransition back to, and a dominant preparation of, the home key, the arrival of which is confirmed at the beginning of the third ritornello and third solo (or the recapitulation).

These basic facts are supremely important for the way music is experienced: the second half of a composition is felt to be more than a mere repetition of the first half because it is experienced as a resolution of the disturbance introduced by structural modulation. But while undeniably important, these harmonic events are too schematic and predictable to be of much interest. The individual, unique character of a composition resides in the melodic (thematic and motivic) content that fills its phrases. It is on this content that composer and listener alike primarily concentrate.

This is particularly true of a concerto allegro. Here a unique feature of the first half is that the two periods are not identical: the first solo, which modulates, cannot be a mere repetition of the first ritornello, which does not modulate. The thematic and motivic content of the corresponding phrases of these two periods can be similar, but they usually differ somewhat. These differences pose a problem in the second half of the form: since it, unlike the first half, contains only one regular period, all the melodic materials introduced in the first two periods somehow have to be accommodated and ordered in the final solo. The opening ritornello and solo provoke the question: How can these diverse materials be synthesized in a single period? The final solo answers the question. It is this question and answer that draw our attention. Here, again, the temporal order of events is essential. The composer's task is not simply to accommodate all the materials of the first two periods in the final one. It is, rather, to find a suitable, convincing, and logical temporal order in which to present the materials.

The general principle governing this temporal logic relates to the presence of function slots. The job of the first and third phrases is to provide a suitable beginning for, respectively, the whole period and its second half—to establish the subject and key of the discourse to follow. An antecedent-consequent phrase does this job particularly well, and more often than not it is a phrase of this sort that fills these two function slots. The job of the second phrase is to divide the period into two halves and prepare the arrival of the second half. An antecedent-consequent phrase would be inappropriate here. Something more flexible and capable of motivic fragmentation and tonal modulation is needed to get from one subject and key to the next. Finally, the job of the fourth phrase is to provide a suitable ending for the whole. At this point the composition no longer needs a new subject of discourse; the appropriate phrase here, whether of the antecedent-consequent variety or not, need not be individually profiled but should contain emphatic cadential figures. Thus phrases of the first two periods, when recapitulated and synthesized in the last period, will reappear in the same function slot in which they had originally been introduced. When the third phrases of the first two periods get different thematic contents, for example, both themes will reappear in the third-phrase position in the last period. This rule has exceptions. But we need to understand such rules of the game before we can observe Mozart at play. This is always a riveting experience, whether he follows the rules or breaks them.

Among Mozart's instrumental compositions, his concertos stand out for their profusion of melodic invention. If the austere point of the fugue was to derive the whole discourse from a single idea, the ethos of the concerto is more relaxed and promiscuous: the more ideas, the merrier. The main focus of interest in the concerto allegros is the order in which melodic ideas are presented within each of the story's three tellings—the opening ritornello, the exposition, and the recapitulation—and playing with the order makes each of the tellings progressively more complete and logical. To demonstrate the full range of inventive solutions Mozart finds in playing this game would explode the limits of this book, but I can suggest something of the range by concentrating on a single radical movement from the piano concerto allegros.

No other movement departs as far from the generic norms as the Allegro of the Piano Concerto in C Minor, K. 491, dated 24 March 1786; hence none demonstrates more fully the extent of flexibility with which these may be treated.

The movement presents a unique case of formal extension: Mozart not only filled the individual function slots with several phrases but also repeated the entire sequence of slots. Table 3 shows the corresponding events of first ritornello, exposition, and recapitulation. Only the opening ritornello presents the regular sequence of four phrases or phrase groups. The first phrase of the exposition is missing, somewhat compensated for by a long, elaborate solo lead-in (mm. 100–118). By contrast, the third phrase-group (mm. 147–65) proceeds regularly to the fourth group (mm. 165–200), after which the sequence is repeated: instead of the expected second ritornello, the third phrase returns (mm. 201–20), followed by the return of the fourth phrase (mm. 220–65); only then, at m. 265, does the ritornello appear. In

TABLE 3. Mozart, Piano Concerto in C Minor, K. 491: melodic content of the Allegro

First ritornello												
measure	1	13	29			35	44			63	74	91
event	1.A	2.A	()			()	3.B1			4.A	c	A'

Exposition												
measure	100	118	135		147	165	201		220	241	249	265
event	lead-in	2.A	()		3.B2	4.b1	3.B3		4.A	b2	b2	5.A'

Recapitulation													
measure	362	382	391	410	428	435	444		463	473	486	487	501	509
event	2.A	()	3.B3	B2	4/2.b1	()	3.B1		4.b2	5.A	cad.	c	A'	()

NOTE: In each of the three systems, the first line indicates the measure with the downbeat on which the event marked in the second line begins. In the second line, capital letters mark significant or highly profiled melodic content—i.e., themes; lowercase letters are reserved for more conventional (transitional or cadential) motifs. Empty parentheses indicate appendices or prefixes whose content is either the same as that of the phrase to which they are attached or conventional. Numbers refer to the four phrases of the periods and the fifth (closing) phrase.

the recapitulation, the first phrase is again lacking, this time without any compensatory lead-ins, and the double sequence of phrases three and four is further complicated—or rather, clarified—because this time the listener does not expect the ritornello earlier than when it in fact comes. The third phrase-group (mm. 391–428) is followed by what begins like the fourth phrase but then transforms in midstream into another second phrase (mm. 428–35); with its appendix (mm. 435–44) because, instead of closing with a full cadence, it gets, like any second phrase—and this is true only of second phrases—a half cadence (m. 435). This is followed by another third phrase (mm. 444–63) and then another fourth phrase (mm. 463–73). Immediately striking about both the exposition and the recapitulation is the drastic abbreviation of the first half (because of the missing first phrase) and the even more drastic amplification of the second half (the sequence of third and fourth phrases occurring not once, but twice). Even without the following ritornellos (the fifth phrase groups) the two "halves" are quite disproportionate.

It is not that the main subject is missing from exposition and recapitulation. Rather, since the main subject appeared twice at the beginning of the opening ritornello—first as the first phrase with a full cadence (mm. 1–13), and then as the second phrase with a half cadence (mm. 13–28)—it is possible to bring it back at the beginnings of the exposition (mm. 118–35) and recapitulation (mm. 362–81) as the second phrase only.

The main subject is also much in evidence in the final section of each of the three ritornellos. A variant of the subject closes each ritornello (mm. 91–99, 265–82, and 501–509, respectively; the haunting appendix-coda that closes the movement, mm. 509–23, is also based on the subject).[20] Moreover, the subject itself, not a variant, opens the fourth phrase of the first ritornello (mm. 63–73) and the fourth phrase of the first solo (mm. 220–41), as well as being reserved in the last ritornello for the pre-cadenza phrase (mm. 473–86). In other words, the final ritornello recapitulates the last phrase-group of the opening ritornello, whereas the second ritornello limits itself only to the final phrase of the other two. Evidently, however, Mozart also wants the main subject toward the end of the exposition; hence its insertion at the beginning of the final phrase of the first solo (mm. 220–41). There it appears to be out of order, as the opening ritornello has led the listener to expect the main subject after, not before, the runs that close the first solo (that is, at m. 265, not 220). This lapse is corrected in the recapitulation, where it appears not before, but after, the soloist's closing runs (that is, at m. 473, not 463).

The larger point here, however, is that the main subject returns toward the end of the three ritornellos, given that it had been dropped in its first-phrase form from the beginnings of the exposition and recapitulation. It is as if Mozart wanted to shift the subject from the beginning, its usual position, closer to the end. This, too, emphasizes the disproportion between the two halves of the story in each of the three tellings.

This shift of balance in the story may be related to the structure of the main subject itself (Example 4). The subject lacks the usual antecedent-consequent balance and instead accumulates chromatic tension in its drive toward the cadence. The emphasized melodic pitches—c' (m. 1), f♯' (m. 4), e♮' (m. 6), d' (m. 8), e♭' (m. 9), f', and g' (m. 12), c" (m. 13)—suggest an ascending C-minor triad, initially destabilized by extreme chromaticism but driving inexorably toward the final c". This drive toward the end is also underscored in the later part of the phrase by the first oboe, in counterpoint, chromatically descending from a♭" to c". The final c" thus becomes the goal for both lines. In its lack of balance and its drive toward the final note the subject thus both prepares and justifies the structural character of the entire movement—its forward drive and emphasis on endings rather than beginnings.

Between the beginnings and endings of the three tellings of the story the movement brings three second subjects (the only such instance in Mozart's music). One second subject appears in the opening ritornello (mm. 44–63),[21] and two more in the exposition (mm. 147–65 and 201–20), each followed by its own closing phrase (mm. 165–200 and 220–65). How the three are to be integrated into the last telling of the story is a question Mozart raises in the first half of the movement. The answer is probably not the one most listeners would expect: in the recapitulation Mozart reverses the order in which he had originally introduced the three phrases.[22] Otherwise, the logic of the recapitulation is impeccable: the two subjects of the first solo are recapitulated side by side and followed by the solo's first closing phrase; thereupon the subject of the opening ritornello is recapitulated separately and followed by the solo's second closing phrase, much abbreviated.

What centrally matters in this movement is not only that Mozart abbreviates the first half of the exposition and recapitulation and expands the second half. More important, he also in effect shifts the principal subject's main appearance (the one closed with a full cadence) from early to later in each section, getting the proper order wrong the first time around and correcting it at the end of the movement. The profusion of second subjects further works to delay the main subject. What all of this adds up to is a structure as tremendously and deliberately lopsided as the main subject itself, featuring a beginning abandoned as quickly as possible and a headlong rush toward the end. The imbalance certainly goes a long way toward explain-

EXAMPLE 4. Mozart, Piano Concerto in C Minor, K. 491, first movement, mm.1–13; with analytic sketch below

ing the Allegro's tremendous forward-directed energy, an energy not even the coda can quite dissipate.

The main interest of a concerto allegro rests with the order in which its melodic ideas are presented: this is the variable surface that focuses the listener's attention, to which punctuation and harmony provide the underlying and stable background. The point of the music is to tell an amusing, moving, and coherent story—a story with a beginning, middle, and end—and to tell it not once, but three times, with each successive version clarifying and closing the gaps left in the preceding version. Mozart's instrumental forms may have their ancestry in the circular Baroque patters of the concerto and the binary dance, but the composer transforms these patterns in such a way as to unbend the temporal circle into an arrow. The recapitulation is no longer simply a return; it is the necessary outcome, the final closing of gaps and reconciling of differences. The fundamental premise of Mozart's playing is that the linear flow of time from past to future matters: we do not get the point of what we hear unless we pay attention to the temporal order of the ideas.

5   The Hidden Center

The three comedies Mozart wrote with Lorenzo Da Ponte are the largest-scale deployments of Mozart's basic ideal of bipartite symmetrical balance. Each opera is divided into two halves, the first ending with a finale that brings dramatic tension and confusion to its highest pitch, the second half's finale bringing resolution to all the accumulated tension. The close correspondence between scenes and events of the two acts of *Così fan tutte*, in particular, has long been admired by connoisseurs of formal perfection.

Mutatis mutandis, this is true also of the way Mozart shaped many individual numbers in his operas. They are often governed by the same ideal of bipartite balance that forms so many of the instrumental movements. Not that the text and dramatic action are ever negligible factors: Mozart's arias and ensembles are far from simply being sung sonatas. Text and action affect the form in two fundamental ways. First, they profoundly affect the way the listener interprets the significance of the form: comparing the form of two pieces that, if read without regard to text and dramatic function, would seem to resemble each other, might reveal diametrically opposed significance once text and action are restored to the reading. Second, because text and action affect the listener's understanding of musical form, the composer can depart from conventional patterns more freely than is possible in instrumental music. How text and action affect form can be exemplified by two justly celebrated ensembles, both formally close to the instrumental sonata but interpreting that form in two very different ways, as well as by three equally celebrated ensembles that show how far behind a composer will leave traditional formal patterns when the dramatic occasion so requires—to show, that is, that a composer can give linear, future-directed time a variety of highly individual shapes.

—

If the point of a simple sonata without a development is to present the same story twice, resolving the problems of the first presentation in the second, this point is exemplified to perfection in the Sextet (No. 19) of *Le nozze di Figaro*.[1] In reshaping Beaumarchais's triumphantly successful and politically scandalous recent comedy, Da Ponte shrewdly used the recitative preceding the Sextet to dispose of the main dramatic business of the trial scene—the revelation that Figaro is the long-lost child of doctor Bartolo and his old servant, Marcellina, which meant that Figaro could no longer be the object of Marcellina's matrimonial ambitions. Traditional eighteenth-century operatic dramaturgy dictated that action be moved forward in recitatives; closed musical numbers were reserved for the characters' static, passionate reactions to changes in their situation brought about by the action. Accordingly, the Sextet might well have been reserved for presenting the reactions of those who had heard the startling revelation. And indeed, the ensemble contrasts the rapturous joy of the three litigants—Marcellina, Bartolo, and Figaro, just turned into a happily reunited family—with the stupefied irritation of Figaro's master, the Count, acting as the judge in his feudal domain, and an assistant judge wholly under his thumb, Don Curzio: the Count, who desired to make Figaro's betrothed, Susanna, his own mistress, had hoped to use Marcellina's legal claim on Figaro (who had promised either to pay off a debt or to marry her) as an instrument of blackmail or, failing that, vengeance.

But giving voice to these two contrasting emotions is just part of the Sextet's function. The ensemble also introduces new action, thus exploding the limits of traditional dramaturgy; there, any new action would have been reserved for the recitative to follow. Instead, Susanna enters with money for the debt, sees Figaro embracing Marcellina, misinterprets what she sees as faithlessness, prepares to leave, boxes his ear when he tries to detain her, and finally, once the situation is explained, reconciles with him and his newly found parents. No praise is too high for Da Ponte's clever decision to set the revelation of Figaro's parentage as a recitative and hold off on showing how Susanna learned of it until the ensemble has begun. To be sure, the dramatic and musical points of gravity do not coincide in the trial scene: what is musically most substantial—the ensemble—is subordinate dramatically. But the crucial difference between the business of the revelation and that of Susanna's brief misunderstanding is that the former requires many words to be made intelligible, whereas Susanna's response, coming as it does after the revelation, needs hardly any words at all; it is mostly a matter of visual gestures and physical action—entrance and motions to leave, ears boxed, and embraces. Unlike the preceding recitative, the Sextet relies more on what the characters are doing on stage than on what they say. Susanna's error could be understood even as pantomime; the revelations about Figaro's parentage could not. Hence the astuteness of waiting to begin the musical number until after the secret is revealed. As a result, what ensues from Susanna's entrance is not only simple to follow (even if one does not catch all of the words) but also utterly predictable and, paradoxically, the more enjoyable for it.

As a result, too, this sequence of events became suitable dramatic material for musical-formal procedures characteristic of Mozart's instrumental music. A sequence of events that is predictable and enjoyable precisely because of that predictability—does this not describe many an instrumental movement? Like a sonata without a development, the Sextet goes twice through a similar sequence of events, getting a "wrong" outcome the first time around (wrong in that it does not bring the sequence to satisfactory closure) and a right one upon repetition (Table 4).

The five personages who are present at the trial from the start and know the outcome—the revelation—before the ensemble begins also know how they feel about this outcome; Marcellina, Bartolo, and Figaro like it, the Count and Don Curzio do not, and none of their positions will change from first to last measure of the Sextet. As he commonly does in his ensembles, Mozart makes sure that the positions are clearly understandable by introducing them successively before presenting them jointly: he uses the first phrase and its appendix (mm. 1–13) for Figaro and his parents to embrace each other, and the second phrase (mm. 14–17) for the Count and Don Curzio to express their surprised irritation; only then, in the appendix to the second phrase (mm. 18–24), does he let the two groups sing together, and he lets the first group dominate the second musically just as they do at this point in the dramatic confrontation. These two groups are still distinct (sing distinct texts) in the last phrase of the exposition (mm. 54–72), and they remain so in the last phrase of the recapitulation as well (mm. 102–36). The difference between the endings of the two storytellings lies in Susanna's position: the first time around she sides with the wrong party and sings with the Count; only on the second try does she return to her proper place at Figaro's side. Showing how she got first into the wrong position and then into the right one is in fact the Sextet's main business.

To ensure that twofold presentation of a similar story or sequence of events is immediately clear, it is important to shape the beginnings similarly, so that the audience will recognize the parallelism right away. Da Ponte

TABLE 4. Mozart, *Le nozze di Figaro*, No. 19 (Sextet): dramatic content

measure	1	10	14	18	25	33	40	45	48	54	67	72
character	M/F/	B	D/C	M/B/F (+D/C)	S	M/B/F (+D/C)	S	S/F		M/B/F+S/D/C		—
theme/motif	1		2	3 (+2)	4	3	5	6	(7)	7		
tonal plan	I			(V)	‡"V"	(V)		‡V				
phrase	1a.FC	()	b.HC	()	HC	()	()	2.()	()	FC	()	()

measure	74	81	90	102	131	136
character	M	S/M/B/ D/C+F	S/M/B/ D/C+F	S/M/B/ F+D/C		—
theme/motif	1	2'	2'	8		
tonal plan	I					
phrase	1a.FC	b.FC	FC	2.FC	()	()

NOTE: The top line lists the measure number that begins the phrase indicated below it; the second line lists the personages involved in the phrase; the third numbers the distinct themes or motifs; the fourth shows the tonal plan; and the fifth marks the cadences that end each phrase.

FC = a phrase closed with a full cadence; HC = a phrase closed with a half cadence; parentheses = a phrase's appendix or prefix; empty parentheses = a phrase's appendix or prefix whose content is either the same as that of the phrase to which it is attached or conventional.

M = Marcellina; F = Figaro; B = Bartolo; D = Don Curzio; C = Count; S = Susanna.

opens both sequences with Marcellina; in the first she encloses Figaro in a maternal embrace ("Riconosci in questo amplesso una madre, amato figlio!" [Beloved son, recognize in this embrace a mother!]), in the second she invites Susanna, too, to embrace her as a mother ("Lo sdegno calmate, mia cara figliuola, sua madre abbraciate, che or vostra sarà" [Calm your indignation, my dear girl, embrace his mother who will now be yours]). He continues the parallelism in the second verbal event in each telling: Don Curzio's constatation, "Ei suo padre, ella sua madre" (He his father, she his mother) in mm. 14–24, is echoed and comically amplified in mm. 81–89, when Susanna insistently repeats the question, "Sua madre?" and gets the steadfast tutti answer, "Sua madre!" (the passage is immediately repeated yet again as "Suo padre? Suo padre!" in mm. 90–102). Only after these two initial parallel events have been established do the two tellings diverge and lead to two different conclusions.

Mozart takes care to make the initial parallelism and eventual divergence of the two sequences even more obvious. As shown in Table 4, each of the four exposition phrases finds a counterpart in the recapitulation (though not one of the appendices and prefixes does, with the possible exception of the final instrumental one, mm. 72–74 and 136–40). But the first two phrases correspond closely (they share thematic-motivic materials); the next two relate only tenuously. The final phrases (mm. 54–72 and 102–36) share only their function—they close their respective periods—and the fact that in each period this is the first time that all of the personages sing at once; otherwise— dramatically, verbally, thematically, and of course also tonally—the two phrases diverge as they should, given that the second telling must correct the false conclusion reached in the first. (This also explains why the second closure is so much longer than the first; at about one-quarter of the length of the Sextet, it closes the whole ensemble, not just its first half.) The phrases that precede the final ones diverge still more (mm. 25–44 plus the prefixes to the following phrase, mm. 45–53, and mm. 90–102): on first hearing it might seem that the only thing they have in common is their function— that of leading to and preparing the outcome that is to follow. And given that the outcome is different in the two cases, these phrases must, of course, diverge.

Susanna's entrance in m. 25 marks a decisive turn in the Sextet: the action begins. Accordingly, the decisive tonal shift also occurs here (Example 5). The first of the two phrases in the second-slot position (mm. 14–17) had been in the tonic key, and its appendix (mm. 18–24) had promised a tonic chord on the downbeat of m. 25. Instead, the music shifts into the unprepared dominant key for the second of the second-slot phrases (mm. 25–33);

the appendix of this phrase (mm. 33–40) in turn promises a move to the properly prepared dominant key. The reason for such dramatic, verbal, and motivic similarity between the two appendices (mm. 18–24 and 33–40) is in the story: It is necessary that Susanna notice that Marcellina and Figaro had lovingly embraced each other even before her entrance. The two phrases are related too, though much more subtly: compare the bass accompaniment in mm. 13–17 and that in mm. 29–33. The similarity of the two second-slot phrases in the exposition probably suggested to Mozart that the second-slot phrase of the recapitulation (mm. 81–89) could simply be

EXAMPLE 5. Mozart, *Le nozze di Figaro*, No. 19 (Sextet), mm. 13–57

EXAMPLE 5 *(continued)*

(continued)

EXAMPLE 5 *(continued)*

EXAMPLE 5 *(continued)*

(continued)

EXAMPLE 5 *(continued)*

EXAMPLE 5 *(continued)*

(continued)

EXAMPLE 5 *(continued)*

repeated (mm. 90–102). The repetition is redundant dramatically and musically, and it conveys no essential new information. But it is there to maintain
as long as possible the parallelism of the exposition and recapitulation—and
to prolong our delight at Susanna's stupefaction—as well as to ensure that
the recapitulation does not end up too short in relation to the exposition.

The only music with no counterpart in the recapitulation is the passage
in mm. 40–53. This is because there is no room in the recapitulation for
dramatic events even remotely like those that took place in the exposition.
Susanna's enraged reaction at the sight of Figaro embracing Marcellina
(mm. 40–44) could not be appropriately set in the expected dominant key
of C major, though it has been properly prepared. Instead, by means of chromatic lines in the first violins and bass, yet another appendix deflects the
expectation toward C minor. As a result, the C major in the prefixes that
follow (mm. 45–53) is at first unsteady as it accompanies the brief strug-

gle between Susanna and Figaro—she trying to leave, he trying to detain her. Only the decisive and audible slap she administers—which clears the wobbly atmosphere like a thunderbolt and which Mozart times for the local dominant chord on the third beat of m. 53, right before the true beginning of the concluding phrase in m. 54—stabilizes C major. The motivic material gradually insinuates itself with similar subtlety: the accompaniment of the phrase that begins in m. 54 is already there in the second prefix (mm. 48–53). Both tonally and motivically m. 54 thus marks the arrival of something that had been struggling to emerge for some time but is only now fully present.

It is clear that text and dramatic action can be used to justify musical-formal features that might seem unmotivated in an instrumental movement: the differences between exposition and recapitulation in the opera are greater than in a typical sonata. But the essential spirit is the same. As in a sonata, a similar sequence of events recurs to make good what went wrong the first time around, and to replace an undesirable outcome with a satisfying one. This throws bright light on a practice that was fashionable around 1800, whereby words were added to preexistent instrumental music to give it concrete meaning.[2] It is usually considered naïve to hear specific personages and actions in an instrumental piece—to attribute to a violin melody, say, the thoughts and action of a Hamlet—but it is easy to sympathize with the impulse behind such attribution. Even if the voices and actions of instrumental music remain unnameable, abstract, and specifically musical, it makes sense to hear in the music a succession of events, a plot. This analogy makes narrative interpretation irresistible; more to the point, it links Mozart's greatest operatic and instrumental triumphs.

—

Of course, sometimes repetition is just repetition. Sometimes steps are retraced not to find the point where it all went wrong so as to do it over again right, but because there is nowhere to go but round and round. Like the *Figaro* Sextet, the Quartet (No. 21) in Mozart's first operatic masterpiece, *Idomeneo* (premiered at the Munich Residenztheater on 29 January 1781) is disposed formally like a sonata. But the dramatic use Mozart makes of the pattern, and hence its temporal meaning, could not be more different in the earlier work.

The differences begin with, and have their source in, the dramaturgy and the disposition of the text. In *Figaro* Da Ponte gave Mozart an ensemble in which something happened and the situation at the end was different from the opening situation; accordingly, he provided a different text for each of the two tellings of the story. Giambattista Varesco—working, as we know from their exceptionally informative correspondence of the period, under close supervision from the Mozarts, father and son—provided a dramaturgically old-fashioned ensemble, one in which nothing happened and the situation of the personages remained unchanged; the number was simply an occasion for them to say how they felt about their situation, just as in a typical *opera seria* aria. Accordingly, it made sense (in this and many other arias in this opera, starting with the first, Ilia's "Padre, germani, addio!") to use the same text for both exposition and recapitulation.

The Quartet comes at the point when fortune is at lowest ebb for all four principal characters. Idomeneo, king of Crete, has ordered his son, Idamante, to leave the island; he is trying to avoid fulfilling the vow he had made to "Nettun spietato" (pitiless Neptune) to sacrifice the first person he meets upon his return, because that person was his son. Idamante, heartbroken because he does not know why his father rejects him, promises that he will leave, "ramingo e solo, morte cercando altrove" (a solitary wanderer, seeking death elsewhere). His beloved, Ilia, a captive Trojan princess, announces that she will accompany him and die with him: "dove tu moja, io morirò" (where you would die, I shall die). Off on the side, Elettra, a princess visiting from Argos whose love Idamante has rejected, mutters, "Quando vendetta avrò?" (When will I have vengeance?). Four distinct sentiments, then, and as usual Mozart introduces them pragmatically one by one to avoid confusion (Table 5). But he also creates two pairs, the young and innocent couple, and the two personages who, whether intentionally or not, threaten their happiness. He gives the first musical idea successively to Idamante and Ilia (mm. 7–28), and the second alternately to Idomeneo and Elettra (mm. 30–34), though Idomeneo's exclamation added to Ilia's phrase (m. 29) shows that his heart is with the young couple. Like their sentiments, Idamante's and Ilia's phrases—his in the tonic key and closed with a full cadence (mm. 7–20), hers modulating toward the dominant minor key and closed with a half cadence (mm. 20–28)—are continuous to such an extent that one hears them as a single unit. Idomeneo's exclamation in m. 29 deflects the music from its trajectory toward the second key, creating another modulating phrase closed with the half cadence needed to get the music tonally back on track (mm. 30–34).

Now the scene is set for all the characters to sing simultaneously, and so they do (Example 6). They share a text that issues in what is surely the most important clause of the whole Quartet, encapsulating what they all have and feel in common: "soffrir più non si può" (one cannot suffer more). The appendix (mm. 35–48), prolonging the just-reached secondary dominant

TABLE 5. Mozart, *Idomeneo*, No. 21 (Quartet): dramatic content

measure	1	7	20	30	35	49
character	—	Ida/	I(+Ido)	Ido/E	I/E/Ida/Ido	I/E/Ida/Ido
theme/motif	(1)	1	→	2	3	3'
tonal plan	I				(V)v	v
phrase	()	FC ⌐ HC	HC	HC	(FC)	FC

‖

measure	68		86	93	123	143
character	Ida/	I(+Ido)+	Ido/E	I/E/Ida/Ido	I/E/Ida/Ido	I/E/Ida/Ido
theme/motif	"1"	+	"2"	3	3'	3'
tonal plan	→			(V)I	i/I	I
phrase	HC			(FC)	FC	HC

‖

measure	154	160
character	Ida	—
theme/motif	(1)	
tonal plan		
phrase	()	(FC)

FC = a phrase closed with a full cadence; HC = a phrase closed with a half cadence; parentheses = a phrase's appendix or prefix; empty parentheses = a phrase whose content is either the same as that of the phrase to which it is attached or conventional. Quotation marks around themes/motifs indicate that these are developed rather than (re)stated.

Ida = Idamante; I = Ilia; Ido = Idomeneo; E = Elettra.

chord, ends with an emphatic and repeated full cadence in the prepared second key of dominant minor (mm. 45 and 48). This ensures that the line will
not escape anyone's attention. What remains to complete the exposition is
a phrase in the second-key area (mm. 49–67). Here again all the personages
share a common text and sing together, prolonging the already expressed
thought, "più fiera sorte, pena maggiore nissun provò" (no one experienced
a more severe fate, a greater anguish), just as the key they sing in prolongs
the local tonic reached just before (in m. 48). Only the thematic idea seems
new at first, but later measures of the phrase (mm. 56–67) prove even on

EXAMPLE 6. Mozart, *Idomeneo*, No. 21 (Quartet), mm. 34–67

EXAMPLE 6 *(continued)*

(continued)

EXAMPLE 6 *(continued)*

EXAMPLE 6 *(continued)*

(continued)

EXAMPLE 6 *(continued)*

first hearing to be an echo of the last part of the preceding appendix (mm. 43–48); this provides the Quartet's central verse with a musical rhyme to match the verbal one.

Mozart now repeats this sequence of verbal and musical events (mm. 68–153) with modifications—some obvious, some less so. The second key area is, of course, now the tonic, but in other respects the recapitulation of mm. 35–67 in mm. 93–142 is quite faithful though much expanded; it is further expanded when the last phrase (mm. 123–42) returns yet again in mm. 143–53. The recapitulation of mm. 7–34 in mm. 68–92 is much less literal: though it preserves the text, its distribution among the characters, and the musical ideas of the exposition, the verbal lines overlap where they did not before, the thematic ideas are modified, and the whole is presented as a single modulating phrase. The resulting effect is as much that of development as of recapitulation; more precisely, this is a recapitulation with a developmentally inflected beginning—a common enough phenomenon.

Despite all these changes, however, the recapitulation is merely repetition. Musically, nothing gets decided and resolved the second time around, not even whether the second key area should be major or minor. In the exposition the anticipated second key area at m. 28 is dominant minor; at m.

34 it is dominant major; at m. 38 it is major again. But the conclusion reached in mm. 45 and 48 is minor, and so is the second key area that begins in m. 49. In the recapitulation the second key area anticipated at mm. 92 and 96 (which correspond to mm. 34 and 38, respectively) is tonic major, and so is the conclusion reached in mm. 119 and 122 (corresponding to mm. 45 and 48), but the pull of the minor is so strong at this point that, were we confronted with tonic minor at mm. 119 and 122, we would not be in the least surprised. And indeed, the second key area begins in m. 123 (corresponding to m. 49) in the minor and only later settles for the major mode; however, the possibility of minor remains alive to the end. Of course this is not surprising, given that the modal mixture was built into the highly chromaticized main theme from the start, and that the theme comes back at the end.

Dramatically, too, the situation of the personages in m. 153 has not changed since m. 67, or m. 7. Formal disposition, which in the *Figaro* Sextet could project the linear flow of time, here projects the sense of hopeless entrapment through circular repetition. The dramatic situation affects our understanding of the music sufficiently to neutralize those features of the musical form (modifications of the original story at second telling) that might otherwise suggest a motion forward. But just to make sure, Mozart, in a formal masterstroke, hermetically closes the circle with a framing device: he brings back the opening orchestral prefix (mm. 1–6) that anticipated Idamante's first verse, "Andrò ramingo e solo" (mm. 7–11), at the end (mm. 154–59), this time with Idamante repeating yet again his opening words (followed by a closing orchestral appendix in mm. 160–66), thus anticipating the eternity of the young hero's solitary rounds.

—

There is no denying that Mozart's language, unlike Bach's, is better suited to projecting a linear temporal flow than a sense of eternity or circularity. Similarly as in the *Idomeneo* Quartet, the Quartet (No. 9) from *Don Giovanni* (the opera received its premiere at the Prague National Theater on 29 October 1787) returns to its opening theme at the end. There, however, the effect is very different—representing not a situation without exit but one subtly transformed from what it had been at the beginning.

For much of its duration, the Quartet behaves like a sonata: there is a regular four-phrase "exposition" (with the phrases beginning, respectively, in mm. 1, 29 [where the modulation starts], 37 [the second key area], and 41), and this is followed by a "development" (mm. 49–68)—though nothing gets developed here; it is, rather, a retransition. But although what follows returns to, and stays in, the main key of the ensemble as a proper recapitulation should, it returns neither to the text nor, at least at first, to the thematic material of the exposition.

The Quartet is another trial scene of sorts. It starts with Donna Elvira's sudden appearance, interrupting a conversation between Don Giovanni and his betrothed friends Donna Anna and Don Ottavio. "Unhappy woman," Elvira tells Anna, "do not trust this scoundrel! This cruel man once betrayed me; he wants to betray you too" (Non ti fidar, o misera, di quel ribaldo cor! Me già tradì quel barbaro: te vuol tradir ancor). Don Giovanni takes his friends aside and tells them that "the poor girl is crazy" (La povera ragazza è pazza), but Elvira's "noble appearance" (aspetto nobile) and "sweet majesty" (dolce maestà) have made an impression: her opening phrase (mm. 1–9), likewise noble, majestic, and heartbroken, reverberates in the minds of her listeners (Example 7a). The phrase's ending (mm. 8–9) echoes through the orchestra (mm. 9–12) even as Anna and Ottavio repeat it (mm. 10–19); it echoes again in the orchestra at the end of their repetition (mm. 17–19) and even enters into counterpoint with Giovanni's attempted diversion (mm. 23–28). (As often in Mozart—or the music of any skillful opera composer— the accompaniment offers additional insight into what is happening in the minds of the characters.) The rest of the Quartet is a struggle between Elvira and Giovanni to gain their listeners' sympathy, a struggle between Elvira trying to strengthen the impression she first made and Giovanni attempting to erase it. Initially it appears that Giovanni might succeed. The beginning of the "recapitulation" (from m. 68 on) is dominated by a rapid-patter argument between him and Elvira, which Anna and Ottavio observe from the background (Example 7b). But by the middle of their last phrase (from m. 79 on) it becomes clear that the impression Elvira had made was indelible: as Anna and Ottavio gradually recover Elvira's opening phrase (the only music from the exposition to be recapitulated), the patter brawl recedes into the background. Here the return of a main theme at the end of the ensemble means something quite different from what it meant in the *Idomeneo* Quartet. Something decisive has happened, and the ending of the Quartet finds Anna and Ottavio transformed.

If Mozart feels free to give the linear temporal flow of this *Don Giovanni* Quartet a more individualistic shape than that authorized by sonata conventions, the Act 1 Trio (No. 7) from *Le nozze di Figaro* provides an even more extreme example of this freedom (Table 6). Traces of those conventions are, to be sure, still audible behind the Trio's surface: the first fifty-seven measures could easily be read in terms of an exposition with main key area (mm. 1–15), transition (mm. 16–43), and second key area (mm. 43–57); the Count's recitative at the center (mm. 122–46) could stand in for

EXAMPLE 7. Mozart, *Don Giovanni*, No. 9 (Quartet)

a. Mm. 1–28

(continued)

EXAMPLE 7 *(continued)*

EXAMPLE 7 *(continued)*

mie - i; la - scia - te - mi con le - i,

for - se si cal - me - rà, for - - se si __ cal - me - rà.

b. Mm. 68–88

Don Giovanni (piano a Donna Elvira)

Zit - to, zit - to, che la gen - te si ra - du - na a noi d'in -

tor - no, sia - te un po - co più pru - den - te, vi fa - re - te cri - ti -

(continued)

EXAMPLE 7 *(continued)*

EXAMPLE 7 *(continued)*

(continued)

EXAMPLE 7 *(continued)*

EXAMPLE 7 *(continued)*

(continued)

EXAMPLE 7 (continued)

TABLE 6. Mozart, *Le nozze di Figaro*, No. 7 (Trio): dramatic content

measure	1	4	16	24	28	43	58	70	85	93	101	110	116	122	147	168	176	183	191	202	214
character	—	C	B	S	C+B+S	B/C	B+S	B/C	B	S	C+S/B			C	C+S+B	S/B/C	B	C+S+B	S/B/C		
theme/motif	1	1	2	3	"1+2+3"	4	3'	4	2	3	1			Recit.	1	4	2	1	4		
tonal plan	I	I	(V)	(V)	↓(V)→V	V	→	→iIV	→	(V)	I	(V)			I						
phrase	()	FC	HC	()	()	FC	HC	FC	HC	()	FC⌣HC	HC	()		FC	HC	FC			()	()

FC = a phrase closed with a full cadence; HC = a phrase closed with a half cadence; parentheses = a phrase's appendix or prefix; empty parentheses = a phrase whose content is either the same as that of the phrase to which it is attached or conventional. Quotation marks around themes/motifs indicate that these are developed rather than (re)stated.

C = Count; B = Basilio; S = Susanna.

a development; and what follows (mm. 147–221) recapitulates most of the ex-position's ideas in the main key. But that would be a normalizing reading—correct enough but useful only to the extent that it profiles all the more clearly the features that cannot be normalized or assimilated to sonata con-ventions. Those features raise the questions: What is the function of the mu-sic between the exposition and the "development" in mm. 58–121? What is an accompanied recitative doing at the center of an ensemble? Why is it not possible to map the successive events of the recapitulation onto those of the exposition?

The Trio is a story of a disaster waiting to happen—and then happening. Strictly speaking, it is not a trio but a quartet in which one of the central personages scarcely dares to breathe, let alone speak. As the Trio begins, Cherubino, the Count's page, who is afflicted by the hormonal upheaval of early adolescence and hence in thrall to every woman in the palace, is curled up inside a large armchair, hidden by Susanna's dress; the Count, equally, and more dangerously, devoted to the prettier womenfolk around, is un-aware of the page's presence and emerges from behind the armchair, where he has been hiding. They are in a room assigned to Susanna and Figaro, and neither has any reason to be there alone with Susanna. (Beaumarchais uses props with a breathtaking directness and economy worthy of Aeschylus's red carpet in *Agamemnon:* the armchair in the as yet barely furnished room stands in for the nuptial bed the Count had promised the young couple, the contents of which the two men would gladly share with Figaro, and around which they circle like two dogs in heat; and to be under Susanna's dress is quite literally what they would like most.) The Count is sufficiently annoyed with the rumors he has just overheard, rumors that the page may be im-modestly eyeing the Countess, to want to banish the seducer from his do-mains at once. The gossip is spread by the music master, Basilio, who does have a legitimate reason for being there, since he acts as the Count's pro-curer. (Basilio's function in the Trio is similar to Don Curzio's in the Sextet; indeed, in the first performances both roles were created by the same singer. Both Basilio and Don Curzio are wholly the Count's men, but Basilio takes a more active pleasure in behaving maliciously toward all, the Count in-cluded, and goads his master about the page whenever there is the slight-est danger that the Count might forget the subject.) Only Susanna and the audience are aware of Cherubino's presence in the chair. He is the silent cen-ter of attention, all the more present for being covered and invisible. The audience knows from the start that he will be discovered, or rather, uncov-ered; it is only a matter of how and when. Here, as in a sonata, the partial

predictability of events only intensifies the pleasure, just as the sense of menace intensifies and complicates the comic effect.

The brilliant subtlety with which Beaumarchais–Da Ponte and Mozart
set up the Count's discovering Cherubino in the central recitative never fails
to take one's breath away, just as the actual discovery itself takes away the
Count's. In a short narrative the Count tells Susanna and Basilio that yesterday he had discovered the page hidden under a table in the room of Susanna's underage cousin, Barbarina, another object of both men's attentions.
Demonstrating how he had made this discovery by gently lifting the table-
cloth, the Count lifts the fateful dress from the armchair. The way in which
past and present, the imagined and the real, the narrated and the enacted, touch
one another and come together in a single moment is positively vertiginous—
and not only for those on stage. A seemingly simple gesture enacted in the
Now of the opera's fictional world is not simple at all because at the same
time it represents a gesture performed yesterday, Then. It is a moment where
art reflects on itself: the representation of an imaginary world that at the
same time lays bare the real world—it is hard to think of a better image of
what art is about.

In setting this scene (Example 8) Mozart matches the subtlety of his
dramatist, who imposed two tasks on the composer: first, to differentiate
clearly between the past tense of the events narrated by the Count and the
surrounding present of the events in the opening and closing sections of the
Trio; and second, to bring the two tenses together at the end. Mozart's setting shows how thoroughly he understood the task. He set the Count's narrative as an accompanied recitative, thus sharply distinguishing it from the
textures on either side of it. Further, he suspended the recitative between
two dominant chords, each followed by a fermata: the first (m. 121) coincides with the present tense of the real world on stage coming to a stand-
still; the second (m. 146) picks up where the first left off, and afterward the
interrupted flow of time resumes. Between the two fermatas the present
hangs suspended, and a window opens on the past. The window's closing
and the return of the present happen gradually—past and present overlap
for a moment. The Trio's meter and tempo are reestablished in m. 129, precisely the point when the Count begins to reenact his fateful gesture; at the
very moment he completes the gesture, in m. 138, harmony returns to the
dominant chord that had marked the suspension of the present in m. 121.
(The rest of the section, mm. 139–46, is an appendix prolonging this dominant.) It is here, at m. 138, that past and present meet.

Were the Count a more self-reflective person, he would realize that what

EXAMPLE 8. Mozart, *Le nozze di Figaro*, No. 7 (Trio), mm. 121–46

EXAMPLE 8 *(continued)*

he discovered under the robe was himself, more innocent because younger and not as dangerous because less powerful, but unmistakably the same erotically driven self. Fast-forward fifteen or twenty years, and Cherubino will be no different from the Count; already their interests overlap to a remarkable extent. But at this point the Count is incapable of such insight. Instead, with the logic of the house despot that he is, he shifts the focus of his anger from the page to the only person in the room who is completely innocent, Susanna. This shift constitutes the main content of the Trio's action, a fact that by necessity alters the situation in the recapitulation from what it had been in the exposition. The main thematic idea of the Trio—the idea that at beginning and end of the exposition twice expressed the Count's

order that the page be banished (mm. 4–15: "Tosto andate e scacciate il se-
duttor" [Go at once and chase the seducer off] and 101–9: "Parta, parta il
damerino!" [The dandy must depart!])—now in m. 147 opens the recapitulation; but this time the Count's jealous attention is unmistakably fixed
on the lovely chambermaid: "Onestissima signora, or capisco come va"
(Most honest lady, now I understand what's happening). Recapitulation is
possible, because the Count is again threatening one of his dependents, as
he had at the beginning. But this recapitulation is not a simple repetition;
the threat is now differently directed.

Unlike in the exposition, where the dramatic situation was changing con-
stantly, nothing changes in the recapitulation from beginning to end; for
this reason mapping the successive events of the latter onto those of the
former would have been neither possible nor desirable. Mozart combines
into a single phrase (mm. 147–75; Table 6) the two main thematic ideas that
in the exposition had articulated the home and second key areas, and he follows this with one more hypocritical reminder to the Count from Basilio
(mm. 176–82): "Ah del paggio quel che ho detto, era solo un mio sospetto"
(What I said about the page was only my suspicion), concluding with an
abbreviated repetition of the phrase that combined the two main themes
(mm. 183–201 = mm. 160–75) as well as two appendices. The Count accuses;
Basilio goads him on; Susanna is reduced to passive despondency. The only
important exposition theme missing from the recapitulation is the one associated with Susanna and her active attempts to forestall the disaster.

The menace over Susanna's head, explicit in the recapitulation, was of
course already present in the exposition, but there it was, so to speak, kept
under cover. The musical material in mm. 58–121, which would be superfluous for a sonata exposition, serves entirely to prolong the sense of threat
and depict its gathering strength. Susanna almost faints from fright (or,
rather, pretends to faint) on seeing and hearing the Count emerge from behind the armchair. This is the first action in the Trio, the first situation change,
and it completes in m. 43 the transition to the second key that had begun
in m. 16. The effect is for the first time to switch the Count's (and Basilio's)
attention away from the page and to her. The two men respond to her action, offering her support (mm. 43–57); this is the first time in the Trio that
they sing the same text together and, being a reaction to a new situation
rather than another change of the situation, this passage requires not modulation but rather the stability of a new, second key area. As usual, Mozart
times the events precisely: Susanna falls into the arms of the two men at
the instant the harmony reaches the second key, at the downbeat of m. 43.
At this point their solicitation for her is about as real as her fainting (they

use the opportunity to feel her beating heart); never again in the Trio will they be as supportive as they are now.

Were this an orthodox exposition, it could close right there, at the end of the men's phrase, in m. 57. Instead, a second tonal transition accompanies the Trio's second action (mm. 58–69), when the men attempt to deposit Susanna on the fatal armchair and she revives just in time to order them out. Their reaction (mm. 70–84) is accompanied by the thematic idea and key stability of the previous reaction (mm. 43–57), but with a subtle difference. In the earlier passage the key prepared by the transition was F major (the dominant), and F major duly arrived in m. 43. Now the prepared key is G minor (the submediant), but instead of G minor arriving in m. 70 it is G minor's submediant, E♭ major. The deceptive tonal relationship infuses a sinister, threatening undertone into the men's overtly solicitous words ("Siamo qui per aiutarti" [We are here to help you]) that was not there before. Mozart extends the exposition primarily to show this growing menace, and he includes two second-key areas rather than just one. (What follows is a retransition back to the tonic, mm. 85–100, and what at first sounds like a recapitulation—both the main key and the principal subject reappear in m. 101—but quickly reveals itself to be setting up the half cadence that precedes the central recitative.) This menace will become explicit in the recapitulation, where the men's music—heard twice in nontonic keys in the exposition—now returns twice in the tonic (mm. 168–75, 191–201). No matter how far he may stray from sonata conventions, Mozart's unerring sense of proportion and balance holds.

—

When reading the *Figaro* Trio it is possible to use, however approximately, sonata terms such as exposition and recapitulation. Not even approximate usage is possible in the case of the Sextet (No. 19) from the second act of *Don Giovanni*, the most complex and individual of Mozart's ensembles and the one furthest removed from any sonata conventions.

Psychologically, too, the Sextet represents a more complicated situation than those previously discussed; here the protagonists are in the grip of sentiments they themselves find hard to articulate, avow, or even understand, and the scene is calculated to make the audience feel some of their moral confusion and discomfort. But if the psychological effects of action are complex here, the action itself is simple. The main dramatic point of the ensemble is the unmasking, or rather uncovering, of Leporello, who had been disguised as his master, Don Giovanni, "giovane cavaliere estremamente licenzioso" (an extremely licentious young gentleman), as the list of the personages

characterizes him. When the discovery occurs and the stage, a courtyard of
Donna Anna's house, which had been dark, becomes brightly lit, the expected
resolution and clarity do not happen; instead, everyone ends up even more
uneasy and uncomfortable than they were at the outset. Don Giovanni is
the only main protagonist of the opera who does not take part in the ensemble. All except Leporello thought they had found Don Giovanni, and,
with the further exception of Donna Elvira, all thought they could now punish him with death. The discovery of Leporello is especially disappointing
to Elvira, who finds herself yet again deceived and abused (it was Don Giovanni who had induced his servant to assume the disguise and seduce Elvira);
the discovery is also disappointing to the two other women who have been
Don Giovanni's victims, the aristocratic Donna Anna and the peasant girl
Zerlina, and to the men to whom they are betrothed, Don Ottavio and
Masetto. The discovery of Leporello under his master's clothes brings no
resolution to their quest; on the contrary, it increases the pain they all feel,
and this pain determines both the emotional tone and the musical shape of
the Sextet. Sonata conventions, which require resolution and clarity, would
obviously not do here.

Accordingly, Mozart arranges the Sextet in four broad sections—each
marking a stage in the dramatic development, each filled with different musical ideas, and each held together by a different key (Table 7). The three
participating couples enter the stage successively in the first three sections.
In the first, Donna Elvira and Leporello are alone in the dark courtyard: she
(mm. 1–13) is frightened by being "sola in buio loco" (alone in the dark)
and assailed by thoughts of death (thoughts that will occur to other protagonists of this scene, too); he (mm. 14–27) is searching for a way to get
away from her. His near escape is thwarted by the entrance of Donna Anna
and Don Ottavio, accompanied by servants carrying lights. The justly celebrated simple, four-measure instrumental transition between the two sections (mm. 27–30) makes the gathering light audible by moving a step down
from the opening's dark, three-flat key of E♭ to the new, much brighter, two-
sharp key of D, whose brilliance Mozart underscored with timbres of softly
played trumpets and timpani.

Donna Anna and Don Ottavio are closer to one another than Donna Elvira
and the dissimulating Leporello could possibly be, and their quiet private
colloquy (they have not yet noticed Elvira's and Leporello's presence and
do not know that they are being overheard) shows that they have a subject
in common—her grief over the recent death of her father, whom Don Giovanni had killed on this very spot after attempting to seduce, or rather, rape,
Donna Anna. Donna Anna and Don Ottavio do not need separate musical

TABLE 7. Mozart, *Don Giovanni*, No. 19 (Sextet): dramatic content

	Andante															Molto allegro				
measure	1	3	14	26	27	31	45	61	69	70	76	80	99	114	121	131	185	240	259	271
character	—	E	L		—	O	A	E/L		A/Z/O/M	E	E+A/Z/O/M	L	A/Z/O/M/E		L+A/Z/O/M/E				
theme/motif		1	2			3		4		5	4		6	7	4	8				
tonal plan	I	→V	V		→VII	VII	vii→vi	vi		i	(V)	i→v	v	→III→	(V)‡ / (V)‡‡	I				
phrase	1.()	FC	FC	()	2.()	FC	FC	3.FC	()	HC	()	FC	H̶C̶	HC	()	4.FC	FC	()	()	()

FC = a phrase closed with a full cadence; HC = a phrase closed with a half cadence; H̶C̶ = a phrase ending with a deceptive cadence; parentheses = a phrase's appendix or prefix; empty parentheses = a phrase whose content is either the same as that of the phrase to which it is attached or conventional.
E = Donna Elvira; L = Leporello; O = Don Ottavio; A = Donna Anna; Z = Zerlina; M = Masetto.

ideas, and their successive cantilenas can be supported by a common accompanimental figure. Tonal contrast alone suffices to convey such distance as exists between them. Don Ottavio (mm. 31–45) asks his betrothed to put her grief behind her, and he keeps his plea in the positive D major introduced by the preceding transition. But there are wounds that only death can heal, and Donna Anna (mm. 45–61), like Elvira, thinks of death ("sola morte . . . il mio pianto può finir" [only death . . . can end my weeping]); the simple nobility of her utterance leaves no doubt that her emotion is more authentic than the conventional exaggeration of an *opera seria* heroine. Her phrase changes the mode to minor and then slowly modulates down another step, to C minor.

It is this key that governs the third, dramatically central and most evolved, section of the Sextet (mm. 61–130), the only portion of the ensemble in which something actually happens. Before this point the only event was the entrance of Donna Anna and Don Ottavio, which occurred between sections, and nothing will happen in the concluding Molto Allegro. This is also the only section that brings a genuine tonal unfolding of the local key area of C minor, involving motion away from and then back to the tonic: the tonic key area (mm. 61–80) is followed by a modulation to the minor dominant (mm. 80–98), a minor dominant area (mm. 99–114), and a retransition back toward the tonic (mm. 114–30).

The tonal changes correlate with some of the turning points in the action. The initial tonic accompanies Donna Elvira's and Leporello's attempt to slip away unnoticed (mm. 61–70); this is thwarted by the entrance of Zerlina and Masetto, their discovery of "Don Giovanni," and the demand for immediate retribution from both aggrieved couples—Donna Anna and Don Ottavio, Zerlina and Masetto—singing together for the first time (mm. 70–76): "Ah mora il perfido che m'ha tradito!" (Ah, death to the perfidious man who has betrayed me!). Thoughts of death infect more and more characters in the ensemble. Donna Elvira's plea (mm. 76–80): "È mio marito! Pietà!" (He is my husband! Have mercy!) prolongs the dominant of the half cadence that closes their phrase. Only at this point does Mozart introduce a change of key. Modulation to the minor dominant conveys the *sotto voce* confused surprise with which the two couples greet Donna Elvira—surprise at her being there and perhaps at her defending the "perfido"— her repeated pleas for mercy, and their full-voiced forte refusal (mm. 80–98): "No! Morrà!" (No! He will die!). Leporello uses his minor-dominant phrase to uncover himself and tearfully beg for his life (mm. 99–114). Given that the uncovering is the central event of the Sextet, it is appropriate that the deceptive cadence closing Leporello's phrase, which simultaneously opens the stupefied *sotto voce* response of the other five personages, is the ensemble's most striking tonal event. This deceptive cadence—perhaps the most affecting use to which this simple device has ever been put—initiates a retransition back to the local C-minor tonic (mm. 114–30).

Mozart's tonal planning of the Sextet's central section is clear: he reserved the two moments marking a change in tonal direction—the beginning of the modulation away from the tonic in m. 80 and the beginning of the retransition back to the tonic in m. 114—for the two moments of surprise in the face of a revelation just produced: the first one by Donna Elvira, the second by Leporello. Further, he made sure that the impact of the second surprise is stronger than that of the first by adroit use of the deceptive cadence. This takes even Donna Elvira aback, so that by the end of the section the number of characters sucked into the whirlwind of confusion and dismay has grown from four to five. It is crucial to note that this kind of tonal planning stands Mozart's standard usage on its head. Normally a modulation conveys the sense that a situation is changing, and the new key is reached when the personages are ready to react to the new situation just produced. Here it is the reverse: the central events happen within the stable key areas (Elvira reveals her presence in the tonic, Leporello reveals his in the dominant), and the modulations begin immediately afterward, when the remaining characters begin to react to the new developments (they express their surprise at the presence first of Elvira and then of Leporello). This reversal of standard usage suggests that what happens in the external world serves merely as a trigger; the true scene of action here is interior. It is as if the personages of the Sextet were dreaming a collective nightmare, trapped in a labyrinth from which they see no exit—which, on the contrary, grows ever more confusing. The real action is the increasing vertigo the characters experience under the impact of accumulating shocks.

Mozart further escalates the sense of entrapment in this section of the Sextet with the use of recurring motivic material. As Donna Elvira and Leporello tiptoe toward a door, trying to leave the courtyard unnoticed, the dotted rhythm of their vocal lines and of the accompanying strings introduces an idea that becomes the section's refrain (mm. 61–70). The rhythm had made an earlier, tentative, appearance with Leporello's first attempt (in mm. 14–27) to find "questa porta sciagurata" (this damned door), but only now does it come to the fore and dominate the music unmistakably. In the central section this music is heard again, twice. It accompanies Donna Elvira's asking the two couples to show mercy to her husband and their subsequent surprise and refusal (mm. 76–98). And it closes the section when, after Leporello's revelation, the two couples and Donna Elvira are reduced to saying,

"Stupido resto" (I am stupefied; mm. 121–30). The motif that made its tentative appearance at Leporello's first attempt to find an exit and became explicit with his second attempt is finally taken up by the other personages as well. They may not be looking for an exit literally, but they feel no less trapped than he does. Moreover, what for him is a dangerous but external situation, they have internalized as a fundamental existential predicament.

They are stupefied and will remain frozen in dismayed torpor until the end. The final section of the Sextet, the Molto Allegro, is long and fast, but it goes nowhere; it merely turns round and round furiously, like the "Mille torbidi pensieri" (thousand troubled thoughts) that, each personage repeats again and again, "mi s'aggiran per la testa" (ramble through my head). They stay in one key throughout, not the C minor promised by the way the preceding section had ended but the E♭ major of the ensemble's opening. And they utter one phrase only, repeating most of it (mm. 192–229 take up mm. 147–84 again), and closing with a few appendices. In this ensemble neither Leporello nor the others ever find the exit. Like the finale that closes the first half of an opera buffa, the end of the Sextet finds nothing resolved and no satisfactory conclusion.

The tonal progression that governs the Sextet—from the I of the Elvira-Leporello opening section (mm. 1–27) to the VII/vii of the Anna-Ottavio colloquy (mm. 27–61), on to the vi of the central section (mm. 61–130), and back to I for the closing Molto Allegro (mm. 131–277)—provides the general shape and direction here. Conspicuously missing from this progression is V, and it is missing in two ways. Not only is there no section unified by the dominant key, which the descent from I through VII/vii to vi has led the listener to expect, but there is not even something as basic as a local dominant area or chord preparing the return of the tonic in m. 131: the dominant appendix in mm. 121–30 prepares the submediant, not the tonic, with the result that when the tonic does come, it is unexpected and unwanted. In a musical language in which the dominant-tonic relationship is the cornerstone of structural solidity, clarity, resolution, and closure, this double absence of the dominant is bound to be conspicuous and significant, and to produce precisely the effect it brings about here—a sense of unease and deception. Musical form, the Sextet shows, may be temporal and linear, but the line may lead to nowhere in particular—or to confusion and dismay—rather than to triumphant clarity.

6 Between Incoherence and Inauthenticity

Don Giovanni and Faust

The Don Juans have terrible moments of emptiness in their lives
and a bitter old age; but most men do not reach old age.
—STENDHAL, *On Love*

"Carpe diem." He seized the day, but when in the evening he
glanced at his captive, he saw the night.
—ADAM ZAGAJEWSKI, "Antennas in the Rain"

The music would have to have the character of *Don Giovanni;*
Mozart should have composed *Faust.*
—JOHANN PETER ECKERMANN, *Gespräche mit Goethe,*
   12 February 1829

Why are we moderns so scattered, why excited by demands
which we can neither reach nor fulfill!
—JOHANN WOLFGANG VON GOETHE, *Italienische Reise*

Listeners will find themselves linking the effect of irresolution, nightmarish
entrapment, unease, and deception in the *Don Giovanni* Sextet, which is
caused by the conspicuous absence of the dominant (conspicuous, because
the dominant is implied by the tonal structure, as well as the basic proper-
ties of the musical language used), with the equally conspicuous absence of
Don Giovanni. Of the opera's personages still living at that point, he is the
only one absent from the stage, yet he is on everyone's mind. All except
Leporello actually believe him to be there. Moreover, he is not only present
in everyone's thoughts but represented, in the complete sense of the term,
by his servant—his comic sidekick and double. (From the start, Leporello
had wanted to be like his master: "Voglio far il gentiluomo" [I want to play
the gentleman]. Now he is getting his wish.) Like the dominant, Don Giovanni both is, and is not, there.

The sacrificial structure of the scene is unmistakable: a victim about to
be killed, surrounded by an assembled community, with a representative of
that community ready to strike the fatal blow; a stage direction mentions
Don Ottavio "in atto di ucciderlo" (about to kill him). The scene is familiar

from other plays and operas, *Idomeneo* for instance. In *Don Giovanni* the two couples, from opposite social poles of the opera's microsociety, are in no doubt about what they intend for the captured scapegoat; only Donna Elvira, who hopes until the last to save her husband, does not join in their call: "Morrà!" (He will die!). But their intention is thwarted. The intended victim is not there; his representative, Leporello, at most deserves a thrashing. The Sextet cannot come to a satisfying closure because of this aborted sacrifice. The link between Don Giovanni's absence and the missing dominant is close indeed.

A satisfying closure must wait until, literally, the end. Only in the final scene, immediately after Don Giovanni is, in the words of a stage direction, "inghiottito dalla terra" (swallowed up by the earth), do the six personages of the ensemble gather on stage one last time. What Masetto has not been able to accomplish earlier in Act 2, what Don Ottavio has not been able to accomplish most recently during the Sextet, has now been accomplished by a larger, superhuman power represented by the statue of Donna Anna's father, the Commandant, whom Don Giovanni had killed in the first scene of the opera. All along they may have suspected that it would require more than human power: the only other time they had all surrounded Don Giovanni, in his ballroom at the end of Act 1, they were unable to do more than threaten him vaguely with "il tuon della vendetta che ti fischia intorno intorno" (the sound of vengeance that whistles around you) and hope that heaven would do what needed to be done, "sul tuo capo in questo giorno il suo fulmine cadrà" (its thunderbolt will fall upon your head this day). Heaven obliged, if not immediately, by sending the statue.

The statue's entrance marks the return to both the opening key of the opera, D minor, and, famously, the opening Andante introduction to the Overture. The beginning of the scene recapitulates almost exactly the entire introduction to the Overture. Less obvious is that Mozart may have chosen his most vivid gestures here to match the aural clues in the threats at the end of Act 1—now materialized, as it were. The thunderbolt then anticipated is heard now in the two crushing chords that mark the statue's entrance in mm. 433–36, corresponding to the two chords in mm. 1–4. The initial exchange of civilities in mm. 437–53 between the stone guest and his host (always accompanied by his terrified servant) follows the succession of motifs in mm. 5–23. Similarly, the conversation and modulation to the minor dominant in mm. 454–86 follow the content of the remaining phrase of the introduction, mm. 23–31—content dominated by a stately dotted rhythm associated with the statue that is as inexorable as the fate promised at the end of Act 1; Mozart confirms the link with whistling scales in the flutes and first violins to remind the listener of the threatened "sound of vengeance that whistles around you." Moreover, he amplifies the orchestra of the Overture with three trombones, the operatic sign of the numinous. But even without this sonorous supplement, the grand recapitulation itself, creating a frame around the opera, suggests the intrusion of or breakthrough to a different order of time. It is as if the normal, mundane, linear temporality of the opera's plot were being embedded in circular, divine time—as if the eternal order whose help was invoked at the end of Act 1 were reestablishing itself and claiming its due.

The phrase that follows in mm. 487–516 remains dominated by the Commandant's dotted rhythm and continues the modulation, now in the direction of the minor subdominant. This tonal goal is reached at the moment when, to Leporello's dismay, his master accepts the statue's return invitation: "Non ho timor: verrò!" (I have no fear: I shall come!). Don Giovanni's undeniable courage on this occasion fulfills another promise from the end of Act 1: "se cadesse ancor il mondo, nulla mai temer mi fa" (even if the world, too, should fall [on my head], nothing will ever make me afraid). The stage is set both for the final reckoning and for a return to the tonic (Example 9). Even with the statue's handshake sending hellish cold through his body, Don Giovanni responds to the exhortation that he repent with a firm "No, no, ch'io non mi pento, vanne lontan da me!" ("No, no, I don't repent, go away from me!"). The conclusion of his refusal coincides with the half cadence on the dominant of the home key in m. 532. The ensuing back and forth—"Pentiti!" "No!" "Sì!" "No!" (Repent! No! Yes! No!)—again ends on the dominant, coinciding with Don Giovanni's last *gran rifiuto* in m. 548; consequently the struggle in mm. 532–548 is heard as the elaboration of a prolonged dominant chord. When Don Giovanni's time is up the Commandant leaves, and the long-prepared D-minor tonic returns (m. 554).

This entire section abounds with echoes from the beginning of the opera—this time not from the Overture but from the scene of Don Giovanni's duel with the Commandant in the Introduction of Act 1 (Example 10). A comparison of the Commandant's repeated demand, "Pentiti!" (Repent!; No. 24, mm. 533–35, 538, 540), with his earlier insistent "Battiti!" (Fight!; No. 1, mm. 141–42, 157) reveals, for instance, how the incisive rhythmic profile of the figure in the first violin and bass, which traces the path of their crossing swords (No. 1, mm. 167–75), reappears in the bass part during the final verbal duel (No. 24, mm. 525–48). Even more compelling is the subtle but unmistakable way in which the Commandant's decision that Don Giovanni's time is up—this punctuated by a slow, deliberate, powerful D-minor cadence (No. 24, mm. 549–54)—answers the emphatic D-minor

EXAMPLE 9. Mozart, *Don Giovanni*, No. 24 (Act 2, Finale), mm. 517–54

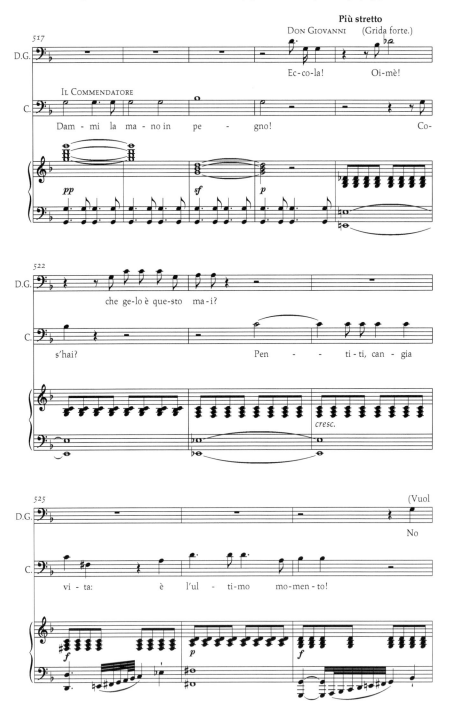

EXAMPLE 9 *(continued)*

(continued)

EXAMPLE 9 *(continued)*

EXAMPLE 9 *(continued)*

EXAMPLE 10. Mozart, *Don Giovanni*, No. 1 (Act 1, Introduzione), mm. 135–75

(continued)

EXAMPLE 10 *(continued)*

EXAMPLE 10 *(continued)*

cadence that earlier had marked Don Giovanni's fateful decision to accept the Commandant's challenge and fight (No. 1, mm. 160–66). Here, too, the musical echoes suggest that Don Giovanni's fate was already sealed at that point, that, *sub specie aeternitatis,* the passage of terrestrial time between the night in front of Donna Anna's house and the night in Don Giovanni's dining room is trivial and insignificant. The Allegro that closes the scene (mm. 554–602) never leaves D minor. Rather, in prolonging the final tonic, it prolongs the moment of damnation. A stage direction tells us of a "tremuoto" (earthquake) at the point when Don Giovanni, greeted by a subterranean chorus, "is swallowed up by the earth." It is as if at the end of Act 1 he had unwittingly predicted the fate that ultimately overtakes him, the world falling on his head.

The story might end right here, and in a sense it does. But just as the D-minor Andante in the Overture was followed by a D-major Molto Allegro, so here too there follows a final scene that assembles all the survivors on stage and tonally represents an elaborate plagal cadence in D major: first an Allegro Assai in G, mm. 603–711, in which Leporello relates as best he can what has just happened; then a Larghetto in G with retransition at the end, mm. 712–55, in which they all make plans for the future: "or che tutti . . . vendicati siam dal cielo" (now that we are all . . . avenged by heaven); and finally a Presto in D, mm. 756–871, in which they all pronounce the moral—"l'antichissima canzon" (the most ancient song)—according to which "Questo è il fin di chi fa mal! E de' perfidi la morte alla vita è sempre ugual!" (This is the end of the evildoer! And the death of perfidious people is always like their life!). Belief that whoever does evil in this life will be appropriately punished in the next is a doctrine with which subtle Christian theologians of all denominations might find any number of problems, but it certainly satisfies the hope, entertained since time immemorial, that justice, contrary to all evidence, rules the world after all.

It makes sense, then, to hear the grand dominant-tonic cadence in D minor in mm. 532–54—where the dominant articulates Don Giovanni's "No!" and the tonic his resulting downfall—as the final structural cadence of the opera, and the plagally organized final scene in D major as a coda to the final cadence. Together, these passages provide the opera with the emphatic closure missing in the Sextet. The dominant was missing there because no closure short of Don Giovanni's death would have satisfied the community represented on stage, and that was impossible without two essential ingredients: Don Giovanni himself and a supernatural force capable of accomplishing what the community was incapable of doing on its own.

In my reading the Sextet is a failed rehearsal for the sacrifice in which the community would offer Don Giovanni on the altar of eternal justice, a sacrifice that takes place only at the end of the opera. The questions arise: Why is the sacrifice needed in the first place? And why is human justice not enough—why is supernatural intervention necessary?

⸻

Each of the personages of the Sextet has a clearly defined personal and communal identity; the audience knows each of their social roles and understands their characters. The remaining two personages of the opera, Don Giovanni and the Commandant, are different. Of course they too have characters and social stations. But, unlike the others, they stand for and personify larger, supraindividual, abstract forces; they serve as allegories—or rather, each blends his individual personal and social characteristics and his allegorical meaning into what in the currently unfashionable language of that era was called a symbol.

Don Giovanni, a young Spanish nobleman, is brave, devoid of scruples, and "extremely licentious" (estremamente licenzioso), but that is not all he is. His pursuit of sexual pleasure is so energetic and single-minded, his results, carefully catalogued by Leporello, so far beyond those achieved by even his most successful real-life competitor, Giacomo Casanova—in Spain alone, Leporello notes, "there are already a thousand and three" (son già mille e tre)—that, without ceasing to be a "real" man, he becomes an embodiment of sexual desire itself. The issue in *Don Giovanni,* Kierkegaard observed, "is not desire in a particular individual but desire as a principle. . . . The expression of this idea is Don Juan." Later in the same essay he writes, "Don Juan continually hovers between being idea—that is, power, life—and being an individual. . . . But when he is conceived in music, then I do not have the particular individual, then I have a force of nature."[1] The defining characteristic of this desire is limitlessness. Don Giovanni's greatest ambition—his only ambition—is further to extend the list of his conquests: "You must augment my list tomorrow morning by a dozen" (Ah la mia lista doman mattina d'una decina devi aumentar), he tells Leporello. And yet he does not lust for anyone in particular; as Leporello observes, "It does not matter to him if she be rich, if she be ugly, if she be beautiful" (Non si picca se sia ricca, se sia brutta, se sia bella). Don Giovanni's desire knows no limits; it is desire for its own sake. This is why the story is one of the quintessentially modern myths. If the liberal Lockean strand in modernity accepts and celebrates the unlimited nature of human desire, our endlessly acquisitive stance, Don Giovanni is the mythical hero of this strand—the paradigmatic libertine but also the paradigmatic liberal. It is no accident that Mozart gave tremendous resonance to the words with which Don Giovanni greets the guests entering his ballroom—words that looked sufficiently innocuous in the libretto to have escaped the censor's attention—by setting them as a long, majestic march in C major, complete with blazing trumpets and timpani: "It is open for all, long live liberty!" (È aperto a tutti quanti, viva la libertà!).

"Viva la libertà!" His guests repeat his words loudly and enthusiastically, again and again—even Donna Anna, Donna Elvira, and Don Ottavio, who are neither libertines nor, probably, liberals and should have known better. (Zerlina and Masetto would have joined in too, if they had not already been inside, within Don Giovanni's realm of liberty.) They cannot resist because, liberal or not, they, like everyone else, value freedom. On reflection, they will reject their host's one-sided, single-minded devotion to freedom and nothing but freedom, but they too feel the attraction.

The famous ballroom scene that follows immediately upon their entrance is a graphic demonstration of what is wrong with liberty as understood by their host. A liberal society can function peacefully and harmoniously only so long as everyone recognizes that individual freedom has limits defined both by law and by some version of the precept of doing unto others as we would have them do unto us. Don Giovanni, however, is a free rider who does not recognize limits; his attempt to force Zerlina into a side room unbalances and then stalls the harmonious turns of three simultaneous dances—the noble menuetto, middle-class contradanza, and peasant Teitsch—whose simultaneity constitutes a perfect image of successful social cooperation across the lines dividing the estates broken by willful aristocratic license.

However, absolute, unlimited freedom is destructive of more than society. It also defeats the attempt to create a coherent self. Thus not only the community but Don Giovanni himself becomes its victim. "Victim" is not quite accurate here, of course, for Don Giovanni does not actually want to be a self. Only someone who aspires to acquiring a coherent self through autonomous self-mastery would recognize loss of self as defeat. A self is defined by commitment to some set of aims and norms, and without limits it dissolves into a whirlwind of infinite and often conflicting desires. Don Giovanni is committed to nothing, not even to the demands of prudence. He listens only to the latest promptings of desire. This is why, as many critics have observed, it is so hard to pin him down, to know who he is—there is no "who" there. Even musically, as has been often noted, he lacks a personality of his own, tending rather to adopt the gestures and habits of his interlocutors.[2] He should be the patron saint of the many enthusiastic French imitators of later Heidegger's anti-humanism for whom autonomy is a trap to be avoided and who sing praises of the end of man and the dispersal of the subject.

Kierkegaard brilliantly recognized that Don Giovanni lives only in the present; his existence as he experiences and understands it is a series of Nows—not a story but a catalogue or list. (The episodic, loose structure of Da Ponte's libretto—often, and in my view superficially, criticized—is well suited for capturing this sort of existence.) So far in this book I have considered only two temporal possibilities, that of existing in God's eternity or existing in human time. Don Giovanni shows that there is a third possibility. Perhaps he was a maximalist who wanted all or nothing. It is as if he told himself, if I cannot have God's eternity, I won't accept the pitiful compromise of my community's linear time either. Possibly he was impressed with Hume's theory of the self's dissolution into an ever-changing bundle of perceptions. It might even appear that he would have preferred to revert to the prelapsarian state of animals and give up the capacity for symbolic thought that differentiates fallen man from the rest of the animal kingdom; for it is this that lifts man from the sensuous immediacy of Now into the mediated reflection where imagination can engage in projecting the future and recalling the past. This, however, is not quite accurate either, since, unlike animals, Don Giovanni is not driven by the instinct of self-preservation. Nor does he, unlike most humans, pursue self-preservation out of prudence. It is indifference and contempt for death that lifts him above the status of a mere animal or that of an *homme moyen sensuel,* giving him instead something of a heroic aura. This is also what differentiates him from Leporello, who so yearns to be a gentleman like his master but cannot, because self-preservation overrides all of his other desires. Leporello does not even pretend to heroism and must settle for being a shabby and mildly despicable double of his master. But—and this is his one redeeming feature—he has an inkling that he might be despicable, a nascent moral sense; his master's self-understanding, by contrast, is wholly beyond such notions as good and evil.

The wish to be like Don Giovanni is not, however, Leporello's alone. For in addition to being a "giovane cavaliere estremamente licenzioso," Don Giovanni also personifies the unlimited desire of the modern subject, and to some extent, however dimly, each of the other five personages of the Sextet recognizes the force of that desire. "The very secret of this opera," says Kierkegaard, "is that its hero is also the force in the other characters. Don Giovanni's life is the life principle in them."[3] At bottom, he symbolizes their infinite freedom, and, appropriately, they enter his house rhapsodizing liberty. But they also recognize that unlimited freedom would make impossible the lives they want to live. They do not want to live only in the Now but want to have a future and a past as well. If each is to be more than a catalogue, if each is to be allowed to build a coherent self with a life story, and if together they are to form a functioning community, they need to place limits on freedom and supplement it with autonomy—that is, sacrifice a part of what Don Giovanni stands for.

And indeed, the first thing they do once they learn that he has been sacrificed is to outline their future projects: Don Ottavio will marry Donna Anna, after granting her the year of mourning she requests; Donna Elvira will finish her days in seclusion; Zerlina and Masetto will go home to have dinner together; and Leporello will go to a tavern to find himself a better master. The prose of the world replaces the poetry of myth. Life can go on now, stripped of some enchantment and much heroism, but it is life all the same. Invariably the opera's end leaves the audience with ambivalence. Something of genuine value has disappeared from the scene. The sacrifice may have been necessary but not without something lost in the process.[4]

Although it may flatter our sense of superiority, there are dangers in succumbing to this bleak mood of sophisticated disenchantment. First, we may be attributing to Don Giovanni more of a heroic status than he really deserves, thus needlessly glamorizing evil. A hero must overcome the fear of death, but whereas for animals the fear is instinctual and for rational creatures it is a product of their ability to envisage the future, there is no evidence that Don Giovanni had to struggle either with natural instinct or rational imagination—we simply do not know one way or the other. Recall, too, that in our own time the most obvious incarnation of infinite desire is the Consumer, much vilified by such Rousseauist critics of liberalism as Adorno but not a figure noted for heroic or demonic qualities. Hence the second danger: that we overlook the complete egoism inherent in the erotic force that drives this hero. Don Giovanni has no interest in the individualities of his women. For him, they are interchangeable occasions rather than persons: as his servant crudely explains to Donna Elvira, "provided she wears a skirt, you know what he does" (purchè porti la gonnella, voi sapete quel che fa). Don Giovanni's eros is without a trace of agape. But a mixture of eros and agape—or rather, ideally, eros saved by agape, to use the remarkable formula of Denis de Rougemont—is precisely what in the end will drive the relationships within this community.[5] Love is probably beyond Leporello's horizon, and it might be too late for the repeatedly humiliated Donna Elvira, but for the other four the miracle and grace of mutually bestowed love, whether in the exalted mode of Donna Anna and Don Ottavio (and I see no good reason to join the long line of those who doubt Anna's love for

Ottavio, nor to despise Ottavio's profound devotion to Anna as a bloodless and conventional attitude of a weak and ineffectual man) or in the down-to-earth mode of Zerlina and Masetto, is the best, the only, thing with which to face down the indifference of all-devouring time and death. Don Giovanni's is not a viable alternative. Ultimately he is less interesting as a person (he hardly is a person) than as a personification of a force also present within the other six. If anything were to justify a bleak response to the end of the opera it is that we recognize in Eros an indispensable god, and a power as creative as it is disruptive.

The sacrifice attempted in the Sextet and completed in the second Finale was needed not just because Don Giovanni was a disturber of public order and peace. In killing Don Giovanni, all members of this community—and the community at large—killed, or rather, limited, something within themselves so as to make better, more autonomous, more fully human individuals and communities possible. Just as the Count in the *Figaro* Trio should recognize an aspect of his younger self in the uncovered Page, so should the figures in the *Don Giovanni* Sextet recognize that the sacrificial victim they think they have surrounded is in part created in their own image. Don Giovanni is their hidden secret, something they need to repress if they are to go on with their lives, individually and together. He shows them a central aspect of who they are, just as Cherubino shows the Count something of who he (the Count) is. But the Sextet probes deeper than the Trio, for here the act of uncovering reveals not a presence but an absence: the nothing, the non-self, that Don Giovanni stands for.

A question arises, of course, as to why the Sextet personages do not or cannot perform the sacrifice on their own; why do they need the Statue to do it for them? This community is sufficiently civilized—though just barely—to know that there is a difference between a personal vendetta and impersonal justice: were Don Giovanni to be killed by Don Ottavio or Masetto, or even by everyone surrounding him at the end of the first Finale, this would not meet the requirements of justice. More to the point, however, assuming we accept that Don Giovanni is a spiritual principle rather than a person, it makes poetic sense that his downfall should be due to another spiritual principle—this one personified in the returning statue of the Commandant.

What is significant here is the return. Don Giovanni, living only in the Now, refuses to acknowledge the links connecting his present with past and future, links on which the coherent individual and collective identities of those around him are built. When he refuses to acknowledge the relevance and authority of the past that is represented in the figure of the returning

Commandant, this refusal spells his annihilation, the end to any hope that he might ever become a Who. Thus it is more than a purely formal gesture on Mozart's part when he sets the Commandant's return as a grand recapitulation connecting the opera's beginning with its end. Moreover, as in the concertos, the recapitulation is no mere repetition; it is only the second Finale that reveals the full sense of the musical events originally heard in the Overture. The musical recapitulation that frames the opera and the dramatic reassertion of the authority of linear time in the figure of the returning Commandant are two aspects of the same thing: a vote of authorial confidence, if you will, in the choices made by Anna and Ottavio, Zerlina and Masetto.

It is a mistake to read too much into the supernatural intrusion in the opera's denouement. The principle embodied in the Statue, that of submission to the authority of linear time, which is prerequisite to making self-identity possible, is supernatural because it is spiritual and because nonhuman nature is not subject to it. Someone like Don Giovanni, living entirely by the natural impulses of the moment, will not recognize it. Whether, over and above this, the Statue should be considered the tool of a personal divinity dispensing eternal justice and suspending the operation of the laws of physics at will, is an open, and ultimately not very interesting, question. It certainly does not much interest the two couples who, even though they did not witness the catastrophe, easily accept the confused account of the only witness, Leporello (whom they know to be a consummate liar), and circumstantial corroborating evidence from Donna Elvira (whom they know to be easily deceived). They want to resume their lives, and all they need at this point is some confidence that theirs is not the purely natural world in which the stronger always overwhelm the weaker—that the supernatural order of love and justice to which they are committed has a chance. As for the audience, we too have witnessed the Statue's visit but, not belonging to the world of the opera, are free to interpret as we please, either literally (whatever that might mean) or as an allegory. We need to believe the same thing the two couples believe, but what matters to us is the real world, not the world of the stage; about our world we probably have as much assurance as they have about theirs, and accept this assurance just as readily.

Whether a personal God underwrote the outcome of the opera or not seems beside the point, because in this story, unlike in the Passion story, the sacrificial victim is not the Son of God but rather something within each member of the community—another reason why the story of Don Giovanni is a quintessentially modern myth. This story is about laying the foundations of individual and collective autonomy, not about God's paying a debt incurred by Adam—a story, in other words, about how human beings pulled themselves up by their bootstraps instead of having Someone Else tie their boots for them.

—

From this standpoint, the similarities and differences between *Don Giovanni* and *Le nozze di Figaro* are both remarkable and instructive. *Figaro,* too, features one figure who is simultaneously a "real" personage and a personification of the erotic force that makes the little world of Count Almaviva's country house go round: Cherubino, the teenage page whose very name suggests a winged child, Eros—an immature, lighter, more poetic, and less dangerous version of Don Giovanni. Kierkegaard got it right when he said, "The Page is the eventual Don Giovanni."[6] Mozart intimates the same in Don Giovanni's supper scene: he has the stage orchestra warn Don Giovanni with music from *Figaro* taken from the scene in which Figaro had warned the Page that the time is fast approaching when he will no longer be able to disturb women's peace of mind. And the Count shows a Cherubino grown up, with social power but without allegorical depth, a figure at once more banal and more predatory. It is as if in the Page and the Count we see the figure of Don Giovanni split into two.

The impression left at the conclusion of *Figaro* is that whereas Cherubino may continue to circulate freely, animating his world, the Count needs to be domesticated, delimited, in some way. In the final scene of the opera the Count, who believes he has just caught the Countess *in flagrante* with his own valet, Figaro, calls all of his people together to witness her disgrace. They come, with arms and lit torches. One by one the presumed Countess (in reality her chambermaid, Susanna, in disguise), Figaro, and finally all who have gathered beg the Count to forgive her. His repeated Nos are as forceful as those of Don Giovanni at a comparable moment just before the denouement of that opera. Then the real Countess appears. What follows takes just six lines of the libretto (and only twenty-five Andante G-major measures of the score): Count, "Countess, forgive me, forgive me, forgive me!" (Contessa, perdono, / Perdono, perdono! [4 measures]); Countess, "I am more tractable [than you] and say Yes [to your Nos]" (Più docile io sono, / E dico di sì [6 measures]); All [repeating the Countess's music and then adding some elaboration], "Ah! Thus we shall all be satisfied" (Ah tutti contenti / Saremo così [15 measures]). Forgiveness is requested and granted with minimum fuss and utmost simplicity. The music, beautiful and solemn and without a trace of bitterness or irony, is faithful to the libretto's simplicity, and it is a marvel of tact: Mozart neither emphasized nor undermined the words, and as a result the resolution is as believable, persuasive, and satisfying as it would be without music.[7]

The resolution of *Figaro* could not be further from the noise and fury of the *Don Giovanni* denouement. In *Figaro* there is no struggle, the Countess does not hesitate even for a moment. The Andante, sandwiched between a bustling Allegro assai in G and the even more conventionally bustling tutti of the Allegro assai in D that ends the opera, is exceedingly short to resolve a long, complex plot—too short to resolve anything, really. Furthermore, unlike the *Don Giovanni* denouement, the one in *Figaro* lacks the single most indispensable component of any musical resolution—an emphatic final cadence. The denouement of *Figaro* takes place within the subdominant section preceding the final tonic tutti but contains nothing like the final cadence that closes *Don Giovanni* at the departure of the Commandant.

Figaro lacks a convincing musical and dramatic closure, any sense that its conflicts have been successfully resolved. Yet what is lacking—greater length, stronger emphasis, above all a powerful dominant-tonic cadence— in no way undermines the sincerity with which in the Andante forgiveness is requested, granted, and witnessed. This is because Mozart creates a sense that the Andante takes place in an altogether different order of time than that of the surrounding Allegros. In purely musical terms the Andante is a parenthesis: it could be lifted out of the score, and the two Allegros seamlessly joined together, without infringing on grammatical correctness. As a result its brevity is an illusion: it is, in fact, neither brief nor long; it is timeless—an atemporal moment of contemplation that interrupts the flow of linear time, the one moment in the whole *Folle journée* (Beaumarchais's title) in which all those present drop their busy plots and counterplots to savor a moment of insight into the world as it should be. With the blessing of their community, the Count and Countess put the crazy day behind them and enact a utopia of loving reconciliation. Nothing gets resolved in their world, no satisfactory or permanent solution has been made available. The spirit of this ending is not a triumphant belief in living happily ever after but the less deluded one of taking one (crazy) day at a time: "Only love can end in contentment and gaiety this day of torments, caprices, and folly" (Questo giorno di tormenti / Di capricci e di follia / In contenti e in allegria / Solo amor può terminar). Here too, eros has been saved by agape—if not in the real world as it is, then in the utopian world as it ought to be.

In *Figaro*, as in the Passion, human history culminates in an act of loving grace. But unlike the divine act of grace that reconciled humanity with

God, this grace has a wholly human source, and its effects are finite, likely to last a finite length of time—perhaps no longer than a day. Human finitude and contingency are accepted, as is the imperfect human capacity to effect reconciliation, but only in time, not out of it.

The end of *Figaro* may be at once shallower and wiser than that of *Don Giovanni*—which, *nota bene*, is not necessarily a contradiction. It seems shallower because the separate characters of Cherubino and the Count suggest that the creative and destructive sides of the will can be neatly and easily separated and kept apart; the figure of Don Giovanni shows just how inseparably intertwined creation and destruction really are, and how difficult and painful the attempts to impose necessary limits on infinite desire. *Figaro* offers the utopian hope that it is possible to reconcile the world as it is with the world as it should be: just as evil has its origin in human decisions and actions, so the eradication of evil is a matter of human decisions and actions. *Don Giovanni*'s vision is more tragic, suggesting that both evil and good spring from the same source, and hence that eradication of evil may be a more difficult task than *Figaro*'s utopia promises.

But the ending of *Figaro* is wiser because it steers clear of radical, revolutionary solutions to human days of folly. Napoleon saw the Revolution prefigured in Beaumarchais's comedy, and Danton opined in 1789 that "Figaro killed nobility" (Figaro a tué la noblesse).[8] Of the two operas, *Don Giovanni* is the more revolutionary one in spirit, the one more ready to accept radical solutions and to kill nobility in the name of moving forward and, at a deeper level, to recognize that suffering will necessarily accompany any such forward motion. Mozart's *Figaro*, for all the menace of Figaro's "Se vuol ballare," ultimately goes for piecemeal reform and social harmony, not revolution; in view of what happened in France only a few years later, the concluding vision of loving reconciliation would seem hopelessly naïve were it not for how frankly its utopian status is displayed.

The combination of tragic depth and radicalism in *Don Giovanni* naturally made it Mozart's central achievement in the view of the romantics. To the narrator of E. T. A. Hoffmann's 1812 story "Don Juan" it was obvious that none of the accidental dinner companions praising the *Don Giovanni* performance they had all witnessed "had any notion of the true meaning of this opera of operas." "Only a romantic spirit can penetrate the Romantic," the poet-narrator tells himself.[9] Don Juan, if taken literally would, he thinks, be a banal figure devoid of any serious interest; however, Mozart's music has too much depth and intensity to allow such a literal interpretation of the hero and subject—it urges a nonliteral, allegorical reading. So far I find myself in agreement with the narrator's thinking: the seriousness of Mozart's tone is such that we must either diagnose a disjunction between the music and its frivolous subject (a common criticism of the opera from the start) or claim that the music elevates the subject and thus eliminates the disjunction.

In Hoffmann's reading, Don Juan personifies the infinite desire for transcendence; he is a superhuman hero who refuses human finitude and longs for the divine: "Nature fashioned Juan . . . giving him all that brings man close to Divinity, raises him above the crowd. . . . [His is] that striving toward perfection which manifests . . . [man's] divine nature."[10] He seeks the transcendent divine, and, since no earthly object can possibly satisfy his desire, he must abandon each woman as soon as she has been seduced:

> In Don Juan's soul the Hereditary Fiend cunningly implanted the thought that through love, through the enjoyment of woman, he could attain on earth that which dwells in our breast as a heavenly promise only, that very longing for the infinite which links us directly to the overworld. Fleeting restlessly from one beautiful woman to another more beautiful . . . ; believing himself always deceived in his choice, yet always hoping to discover the utopia of final satisfaction, Juan was doomed to find earthly life dull and shallow to the end.

Thus contempt for the human condition of finitude becomes the obverse of the desire for transcendence:

> The enjoyment of woman was not even any longer a satisfaction to his senses, but merely a cynical mockery against Nature and the Creator. He was driven onward by a deep contempt for the common features of life, to which he felt superior, and by sardonic laughter at men who expected to find in happy love and its homely community of feeling the fulfillment of the highest wishes that Nature has treacherously planted in our hearts.

Don Juan ultimately rejects the creator of a self-contradictory creature endowed with a desire that cannot be satisfied, and he ends as the enemy of "a Being who seemed to him as one maliciously rejoicing in the misery of the creatures whom he makes and sports with as in a cruel game."

Hoffmann's Don Juan personifies infinite longing for the divine; he is an amorous mystic desiring to transcend the human condition of finitude, yet he is human and hence necessarily frustrated in his highest aspirations—a rebel who turned against God for making him want what he could not have (and who forgot that God's promise of reconciliation was to be fulfilled not on earth but only in heaven). Hoffmann's view captures something essential about Mozart's hero that explodes the limits of *Figaro*'s world, where the inescapable finitude of the human condition is accepted and even embraced. Since we are indeed finite creatures, the world of *Figaro* may well be the best available to us, but from the standpoint of a certain kind of max-imalist (Don Giovanni and, for those who believe Hoffmann, Donna Anna) that world is only second best, and it represents an unacceptable compro-mise. Our (their) predicament is that we can imagine, but not realize, the poetry of the best world, in which we would be able to abandon our finitude and transgress all limits; hence we (they) find the second-best world prosaic. It is a predicament resulting from misplaced religious longing—misplaced because it demands from the here and now what has been promised only for the hereafter. Attempts to realize on earth what is possible only in heaven inevitably end in mayhem and death: Don Giovanni's do, as do any attempts to realize utopia, for to attempt is to forget the definition of utopia. The only sensible way to live while on earth is according to the laws of *Figaro*. But a world in which we cannot remember or comprehend Don Giovanni's hunger for transcendence would be a sadly diminished and flattened one. Thus we try to live according to *Figaro* but with a self-understanding bequeathed to us by *Don Giovanni*, a memory of our inescapably tragic predicament, an awareness of our homelessness on earth.

But what if Hoffmann overinterpreted Mozart's hero; what if Don Gio-vanni is not a metaphysical rebel but only a force of nature, a personification of limitless desire? In that case his choosing a way of life so at variance with the way of life chosen by all the others—Anna and Ottavio, Zerlina and Masetto, the Countess and the Count, Susanna and Figaro—is, if anything, even grimmer. To live according to nature is to accept a world that is com-pletely amoral: nature is the realm where might is right, the strong devour the weak, and the weak perish so that the strong may survive. In Don Gio-vanni's Hobbesian world—Da Ponte and Mozart make this clear right from the outset, lest we, like Elvira, Zerlina, Leporello, and countless others, suc-cumb too easily to his seductive charm—daughters get raped and fathers murdered. Leporello spells this out on the spot: "Bravo: two charming under-takings! To force the daughter, and to kill the father" (Bravo: due imprese leggiadre! Sforzar la figlia, ed ammazzar il padre). When what Don Gio-vanni reveals turns out to be not a mocking divinity but the Darwinian bleak-ness of nature, then too the world of *Figaro* represents our best answer: eros saved by agape and the grace of mutually bestowed love transfigure, if only provisionally for a day, the amoral neutrality of nature, making it bearable for humans.

Kierkegaard's interpretation of *Don Giovanni* is not flawless, but surely no one in the history of the opera's reception, not even Hoffmann, has been able to match its richness and depth. It is also an interpretation that resonates particularly closely with the perspective from which I discuss the opera here.

In Kierkegaard's famous 1843 essay on the opera, "The Immediate Erotic Stages or the Musical-Erotic" from *Either/Or,* Don Juan is celebrated as the embodiment of sensuous immediacy.[11] Kierkegaard thinks in terms of the opposition between sensuality and spirit. What is essential about the sensuous (or "sensuous-erotic") is that it is experienced immediately. This lack of mediation results in two essential features of the sensuous. First, the sensuous is "abstract" or "indeterminate" (Kierkegaard clearly knew his Hegel): not one of the experienced instants refers to anything else or any other instant; each is unique, without a meaning that could be grasped by a concept and thereby related to other instants falling under that concept. "Reflection is implicit in language, and therefore language cannot express the immediate. . . . The immediate is the indeterminate, and therefore language cannot grasp it." Second, the sensuous is experienced in the present, and, strictly speaking, the present is the only dimension of time it knows: the sensuous "exists in a succession of instants." The sensuous "is power, life, movement, continual unrest, continual succession. But this unrest, this succession, does not enrich it; it continually remains the same." Further, "sensuous love is not faithful but totally faithless; it loves not one but all—that is, it seduces all. It is indeed only in the moment, but . . . that moment is the sum of moments." For Don Juan, "everything is merely an affair of the moment. . . . In the same moment everything is over, and the same thing repeats itself indefinitely. . . . The essential is completely abstract femininity. . . . Sensuous love is disappearance in time." By contrast, the spiritual (or, as we would say, rational) is not experienced immediately but only as mediated experience, and its proper medium is language. As a result, each present instant becomes determinate and acquires a meaningful relationship—mediated by a concept—to many other absent instants. Moreover, this relationship between what is present and what is absent opens up all three dimensions of time, connecting the present instant to instants in the past and future: one is no longer confined to a continual succession of Nows.

The opposition between sensuality and spirit defines two opposed ways of existing—the aesthetic and the ethical: the former embodied in the figure of Don Juan, whose life is a continual succession of meaningless, aesthetic (that is, sensuous) Nows; the latter in that of Judge William (Kierkegaard's invention), in whose life every Now is judged and hence meaningfully related to a past and a future according to an ethical system of responsibilities and rights. Judge William's life can become a coherent narrative—a story rather than a chronicle or catalogue of one thing after another. (Don Juan and Judge William are, one assumes, ideal types, since it is hard to imagine that a real person could embody in a pure form either of these two ways of existing; in reality it is a matter of one principle's predominating over the other.) Our earthly destiny involves the choice, the Either/Or, between these two ways of being. To avoid a possible misunderstanding, Kierkegaard issues a reminder:

> Rather than designating the choice between good and evil, my Either/ Or designates the choice by which one chooses good and evil or rules them out. Here the question is under what qualifications one will view all existence and personally live. That the person who chooses good and evil chooses the good is indeed true, but only later does this become manifest, for the esthetic is not evil but the indifferent.[12]

Obviously Kierkegaard's two ways correspond closely to the two strands in modernity that I identified in the Interlude. The modern moral-political outlook is an unstable compound of freedom and autonomy, an irreconcilable quarrel between those who cherish freedom of the will from causal determination and those who emphasize the importance of autonomy of the will, that is, rational self-determination. Don Juan is the quintessential libertine liberal, someone whose outlook maximizes freedom and minimizes autonomy, just as Judge William stands for those moralist democrats who maximize autonomy and minimize freedom. Their ways of existence consequently suffer from the Janus dangers of incoherence and inauthenticity: Don Juan, reluctant to accept limits to his freedom, is unable (or, rather, unwilling) to make a coherent, meaningful story of his life (Don Giovanni's "life is a sum of . . . moments that have no coherence);"[13] Judge William, committed to a system of communally shared norms, runs the risk that the story of his life will be scripted by someone else and thus not truly his own.

In the Interlude I contrasted two components of the modern view of how our earthly lives should be lived with the Christian outlook that relativizes our earthly existence in terms of eschatological destiny. Kierkegaard, too, ultimately finds his earthly Either/Or insufficient and leaps into the otherworldly Neither of the Christian faith. Of particular interest in the context of this discussion is that each of the three existential options—aesthetic; ethical; religious—emphasizes a different temporality, and each can be correlated with the three kinds of love analyzed by Augustine.

From the Augustinian perspective, what is essential about Don Giovanni is not only that his life is a catalogue of Nows but also that the only object of his love is himself. As he puts it, with characteristic honesty and uncharacteristic coarseness: "Since I am spending my money, I want to enjoy myself" (Già che spendo i miei danari, io mi voglio divertir). He lives as if the world contained many objects of desire but only one desiring subject—himself; the status of his women is no different from that of his supper. The ethical man, by contrast, not only makes his life into a coherent story that meaningfully relates each moment of present to both past and future; he also thinks of himself as one desiring subject among many and cannot exist outside of a community providing him with the norms that bind his past, present, and future. Thus he loves not only himself but also his neighbor.

Augustine objected neither to the love of self nor, certainly, to the love of neighbor; he thought, however, that a well-directed love proceeds from self to neighbor and hence from neighbor to God, each subsequent object of desire subsuming and transcending the previous one. He also believed that ill-directed love arrests the movement of desire before it reaches the final, supreme, unconditional, and eternally unchangeable good, thereby transforming self-love into selfish cupidity, or charity toward one's neighbor into idolatry. Only love of the unchangeable Creator can provide His creatures with secure happiness; otherwise they will forever be agitated by desire. This is why, for an individual, love of one's neighbor is not enough. Similarly, stable unity and harmony are possible in a community only when all of its members are bound by a shared, noncompetitive desire for a common object—and only God is the suitable object of love of this kind.

Like Augustine, Kierkegaard eventually transcended his Either/Or for a place beyond cupidity or idolatry. Neither *Figaro* nor *Don Giovanni* makes that leap. In both operas, all that matters is earthly existence; eschatology is beyond their horizon. This makes them into essentially modern artworks. The existential option represented by faith involves a premodern privileging of divine eternity over human time. Whereas self-loving Don Giovanni lives only in the present, and neighbor-loving Judge William lives in linear time, the God-loving man of faith lives in a linear time that is relativized and subsumed by an all-encompassing eternity.

Kierkegaard occasionally goes astray, usually whenever, in too close imitation of Hegel, he becomes obsessively systematic. He is overly schematic, for example, when, having recognized in language the medium of spirit, he claims that the sensuous-erotic can be "expressed and presented in its immediacy . . . only in music."[14] Presumably he makes this claim because music, like the sensuous, is only "a succession of instants." And, indeed, he elaborates that "in elemental sensuous-erotic originality, music has its absolute theme," just as sculpture has it in "human beauty" and painting in "celestially transfigured beauty."

There is no denying that much, perhaps most, music—in Europe and elsewhere—is a succession of Nows; to this extent Kierkegaard's point is well taken. But it does not apply to all music, and it quite emphatically does not apply to the music of Mozart—particularly *Don Giovanni*. All three kinds of temporality can be embodied in music; music can be a succession of Nows, but it can also aspire to suggest God's eternity or human linear time. True, "music does not exist except in the moment it is performed."[15] But it may configure its individual moments into a story and need not remain a mere catalogue of moments. To understand a moment of music in *Don Giovanni*, for example, may require that we remember the past and recognize behind one moment something heard previously. This becomes true at the largest possible scale, the opera as a whole, when the Commandant's return in the finale brings the return of music from the Overture. But it is also frequently the case at the smaller scale of individual numbers.

In the Act 1 Quartet discussed in Chapter 5 (see Examples 7a and 7b) the dramatic situation resembles a trial in which the accuser (Donna Elvira) and the accused (Don Giovanni) compete for the hearts and minds of the judges (Donna Anna and Don Ottavio). Close to the conclusion of the ensemble these judges—at first (from m. 74 on) gradually and almost imperceptibly, but then (from m. 79 on) more and more emphatically—take over the melody of the phrase with which Elvira had initially stated her accusation (mm. 1–9); clearly her message was the more convincing of the two, and they end up ignoring Don Giovanni's desperate cover-up patter without even having to use language to say so. The music here is more that a succession of instants, and we in the audience recognize the past in the present because the music forces us to take the linearity of time seriously.

Kierkegaard is right about Don Giovanni but wrong about the music when he says: "Words . . . are not suitable for him, for then he immediately becomes a reflective individual. He does not have that kind of continuance at all but hurries on in an eternal vanishing, just like the music, which is over as soon as the sound has stopped."[16] But Kierkegaard is forgetting the power of memory—our memory: Don Giovanni may not be reflective, but we are; and some music imposes reflection on us, forcing us to recall and recognize the past in the present.

Kierkegaard goes astray too when, again in a Hegelian fashion, he claims that *Don Giovanni* represents the perfect correlation of form and subject matter that is the mark of a classic work of art.[17] Similarly, he is surely one-sided when he proclaims that, because Christianity defined the sensuous-erotic as excluded by spirit, music is "the art Christianity posits in excluding it from itself. . . . In other words, music is the demonic."[18] Kierkegaard, in saying this, is privileging only the hellish cacophony that devils make and forgetting the music of the angels—forgetting that music is in fact the only art practiced in heaven. But Kierkegaard's tributes to the spirit of system are minor flaws when compared with what he gets right: the peculiar temporality of Don Juan's existence in the present moment only.

—

To a very considerable extent this is also the temporality of Goethe's Faust. In fact, as of the early nineteenth century Faust and Don Juan have frequently been associated.[19] The very term *moment*, or *instant* (Augenblick), plays a key role in the "wager" (die Wette; line 1698) that Faust proposes to the devil:

> If on a bed of sloth I ever lie contented,
> may I be done for then and there!
> If ever you, with lies and flattery,
> can lull me into self-complacency
> or dupe me with a life of pleasure,
> may that day be the last for me![20]

Faust immediately follows this with an interpretation that contains the key term:

> If I should ever say to any moment:
> Tarry, remain!—you are so fair!
> then you may lay your fetters on me,
> then I will gladly be destroyed!
> Then they can toll the passing bell,
> your obligations then be ended—
> the clock may stop, its hand may fall,
> and time at last for me be over![21]

Shortly thereafter he adds yet a further explanation:

> If I stagnate, I am a slave—
> why should I care if yours or someone else's?[22]

Decades later, toward the end of his life, Faust recalls the term when, during his encounter with Care (Sorge), he spells out his idea of how a man should live:

> . . . let him not break stride
> but, keeping on, find all life's pains and joys,
> always, in every moment, never satisfied![23]

The key term and the wager are recalled yet again in Faust's final words:

> If only I might see that people's teeming life,
> share their autonomy on unencumbered soil;

then, to the moment, I could say:
tarry a while, you are so fair—
the traces of my days on earth
will survive into eternity!—
Envisioning those heights of happiness,
I now enjoy my highest moment.[24]

And at that instant he falls and dies, "Augenblick" being his last word.

Faust's pact with Mephisto does not take the traditional form whereby the devil serves a man on earth, fulfilling his desires by supernatural means, in return for the man's servitude to him after death. Rather, Faust and Mephisto make a wager whose outcome is uncertain: in accordance with tradition, Mephisto is to serve Faust during his lifetime, but whether he will get the man's soul afterward depends on a highly ambiguous formula. Faust proposes that he shall agree to die should he ever become lazily self-satisfied. He couches his proposal in strictly temporal terms: should he ever wish a beautiful instant to remain—that is, should he ever wish to arrest the flow of linear time—then may time stop for him altogether. Goethe makes clear that Faust equates stagnation with slavery and slavery with death.

What is to follow death, if anything, is not spelled out, nor does it seem to interest Faust much; only his saying to Mephisto, "then you may lay your fetters on me," and his later remark that he does not care whose slave he becomes once he stagnates, suggests that the devil may expect Faust's eternal servitude after death, as in the traditional pact. Before Faust proposed his wager, Mephisto had offered him the traditional pact:

I'll bind myself to serve you *here,*
be at your beck and call without respite;
and if or when we meet again *beyond,*
then you will do the same for me.[25]

But Faust's answer could not be more explicit, and it is the answer of a thoroughly modern subject:

With the Beyond I cannot be much bothered;
once you annihilate this world,
the other can have its turn at existing.
This earth's the source of all my joys,
and this sun shines upon my sorrows;
if ever I can be divorced from them,
it cannot matter what then happens.[26]

This is the position he will maintain to the end, as is clear in the colloquy he has with Care shortly before he dies:

I know this mortal sphere sufficiently,
and there's no seeing into the Beyond;
he is a fool who casts a sheep's eye at it,
invents himself some peers above the clouds—
let him stand firm and look at what's around him:
no good and able man finds this world mute!
What need has he to float into eternity—
the things he knows are tangible![27]

On this point, at least, to judge by a conversation with Goethe that Eckermann reported from 25 February 1824, the position taken by the elderly Faust seems to have overlapped with the position taken by the elderly Goethe: "'Preoccupation with ideas of immortality,' continued Goethe, 'is something for the upper classes, in particular for women who have nothing to do. An able man, however, who plans to make something respectable of himself here and who, therefore, has to strive, fight, and act every day, leaves the future world to its own devices, and is active and useful in this one.'"[28] In short, while it is clear what would make Faust lose the wager, it is not clear whether his losing it, that is, his damnation, would involve just death or something worse. The devil may care and expect something more, but to Faust the afterlife is of no concern.

The difference between the wager in Goethe's tragedy and the traditional devil's pact may seem small, but it is essential. Whatever the actual nature of the fate that overtakes Goethe's Faust, his damnation does not automatically follow from having used Mephisto's services. Rather, damnation, if it occurred, would result from how Faust has lived. Both divergences from the traditional story are indispensable to understanding who Goethe's Faust is and what he stands for.

Let us consider first why it is that Faust's use of Mephisto's services is not grounds for damnation. In the "Prologue in Heaven" ("Prolog im Himmel") that precedes the presentation of Faust's earthly story (and which, together with the epilogue that follows this presentation—the "Mountain Gorges, Forest, Rocks," or "Bergschluchten, Wald, Fels" scene—provides the framework of metaphysical presuppositions according to which we are to understand and evaluate the life of the hero), the Lord implies that he considers the devil to be man's indispensable companion. "I have no hate for creatures of your kind," he tells Mephistopheles,

Of all the spirits of negation
rogues like you bother me the least.
Human activity slackens all too easily,
and people soon are prone to rest on any terms;

that's why I like to give them the companion
who functions as a prod and does a job as devil.[29]

Goethe's is a thoroughly modern Lord. Indifferent to such notions as good, evil, and sin—no wonder Nietzsche adored this poet—he wants man to be active and creative, never to cease striving, and he sets no goals or limits to the striving; to find both the goals and limits is, presumably, also man's business, part of what is meant by striving. It does not trouble this Lord that man will err while he strives: "men err as long as they keep striving." On the contrary, as the Angels famously say while carrying Faust's immortal part upward in the final scene, "for him whose striving never ceases / we can provide redemption."[30] In this Lord's universe the only real sin is to stop striving.

But man seems to be lazy by nature and needs the devil—the spirit of negation—to destroy his comfortable rest and spur him into action: to negate what is, to consider it worthless, is to awaken the desire for what is not but could be. If man is to be creative, he needs to be dissatisfied with the status quo. Evil is needed, if good is to appear. In this sense, too, destruction and creation are but two sides of one coin: destruction is needed to make room for creation. This may be the place to recall Goethe's dictum from "Selige Sehnsucht" in *West-östlicher Divan:* "Die and become!" The emphasis here is on becoming at the expense of being: "And as long as you don't have it, / this: Die and become! / you are only a dim guest / on the dark earth."[31] Goethe often sounds like a prophet of modern society, with its economy of creative destruction. Certainly Mephisto's self-description fits the Lord's understanding of the devil's role in the universal economy. He is, he says, "a part of that force / which, always willing evil, always produces good." He becomes more specific as he continues:

I am the spirit of Eternal Negation,
and rightly so, since all that gains existence
is only fit to be destroyed; that's why
it would be best if nothing ever got created [on this one point, the devil
    and the Lord part company].
Accordingly, my essence is
what you call sin, destruction,
or—to speak plainly—Evil.[32]

Men call the devil "sin" and "evil," but in Goethe, Faust's association with Mephisto is necessary if he is to fulfill his earthly calling to be active and creative.

Yet it would be a mistake to take Mephisto literally as a power external to humanity. He is, rather, a power within us and an aspect of who we are and of who Faust is—a distillation of the spirit of negation, and of rest-lessness and dissatisfaction with what is. Indeed, the doctor is dissatisfied and restless even before his encounter with the devil; he does not need the devil to awaken him from self-satisfied slumber. For Faust, Mephisto will serve merely as tool and enabler—almost a shabbily comic double like Leporello. Indeed, he is much like Leporello in keeping an ever sharp eye out for his own sexual advantage even as he helps his master—as is evi-dent in his encounters with Margarete's friend Martha, with the assorted Germanic witches of the medieval-romantic Walpurgisnacht, with the Greek nymphs of the classical one, and finally with the rosy-bottomed an-gels that carry away Faust's soul and distract Mephisto with unmistakably homoerotic longings. He is much like Leporello, too, in delivering all of the play's funny lines, though his intelligent cynicism is deeper and hence more chilling than that of Don Giovanni's servant. And he is also like Leporello, finally, in maintaining his shabbily comic tone clear to the end, when Faust's soul is at stake.

Next let us consider what would for this Lord be grounds for damnation: not necessarily any one specific evil deed or sin but the cessation of activ-ity, the end of striving, the self-satisfied rest. Seen thus, the conditions of the wager Faust proposes to Mephisto are likely to be concordant with the Lord's wishes. These conditions also account for the peculiar temporality of Faust's promise that should he "ever say to any moment: / Tarry, remain!— you are so fair! / then you may lay your fetters on me, / then I will gladly be destroyed!" He promises never to rest satisfied with what he has ac-complished, never to wish for a moment to become permanent, never to cease striving and moving forward. But not to want even a single moment of one's life to remain is never to recognize anything as worthy of permanence, to avoid all lasting commitment—and this is equivalent to making one's life a continual succession of Nows, in other words a catalogue of chaotic de-sires pursued one moment and abandoned the next. The alternative is to make of one's life a coherent narrative, a *Bildungsroman* of becoming a ma-ture, ethical, and committed person who knows which desires to pursue and which to avoid—a person with lifetime projects. But Faust aspires to a life temporally structured very much like Don Giovanni's, a life only in the present, without binding commitments, responsibilities from the past, or promises for the future. In Kierkegaard's terms Faust's is an aesthetic, not an ethical existence, let alone a religious one.

Accordingly Faust, like Don Giovanni, can in the end look back on his life and believe that he has kept his promise and remained paradoxically consis-tent in his inconsistency, committed to a lack of commitment. He tells Care,

I've never tarried anywhere;
I snatched from fortune what I wanted,
what did not please me I let go,
and disregarded what eluded me.
I've only had desires to fulfill them,
then wished anew, and so I've stormed again
my way through life . . . [33]

Like Don Giovanni, he shows no ethical self-awareness or trace of conscience. When he learns of Margarete's imprisonment he reproaches only
Mephisto—not himself. (Though in a sense, of course, Mephisto is himself.) In the opening scene of Part 2 his restoration and healing in the after-
math of Margarete's catastrophe brings no soul-searching with it; it is a simple biological process of forgetting, an undeserved mercy bestowed by
nature—and prefiguring the equally undeserved mercy the Lord will be-
stow after death. At the end of his life, in the encounter with Care, he rejects everything she stands for; not only thoughts of death and the beyond
but also any stirring of conscience that might impose limits on his cease-
less activity. It is his carelessness and lack of ethical awareness that makes
him—metaphorically and, finally, also literally—blind. Like Mozart's opera,
Goethe's drama is not a *Bildungsroman;* in neither work does the hero ever
become an ethical being, hence in neither can he undergo any process of
ethical self-discovery or improvement.

Obviously there is a necessary connection between wishing to live only
in the present and rejecting limits to personal freedom. Faust and Don Giovanni also share the desire for absolute freedom. In Faust's view, to commit
to any kind of permanence is to give up freedom and become enslaved. The
indispensable proximity of active creativity and destructive negation, as seen
in the connection between Faust and Mephisto, is clearly related to the wish
to escape all limits. Moreover, aspiration to absolute freedom, pursuit of desire without limits, the paradoxical commitment to a lack of commitment,
the privileging of becoming over being—all of these belong to the modern
outlook. (Goethe, who recognized this aspiration as particularly characteristic of the most recent poetry, embodied it in the Lord-Byron-inspired figure
of Euphorion, son of Helen and Faust and thus an allegory of modern poetry as offspring of ancient classicism and medieval romanticism.)[34] And it
is this aspect of modernity that is embodied in the stories of Don Juan and
Faust, perhaps the only truly modern myths we have. It goes without saying that the definitive versions of these myths are Mozart's and Goethe's,
respectively.

Goethe's lifelong obsession with the nearly contemporaneous Mozart, and especially with Mozart's operas, is copiously documented.[35] As late as 1830 he was still reminiscing about a concert in Frankfurt in 1763 "of the little man with his wig and sword" (des kleinen Mannes in seiner Frisur und Degen).[36] Mozart's place in Goethe's private artistic pantheon was at the pinnacle, a place shared with only two other masters of their respective medium, Raphael and Shakespeare.[37] And Mozart's operas were central to the repertory of the Weimar theater under Goethe's directorship.[38] They seem to have been no less central to the way the poet thought about the nature of music theater and about his own dramatic projects. For Goethe, Mozart's works—from *Die Entführung aus dem Serail* (1782) to *Die Zauberflöte* (1791)—were objects to imitate, emulate, and compete with; and always there was the sense that the composer had been there before and done it better. Goethe's description of how the 1785 Weimar production of the *Abduction* influenced his own 1784 *Singspiel* project with Philipp Christoph Kayser is emblematic: "All our endeavour to confine ourselves to what is simple and limited was lost when Mozart appeared. *Die Entführung aus dem Serail* conquered all, and our own carefully written piece has never been so much as mentioned in theatre circles."[39]

The spirit of music theater—both opera and oratorio—presides to an unprecedented degree over *Faust*, especially over its second part. Long sections of the tragedy read like a libretto waiting for a composer: in Part 1 the grotesque medieval *Singspiel* of the "Walpurgisnacht"; and in Part 2 the Renaissance masque of the "Mummenschanz" (Masquerade) scene in Act 1; the "Klassische Walpurgisnacht" of Act 2; the modern melodrama (9679–9938) of the "Arkadien" scene in Act 3; and arguably also the visionary oratorio of the final "Bergschluchten" scene (or so it seemed to a number of musicians, most notably to Mahler). I shall return to the traces throughout Faust of Goethe's long involvement with *The Magic Flute*. But, judging by Goethe's letter to Schiller of 30 December 1797, *Don Giovanni* represented the benchmark for what opera was capable of achieving: "The hope which you entertained for the opera you would have seen fulfilled to a high degree in *Don Juan* recently; however, this piece too stands quite alone, and all prospect of something similar has been frustrated by Mozart's death."[40] Hence it was not simply Mozart, but the Mozart who had composed *Don Giovanni*, whom Goethe named as the ideal composer of *Faust*: "The music would have to have the character of *Don Giovanni*; Mozart should have composed *Faust*."[41] What Goethe required above all was the musical representation of "what is repulsive, repugnant, dreadful" (das Abstoßende, Widerwärtige, Furchtbare). The similarity of subject matter called for music of similar character.

But the two figures and the two myths are hardly identical. To begin with, Faust intensifies and generalizes Don Giovanni's way of life in that his desires, unlike Don Giovanni's, are not exclusively sexual. Erotic conquests are centrally important in Faust's story, too: the seduction of Margarete is the main event that shatters the narrow middle-class world of Faust's exploits in Part 1; and once he enters the larger world in Part 2, Faust's main deed before he begins the final phase of his life is to seduce Helen of Troy. But Faust is driven by something deeper than mere erotic drive. We first meet the doctor at the point in his life when, disillusioned and dissatisfied, he abandons his obsessive pursuit of academic knowledge and turns from *vita contemplativa* to *vita activa:* what he desires now is not the contemplation of desiccated truth mediated through concepts but life—unmediated experience of the world through action. He wants to trade theory for practice, cognition for will, and truth for power:

> The thread of thought is torn asunder,
> and I am surfeited with knowledge still.
> Let us sate the fervors of passion
> in depths of sensuality!
> . . . .
> Let's plunge into the torrents of time,
> into the whirl of eventful existence!
> There, as chance wills,
> let pain and pleasure,
> success and frustration, alternate;
> unceasing activity alone reveals our worth.
> . . . .
> Henceforth my heart, cured of its thirst for knowledge,
> will welcome pain and suffering
> and I'm resolved my inmost being
> shall share in what's the lot of all mankind,
> that I shall understand their heights and depths,
> shall fill my heart with all their joys and griefs,
> and so expand my self to theirs
> and, like them, suffer shipwreck too.[42]

Faust wants the full measure of experience. By comparison, the figure of Don Juan, pursuing only sexual gratification, is rather limited, even banal.

In both figures the creative and the destructive sides are inextricably linked, but the narrow sphere of Don Juan's desires therefore also delimits the amount of damage he is likely to do; Faust is infinitely more predatory and dangerous. Unlike Don Juan, Faust at the end of his life does, for the first and only time, commit himself to an enduring task—the grandiose project of reclaiming land from the sea—and it is here that the sinister ambiguity of this figure is most clearly apparent.

Only once, in his last monologue, does Faust suggest that the purpose of his project is human happiness or advancement:

> If I can furnish space for many millions
> to live—not safe, I know, but free to work.
> . . . .
> creating here inside a land of Eden—
> . . . .
> If only I might see that people's teeming life,
> share their autonomy on unencumbered soil.[43]

He would furnish men with a new paradise, one in which, to be sure, they would have to work and defend themselves—"he, only, merits freedom and existence / who wins them every day anew"—but one nevertheless in which they would be free, autonomous, and able to flourish.[44]

Even taken at face value, however, Faust's words elsewhere, to say nothing of his deeds, suggest that what drives him first and foremost is the pure will to power, limitless power over nature and men. His utopian hope to create a paradise on earth may be genuine, but to bring this dream about he ruthlessly destroys real lives in the real world, creating a nightmare. Old Faust contemplating his project brings to mind figures like Stalin contemplating the construction of the White Sea canal, or, for that matter, Peter the Great contemplating the construction of his new capital on the northern swamps; Faust's paradise is one of those characteristically modern, grandiose projects of a despotic will who uses slave labor and is prepared to subjugate nature at an unspeakable cost in human lives.

In wresting land from the sea, Faust feels like the creator of his domain and behaves as its absolute sovereign; he shares power with no one, not even the two principal powers of premodern Europe: the Emperor, who had originally given him the land as fiefdom, and the Church. His is a quintessentially modern dominion—future-oriented, unrooted in the past, and without tradition. Of course no land is truly virgin or empty, passively awaiting the colonist's shaping will. Prospero found Caliban waiting for him on the "uninhabited island" of his exile. Faust's realm, too, contains a last vestige of what had been there before his arrival: the premodern Christian world of the old couple Philemon and Baucis, who live in the shade of a decaying small chapel. This world has not yet entered historical time and knows no striving or progress, but it is hospitable to traveling strangers and "trusting in our fathers' God." Above all, this world recognizes the usurper's modernizing project as "a counterfeit of Eden" (or, to translate less tendentiously, "a paradisiacal image" [ein paradiesisch Bild; 11086]), and it is aware of the human sacrifices required to bring it about: "Human lives were sacrificed, / groans of torment filled the darkness; / fires flowed down to the sea— / there, at dawn, was a canal."[45]

This last speck of the traditional world vexes Faust quite out of proportion to its insignificant size and power because it shows his limitations: "Ostensibly my realm is boundless, / but at my back vexation, taunting." He feels particularly oppressed by the sound of the little chapel bell that marks the cyclic, sacred time of baptisms and burials and reduces his profane time of progressive life projects to insignificance: "How to rid myself of this obsession— / the bell will ring, and I'll be frantic!"[46] With diabolical precision and cynical irony, Mephistopheles puts his finger on what annoys Faust:

> And yet that damned ding-dong-ding-dong,
> casting its damp pall on serenest evening skies,
> intrudes itself upon whatever happens
> from first immersion to interment,
> as if, between that ding and dong,
> life were a dream to be forgotten.[47]

He follows with the obvious suggestion that Faust leave matters to the secret police chief he has now become: "Why let yourself be bothered so by this? / You surely know, by now, how best to colonize." And at Faust's order ("So be it! Go and rid me of their presence!"), Mephistopheles departs with his henchmen to rid Faust of the vexing presence, killing the old couple and their guest and burning down their cottage and chapel. Characteristically, Faust feels no remorse; rather, Mephisto is to blame for this "wild, senseless savagery": "I wanted an exchange, not theft," he claims, conveniently forgetting that he had authorized the use of violence to bring about the exchange. Faust dreams of standing on free soil with a free people, but the actual foundations of his utopian project are violence and enslavement of colonized natives and mobilized mass labor: "Prompt effort and strict discipline / will guarantee superb rewards; / to complete a task that's so tremendous, / working as one is worth a thousand hands."[48]

Old Faust's unlimited will to power ("the few trees spoil, because I do not own them, / everything that I possess on earth") makes Don Giovanni's limitless lust (mille e tre) seem harmless by comparison.[49] But there is yet another difference between the two heroes: Don Giovanni ends "punished" (*Il dissoluto punito* was the opera's title); by contrast, Faust's soul is "saved" (gerettet; 11934). To be sure, the significance of this difference should not be exaggerated: ambiguity is the key to both figures. They both deserve punishment and redemption in some measure; the verdict ultimately delivered by their authors is a matter of emphasis, in both cases expected to be received by the audience with doubt.

It is not completely clear who wins the wager in the end. Mephisto considers himself the winner because Faust's final monologue envisions saying to the moment, "tarry a while, you are so fair" (11582). But Faust could legitimately object that he had spoken hypothetically about a highly uncertain future: "If only I might see that people's teeming life, / share their autonomy on unencumbered soil; / then, to the moment, I could say: / tarry . . ." (11579–81). In any case, whether Faust wins or loses his wager with the devil is immaterial to his eschatological destiny. To the end Faust lives up to his Lord's wish that human activity never slacken, even if constant striving might lead to errors, as it inevitably will. For Faust's Lord (and presumably for Goethe too), this was justification enough. This is not to say that Goethe is indifferent to Faust's errors: from the destruction of Margarete, her family, and her world, to the destruction of Philemon and Baucis, their guest, and their world, Faust's crimes in Goethe's retelling remain unredeemed by guilt or remorse; still worse, Faust's crimes are unredeemed by improvement or any sense that the hero is learning from his errors and becoming wiser. The dying Faust does reach a genuinely wise conclusion in his last moment: "It is the final wisdom we can reach: / he, only, merits freedom and existence / who wins them every day anew." But even this final wisdom is undermined by its context: only a moment earlier, Faust had urged his overseer to use every means ("make payments, offer bonuses, conscript them!") to spur the effort of his laborers.[50] Forced labor is the bedrock on which the sage is building his freedom and existence. (With Faust it is rarely possible to separate nuggets of wisdom out of the torrents of grandiloquence.) The lack of genuine development—the sense that Faust's striving may be incessant but has no purpose beyond itself—makes Faust's redemption utterly unjustified by any conceivable earthly standard.

The old Faust can on occasion (in particular, when he brushes aside idle thoughts of the unknowable beyond) sound remarkably like the old Goethe—a cold, ministerially impassive, Talleyrand-like figure; one would contemplate the prospect of inhabiting Goethe's despotic little Weimar with no greater enthusiasm than that with which Baucis contemplated Faust's offer to resettle her in his marshland.[51] But Goethe and Faust are far from identical. Old Goethe knew full well what Faust's problem was: "Nothing is more sad to see than the sudden striving for the unconditional in this thoroughly conditional world," he observed in 1830.[52] Similarly, "[it is] precisely the limitless striving, the unconditional passion, that drives us away from the world; the only satisfaction that remains for it when insurmountable obstacles appear is despair, the only repose—death." Finally, and most incisively: "Unconditional activity, of whatever kind, in the end makes one bankrupt." In part Goethe may be directing these strictures against metaphysical longings for the beyond, but only in part: he is not focused on idle longing for another world but on activity and striving in this one. What he condemns, of course, is not striving itself but the lack of limits on desire.

It must remain open whether the limits Goethe had in mind were specifically moral limits or simply limits resulting from circumstances. Is it a flaw in Goethe that to know how he personally would have judged someone like Faust requires turning to his private pronouncements? From the start Goethe had a knack for bringing characters to life—characters who are monumentally obnoxious, even repulsive, and yet also attractive—and then leaving the task of judging them to his readers. Faust is only the last in a line that began with Werther (last and infinitely less attractive than Werther, whose youth provides at least some excuse; there is no such excuse for Doctor Faust, the aging, burned-out academic, disillusioned with knowledge and greedy for experiences heretofore lacking in his life). Perhaps the artist's instinct was correct when it suggested that showing was enough, and that pronouncing a judgment on what is shown would have cast a pall of moralizing didacticism over the work. We cannot blame the poet for not delivering a moral judgment on a hero who at the end of his life can look back at a string of unregretted crimes and not a single worthwhile achievement. We certainly cannot blame the poet for those readers—and between Goethe's time and ours there were many—for whom Faust personified the triumph of progressive modernity, whether what they had in mind was the triumph of the West, the German nation, or international socialism.[53] Those readers forgot what Goethe knew: that incessant striving may be a necessary condition of a praiseworthy life but cannot suffice by itself. It is unclear whether Goethe also knew that striving even when limited by commitment to a goal cannot suffice—consider old Faust's single-minded pursuit of his land-reclamation project; and the poet's worship of Napoleon (for him a figure as great as Raphael, Mozart, and Shakespeare) does not inspire confidence in this respect.[54] We know that specifically moral limits on desire are needed as well. Without them, there would be no way of knowing why we blame the highly conscientious Ukrainian activities of Hitler's *Einsatzgruppen,* and we might be tempted to accept the murder of Philemon and Baucis as a tragic but necessary price of progress.

Be that as it may, Goethe could have had no illusions about the ultimate bankruptcy of his hero's limitless earthly strivings or about Faust's inability to recognize guilt and feel remorse. Nothing could save Faust, given that he had neither good works nor faith to plead for him. Perhaps Faust's incessant striving ultimately brought about the salvation of his soul but certainly not deservedly so. That instance of redemption is an act not of divine justice but rather of God's unmerited mercy, of the "eternally feminine" love that meets and complements man's striving (Das Ewig-Weibliche; 12110). Goethe's Lord, we have seen from the beginning, has no interest in moral issues; his beyond, unlike Dante's, where the good are rewarded and the wicked punished, is where a loving Yes is said to all of God's creation—even the part that fell and was separated from the Creator.[55] If any realm in this universe is fit for moral questions—fundamentally the question of proper limits on desire—it is the earth. And from the earthly perspective, unconditional activity ultimately bankrupts the perpetrator. Whether Goethe also viewed this bankruptcy as a moral one, remains, again, an open question.

If, despite traditional mores and Faust's earthly bankruptcy, Goethe allowed his hero a redemption in the beyond, it was probably because even more than limitless striving Goethe feared the self-contented sloth—the opposite of creation, the devil's empty nothingness ("it would be best if nothing ever got created"; 1341). Goethe evidently thought that, when all is said and done, something is better than nothing, and that human activity—self-assertion, creation—is all that can be opposed to ever-threatening entropy, descent into chaos, death, and nothingness. (But *is* Faust's something better than nothing? I rather doubt it.) In the world of *Faust* (again unlike that of Dante's *Commedia*) and in our modern world, humans cannot count on the beyond for help or justice: all help and justice have to come from ourselves. All we can hope for from the beyond is a loving Yes, extended to all creation.

But of course the "beyond" is only a metaphor, since unconditional reality remains "indescribable" in our thoroughly conditional and "transitory" world (these terms recalled from the Chorus mysticus that closes the drama); and metaphors are all we have at our disposal. Goethe uses the repertoire of Catholic images and stories just as he uses Greek mythology—as so many metaphors to hint at the indescribable.[56] His attitude is captured in the following pronouncement: "In Homer the human world is reflected once again in the Olympus that hovers like a fata morgana over the earthly world. This mirroring is a good thing in any poetic work, because it brings forth a totality and at the same time is a real human need. This is also true in Catholicism."[57] Goethe similarly explained the presence of the Catholic figures in the final scene to Eckermann on 6 June 1831: "By the way, you will admit that . . . , dealing with such supersensuous, barely graspable things, I might have easily lost myself in vagueness, had I not given my poetic intuitions a salutary limiting form and solidity by means of the sharply delineated figures and images of the Christian church."[58] Goethe's "beyond," too, along with the "redemption" it delivers, is a metaphor for our human hope that something is better than nothing; the Yes extended to all creation is ultimately our own Yes. (Here, again, is reason for Nietzsche's enthusiasm for the poet.)

In *Faust* Goethe delivered a highly attenuated and nuanced vote of confidence in modernity: he was fully—indeed, prophetically—aware of its destructive potential, but he saw nothing better on offer. His hero's final redemption should not blind us to the fact that his story is titled not *Commedia* but *eine Tragödie*. The affirmative Yes at the end feels strained because we experience Mephistopheles' No as a genuine temptation (Schopenhauer expressed this temptation even before *Faust* was completed); we are genuinely tempted because Goethe painted such a relentlessly bleak picture of the human world, a world in which the only hospitable enclaves are provided by the premodern naïves, among them Margarete and Baucis.

Translated into temporal terms, Goethe's recipe of conditional activity and limited (though never-ending) striving amounts to a recognition that what we humans need while on earth is not eternity—that is for the gods, or for afterlife in the unconditional world, for which we may hope, if we wish, but should not confuse with its "many-hued reflection" (farbige[r] Abglanz; 4727), our thoroughly conditional here and now. Nor do we need constant scattering in the Now of the present instant—that is for animals. Rather, what we need is something in between—the relative durability and permanence of civilization, freedom and existence won anew every day, and eternity made to human measure. The only alternative to this modest, limited something is nothing. By and large, says old Goethe in his final wisdom, the world is a slaughterhouse made mostly to our own design: make the best of it, he says, because nothing else is available—and it is better than nothing.

If, despite all the affinities that link the heroes of *Faust* and *Don Giovanni*, the view of the human world and prospects in *Faust* is so much less optimistic, so much more disenchanted, than the view in *Don Giovanni* (let alone in *Figaro*), this is not only because Goethe in 1831, unlike Mozart in 1787, was an old man who had seen and understood much. It is also because between 1787 and 1831 an old world had died and a new one come into being in a way that Goethe evidently did not think warranted more than guarded optimism.

7 *Die Zauberflöte,* or the Self-Assertion of the Moderns

The Magic Flute was Mozart's only major Viennese opera not sponsored by the court or prepared for the Burgtheater.[1] The Theater auf der Wieden, in existence since 1787 and directed by Emanuel Schikaneder since 1789, was a modern capitalist venture that had a rich private backer rather than the state behind it. One of several suburban venues that had sprung up in the 1780s, it had a frequently parodic relationship to the court theater and furthered the Viennese tradition of popular entertainment with an eclectic repertory of spoken plays and operas in German. (The Theater an der Wien which replaced it in 1801, and still exists today, would in 1805 host the premiere of the first version of Beethoven's *Fidelio*.) Capable of accommodating nearly one thousand spectators, it cultivated an eclectic audience to match, spanning the popular classes and the aristocracy.

An extraordinary proximity of high and low culture determines the fundamental tone of *The Magic Flute*. The conjunction of the "Egyptian" mysteries of the Masonic religion of humanity with the *Hanswurst* clowning of the opera's most memorable character, Papageno (the role created by Schikaneder himself), which was immediately noted, is epitomized in the Overture, where Mozart treats the patter of the comic bass with the learned fugal and contrapuntal seriousness of sacred music.[2] This proximity of high and low culture has delighted and offended in equal measure ever since.[3] A truly successful conjunction of the highest art with the genuinely popular is a rare and precious event in European culture. For the duration of the opera's run, Schikaneder's theater became the new Globe.

Prince Tamino, assisted by the birdcatcher Papageno, embarks on a mission to rescue Pamina, the girl he loves and daughter of the Queen of the Night. Pamina has been abducted by Sarastro, "a powerful, evil demon" (ein mächtiger, böser Dämon), who holds her captive in his castle. The mission fails, as the would-be rescuers are discovered and arrested by Monostatos, a Moor who runs Sarastro's security service and lusts for Pamina himself. Sarastro, however, turns out to be not an inhuman tyrant but a benevolent ruler and high priest in the temple of wisdom. Unwilling to force Pamina to love him, he surrenders her to Tamino.

Had the story concluded, as well it might, at the end of Act 1, *The Magic Flute* would have repeated the plot of Mozart's earlier 1782 Singspiel, *The Abduction from the Seraglio*, where the mission of Belmonte and his servant Pedrillo to rescue his beloved Konstanze from slavery in the seraglio of Pasha Selim is similarly thwarted by the Pasha's overseer, Osmin, but ends well thanks to the Pasha's magnanimity. But *The Magic Flute* does not end at this point. Act 2 serves as a sequel to the plot of Act 1, and the rescue opera is thereby transformed into a *Bildungs*-drama. If Act 1 replays *The Abduction*, Act 2 takes up issues from Mozart's one great, serious Italian opera, *Idomeneo* of 1781. In *Idomeneo* a young prince, Idamante, and an enemy princess, Ilia, must go through trials that show them ready and willing to face death before they are found worthy of each other and can succeed to the throne of his father. (Idamante even manages to slay the monster which, at the beginning of *The Magic Flute*, had nearly destroyed Tamino.) In *The Magic Flute* Tamino and Pamina are not granted the facile, unearned happy end of Belmonte and Konstanze. Rather, like Idamante and Ilia, they must undergo trials, including the trial of separation, and overcome the fear of death to show themselves worthy of marriage, initiation into Sarastro's brotherhood, and future leadership. What begins as a story of a young man attempting to rescue his sweetheart and landing in a situation from which he himself has to be rescued ends as a story of how two confused young people become mature, strong, and wise enough to earn a new life for themselves and their chosen community.[4]

Critics have long complained about the "break" in the story: the wronged mother turns out to be evil, the tyrant turns out to be good. But the break is not the problem; it is the point. *The Magic Flute* is about a reversal of values brought about by the passing of the old regime, in which the young and powerless depended for their happiness on the mercy of the old and powerful, and its replacement by a new order, in which the happiness of the young depends on their own acts and choices. It is, to use Ivan Nagel's illuminating formula, about autonomy replacing mercy. At the end of Act 1 everybody's future depends on Sarastro and the Queen. In Act 2 the future hangs on the efforts of the young—on their ability to raise themselves from the status of "princes" to the more universal condition of "men." (At their first encounter, when Tamino asks Papageno who he is, Papageno answers,

"A man, like you" [Ein Mensch, wie du]; at this point Tamino introduces himself as a "prince." By the beginning of Act 2, when one of the priests worries about Tamino's being a prince, Sarastro answers, "More, he is a man!" [Noch mehr—Er ist Mensch!].

But the opera is about more than replacing the rule of mercy with the rule of autonomy: it is also about the transition from a world at war to a world at peace. In this it again resembles *Idomeneo*, where the marriage of the Cretan prince and the captive Trojan princess after the fall of Troy reestablishes universal peace (although in the cosmic perspective of *The Magic Flute* the war between Europe and Asia might appear as a merely local conflict). From Rousseau through Hegel and Marx, one of the great myths, or metanarratives, of modernity is about the world that was once whole, was torn asunder and internally split, but will in future be put together again. *The Magic Flute* stages one version of this myth. While the husband of the Queen of the Night still lived, owner of the "all-consuming circle of the sun" (der alles verzehrende Sonnenkreis), the world was whole. Then moon and sun, male and female, were united. On his deathbed the husband bequeathed the circle of the sun to Sarastro and his initiates, ordering his Queen and their daughter to submit to the guidance of the wise men. But the Queen does not wish to submit; she wants to destroy the brotherhood, wrest the circle of the sun for herself, and rule alone. It is this warring world—the world of Sarastro and the Queen, sun and moon, male and female—that the union between the young, Sarastro's disciple and the Queen's daughter, is supposed to heal and make whole once again. (The moral cosmogony of *The Magic Flute*, incidentally, parallels to some extent that of *Faust*. When Mephistopheles first introduced himself to Faust he explained that "I'm a part of the Part that first was all, / part of the Darkness that gave birth to Light— / proud Light, that now contests the senior rank / of Mother Night, disputes her rights to space.")[5]

But why should a world whole and at peace be more desirable than a world asunder and at war? The six main personages of the opera form three pairs. Whereas Sarastro's counterpart is the Queen, and Tamino's is Pamina, Papageno finds his in Monostatos. These two characters are two versions of *l'homme moyen sensuel*: devoid of higher spiritual ideals and aspirations, not tempted by enlightenment and wisdom, they care mainly about satisfying their bodily appetites. (It is because he is a Rousseauist natural man who has never fallen into civilization that Papageno does not need to follow Tamino through the purifying, enlightening, civilization-healing trials.) At their first encounter Papageno and Monostatos are like mirror images of each other—a noble savage and a Caliban face to face, both equally scared by what they see. Lust is what they have in common. What distinguishes them is that Papageno longs for a willing Papagena with whom to establish a family, whereas Monostatos has no realistic prospect of winning Pamina's heart and hence cannot separate his desire for her from thoughts of coercion, rape, and murder. The distinction is in their very names, Papageno's suggesting—beyond the obvious association with *Papagei* (parrot)—paternity and generation; Monostatos's suggesting solitary existence. This distinction makes all the difference. Papageno can sing a duet with Pamina in which his desire is ennobled: "There is nothing more noble than woman and man" (nichts Edlers sei, als Weib und Mann—or, in Auden's and Kallman's paraphrase, "The highest goal of Nature's life / Is the sweet joy of man and wife"). Monostatos can sing about his desire only while Pamina is asleep; and even he knows that there is nothing noble in his wish to violate her, since he tells the moon: "Close your eyes, if it disgusts you too much!" (Sollt' es dich zu sehr verdrießen, o so mach die Augen zu!). Papageno begins in the Queen's service but ends in the realm of Sarastro. Monostatos's trajectory runs in the opposite direction: unable to get Pamina while he is in Sarastro's service, he switches sides. Monostatos can only thrive in a world at war, since there no one need be fastidious in choosing allies; even Sarastro had needed security police. By contrast, peace makes the world safe for Papageno, and making the world safe for Papageno rather than for Monostatos is the goal of human history as told in *The Magic Flute*—and told well: the twentieth century, which Nietzsche predicted would be the age of war between competing philosophies, turned out to be the age of struggle between Monostatos and Papageno.

As in any story of *Bildung*, confusion about values gradually gives way to increasing clarity. And from the start there is no doubt that not only Tamino and Pamina but also the audience will be educated and initiated: the opening three measures of the Overture serve both as the traditional theatrical gesture of knocking on the wooden planks of the stage to demand silence and as anticipation of the threefold chord of the Priests' horns that will accompany the initiation ceremonies of Act 2. The theatrical event is the initiation rite that it represents. The "problem" of the opera, if it has one, is not the midstream reversal of Sarastro's and the Queen's moral status. Rather, the problem lies in how we are to understand the conclusion to the cosmic conflict between the Queen and Sarastro, female and male, darkness of night and light of day, nature, with its elemental passions, and culture, with its controlling reasons, of superstition and truth, vice and virtue, vengeance and forgiveness, death and love? Does the conflict end with the total victory of day over night? This is suggested by the imagery of the final scene, where the defeated Queen is "hurled down into the eternal night" (gestürzet in ewige Nacht) and Sarastro announces that "the rays of sun drive the night away" (die Strahlen der Sonne vertreiben die Nacht). Or does it end with reconciliation and harmony between opposing principles, as suggested by the union of Pamina and Tamino?

The logic of the plot, which drives toward a dynastic marriage and youth taking over from the older generation (to say nothing of our own wishful thinking), supports the second reading; Sarastro's concluding apotheosis in the blazing light of sun would seem to support the first. But what is a post-totalitarian audience to make of the total victory of a leader who makes his first entrance on a triumphal chariot pulled by six lions while the adoring crowd sings, "Long live Sarastro! He is the one to whom we surrender with joy! . . . He is our idol" (Es lebe Sarastro, Sarastro soll leben! Er ist es, dem wir uns mit Freuden ergeben! . . . Er ist unser Abgott). Today we are chilled by a leader who says, "He whom such precepts do not please, does not deserve to be human" (Wen solche Lehren nicht erfreun, verdienet nicht ein Mensch zu sein). For that matter, how could early audiences have contemplated the prospect of such a victory so calmly, when fewer than two years after the opera's premiere Europe was to witness the rise of Robespierre? Isaiah Berlin, writing in 1958, judged Sarastro's polity to be "despotism, albeit by the best or the wisest."[6] A stanza from Joseph Brodsky's "The Berlin Wall Tune" also comes to mind: "Behind this wall throbs a local flag / against whose yellow, red, and black / Compass and Hammer proclaim the true / Masonic dream's breakthrough."[7] The modern outlook is an unstable compound of aspirations for unlimited individual freedom and aspirations for self-limiting collective autonomy. It is to be feared that in Sarastro's realm individual freedom would be sacrificed on the altar of the brotherhood's collective autonomy, the claims of *fraternité* trumping those of *liberté*.

Better to hope that the union of the young initiates may bring night back into harmonious relation with day (and that Pamina may further civilize the well-meaning but comically misogynist priesthood).[8] Although this harmonious outcome is not guaranteed by the libretto, it is not entirely inconsistent with it either, provided one does not confuse reconciliation with equality. The only problem with the Queen is, after all, not that she exists but that she refuses to submit: in a Platonic universe, unbridled natural passions should be controlled by reason. (Curiously, though, during their trials it is Pamina who leads Tamino.) The central portal of the Temple of Wisdom is flanked by the doors of Nature and Reason; wisdom presupposes that nature not be abandoned or suppressed but transcended in culture. Instead of being annihilated, the Queen, one imagines, is left to wander the subterranean passages beneath the temple.

Music is the symbol of the harmonious reconciliation in which nature is transcended by culture. While making their way through the life-threatening elements of fire and water, Pamina and Tamino are protected by the sound of a magic flute carved by Pamina's father from a "thousand-year-old oak" (tausendjähr'ge Eiche)—presumably the mythic tree of life. This sound now tames brute, inanimate, elemental nature, just as it tamed wild beasts in Act 1.

Using the power of music to wrest new life from the clutches of death, Tamino is a new Orpheus—new both because he is successful and because his music is instrumental rather than vocal (he is an Orpheus who does not sing). His success is an index of the unique moment of political and cultural optimism between 1789 and 1793. The optimistic belief then—that the earth can be refashioned so as to be, in the words that end Act 1 and recur in the second finale, "a realm of heaven, and mortals equal to gods" (ein Himmelreich und Sterbliche den Göttern gleich)—was unthinkable two hundred years earlier, when Monteverdi's Orfeo first sang, just as it is difficult to recapture today.[9] What is novel about this Orpheus's music, the fact that it is instrumental rather than vocal, is related to another revolution, aesthetic rather than political—one occurring in Vienna rather than Paris, and with Mozart, not Mirabeau, at its center.

It is striking, and for opera by no means customary, that the music in *The Magic Flute* heard by its personages (as opposed to the music heard only by the audience) is entirely instrumental: Tamino's flute, Papageno's glockenspiel and panpipe, the Priests' horns. Just before the magical instruments (the flute and the glockenspiel) appear in the Quintet of Act 1, yet another instrument is introduced: the golden lock attached to the birdcatcher's mouth to keep him from talking. The same sequence of events is repeated in the first three sections of the first finale: first the virtue of silence is extolled, then the virtues of the instruments are demonstrated—the flute taming wild beasts, the glockenspiel taming slaves. Clearly language silenced is a prerequisite for musical magic to happen.

During the two centuries preceding the premiere of *The Magic Flute*, music was thought of as a mimetic art inextricably linked with language and devoted to the representation of human passions: music performed passionate human speech, amplifying its persuasive, rhetorical power. This conception of music, arising simultaneously with the birth of opera, acquired its foundational myth in 1607 with Monteverdi's *L'Orfeo*, whose protagonist's song has persuasive force even over the powers of the underworld.

But by 1791 Haydn and Mozart had produced instrumental music of such high aesthetic interest and in such quantity as to put the mimetic conception of music on the defensive. In the quarter century that followed, this new Viennese music gave rise to a new aesthetic theory. For those like E. T. A. Hoffmann and Arthur Schopenhauer, music, once it is separated from language and hence abstract rather than mimetic, is capable of piercing the veil of phenomena accessible to language and thereby revealing, as no other medium could, the noumenal realm beyond. Music's subject matter is now no longer human passion but infinite totality—the metaphysical ground of being. Tamino's flute, because it intimates this noumenal totality, protects him and Pamina from the phenomenal elements. In *The Magic Flute* modern abstract music achieves a foundational myth of its own. And the abstract, autonomous subject of modern politics—no mere "prince" but now universal "man"—finds his medium in the new, abstract, autonomous art.

Goethe intimated that modernity would turn to instrumental music to replace traditional religious-literary myths of the past that had lost their validity. In the opera at the center of the Arcadian scene of the Helen act in *Faust II* (lines 9679–9938) he calls for "pleasing, purely melodic music of stringed instruments" (ein reizendes, reinmelodisches Saitenspiel), to which "all listen attentively, and soon seem deeply affected by it" (alle merken auf und scheinen bald inning gerührt [stage direction before 9679]). Mephistopheles thereupon tells the Chorus of captive Trojan women following Helen:

> Hear those strains of lovely music,
> liberate yourselves from myth!
> Do not cling to ancient gods—
> a sorry lot that's now passé.
> What you say, no more has meaning;
> we today are more exacting:
> nothing can affect our hearts
> that does not have its source in feeling.[10]

Abstract modern music, generating from the interiority of the individual composer and affecting the interiority of its listeners, will replace the stories of ancient gods, which are no longer meaningful. The women confirm Mephisto's diagnosis of the new regime of interiority (lines 9693–94): "We find within ourselves / what the world will not provide" (Wir im eignen Herzen finden / Was die ganze Welt versagt). From the beginning, Faust has been affirming that self, not tradition, is the only valid source of values: "There's nothing you can gain refreshment from / except what has its source in your own soul" (Erquickung hast du nicht gewonnen, / Wenn sie dir nicht aus eigner Seele quillt [568–69]). The wordless narratives of instrumental music step in to replace traditional myths because modern people, newly autonomous, do not want either their individual or their collective identities to be pre-scripted; they prefer to script them themselves as they see fit. The abstract scenarios of instrumental music can be filled with a great variety of contents, giving the moderns the flexibility they need while providing their stories with authenticating emotional intensity.[11]

On 6 November 1791, after hearing the twenty-fourth performance of *The Magic Flute,* Count Karl von Zinzendorf noted in his diary: "The music and the stage-designs are pretty, the rest an incredible farce. A huge audience."[12] This summarizes in a nutshell the reception of *The Magic Flute* from Mozart's day to our own: a great popular success, and with connoisseurs loving the music, perhaps admiring Schikaneder's stagecraft, but heaping scorn on the libretto. Stung by the criticism, Schikaneder stressed in 1795 that this was an opera he had "thought through diligently with the late Mozart"—a credible claim, given that the composer generally took great interest in the shaping of his libretti.[13] The most independent minds of the age—among them Goethe, Beethoven, and Hegel—disagreed with those who criticized the libretto. Hegel, in his lectures on *Aesthetics,* argued that in opera "music is the chief thing, though its content is given to it by poetry," and that a good libretto, steering clear both of trivial, worthless feelings and of excessive profundity, should provide the composer with "only a general foundation on which he can erect his building."[14] "How often," he added, "have we not heard chatter to the effect that the libretto of *The Magic Flute* is really lamentable, and yet this 'bungling compilation' is amongst the finest opera libretti."

Theorists stressed that modern music remained nonmimetic even when combined with language. Hoffmann and Schopenhauer believed that in opera the words served merely to provide a finite and random example for the universal, infinite content of the music. Hegel, on the other hand, believed that the text was there to create "for our minds a better idea of what the artist [composer] has chosen as the subject of his work."[15] Schikaneder's dramaturgy, in any case, stressed the nonverbal; even his detractors admired his skill in working out scenic effects. In creating magic in the libretto he relied more on spectacular scenery transformations than on poetry. The most potent indication of the music's content was not in the words but in the final transformation of darkness—the darkness out of which the Queen had mounted her assault on the temple—into the light of Tamino's and Pamina's initiation. The true "problem" of this opera is that the spectacular and auricular overwhelm the verbal, thus undermining explicit textual claims for the primacy of *logos* over appetites, senses, and passions. Platonism/Kantianism is preached but not practiced here.[16]

The essential content of the opera is transition from the confusion and darkness of minor to the clarity and brightness of parallel major. Mozart had already rehearsed this abstract but potently suggestive scenario in 1785, in the introduction to the "Dissonance" String Quartet in C Major, K. 465. Now he gives it a full-scale treatment: having created a trajectory from C minor to C major in Act 1, he also, and more crucially, reproduces the same tonal trajectory in the central trial scene of the second finale, the opera's denouement—which extends from the archaic Bachian counterpoint of the two Armored Men to the modern homophonic chorus that celebrates the triumph of the noble couple; the breakthrough to C major is achieved at the very moment when all speech is silenced to give way to the sound of Tamino's flute as it subdues the elements. Purely instrumental music, not language, accompanies the crucial step of emerging from obscurantism to enlightenment, thus linking the emancipation of instrumental music to the emancipation of humanity.

But to exemplify the utopian hope expressed in the music with the transition on stage from confusion and darkness to final clarity and light was to offer allegorizing interpreters an irresistible temptation. By 1794 three principal readings were in place.[17] In the French-occupied Rheinland an anonymous critic described Schikaneder and Mozart as Jacobin demagogues in the service of the Revolution, and the opera as an allegory of wise legislation (Sarastro) liberating the French people (Tamino) from royal despotism (the Queen)—Pamina, liberty, is the daughter of despotism. From Austria, alarmed by the French Revolution, came the anti-Jacobin reading of Johann Valentin Eybel: the philosophy of the Jacobins (the Queen) gives birth to the republic (Pamina), whom divine wisdom (Sarastro) abducts until the night is driven away and the light of legitimacy reestablished with the marriage of the republic and a royal prince (Tamino).[18] From Prussia, attached to legitimacy but not frightened by the Enlightenment, came the first outlines of a Masonic reading (Schikaneder's and Mozart's Masonic sympathies are indeed well documented): Ludwig von Batzko, in a performance review from Königsberg published in the Weimar *Journal des Luxus und der Moden*, emphasized the primordial struggle of light and darkness, good and evil, enlightenment and prejudice, with an attendant suggestion that these were Masonic themes. By the second half of the nineteenth century this allegorical interpretation won over all others; in the 1860s, for example, liberals who worshipped the enlightened, reforming 1780s regime of Joseph II were seeing the opera as the story of the emperor's struggles with the Church. The flood of Masonic-colored interpretations continues to this day.

The amalgam of diverse generic traditions that makes up *The Magic Flute*—including baroque-improvised Viennese popular theater, the fairy tales of Wieland, the dramatic fables of Gozzi, the scenic machinery wonders of baroque opera that, though no longer fashionable at court, were all the rage in the suburbs, and, of course, the Singspiel—determined its unique compound of high-minded solemnity and low clowning, of the sublime and the comic. Those diverse traditions soon coalesced into two main strands that went their different ways: the popular Viennese spoken comedy of Nestroy (who, incidentally, debuted as Sarastro) and the German Romantic opera of Weber. The artistic heirs of Mozart's "German opera" (as the composer called it to suggest that he was aiming higher than mere Singspiel)—among operas Beethoven's *Fidelio,* Wagner's *Parsifal,* and Hofmannsthal's and Strauss's *Die Frau ohne Schatten* are the principal ones— invariably chose to purify the sublime and leave the comic to parodists.[19] The tendency to monumentalize the serious and eliminate Papageno is also clearly visible in Karl Friedrich Schinkel's celebrated stage sets for the Berlin production of 1816.

Beethoven is said to have considered this the greatest of Mozart's operas, and this is confirmed by not only the score but also the subject matter of *Fidelio.*[20] Beethoven's heroine, descending to an underground jail to liberate her imprisoned husband, Florestan, is both a daughter of Alcestis and a younger sister of the Pamina who successfully led Tamino from the threatening underground labyrinth of their trials into the open. Even more important, Beethoven reproduces the underlying minor-to-major, darkness-to-light emancipation scenario of Mozart's opera in Act 2 of the final 1814 version of *Fidelio:* there the trajectory is from the dungeon and the act's first words, Florestan's "God, how dark it is!" (Gott! welch' Dunkel hier!), to the light of day and the first words of the triumphant C-major open-air Finale, the Prisoners and the People singing "Long live the day!" (Heil sei dem Tag!). (The link between Mozart's and Beethoven's enactments of this optimistic scenario is Haydn's celebrated Prologue to *The Creation* of 1798, in which triumphant C major emerges from nebulous tonal chaos with the words "Let there be light, and there was Light" [Es werde Licht, und es ward Licht]. As Count Waldstein prophesized in an entry in the composer's personal album in 1792, in Vienna Beethoven did "receive *the spirit of Mozart from the hands of Haydn.*")[21] Beethoven also used the scenario in his Fifth (1807–1808) and Ninth (1822–1824) Symphonies, as well as in the *Egmont*

Overture (1809–1810), and it became the exemplary archetypal plot of Austro-German absolute music until, in Adrian Leverkühn's words, the pessimistic, valedictory symphonic finales of Brahms and Mahler "revoked the Ninth."[22] The Ninth, culminating in a utopian vision of the universal brotherhood of men, can be thought of as one last nostalgic glance at the ideal of Sarastro's fraternity.

Understandably there were bound to be sequels to an immensely popular piece like *The Magic Flute,* whose own second act is a sequel of sorts to the first: like the French Revolution, the struggle between light and darkness is difficult to conclude.[23] Schikaneder himself came up with a moderately successful continuation of the story in 1798, titled *Das Labyrinth, oder: Der Kampf mit den Elementen,* which was set to music by Peter von Winter. But the spectral presence of *The Magic Flute* is most haunting in Goethe's oeuvre. Goethe's production of *The Magic Flute* in Weimar, which premiered on 16 January 1794, achieved more performances than any other work he staged there during his directorship of the Court Theater.[24] Although Goethe admitted to Eckermann on 13 April 1823 that the libretto's "improbabilities and jokes" were not to everyone's taste, he defended Schikaneder as someone who "understood the art of working with contrasts and of bringing about great theatrical effects."[25] In any case, Goethe spared the Weimar audience all of the Viennese improbabilities and jokes: Goethe's future brother-in-law, Christian August Vulpius, adapted the libretto for German Protestant sensibilities.[26] And surely Goethe found the Masonic symbolism of the libretto congenial—Sarastro's brotherhood has a lot in common with the "Tower Society" in *Wilhelm Meister.*

In 1798 Goethe abandoned the hope of completing his own sequel, *Der Zauberflöte zweiter Teil,* but he thought well enough of the fragmentary "sketch of a dramatic fable" (the original Gozzian subtitle) to include it in his *Gesammelte Werke* of 1807–1808.[27] And traces of the fragment's substance and form are everywhere in Goethe's later work, above all in *Faust II,* a magic opera in its own right (Goethe himself commented on the proximity of the Helen act, in particular, to Mozart's opera).[28] Goethe's conception of the figure of Genius—Tamino's and Pamina's son—is an early version of Euphorion, the son of Faust and Helen; he is both personification of modern poetry born of the encounter of the classic and romantic worlds, and the elusive erotic spirit of creativity in whom the affinity of beauty and death becomes visible (the Euphorion who overreaches is the Lord Byron who ends up destroying himself). But the projected sequel was doomed from the start: the only composer who might have brought it to life—Goethe's ideal composer for *Faust,* too, as we know—was no longer alive. The popular view of

Mozart as "eternal child"[29] may have entered into Goethe's decision to end the published fragment with a singularly moving image of the child Genius escaping from his sarcophagus like a butterfly from a cocoon. Set free not by the sound of the flute but by his parents' speech, the winged child melts like Ariel into thin air. Thus Goethe in his aborted sequel lamented the disappearance of the one artist whose presence was necessary for the work ever to be completed.

Between Utopia and Melancholy

Beethoven and the Aesthetic State

"And what music do you prefer?"
  "Oh, German music; that which makes you dream."
—GUSTAVE FLAUBERT, *Madame Bovary*

The music of Beethoven often appears like a deeply moved *contemplation* at an unexpected rehearing of a piece one thought had been long lost, "Innocence in Tones"; it is music *about* music. In the song of beggars and children on the street, in the monotone melodies of wandering Italians, in a dance at a village inn or in the nights of the carnival—there he discovered his "melodies": he collects them like a bee, snatching here and there a sound, a short progression. For him these are transfigured *recollections* from the "better world": similarly as Plato thought about the ideas.
—FRIEDRICH NIETZSCHE, "Der Wanderer und sein Schatten"

There is no vita contemplativa; there are only moments of contemplative activity abstracted and rescued from the flow of curiosity and contrivance. Poetry is a sort of truancy, a dream within the dream of life, a wild flower planted among our wheat.
—MICHAEL OAKESHOTT, *The Voice of Poetry*
  in the Conversation of Mankind: An Essay

THE MAIN THEME of the Adagio from Beethoven's Piano Sonata in C Major, op. 2, no. 3 (mm. 1–11), is a simple phrase (Example 11). The theme balances a four-measure antecedent with a consequent whose essential five measures (the phrase is elided with the next one beginning in m. 11) are expanded to seven by an internal repetition of the consequent's third and fourth measures. The first measure to be thus repeated, m. 7, marks the only ripple on the otherwise regular metric surface of the phrase: everything in it happens one sixteenth note too early. When the melody is repeated in the left hand in m. 9, the right-hand counterpoint shows what its correct metric placement should have been.

EXAMPLE 11. Beethoven, Piano Sonata in C Major, op. 2, no. 3, second movement, mm. 1–11

During the third and last repetition of the theme (mm. 67–77; Example 12), something goes wrong at the very spot where the ripple had first occurred: in the first measure of the consequent (m. 71) the pianist "accidentally" hits a second-inversion C♯-minor chord, instead of the expected C♯⁷. Annoyed, he covers up the mishap with a blustering fortissimo bravado, this time not a sixteenth but a thirty-second note too early, pretending that a 6/4 suspension of the G♯-major chord is what he wanted all along, adding an arpeggio for good measure when the suspension gets resolved, and skipping the second measure of the consequent altogether. After this brief one-measure outburst (m. 72), the theme continues in piano as if nothing had happened.

But something did happen. The two fortissimo chords wrenched the discourse for a moment to a different ontological level. Throughout the Adagio the pianist has been performing the expected role of a real musical actor impersonating an imaginary character who by means of musical gestures and speech reveals his mind to an audience. In this accustomed role the pianist

EXAMPLE 12. Beethoven, Piano Sonata in C Major, op. 2, no. 3, second movement, mm. 67–77.

is a transparent medium, invisible and inaudible behind the impersonated character, just as an actor is a transparent medium invisible and inaudible behind the personage he plays. But the pianist's "mistake" on the second beat of m. 71 and its "correction" in the following measure have an effect equivalent to an actor's slipping up and revealing for a moment his own face behind the mask—the face of a real, fallible human being. Because we know that Beethoven wrote most of his piano roles for himself, we can for a brief vertiginous moment catch a glimpse of Beethoven the pianist behind the nameless protagonist of the Adagio. It is this Beethoven (not the protagonist) whom the undeleted expletive of two fortissimo chords characterizes as both impatient (the premature thirty-second!) and violent. But before there is time to reflect that this "Beethoven" might be no less staged than the protagonist himself, he disappears into the impersonated character again.

From very early on Beethoven liked such shifts from one ontological level to another, from the staged imaginary to the equally staged real, and back—as in the Adagio—or, more frequently, in the opposite direction, from the "real" to the "imaginary" and back; that is, from the "real" world of the imaginary personage played by the pianist to a different "imaginary" world into which the mind of the personage momentarily wanders before being recalled to his "reality."

The last presentation of the main theme in the final Rondo from the same sonata (mm. 259–312) contains a similar moment of distraction (Example 13). By m. 281 the theme has developed a full-scale cadenza on a dominant-function 6/4 chord. But the lengthy trill that should close the cadenza wanders off distractedly in m. 295. What then ensues is hesitant groping, a step too high, for the lost V^7. By m. 306 the direction is resumed, and the passage can conclude. The moment of distraction accentuates the usual paradox of cadenzas: the longer the 6/4 chord is embellished with seemingly irrelevant digressions, the stronger the dominant and the more powerful the cadence. The same is true here: the momentary losing of the way strengthens rather than weakens the listener's sense of direction.

Another instance of a cadential drive's being strengthened by momentary loss of direction occurs in the phrase preceding the coda of the final movement of the Piano Sonata in G Major, op. 14, no. 2 (mm. 160³–89; Example 14). In this Scherzo, cast in the form of a simple rondo and composed no later than 1799, the dominant of G major is strengthened by three successive events: first the dominant is lost in a fit of distraction in which the bass moves chromatically up from d' (m. 166) through d#' (m. 169) and e' (m. 171) to f' (m. 177); then the main theme is looked for in the wrong key of F major (mm. 175–81); and finally the proper dominant is regained when the bass traces the earlier chromatic motion, but now in the opposite direction (mm. 181–84).

Yet another case is the main theme of the opening Allegro vivace of the Piano Sonata in A Major, op. 2, no. 2 (mm. 1–32), composed in 1794–1795 (Example 15a). This theme is a complex, balanced phrase with an antecedent articulated by a half cadence in m. 17 whose final chord is prolonged for four measures (mm. 17–20): the impression is that of discourse momentarily stuck in midsentence, requiring a forceful forte recollection of the opening gesture to get going again. At the theme's recapitulation (mm. 225²–52; Example 15b) the antecedent recurs literally, except that the dominant chord on which it got stuck before is now held for only three measures (mm. 242–4). A moment of absentmindedness follows (mm. 245–48), in which the three measures are repeated pianissimo a whole tone lower. What had originally been just a suggestion of getting stuck is now a brief but full-scale derailment. Even more than before, the return (mm. 249–52) is a forceful fortissimo act: the three measures are repeated yet again at a pitch that

EXAMPLE 13. Beethoven, Piano Sonata in C Major, op. 2, no. 3, last movement, mm. 259–312

(continued)

EXAMPLE 13 *(continued)*

EXAMPLE 14. Beethoven, Piano Sonata in G Major, op. 14, no. 2, last movement, mm. 160–89

EXAMPLE 14 *(continued)*

EXAMPLE 15 Beethoven, Piano Sonata in A Major, op. 2, no. 2, first movement

a. Mm. 1–32

(continued)

EXAMPLE 15 *(continued)*

b. Mm. 225–52

EXAMPLE 15 *(continued)*

returns them to the tonic orbit (though there is no telling at first whether the A chord is the tonic or the dominant), the consequent of the main theme is omitted altogether, and the transition phrase begins (m. 252). Unlike the two earlier examples, this time the pianist does not disclose his existence by making a mistake. There is no mistake. Rather, the protagonist momentarily loses direction and wanders off into a distant region and suffers a brief *absence*, from which he needs to recall himself forcefully into his reality.

Such spells of absentmindedness recur frequently in Beethoven's early piano music. In the concluding Rondo of the same sonata, for example, the main theme (Example 16a) consists of four four-measure incises combined to form an eight-measure antecedent, which is followed by an eight-measure consequent. Beethoven could easily have abbreviated this theme by half, into an eight-measure balanced phrase, by making the first incise into an antecedent and the last into its consequent. And indeed, when the theme recurs for the last time before the coda (mm. 135–48; Example 16b) it appears in precisely this form. Well, not precisely: after one and a half measures of the consequent, on the third beat of m. 140, the bass unexpectedly takes a chromatic half step down, whereupon through m. 144 the protagonist is sidetracked on a second-inversion F-major chord, the flat submediant; he recovers his lost train of thought in m. 145 by reversing the chromatic half step in the bass. As a result of this brief sidetracking, what might have been a regular four-measure consequent is parenthetically expanded by six measures (from the second half of m. 140 through the first half of m. 146).

Actually, the protagonist did not lose his train of thought completely, for he manages to hold on to the motivic substance of the theme. But another thought intrudes and, distracting him somewhat, prevents him from immediately completing the consequent. This other thought, a vague recollection of the A-minor tonal region of the Rondo's central episode, is promptly suppressed, but not for long. What is hushed up here is fully worked out in the coda (mm. 148–87; Example 17). There the chromatic bass descent to the dominant, f♯–f–e, in mm. 154–55 is, upon repetition in mm. 157–58, ar-

EXAMPLE 16. Beethoven, Piano Sonata in A Major, op. 2, no. 2, last movement

a. Mm. 1–16

b. Mm. 135–48

EXAMPLE 16 *(continued)*

EXAMPLE 17. Beethoven, Piano Sonata in A Major, op. 2, no. 2, last movement, mm. 148–87

(continued)

EXAMPLE 17 (continued)

EXAMPLE 17 *(continued)*

rested on f. Instead of moving to the expected e, the discourse gets stuck again on a second-inversion chord (B♭ major) in a tonal region that is closer to the A minor of the central episode than to the A major of the main theme. And this time the intruding thought will not be suppressed. After two measures of struggle it comes to the fore in m. 161, where the motivic substance of the central episode surfaces with the fortissimo violence that belongs to it. Only the return of the suppressed episode makes a satisfactory conclusion possible. The long-postponed dominant bass is reached in m. 165—at first as the dominant of A minor, then, in m. 169, as the dominant of A major—and resolved in m. 173. Only then (mm. 173–80) can the main theme be presented as it should have appeared just before the coda, that is, as a simple eight-measure phrase undisturbed by intruding thoughts.

The Rondo of the Piano Sonata in E♭ Major, op. 7, composed in 1796–1797, shows another variant of this scenario. In its last appearance (mm. 142²–66¹) the main theme (Example 18) presents the first three of its four four-measure incises essentially unchanged. The fourth incise, however, is expanded to twelve measures. In m. 155 a single note, B♮, shifts the tonality up a half step, from E♭ major to E major, so that the incise begins in m. 157 in a wrong key. After three measures the protagonist, growing insecure, repeats the third measure, hesitates for half a measure, and then, with a *ffp* gesture that changes the expected f♯¹ to a♭¹¹, returns to E♭ major as briskly as he had left it.

As in the preceding case, the protagonist does not lose his train of thought completely: he retains the motivic substance of the theme, but a half-conscious recollection distracts him for a moment. And again the recollection has to do with the tempestuous central episode of the Rondo—more precisely, with the way the episode was introduced: the second presentation of the main theme (mm. 51–62) dropped the last incise altogether, and a single note in a single measure, the B♮ in m. 63, affected the transition from the E♭ major of the theme to the C minor of the episode that began in m. 64 (Example 19a). This B♮, by implying the episode, now momentarily derails the last presentation of the main theme. Once the derailment has been rectified and the theme completed, and once the threat of the disrupting chromatic B♮ in m. 155 has been contained by the resolving diatonic A♭ in m. 161, it is possible for the motivic content of the episode to return to the surface in the coda (mm. 166–83; Example 19b); there it is expressively transformed into a gentle valediction and, in mm. 169 and 174, rejoices in the security of its B♭s.

Such shifts of ontological level—from the level of the "real" world of the character impersonated by the performer, to the level of an "imaginary" world into which the mind of this personage escapes, and back to "reality"—occur most frequently in music for piano solo (Beethoven was surely well acquainted with C. P. E. Bach's keyboard fantasias). But they also occur in music written for other instruments. The finale of the String Quartet in B♭ Major, op. 18, no. 6, completed in 1800, is an early example of this. There it is significant not only because it is occurring in a string quartet but also because the section being recalled is not necessary to the form, as the central episode in a rondo is. Instead what is recalled, the famous Adagio "La malinconia," is something optional—a slow introduction to the finale that, given its lack of tonal or formal closure, as well as the notation of rhythm in the last measure, cannot be considered an independent second slow movement. The finale, a light Allegretto sonata form without a development, is

EXAMPLE 18. Beethoven, Piano Sonata in E♭ Major, op. 7, last movement, mm. 142–66

EXAMPLE 19. Beethoven, Piano Sonata in E♭ Major, op. 7, last movement

a. Mm. 58–64

b. Mm. 166–83

EXAMPLE 19 *(continued)*

framed by the weighty Adagio on one side and a huge coda on the other. The melancholy, heavy Adagio thoughts return between the recapitulation and the coda, appearing with an opening dominant 6/4 chord (m. 195) that initially suggests a cadenza. The Allegretto has no small difficulty dispelling the Adagio thoughts, and it takes several false starts to get the music back on track with the expected V^7 (m. 219) and I (m. 221). The effect is that of someone whose mind wanders from its present concerns into an imaginary recollected world from which it can only tear itself away with effort. The sizable coda that follows is quite out of proportion to the slight Allegretto, giving the impression of a panicky attempt to talk down the melancholy. Panic is understandable, for melancholy threatens to resurface when the Allegretto slows down to poco Adagio. This time, in the final Prestissimo, melancholy has to be shouted down.

The rondo finale of the Piano Sonata quasi una fantasia in E♭ Major, op. 27, no. 1, composed in 1800–1801, takes the idea first essayed in the quartet one step further by recalling material from another movement, the preceding Adagio con espressione. (The Adagio has its own key and a closed

ABA form, so even though it is connected with the following Allegro vivace by a brief three-measure modulation, and the Allegro follows, like all the successive movements in this sonata, without an interruption, *attacca*, there can be little doubt that it is a separate movement and not a slow introduction to the finale.) The theme of the contemplative Adagio is interpolated into the frantic perpetuum mobile rondo just at the moment when the main theme should occur for the last time; it is literally interpolated, as mm. 256–65 could easily be removed without any loss of coherence. Again the effect is that of a mind suddenly lost in recollections; again the return to the present is somewhat forced; and again the coda-like Presto taking the place of the main rondo theme gives the impression that something needs to be "talked down."

In the first movement of the Piano Sonata in D Minor, op. 31, no. 2, composed in 1802, the experience of being lost in another world is literally thematized: the contrast between two very different worlds is itself the main theme of the movement (mm. 1–21; Example 20).[1] The two Largos that open the antecedent and consequent, respectively, each consist of a first-inversion, arpeggiated, pianissimo triad held with a fermata over a depressed pedal. At the moment of sounding, the triads have no definite harmonic function; this is not defined until the subsequent Allegros. The arpeggiation and fermatas, as well as the pianissimo and pedal, deprive the triads of clear metric definition, and this, too, does not get defined until later. The Largos thus achieve an indefinite, directionless, and timeless quality. They are pure sound—beyond space and time. The Allegros, by contrast, are designed to establish harmonic and metric definition. Their content is the drive to the dominant and the tonic, as well as the downbeat. (Note the accented dominant 6/4-chords on the downbeats of mm. 6 and 13, and note, above all, the explosive quality of the tonal and metric goal of the whole phrase on the downbeat of m. 21.) In the Allegros the mind of the protagonist is drawn from the world beyond back to earth, where the normal laws of directed motion define musical space and time.

But the hold of the world beyond is far from broken. The protagonist is lost in it again at the beginning of the development (mm. 93–98) and, even more profoundly, at the beginning of the recapitulation (mm. 143–71); here the calls from beyond acquire a human voice, as each arpeggiated triad develops into a recitative, always played "con espressione e semplice" over the same pedal as the triad. The other world, the world beyond, turns out to be the world within. And though the protagonist's mind remains in the here and now for the remainder of the movement, the other world is not entirely forgotten: the next movement, the Adagio, opens with an arpeg-

EXAMPLE 20. Beethoven, Piano Sonata in D Minor, op. 31, no. 2, first movement, mm. 1–21

giated triad that sounds less like the beginning of a new discourse than a distant memory of the arpeggiations heard before. And indeed, the arpeggiation is absent when the main theme of the Adagio is recapitulated (compare mm. 43–45 with mm. 1–3).

These spells of absentmindedness in Beethoven's early works—moments of distraction when the mind of the protagonist wanders off and gets lost in "another world"—are rare in the instrumental music he wrote after 1802 and before 1814. The best-known case from these years occurs in the Symphony No. 5 in C Minor, op. 67, composed in 1807–1808. In the opening Allegro con brio, a fermata marks the half cadence in the middle of the main theme (m. 21; Example 21a), allowing the dominant g" in the first violins

EXAMPLE 21. Beethoven, Symphony No. 5 in C Minor, op. 67, first movement

a. Mm. 18–21

EXAMPLE 21 *(continued)*

b. Mm. 265–68

to stand out; in the recapitulation this fermata develops into a one-measure Adagio flourish (m. 268; Example 21b): already in m. 266 the first oboe takes over the melodic lead from the violins and subsequently allows the g" to descend to d" (a detail that Wagner said opened up the meaning of the entire movement for him).[2] The fermata, which in the exposition merely added emphasis to the central point of articulation within the theme, now becomes the scene of a momentary loss of will to go on, coupled with the attempt of something struggling to emerge—a subconscious, private, individual voice embodied in the oboe solo sound that the main tutti discourse is trying to suppress. When the main theme is evoked once more at the end of the coda (mm. 478–502), the pathetically embellished g″ of the first oboe again wants to be heard (mm. 486–87 and 490–91), but is again suppressed.[3]

In the finale of the Fifth Symphony the interpolation of material from the third movement right before the recapitulation (mm. 154–206) likewise has the effect of a past moment's being recollected by a mind that abandons present concerns for that recollected world. This effect had already been explored in two earlier finales, those of the B♭-Major Quartet and the E♭-Major Sonata op. 27, no. 1. What we have in the Fifth Symphony is again a literal interpolation. The music could easily proceed directly from the fortissimo tutti dominant in m. 153 to the fortissimo tutti tonic in m. 207. Instead, fifty-three measures of hushed pianissimo stillness prolong the dominant and allow the individual voice of the first oboe to emerge once more in m. 175; here the oboe picks up the g″ with which the first violins had interrupted in m. 153 and, holding it for nine measures, descends through other tones of the dominant-seventh chord. This interpolation is the opening movement Adagio flourish writ large: both passages prolong the dominant in a momentary loss of the protagonist's will to proceed with the hard-driving and very public discourse, and both do so by allowing a solo oboe to emerge from the tutti and descend from a long-held g″. The difference between the two moments is that this time the oboe voice is not so much interrupted and suppressed as triumphantly integrated into the tutti as the descent from g″ is completed by c″ in m. 217. It is immaterial whether this triumph is perceived to be convincing, unintentionally comic (especially in the logorrheic coda), or, in the opinion of E. T. A. Hoffmann as interpreted by Thomas S. Grey, uncanny. "It is not surprising that Hoffmann should have reacted to the tonic excess of this coda," notes Grey; "critics have continued to voice subdued protests from time to time about this triumph that itself protests too much, that risks bombast and rhetorical overkill. . . . Yet Hoffmann's response here is no rejection of bombast in the name of moderation or *bon goût*. Rather, he suggests that our confidence in the outcome of the movement is undermined by its very vehemence."[4] In any case, the oboe is never heard from again, and the coda makes the impression of someone talking very quickly and loudly in order not to hear what can be heard only in moments of contemplative stillness. This, too, is reminiscent of the finales of the B♭-Major Quartet and the Sonata op. 27, no. 1.

In a more intimate vein, the opening movement coda of the Piano Trio in E♭ Major, op. 70, no. 2, composed in 1808, brings back material from the slow introduction (Example 22a). This, too, is an interpolation, in that m.

EXAMPLE 22. Beethoven, Piano Trio in E♭ Major, op. 70, no. 2, first movement

a. Mm. 219–34

(continued)

EXAMPLE 22 *(continued)*

b. Mm. 53–64

EXAMPLE 22 *(continued)*

c. Mm. 1–8

234 might easily have followed directly on m. 219, in which case it would have resolved the longest-held dominant of the movement. And again the effect is one in which a train of thoughts and actions in the present is interrupted to make room for a recollection of a past moment; this time, however, a few measures at both ends make for a smoother transition between the two levels of reality than in the earlier examples. Moreover, the recollection is subtly prepared in both exposition and recapitulation: the second subject of the Allegro ma non troppo is preceded by an introduction (Example 22b) that is audibly derived from the Poco sostenuto preceding the Allegro movement (Example 22c). What is really new here, however, is the character of the interpolated material. The spare introductory Poco

sostenuto imitation of a short subject, moving by step within a restricted range of pitches and rhythmic values, is calculated to evoke the air of what E. T. A. Hoffmann called "old church music"—the Romantic vision of Palestrinian counterpoint—and to contrast this with the more modern, though rather ancien-régime, Allegro ma non troppo that follows.[5] The subject's return within the *galant* context gives the impression of a music recollecting, in more senses than one, its own past.

For eleven years Beethoven almost entirely ignored the issue I have been following here, but in 1814 his interest revived, and in his late instrumental music he takes up anew the idea of compositionally representing a mind whose attention shifts from the present to "another world" and back. He revisits the scenarios rehearsed in youth, now endowing them with new significance and depth. Again the piano sonata provides the main arena for his explorations.

The first evidence of his renewed interest is a fairly modest form of momentary distraction that happens in the finale of the 1814 Piano Sonata in E Minor, op. 90, right before the last return of the main rondo theme in m. 230. The first return of the main theme and key at the end of the exposition, in m. 70 (Example 23a), was prepared in the usual way by a short, four-measure idea in the dominant key (mm. 60–63), which, when the idea is repeated and varied (mm. 64–69), is transformed into the V^7 chord. Recapitulating this same passage in the tonic key (Example 23b) would obviously move the music in an undesirable direction, toward the subdominant key (mm. 200–210). Beethoven avoids this by means of a deviation to an untonicized flat submediant (mm. 211–14), followed by a tortuous enharmonic modulation back to where he needs to be, the V^7; this is reached in m. 221, and the effect is one of a speaker who momentarily loses, and then quickly regains, his way. Both the dominant's delay and its subsequent length (mm. 221–29) strengthen the effect, so that the last arrival of the main theme is suitably emphatic.

In the opening movement of the Piano Sonata in A♭ Major, op. 110 (1821–1822), the common deviation to the subdominant in the first half of the recapitulation takes an unusually radical form. The main key area of the exposition consists of two phrases (mm. 1–4 and 5–12). In the recapitulation (Example 24) the first of these phrases reappears in the tonic (mm. 56–59); after a three-measure modulatory transition (mm. 60–62) the second phrase begins in the subdominant (m. 63), starts modulating again in the middle (m. 67), and ends in the distant region of the enharmonically notated flat submediant (m. 70). The recapitulation of the transition between the two key areas (mm. 70–87 correspond to mm. 12–28) stays in E major until the

EXAMPLE 23. Beethoven, Piano Sonata in E Minor, op. 90, last movement

a. Mm. 60–71

b. Mm. 200–231

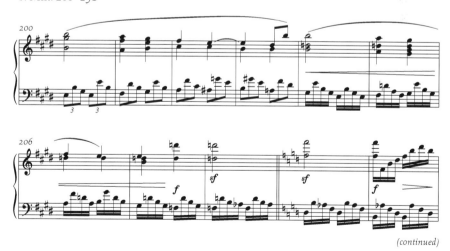

(continued)

EXAMPLE 23 *(continued)*

EXAMPLE 24. Beethoven, Piano Sonata in A♭ Major, op. 110, first movement, mm. 56–87

EXAMPLE 24 *(continued)*

(continued)

EXAMPLE 24 *(continued)*

third beat of m. 77, at which point a wrenching modulation rapidly returns to the tonic area: the music is "on" A♭ major by m. 79 and "in" it by the confirming cadence in m. 87. There is, of course, nothing unusual about the deviation to the subdominant in the first half of a recapitulation. The further deviation to E (or F♭) major, and especially the prolonged stay in it, is another matter. The effect is of a mind that barely manages to stay with the appointed thematic substance of its discourse but is strongly pulled elsewhere and can be pulled back only with effort. The E (or F♭) is forcibly abandoned but not entirely forgotten; this is evident in the flattened rather than natural f's of the final measures of the movement (mm. 114–16).

The opening Allegro con brio ed appassionato of the Piano Sonata in C

Minor, op. 111 (1821–1822), gives another twist to the idea of the subdominant deviation in the recapitulation. In addition to the usual turn toward the subdominant right before the beginning of the transition between the two key areas (m. 100), there is yet another subdominant area within the second theme (mm. 116–35). The moment of Adagio pensiveness (m. 121), which had been immediately shaken off at the corresponding spot in the exposition (m. 55), now develops into something more serious as the mind of the protagonist is dreamily pulled toward the subdominant (mm. 122–23), turns the theme over "on" that key (mm. 124–27), and then gradually returns to the tonic (mm. 128–35).

In the opening movement of the 1820 Piano Sonata in E Major, op. 109, the idea of temporarily losing the way ceases to be just a local effect and becomes an essential element of the structure (Example 25).[6] The Vivace, ma non troppo—kept together by a repetitive Lombard rhythm, motivically unified, and endowed with a clear sense of harmonic direction—is twice interrupted by an Adagio espressivo that sounds like a written-out keyboard improvisation, both motivically undefined and uncertainly groping for harmonic direction. (In a draft Beethoven marked the Adagio espressivo "Fantasie.")[7] On the surface, this is a twice-interrupted character piece that is both rhythmically and motivically unified. Indeed, the movement probably began its life as an independent bagatelle.[8] This surface hides the harmonic—but not the thematic—features of sonata allegro form: the opening Vivace (mm. 1–8) establishes the main theme and key and initiates the modulation to the dominant key; the first Adagio (mm. 9–15) completes the modulation by way of a complex prolongation of the secondary dominant (so complex that it suggests a momentary loss of direction); the second Vivace modulates further and develops the main theme (mm. 16–48) and recapitulates it in the main key (mm. 49–57); the second Adagio (mm. 58–65) reconfirms the main key by way of a prolongation of the dominant again so complex it suggests a loss of direction; and the final Vivace (mm. 66–99) functions as a coda. Forgetting for a moment the actual genesis of the movement, it might be regarded as a sonata allegro that has been transformed into a character piece. Instead of a second-key area clearly articulated by a second theme, it features long preparations of the second key that give the impression of an improvisatory search for a direction momentarily lost.

More far-reaching than moments of distraction are recollections of music from earlier movements, since in such cases the mind of the protagonist is not just threatened with loss of the here and now but actually does lose it in shifting attention from its "real" present to its "imaginary" past. This is the case with the Tempo d'Andante interpolated between the Adagio intro-

EXAMPLE 25. Beethoven, Piano Sonata in E Major, op. 109, first movement, mm. 1–15

EXAMPLE 25 *(continued)*

duction to the Allegro vivace finale and the main body of the finale itself in the 1815 Cello Sonata in C Major, op. 102, no. 1 (mm. 10–20). The return of material from the opening Andante at this point has the usual character of recollection and, with it, the usual effect of binding the individual movements into a single whole.

Like the Adagio of the Cello Sonata, the Langsam und sehnsuchtvoll section of the 1816 Piano Sonata in A Major, op. 101, is another instance where Beethoven amalgamates the functions of a slow movement with those of a slow introduction to a finale. He had two ways of doing this: either by giving the slow introduction to the finale sufficient weight to suggest an almost independent slow movement, as in the B♭-Major String Quartet, op. 18, no. 6; or by sufficiently lightening the slow movement and linking it up with the following finale to suggest an introduction rather than an independent movement, as in the E♭-Major Piano Sonata, op. 27, no. 1. The Piano Sonatas opp. 53 (where the Adagio molto even acquires the label of Introduzione) and 81a offer further celebrated examples. Undermining the autonomy of the slow movement accentuates what is already inherent in such movements, their tendency to represent a moment of reverie, an interruption of and escape from more down-to-earth thoughts and events. More important, the finale of op. 101 resembles the one of op. 102, no. 1, in that it also interpolates a recollection of material from the opening movement between the slow introduction and the main body (mm. 21–32); and it does so with a similar purpose and a similar effect. Whether using one method or the other, Beethoven makes palpable the process of reverie abandoned and return to the here and now, and he does so by forging a transition between tempi, meters, and motivic materials (see op. 102, no. 1/ii/mm. 17–20, and op. 101/iii/mm. 25–32).

On an incomparably larger scale, the same process of gradual awakening—this time from a prolonged reverie of the preceding Adagio sostenuto—is manifested in the slow introduction to the finale fugue of the "Hammerklavier" Sonata in B♭ Major, op. 106, of 1817–1818 (Example 26).

EXAMPLE 26. Beethoven, "Hammerklavier" Sonata in B♭ Major, op. 106, last movement, mm. 1–15

EXAMPLE 26 *(continued)*

The opening gesture of the Largo makes an obvious reference to the final arpeggiated F♯-major triad of the Adagio, but the shift of pitch by a half step down can be likened to the first stirring of waking consciousness.[9] Thereupon the protagonist gradually shakes off the dream and gropingly searches for the light of day—for the tonic key and an appropriate meter, tempo, texture, and motif; the search is held together by the bass descending systematically by thirds (only at the end, at the Prestissimo in m. 10, is the chain of thirds broken) before coming to a successful conclusion with the downbeat of m. 15.[10]

Later in the finale, just before the return of the main key, the relentless fugue is interrupted by music quite unrelated to it in key, motive, texture, dynamics, and every other conceivable parameter (mm. 250–78).[11] The contrast is so strong and complete that the new music—initially imitative and then free three-part counterpoint in even note values played "una corda," "sempre dolce cantabile," and "sempre ligato"—is like a thought intruding upon the consciousness of the protagonist from another sphere, another world. Like the opening of the Piano Trio op. 70, no. 2, this is another Romantic vision of *stile antico* polyphony sharply contrasted with the thoroughly modern polyphony of fugue—a message from, or rather a recollection of, another time: music's past.

The last movement of the Piano Sonata in A♭ Major, op. 110, combines several of the features I have been discussing: amalgamation of the functions of the slow movement and the slow introduction to the finale, recollection of thoughts entertained earlier, and gradual return from the recollected world to the one at hand. The Adagio ma non troppo that opens the finale, the Arioso dolente in A♭ minor (mm. 8–26), which is preceded by a Recitativo in search of the right key, meter, and tempo (mm. 1–7), is saturated with the kind of vocalism calculated to make the strongest possible contrast with the abstract instrumental gestures of the Allegro ma non troppo fugue in A♭ major that constitutes the main body of the movement. The sorrowful lament of the individual human voice is superseded by implacable but also reassuring superhuman order.[12] However, just as the fugue seems to be approaching the final cadence, it is arrested on the V⁷ chord (mm. 110–14), and a variation of the Arioso returns, this time in the unprepared and distant key of G minor (mm. 115–36). The effect, predictably, is one of present business being temporarily abandoned for a recollection of past experience. Return to the present is drawn out over thirty-eight measures (mm. 137–74) during which the expected subject matter, tempo, and key are gradually recovered; the return culminates in the arrested V⁷, and once that is finally properly resolved, the fugue is brought to a victorious conclusion (mm. 175–213). In this scenario, overcoming the painful memory of the Arioso is not experienced as enforced suppression of the individual voice but as liberation from it—a willing defeat and abandonment in favor of more satisfying superindividual order. The tone of triumph at the end rings much more effortlessly and, to my ear, convincingly, than the one that concludes the Fifth Symphony.[13]

Beethoven continued the explorations of his late sonatas in some of the late quartets. In the opening movement of the String Quartet in B♭ Major, op. 130 (1825–1826), the main theme of the Allegro emerges with some difficulty—only after one failed attempt—from a contemplative introductory Adagio ma non troppo (mm. 1–25). When the Adagio is recollected at the beginning of the development, the main theme again has some difficulty reestablishing itself—it now takes two failed attempts (mm. 92b–104). A similar situation also recurs at the beginning of the coda (mm. 213–21). The scenario in which the slow introduction is brought back at the beginning of development and coda goes all the way back to the first movement of the Pathétique Sonata, which Beethoven had completed perhaps as early as 1797–1798. Twenty-eight years later he uses the scenario to show a mind that is reluctant to abandon the realm of actual or recollected contemplation for the here and now.

The central movement of the 1825 String Quartet in A Minor, op. 132, alternates Molto adagio and Andante sections in an ABABA pattern. Here nothing is being recollected. Rather, the protagonist's thoughts oscillate between two worlds so strongly contrasted that they suggest two distinct ontological realms. A worldly modern galant dance in D major twice interrupts thoughts lost in another world, a *stile antico* world, in which a diatonic, consonant, cantus firmus–based counterpoint in F Lydian is so unfocused that C major remains a possible interpretation throughout.[14] The sense of being lost in another world and then twice recalled to this one, which is suggested by the stylistic clues, is confirmed when Beethoven explicitly specifies the content of the Molto adagio as a "Hymn of thanksgiving to the divinity, from a convalescent, in the Lydian mode" (Heiliger Dankgesang eines Genesenen an die Gottheit, in der lydischen Tonart), and that of the Andante as "Feeling new strength" (Neue Kraft fühlend). Indirectly, the inscription suggests that *stile antico* may stand for thoughts focused on the beyond, on the transcendent divine world; this may also be true in other passages where Beethoven makes that reference, including the opening of the Piano Trio op. 70, no. 2, and the music that interrupts the fugue in the finale of the Hammerklavier Sonata.

As a group, the preceding examples are admittedly quite heterogeneous—making up a family rather than a class. What they collectively show, however, is a composer's preoccupation with representing a mind that threatens to lose, or even does lose, its grip on the world at hand as it becomes absorbed in some other order of being. This is music that assumes the existence of two distinct ontological levels—the protagonist's real world and his imagined or remembered world—and that makes palpable the shifts between those two levels. Beethoven's preoccupation with this theme was particularly intense in the piano sonatas of the early and the late periods. But other genres show traces of it too, and even the heroic and public music of the middle years is not entirely free of it.

It is even possible to specify more closely the content of this "other world" that distracts the protagonist from his here and now. An initial clue is in the way Beethoven shapes the experience of time passing. In most cases the normal flow of time, characterized by a fairly regular and orderly succession of events and endowed with a clear sense of tonal direction, is interrupted and then resumed. Inside the interruption—and this is the most fundamental feature of the "other world"—the normal laws governing musical time and space, the sense of directed motion and the concomitant sense of change and time passing, are suspended. At the very least, operation of the normal laws is radically slowed down in relation to the surrounding "real world": the alternative world is not one of action and change but of contemplation of the eternal and timeless.

In some of the most characteristic examples, the contrast between the two worlds is represented by the contrast between two sharply differentiated but familiar kinds of music. Beethoven uses the clash of evoked styles or genres, each with its own traditional associations, to provide clues about the content of the alternative world. There are two particularly suggestive versions of this technique. In the one, exemplified in the Piano Trio op. 70, no. 2, and the String Quartet op. 132, Beethoven evokes *stile antico* in the middle of modern galant music. The contrast here is not only between present and past worlds but between the secular and the sacred, where the "other world" is characterized more specifically as the divine world beyond. But there are also cases that seem to point in the opposite direction, where, as in the Piano Sonatas op. 31, no. 2, and op. 110, unexpectedly vocal gestures appear in the middle of more idiomatically instrumental music. The "other world" here is revealed not as the divine world beyond but as the individual private world within.

Beethoven provided yet another kind of clue to the specific content of the "other world" in his verbal inscriptions in the scores. Sometimes these do no more than name the styles or genres of the music and characterize its expressive range; the terms "recitativo" and "arioso dolente" perform this function in op. 110. Occasionally, though rarely, the inscriptions tell us more: for example, that the introduction to the finale of op. 18, no. 6 has to do with "La malinconia"; or that the central movement of op. 132 is a "Heiliger Dankgesang eines Genesenen an die Gottheit." Intriguingly, these two last-named clues also point in two opposed directions, within and beyond. The contents of the thoughts that escape from the protagonist's here and now are either his own heart (his individual temperament and state of mind) or divinity.

Even more specific clues can be found in vocal and dramatic music. *Fidelio* (the *Leonore* of 1804–1805, revised in 1805–1806, and then revised again, with new title, in 1814) contains two particularly striking moments of stillness and abstraction from the ongoing course of affairs.[15] The four-part Andante sostenuto canon of the Act 1 Quartet (No. 3), which is completely static tonally and regular in its eight-measure phrasing, freezes all sense of change and the passage of time. At the Quartet's end the dramatic clock shows the same time as at the beginning. What happens in between is a timeless moment of inward reflection: only the audience is allowed to overhear the personages as each communes silently with her- or himself—"für sich," as the stage direction has it. Just before the Quartet begins, Rocco asks Leonore, "Do you think I cannot see into your heart?" (Meinst du, ich kann dir nicht in's Herz sehen?). But indeed, he cannot; nor can the other personages, Marzelline and Jaquino. Only Leonore and we in the audience can do so. In the Quartet the content of timelessness is inwardness. While the normal flow of time is suspended, the personages turn from one another and from the world to sink into their individual thoughts.

Another moment of stillness is the penultimate section of the C-major Finale of Act 2 (No. 16), the Sostenuto assai in F major, where a slower tempo and the subdominant precedes the final tonic jubilation. This is, almost literally, a moment of time frozen: "What a moment!" (Welch' ein Augenblick!), says Leonore, and her words are echoed by the remaining personages of the quintet—Florestan, Don Fernando, Marzelline, and Rocco—and by the chorus of the people. The moment immediately follows the drama's last action, when Leonore unlocked Florestan's chains; their fall to the ground is graphically depicted by the tonal fall four steps down the circle of fifths, from A to F major. Only with the jubilant turn to the final tonic section, when time unfreezes, do the personages once again begin to address one another: they are back in the real world they share. But in the timeless moment of the Sostenuto assai they do not address one another; they are not world-directed but turned only toward God, to whom they address their "Oh, God, oh, what a moment!" (O Gott, o welch' ein Augenblick!). The Sostenuto assai shares with the Act 1 Andante sostenuto Quartet a suspension of normal time flow, a similarly slow tempo, and the soundscape of pizzicato strings. But whereas in the Quartet each personage was alone ("für sich") and inward directed, now in the Sostenuto assai all share the same thought and direct it beyond.

For those who feel qualms about using verbal and dramatic clues in the search for the specific content of musical phenomena, it might be useful to recall the finale of the String Quartet in F Major, op. 135 (1826), where the head motifs of the introductory Grave and the following Allegro are set to words that introduce the movement as "the resolution reached with difficulty" (Der schwer gefasste Entschluss): "Must it be? It must be! It must be!" (Muss es sein? Es muss sein! Es muss sein!). The finale of Symphony No. 9 in D Minor, op. 125 (1822–1824), too, seems designed to demonstrate the legitimacy of this sort of interpretive practice. Here Beethoven briefly retraces the essential outline of the movement's initial instrumental section (through m. 207) at the beginning of the following vocal section, so that the voices seem to spell out what had previously been implicit in the music. Beethoven behaves here like his own Momigny.[16] The essential scenario is one of gradual awakening or transition, from one world to another—not unlike the way several other finales begin, that of the Hammerklavier Sonata in particular. In the Symphony the transition is from instrumental to vocal gestures, and from a tempestuous, angry tone to one of quiet but intense elation. The terror-inspiring noise of the winds and timpani gives way to low-string recitative (mm. 1–29), as do the snatches of the three earlier instrumental movements recollected one by one (mm. 30–91). Meanwhile the new tone and the new tune struggle to emerge, first from within the recitative itself (mm. 44–47), then independently of it in the woodwinds (mm. 77–80). By m. 92 the new tone succeeds, and the recitative is replaced by a song—a strophic communal hymn-march, intoned monophonically by the same voice that had pronounced the recitative before being picked up by more and more participants. After this breaks up (m. 208) a much-abbreviated recapitulation of the most essential events occurs, in which the same terror-inspiring orchestral noise is subdued by the same low-tessitura recitative; this in turn gives way to the same strophic communal hymn intoned, as before, by the soloist who had sung the recitative, with more participants joining in later. The text of the baritone recitative specifies the implicit content of this scenario: "Oh, friends, not these tones! Let us instead tune our voices more pleasantly and joyfully" (O Freunde, nicht diese Töne! sondern laßt uns angenehmere anstimmen, und freudenvollere). And indeed, what follows is the Ode to "Freude."[17]

—

Beethoven gives us various clues, then, to the content of that "other world" to which his protagonist is drawn. The most fundamental feature of that world is that in it the normal laws governing musical time and space are suspended, or at least drastically slowed down in relation to the surrounding "real world." This other, alternative, world is not the world of action but of contemplation. The object of contemplation during the suspension of normal time is either the interiority of the individual mind or God—either the world within or the world beyond.

What is the significance of Beethoven's preoccupation? What sense can be made of the fact that this artist, working at this time and place, was concerned to provide himself and his audiences with aural images of this sort?

I shall consider the particularity of the artist first. Beethoven's habit of temporarily escaping from normal social intercourse, to lose himself in fits of abstraction, was sufficiently striking for his contemporaries to have noticed it already in his Bonn years, when Frau Hélène von Breuning repeatedly remarked, "He has his *raptus* again."[18] May we then conclude that in his early piano music, a collection of roles he wrote with himself as actor in mind, Beethoven was representing his own mental processes—that, like our rock-and-rollers, he was "expressing himself," putting his own person on display? Perhaps. But let us not forget that the Latin word *persona* comes from the Etruscan *phersu*, meaning "mask." All we know is that the personages represented in Beethoven's early piano music and the persona the composer staged in so-called "real life," for Frau von Breuning and his other Bonn acquaintances, were equally given to fits of abstraction. Or do we know even that much? What if Frau von Breuning heard Beethoven improvise and confused a mask with the person? What if Beethoven confused them himself? What if he had been trying on different roles and masks to find out which fit him best—was using his art not so much to express himself (at the beginning, there is not all that much to express, after all) as to create himself, or discover who he actually was?

These cautionary questions are worth keeping in mind in entering the slippery no-man's-land between art and life, a territory ruled by the figure of analogy, or structural homology, between lived and imagined experience. The questions should not make us shy away from this territory (that would be equivalent to lapsing into the twin sins of a formalism that notices the text but not its various contexts, and interpretation that pursues contexts so merrily as to lose sight of the text altogether). There would be little point in paying attention to represented imaginary experiences if one were never allowed to compare them with one's own actual lived experiences. Much of the significance that art has for us is born at the intersection between imaginary and real experience. And what is true for us is no less true for the artist and his initial audiences.

More central, surely, to Beethoven's growing sense of self than any tendency to abstraction was his recognition at some point—probably in his late twenties—that his deafness was progressing and very likely incurable. A certain degree of existential isolation from others is built into the very structure of human consciousness: if we do not want others to know about a state of affairs obtaining in the outside world we share with them, we must try and hide it; but if we do not want them to know what goes on in our own mind, we do not need to do anything (to be sure, there are situations in which not doing anything requires quite a bit of effort). The conviction that our states of mind are more privately ours than anything else in the world, more so even than our bodies, lies at the foundation of our sense of uniqueness and distinction from others. But blindness or deafness are catastrophes that may transform this natural sense of separation into a profound sense of existential isolation: after all, we take in the world shared with fellow humans primarily through our eyes and ears. Someone growing deaf or blind is bound to be more acutely aware than others that the private world within and the public world without are two distinct realms.

Beethoven's known pronouncements on the subject of his affliction do not register any noticeable fear that the growing deafness might impair his ability to compose, though he does seem to have considered the effect it might have on his reputation as a musician or his ability to perform. He understood that the condition would above all isolate him socially. In reading the Heiligenstadt Testament of October 1802, the principal record of his reaction to his deteriorating hearing, one is struck by how little concern this musician—who was first and foremost a composer—shows for the effect his malady might have on his ability to ply his craft, and how greatly he is preoccupied with his human relations. "Oh you men who think or say that I am malevolent, stubborn, or misanthropic," he begins—not, Oh you men who think or say that my music is not user-friendly but willful and incomprehensible.[19] Directly after mentioning "the prospect of *a lasting malady*" he continues: "Though born with a fiery, active temperament, even susceptible to the diversions of society, I was soon compelled to withdraw myself, to live life alone." And later: "For me there can be no relaxation with my fellow men, no refined conversations, no mutual exchange of ideas. I must live almost alone, like one who has been banished." In the whole document there is not a trace of anxiety that his art might suffer. On the contrary, his art is what saves him and compensates for the loss of human fellowship: "A little more of that and I would have ended my life—it was only *my art* that held me back. Ah, it seemed to me impossible to leave the world until I had brought forth all that I felt was within me."

Maynard Solomon has shrewdly observed that the Testament is "a carefully revised 'fair copy' which has been scrubbed clean of much of its original emotion."[20] The document is all the more compelling for representing not a spontaneous, possibly momentary, reaction to a misfortune but rather a carefully considered response. That this response became Beethoven's permanent resolve is evident from the similarity between the pronouncements of the Testament and those in letters and documents from later periods of his life. Thus a letter of 1810 reads: "So be it then: for you, poor B[eethoven], there is no happiness in the outer world, you must create it in yourself. Only in the ideal world can you find friends."[21] Even more revealing, perhaps, are the entries in the private *Tagebuch* that Beethoven kept between 1812 and 1818. An entry of 1812 reads: "You must not be a *human being, not for yourself, but only for others:* for you there is no longer any happiness except within yourself, in your art. O God! give me strength to conquer myself, nothing at all must fetter me to life."[22] In 1815 Beethoven notes: "Everything that is called life should be sacrificed to the sublime and be a sanctuary of art." Similarly, a year later: "Live only in your art, for you are so limited by your senses. This is nevertheless the *only existence* for you." And in 1818: "Sacrifice once and for all the trivialities of social life to your art."

We do not choose our fate, but we do, to a certain extent, have a choice over the manner in which we meet fate and the sense we make of it. Beethoven did not choose his malady, nor did he choose to interpret it as a threat to his calling. But he did choose to see it as banishment from the human world to that of art. Momentary fits of abstraction deepened into a permanent existential condition. Indeed, in Beethoven's mind there was a connection between the two stages. In the earliest communication from him on the subject, a letter of 29 June 1801 to Franz Wegeler in Bonn, he wrote: "It is surprising that some people have never noticed my deafness; but since I have always been liable to fits of absentmindedness, they attribute my hardness of hearing to that."[23]

It is not unreasonable to suppose that Beethoven's deafness, in combination with his extraordinary musical powers, contributed to his feeling a profound cleft between the world without—the public realm of human fellowship and sociability—and the world within, the private realm of the mind and art. If so, Beethoven would have resonated to the idea of creating aural images of a mind torn between two distinct ontological regions. Music lends itself to self-exploration and self-revelation; in that medium he would be able to try on different masks and rehearse, by means of fictional personages, different ways in which a fate like his might be met, and thus he would learn what kind of a person he was or wanted to be. For Beethoven, given that his private realm of the mind was filled with art, moments when fictional personages are distracted or absorbed in their own thoughts thus stand metonymically for the whole of his art.

—

In this context the specific features of the "other world" take on a new light. In this realm, in which a Beethovenian protagonist gets lost when his "real world" loses its hold on him, the normal flow of time is suspended—it is the realm of contemplation rather than action. This description overlaps remarkably well with the structure of aesthetic experience as Kant conceived it. Kant taught that when the mind is engaged in the activity of knowing, when it experiences the objective world, it must perceive objects in space and time, must synthesize the data of perception in imagination, and must think the synthesized images through concepts applied in understanding. This account of the structure of objective experience implies that behind the objective, knowable world of *phenomena* lies a completely unknowable realm of *noumena*—things as they are in themselves, undisturbed by the mental activities of perception, imagination, and understanding that provide whatever it is that affects our senses in the first place. Moreover, the *noumenon*—unknowable and not subject to perceptual forms of space and time—is nevertheless implied not only by our cognitive experience, our experience of the objective world, but also by our moral experience, our conviction that we are endowed with free will and have the power to do our duty even when it conflicts with our desire. This suggests that man is simultaneously a phenomenon, a natural object governed by causality like all other phenomena, and a noumenon, a morally free active subject independent of the causal order of nature.

Although the mind, in knowing the objective world, fits appropriate concepts with particular images, there are situations where no such fit is possible. One such situation is when reason finds a legitimate regulative use for its ideas—that is, concepts such as world, soul, or God—for which, because they refer to infinite entities, no adequate images can be found. The opposite situation is also possible: one may have, and find legitimate use for, the so-called aesthetic ideas presented in art, that is, representations for which no adequate concepts can be found since they strive to go beyond the limits of all possible experience. "But, by an aesthetic idea," writes Kant, "I mean that representation of the imagination which induces much thought, yet without the possibility of any definite thought whatever, i.e., *concept*, being adequate to it, and which language, consequently, can never get quite on level terms with or render completely intelligible."[24] And further: "Beauty (whether it be of nature or of art) may in general be termed the *expression* of aesthetic ideas." It is one of the functions of art to embody such ideas, to represent that which cannot be represented, to provide hints of the transcendent realm. The *noumenon*, implied by our cognitive experience of the objective world and our moral experience of freedom, is also intimated in our aesthetic experience, in the contemplation of art.

In Beethoven's lifetime the phenomenal-noumenal split was hotly debated in German philosophical circles but readily accepted by the broader intellectual opinion, for it gave new life to thinking in terms of two distinct ontological realms—a point of view that European culture, with its Platonic and Christian roots, had long embraced. A kind of soft Kantianism suffused the intellectual life of the period (somewhat akin to the soft Freudianism and Marxism that until recently suffused our own), providing the educated and half-educated with a repertoire of ready-made notions and images that could be taken for granted without necessarily being examined. Similarly, the thought that art may provide intimations of the transcendental realm was bound to be attractive to artists who, newly emancipated from the comforts and certainties of ecclesiastical or courtly servitude, were now subject to both the opportunities and rigors of the market and thus in search of a legitimating social function. Musicians were to be the greatest beneficiaries of this thought: still during Beethoven's lifetime, E. T. A. Hoffmann and Arthur Schopenhauer argued independently of each other that music is particularly well suited to disclose the noumenal.[25]

Beethoven's stance on this matter is most famously documented in his enthusiastic notation in a conversation book of early February 1820: "The moral law within us, and the starry heavens above us Kant!!!" (das Moralische Gesez in unß, u. der gestirnte Himel über unß Kant!!!).[26] The "gestirnte Himmel über uns" resonates with the Ninth Symphony's "Sternenzelt" (starry tent) above which "muß ein lieber Vater wohnen" (must dwell a loving father). In Kant's shorthand for the moral and cognitive experiences that hint at something transcendent, Beethoven found the formula for his own double-faced transcendent realm—the world within and the world beyond.

This intellectual climate provides a vantage point for considering the significance—both for this particular composer and for some of the listeners at that particular time and place—of Beethoven's preoccupation with representing a mind drawn from this world to the contemplation of its own interiority or matters divine. From this perspective, Beethoven's music may have been heard as occasionally staging its own mode of reception, dramatizing the act of aesthetic contemplation and absorption in the transcendent realm disclosed by art, in short, as embodying the aesthetic state itself. Nietzsche's intuition was unerring: Beethoven not only writes "music *about* music," he also writes music about hearing music.[27]

For an early nineteenth-century artist and intellectual who had accepted these Kantian notions and images, there were, roughly speaking, two ways of dealing with the phenomenal-noumenal division (roughly speaking, because in practice the two ways of proceeding were endlessly and variously combined). One was to experience the split as a painful fissure—between the actually existing world, the world as it was; and the ideal world, the world as it should be—and to attempt to heal that ontological wound and bring the actual and the ideal into harmony. Rousseau was as important a source for this line of thinking as Kant: Rousseau saw man as originally good and whole, his capacities in harmony and himself in harmony with his fellow men, corrupted by the multiple artificial needs bred by modern civilization; as a result, man, now alienated from himself and his fellows, came to need a force to make him and his society whole again, a bond whose "Zauber bindet wieder, was die Mode streng geteilt" (magic binds again what fashion had strictly divided), ensuring that "alle Menschen werden Brüder" (all men become brothers). This hopeful, modernist, progressive vision of earthly redemption was promised by the finale of the Ninth. The other way to deal with the split was to find the phenomenal world corrupt beyond any hope of repair and to pine in a reactionary and more or less explicitly Christian fashion for escape—to hope, with Florestan, for "Lohn in bessern Welten" (recompense in better worlds).

As Nietzsche put it: "Both those spirits of a classical and those of a romantic bent . . . entertain a vision of the future: but the former do so out of a strength of their age, the latter out of its weakness."[28] It would not be entirely wrong to associate the first of the two strategies sketched above with the Weimar classicism of Schiller and the second with the Romantics; not entirely wrong (this was, after all, how Schiller's most enthusiastic readers in the nineteenth century, people like Herzen or Verdi, understood him) but far too neat, too pat. A more nuanced reading of Schiller would reveal some hesitation on his part as to which of the two strategies to adopt. Readers of the *Letters on the Aesthetic Education of Man* have long been aware of this hesitation. It is traditional to read the *Letters* as Schiller's response to the Revolution and its degeneration into the Terror. Schiller envisages that art will help man harmonize the sensuous with the rational, enabling him to overcome the divisions within himself and between him and his fellows: "If man is ever to solve that problem of politics in practice he will have to approach it through the problem of the aesthetic, because it is only through Beauty that man makes his way to Freedom," he announces at the outset.[29] The lesson of the Terror—that an attempt to establish the rule of reason had degenerated into the rule of naked force—suggested to Schiller that a successful revolution required an aesthetic education as preparation for rational self-government. So far Schiller is fully consistent with the first strategy. But by the end of the *Letters* the reader is no longer sure whether the aesthetic state is a school for mankind, preparing it for a disalienated and fulfilled life on earth, or a substitute for a state of political freedom—whether beauty is a stepping stone to freedom, or a true locus of freedom itself—in short, whether Schiller's project is, in Nietzsche's sense, classic or romantic, his freedom the state in which "alle Menschen werden Brüder" or in which one can only dream of a "Lohn in bessern Welten."[30] By the end of the *Letters,* in Hans-Georg Gadamer's view, "in place of the true moral and political freedom, for which art should prepare us, we have the culture of an 'aesthetic state,' an educated society which is interested in art."[31]

It would be a mistake to see Schiller's indecision merely as a peculiarity of his—or German intellectuals'—response to the Terror. The indecisiveness here has deeper roots; it precedes the Revolution itself and transcends the local German response to it. A close cousin of Beethovenian fits of abstraction is the literary genre of reverie made fashionable by Rousseau. As Jean Starobinski has pointed out,

> When he wrote *Émile,* when he took refuge in reverie, Rousseau seemed to have given up hoping for anything more than a respite for the individual. At a crucial moment in which the human mind was discovering the reality of history and its own link with the historical moment, it was almost simultaneously tempted to find its salvation, not in and through history, but apart from it, and almost in contempt of its hitherto inevitable constraint. One whole aspect of Rousseau's work offers his contemporaries a pessimistic reading of history, and the prospect of finding refuge in the solitude of personal existence. This part of Rousseau's writings, though it is not the whole, acted as a guide to superior souls horrified by the way the world was going and seeking happiness in a secret belief in their own innocence. The state of crisis and the age of revolutions were, for the individual, a schism which threw him back on his own autonomy, his difference, and his painful survival in a universe inhabited by death.[32]

The aesthetic as an escape from the practical, from history: from Rousseau through Schopenhauer and beyond, this has remained an enduring option, or temptation, for us moderns. It has endured at least through the middle of the twentieth century, if Michael Oakeshott's testimony is to be believed:

> Practical activity is an endless battle for noble or for squalid but always for illusory ends, a struggle from which the practical self can-

not escape and in which victory is impossible because desire can never be satisfied. . . . To listen to the voice of poetry is to enjoy, not a victory, but a momentary release, a brief enchantment. . . . Having an ear ready for the voice of poetry is to be disposed to choose delight rather than pleasure or virtue or knowledge, a disposition which will reflect itself in practical life in an affection for its intimations of poetry.[33]

The "melancholy of incapacity," Nietzsche's maliciously brilliant formula for Brahms's romantic "yearning and dissatisfaction," forms a hidden strand already in the fabric of Beethoven's art.[34] The traditional image of Beethoven as the tone poet of the heroic Revolutionary and Napoleonic history, while not false, is one-sided.[35] That it is not false is clear from the work that inaugurated his "heroic" period, the *Eroica* Symphony of 1803, with its complex, Goethean intertwining of the Prometheus myth with the figure of Napoleon as emblems of humanity's progressive emancipation to autonomy.[36] But the Beethovenian heroic quest and its temporal teleology have their obverse side in the Beethovenian abstraction out of time. No sooner did music acquire its "classical" ability to represent linear time, than it began "romantically" to undermine and question that ability by exploring moments of timelessness. Significantly, where Mozart tended to separate the two sides, relegating the daydream to the slow movement of an instrumental cycle, Beethoven dramatized their tense coexistence in single movements.[37] Some of the heroic effort and struggle, in fact, seems with him designed to silence and suppress the dreamy side, just as the pointless reverie tends to interrupt the teleological drive. By the same token, no sooner did Europeans begin to realize that autonomous existence in historical time comes at a price than they started to wonder whether it might not be better to live life under the tutelage of an eternal deity or withdrawn in the privacy of timeless interiority. Beethoven shares with Rousseau the duality of being engaged in the historical social world of emancipating autonomous humanity and at the same time being disengaged from it through escape into the realm of individual freedom—the private refuge beyond or within. At the beginning of the modern age the heroic Beethoven stands side by side with Beethoven the dreamer.

With this dual figure I have moved far beyond the simple question of how we should interpret the significance that the Beethovenian images had both for the composer and for his contemporaries. We may by now have left ontological dualisms firmly behind, but the debate over the significance of the aesthetic state as preparation or substitute for a just political one, or more generally, as a utopian unfolding of human possibilities or escape from our most central concerns—this modern debate that began in the new dawn of the Revolution shows no sign of coming to a conclusion, even in our presumably postmodern twilight.

—

Setting Schiller's "Ode to Joy" in the finale of the Ninth Symphony is the one occasion in his late work when Beethoven tried to keep faith with the ideal of engagement in the historical social world of emancipating autonomous humanity—even in the inhospitable context of post-Napoleonic Europe's reassembled monarchies, which allowed most members of the composer's educated audience little room for substantial involvement in public life.

Beethoven cut and restructured the poem so as to project the two principal subjects of the movement: "Freude, schöner Götterfunken," which makes its first appearance in m. 92 and dominates the discourse through m. 594, is resolutely this-worldly in its orientation, marchlike, and centered on the thought that "all men become brothers under your [the joy's] soft wing" (Alle Menschen werden Brüder, Wo dein sanfter Flügel weilt); and "Seid umschlungen, Millionen!" which makes its first appearance in m. 595, dominates the discourse through m. 654, and is otherworldly, hymnlike, and centered on the thought that "brothers—above the starry tent / a dear father must dwell" (Brüder—überm Sternenzelt / Muß ein lieber Vater wohnen). After the climactic double fugue (Allegro energico, sempre ben marcato; mm. 655–729) that unites these two subjects and suggests a vision of universal earthly brotherhood under the loving eye of a transcendent God, and after a brief interlude (mm. 730–62) that comes back to the otherworldly topic, there follows a faster return of the this-worldly subject (Allegro ma non tanto; mm. 763–842), followed in turn by a few measures of an orchestral transition (mm. 843–50) and a still faster coda (Prestissimo; mm. 851–940). This last return of the main subject before the coda climaxes, again, on two cadenza-like moments of timeless Poco adagio abstraction (mm. 810–13 and 832–42; Examples 27a and 27b), the second so absentminded that it wanders off the main key of D major up by three additional sharps and ends up in the completely wrong key of B major. The embellishing turns in the soprano line (mm. 812, 835, and 836), with their echoes in the tenor (m. 838) and bass (m. 839), bring to mind the famous reflective turn of the oboe in the recapitulation of the Fifth Symphony Allegro con brio (see Example 21b).

The crux of the Ninth Symphony seems to me to be hidden right here, in these two Poco adagio moments before the coda. In a world in which one can no longer realistically expect all men to become brothers on earth, the ideal of *fraternité* is displaced into a realm no less transcendent than that

EXAMPLE 27. Beethoven, Symphony No. 9 in D Minor, op. 125, last movement

a. Mm. 806–14

EXAMPLE 27 *(continued)*

(continued)

EXAMPLE 27 *(continued)*

b. Mm. 827–42

EXAMPLE 27 *(continued)*

(continued)

EXAMPLE 27 (continued)

EXAMPLE 27 *(continued)*

(continued)

EXAMPLE 27 *(continued)*

in which the ideal of a loving father must dwell—both equally the subject of wistful nostalgia for original wholeness and utopian longing for the dis-alienated future of restored harmony. It is this melancholy thought that the coda (much too triumphant and noisy, as is usual with Beethoven) tries one last time to suppress and talk down.

This sort of displacement of the ideal is something Beethoven shares with a great many of his contemporaries, not least among them Goethe. As Nicholas Boyle has argued, "the evaporation of the happy ending, the imposition on us by an inscrutable reality of the renunciation of our ideal goal—is the nucleus from which grow nearly all the major works Goethe wrote in the second half of his life."[38] Thinking people in Germany may have reacted to the new reality resulting from Napoleon's wars in a variety of ways, ranging from despair to enthusiasm, but there was not much room for doubt as to what the new reality was: "Partly under the impact of a continental war, the German middle classes had to give up any desire for directly exercising political power in their own name and had, for a century, to reconcile themselves to achieving their advancement only through action at a distance, as the officials of an alien and absolute executive, the monarch." To this situation Goethe, no less than Beethoven, responded by means of a symbolic art in which "the desired object can now be represented . . . either to be lost, though unforgotten, in the past, or to be inaccessible, though secure, in an ideal future."

Hence there was something at once oddly inappropriate and appropriate in the choice of the Ninth Symphony for the famous Leonard Bernstein concert that celebrated the fall of the Berlin Wall in 1989, an event as symbolically charged as the fall of the Bastille two hundred years earlier. If, as I have argued here, the world inaugurated in 1789 was an inherently unstable compound of aspirations to individual *liberté* and collective autonomous *fraternité*, there can be little doubt that the finale of the Ninth extols the brotherhood and not the liberty component of this mixture; in that sense it fit the occasion when the dream of fraternity was put to (a temporary) rest about as well as a solemn Mass would fit a celebration of God's death.[39] And yet the performance, itself a distant echo of the Revolutionary outdoor festivals that were one of the models for the finale in the first place, fit the occasion all the same, because the ideal of fraternity is celebrated in the Ninth, too, as something commemorated rather than actual.

As it happens, most brotherhoods, even universal ones, will find someone who does not fit and must be excluded. The second stanza of Schiller's Ode makes clear that the union he envisages is no different in this respect from Sarastro's brotherhood:

Whoever succeeded in the great game
of winning a friend
or obtaining a lovely woman,
let him join in the jubilation!
Yes—he who calls even a single soul
his own on the globe!
And he who has never known it—let him steal away,
weeping, from this union.[40]

Beethoven's last great project, the late string quartets of 1823–1826, occupies the pole opposite to that of the Ninth Symphony—the pole of the music of those not admitted to the brotherhood of men, not able to call a single soul their own, the music of withdrawal from the unacceptable and non-accepting public world into the privacy of interiority. This world, too, is explored by the wanderer in Schubert's *Winterreise* of 1827—another who has to steal away in tears from human brotherhood, unable to call a single soul on earth his own: "I came here as a stranger and as a stranger I leave" (Fremd bin ich eingezogen, fremd zieh ich wieder aus), he tells us at the outset of his winter journey, describing the existential situation of every one of us with uncommon directness and economy.

Unlike the protagonist of the Ninth, the wanderer puts his faith neither in the past nor in the future—not even in the present. He meets the expectations of the secular emancipation of autonomous mankind with bitter derision ("if there be no God on earth, we ourselves are gods!" [will kein Gott auf Erden sein, sind wir selber Götter!]), and he finds no peaceful refuge in his hallucinatory *rêveries du promeneur solitaire.* As to the outcome of his journey, he can expect none—neither the cyclical renewal of spring nor the consolation of death. To be sure, he does dream of spring, but what he sees when he wakes up are the flowers that frost has painted on window panes, flowers that, should spring come, will melt away rather than bloom. And not even the graveyard has room for him: "Oh, pitiless tavern," he addresses it, "do you yet turn me away?" (O unbarmherzge Schenke, doch weisest du mich ab?).

His is a journey without arrival, a story with no closure. The time of *Winterreise* is neither cyclical nor linear. It is, rather, time that gradually freezes over, like a river, or tears, in winter. Images of liquids that no longer flow, immobilized by ice, accompany the journey from early on: there are the tears that freeze into ice in "Gefrorne Tränen" (No. 3), the frozen heart of the "Erstarrung" (No. 4), the frozen river in "Auf dem Flusse" (No. 7; "My heart, do you recognize your image in this stream?" [Mein Herz, in diesem Bache erkennst du nun dein Bild?]). Indeed, "freezing" (Erstarrung) is the

EXAMPLE 28. Schubert, *Winterreise*, No. 24 ("Der Leiermann"), mm. 1–8

cycle's key image. In the last song, time has congealed almost entirely. The music of "Der Leiermann" (No. 24) is based on the hurdy-gurdy man's single open-fifth tonic drone on each downbeat of the song's sixty-one measures, with accented, coloristic, nonfunctional dominant chords falling frequently but irregularly against it (see its beginning in Example 28). Like the wanderer whose figure is about to merge with his own, the hurdy-gurdy man is going nowhere, just irregularly shuffling on ice from one bare foot to the other, making music no one wants to hear, and remaining as completely, fatalistically, indifferent to others as they are to him: "And he lets it all happen as it will" (Und er läßt es gehen alles, wie es will).

Schubert's *Winterreise* is our civilization's greatest poem of existential estrangement and isolation. The landscape of private interiority it maps out offers no refuge to those who would escape history: the inner world turns out to be as wintry, barren, and desolate as the outer one—empty, with no future, and nowhere to go. After almost two centuries in which we have had time to get accustomed to landscapes such as those painted by Schubert and his progeny, through Beckett and beyond, it is necessary to be reminded that this bleak vision of the human condition and prospects was quite unprecedented at the time, at least in music. But then the hopes embodied in *The Magic Flute* were unprecedented, too. The hopes of a new dawn on earth raised in 1789 were so high that disillusionment, when it set in after the pacification of Europe in 1814–1815, was correspondingly deep. It must also have been particularly painful for the younger generation, who had not even a living memory of hope to fall back on. Both old Beethoven and young

Schubert may have experienced the present, Prince Metternich's heavily po-
liced 1820s, similarly, but, judging by the Ninth and *Winterreise*, there was
an essential difference to their sense of the past and future, a difference in
outlook between someone who had been young in 1789 and someone who
did not come of age until 1814.[41]

From the Olympian heights of old age, Goethe, born some seven years
before Mozart and destined to outlive Schubert by another four, had little
patience for the Romantic poets and their complaints. After one such poet
visited him in Weimar on 21 September 1827, Eckermann on the 24th reported Goethe's comment on the visitor's contemporaries:

> The poets all write as if they were sick and the whole world an
> infirmary. . . . This is a veritable misuse of poetry, which after all
> was actually given us so as to settle the small discords of life and
> to make men satisfied with the world and their condition. But the
> present generation is afraid of any genuine strength, it feels com-
> fortable and poetic only with weakness.[42]

As it happens, this particular poet *was* sick: on the night of 30 September the visitor, back home in Dessau, suffered a fatal heart attack. He was
Wilhelm Müller, the poet of *Winterreise*.

Acknowledgments

Several sections of the book have appeared previously, and I would like to thank the original publishers for permission to reproduce them here:

Sections 1–3 of the Introduction, Chapter 2, and Section 6 of the Interlude use material from my "Time's Arrow and the Advent of Musical Modernity," in Karol Berger and Anthony Newcomb, eds., *Music and the Aesthetics of Modernity: Essays*, Isham Library Papers 6, Harvard Publications in Music 21 (Cambridge: Harvard University Department of Music, 2005), 3–22.

The Prelude contains a few paragraphs that make use of material from my "Concepts and Developments in Music Theory," in *European Music 1520–1640*, ed. James Haar (Woodbridge: The Boydell Press, 2006), 304–28.

Chapter 1 reproduces a few paragraphs from my "Die beiden Arten von Da-Capo-Arien in der Matthäus-Passion," *Bach-Jahrbuch* 92 (2006), 127–59.

Chapter 4 reproduces portions of my "The First-Movement Punctuation Form in Mozart's Piano Concertos," in *Mozart's Piano Concertos: Text, Context, Interpretation*, ed. Neal Zaslaw (Ann Arbor: The University of Michigan Press, 1996), 239–59, and in my "The Thrice-Told Tale: Thematic Narratives in the Allegros of Mozart's Piano Concertos," forthcoming in *Mozart-Jahrbuch* 2007.

Chapter 7 is a revised and expanded version of my "Beyond Language," in *A New History of German Literature*, ed. David E. Wellbery (Cambridge: Harvard University Press, 2004), 445–50.

Sections 1–4 of the Postlude are an expanded version of my "Beethoven and the Aesthetic State," *Beethoven Forum* 7 (1999): 17–44.

My work on this project has been significantly facilitated by a Fellowship from the American Council of Learned Societies, a Donald Andrews Whittier Fellowship from the Stanford Humanities Center, a Residency at the Rockefeller Foundation's Bellagio Study and Conference Center, and a

Robert Lehman Visiting Professorship at Villa I Tatti, the Harvard University Center for Italian Renaissance Studies. I would like to acknowledge with gratitude the generous support of these institutions. I would also like to thank Stephen Hinton, Senior Associate Dean at the Stanford University School of Humanities and Sciences, for providing a subsidy to defray some of the publication costs. Both John Bender with his staff at the Stanford Humanities Center and Joseph Connors and his staff at Villa I Tatti expertly provided the ideal conditions for serious scholarly research and lively exchange of ideas. My particular thanks are due to Kathryn Bosi, the F. Gordon and Elizabeth Morrill Music Librarian at Villa I Tatti, for making her library a supremely congenial and useful research tool, and to Fiorella Superbi Gioffredi, the Curator of the Fototeca Berenson at Villa I Tatti, for her generous help with obtaining some of the illustrations and permissions to reproduce them. In addition, I would like to express my gratitude for help in unforeseen emergencies to Piotr Kłoczowski of the Adam Mickiewicz Museum of Literature in Warsaw, and to my student Blake Stevens.

I have greatly benefited from stimulating input from a number of scholars and friends and would like to express my gratitude to at least some of them here. A dialogue with Andrzej Rapaczyński and Wojciech Karpiński, conducted in more places and over many more years than any one of us is likely to recall, will find echoes in these pages. Conversations with Reinhold Brinkmann, Michał Bristiger, Thomas Grey, Stephen Hinton, Lewis Lockwood, Anthony Newcomb, Maynard Solomon, Richard Taruskin, and James Webster have provided frequent inspiration. I am indebted to David Wellbery and to Christopher Reynolds for having invited me to write the essays that eventually developed respectively into Chapter 7 and the Postlude of this book. At Stanford University, Keith Baker directed me to the work of Marcel Gauchet. Thomas Sheehan's introduction to St. Paul during a meeting of the Philosophical Reading Group, a Stanford faculty seminar conducted by Hans Ulrich Gumbrecht and Robert Harrison, was truly eye-opening. My Stanford students patiently tested some of the hypotheses presented here. Students and colleagues offered insightful reactions when I read some of the chapters as lectures at Cornell, Harvard, Humboldt University in Berlin, the Universities of Basel, Michigan, North Carolina at Chapel Hill, Poznań, Utrecht, and Zurich, as well as at the Charles S. Singleton Center for Italian Studies of the Johns Hopkins University at Villa Spelman in Florence, the Harvard University Center for Italian Renaissance Studies at Villa I Tatti in Florence, the Institute for the Arts of the Polish Academy of Sciences in Warsaw, the International Foundation Mozarteum in Salzburg, and the Rockefeller Foundation's Bellagio Study and Conference Center. Repeatedly, I have been inspired by conversations held during seminars for Swiss doctoral students in musicology at the Fondation Hindemith in Blonay with Hermann Danuser, Anselm Gerhard, Lydia Goehr, Peter Gülke, Hans-Joachim Hinrichsen, Laurenz Lütteken, Anne Shreffler, Leo Treitler, and Luca Zopelli.

Anna Maria Busse Berger and Richard Taruskin, long my best readers, studied the whole manuscript with the right mixture of sympathy and skepticism, as did the anonymous readers for the Press; their comments alerted me to a number of possible misunderstandings and impossible blunders. Two good friends and Bach experts, John Butt and Laurence Dreyfus, offered kind but firm critiques of the three chapters devoted to that composer. I also received valuable comments from Frederick Neuhouser on the Interlude and from Jan Assmann on the *Magic Flute* chapter. Finally, I would like to express profound gratitude to Mary C. Francis, Rose Vekony, and Juliane Brand of the University of California Press for their expert and untiring help in shepherding my text through publication and cleaning it up in countless ways in the process. Not for the first time I feel blessed in having such patient, generous, and acute colleagues and friends.

Notes

INTRODUCTION

1. François-René de Chateaubriand, *Mémoires d'outre-tombe*, bk. 9, ch. 10, trans. Robert Baldick as *The Memoirs* (New York: Alfred A. Knopf, 1961), 174.

2. *The Memoirs*, xxi.

3. G. W. F. Hegel, "Proceedings of the Estates Assembly in the Kingdom of Württemberg 1815–1816," in *Political Writings*, trans. T. M. Knox (Oxford: Clarendon Press, 1964), 282.

4. Ernst Robert Curtius, *European Literature and the Latin Middle Ages*, trans. Willard R. Trask (New York: Harper & Row, 1963), 19–24, 585–96.

5. Curtius, *European Literature*, 20, 23–24, 587.

6. Curtius, *European Literature*, 24.

7. Jacques Le Goff, *L'imaginaire médiéval* (Paris: Gallimard, 1985).

8. Curtius, *European Literature*, 24, 587. Cf. Hans Robert Jauss, "Der literarische Prozess des Modernismus von Rousseau bis Adorno," in *Epochenschwelle und Epochenbewußtsein*, ed. R. Herzog and R. Koselleck (Munich, 1987), 243–68, who similarly locates the origins of modernism in the mid-eighteenth century.

9. Curtius, *European Literature*, 23, 24, 587.

10. Curtius, *European Literature*, 20, 594–95, 16, 595.

11. Curtius, *European Literature*, 23.

12. See, e.g., Daniel K. L. Chua, *Absolute Music and the Construction of Meaning* (Cambridge: Cambridge University Press, 1999).

13. E. T. A. Hoffmann, *Musical Writings: Kreisleriana, The Poet and the Composer, Music Criticism*, ed. David Charlton, trans. Martyn Clarke (Cambridge: Cambridge University Press, 1989), 96–103, 351–76.

14. Hoffmann, *Musical Writings*, 372, 97.

15. Hoffmann, *Musical Writings*, 96.

16. Stephen Jay Gould, *Time's Arrow, Time's Cycle: Myth and Metaphor in the Discovery of Geological Time* (Cambridge: Harvard University Press, 1987).

17. Scott Burnham, *Beethoven Hero* (Princeton: Princeton University Press, 1995).

18. Carolyn Abbate, *Unsung Voices: Opera and Musical Narrative in the Nineteenth Century* (Princeton: Princeton University Press, 1991), 21–29.

19. Carl Dahlhaus, *Nineteenth-Century Music,* trans. J. Bradford Robinson (Berkeley: University of California Press, 1989), 15.

20. G. W. F. Hegel, *Aesthetics: Lectures on Fine Art,* trans. T. M. Knox (Oxford: Clarendon Press, 1975), 7.

21. Cf. Robert L. Marshall, "Bach the Progressive," in *The Music of Johann Sebastian Bach: The Sources, the Style, the Significance* (New York: Schirmer Books, 1989).

22. Richard Taruskin, *The Oxford History of Western Music* (New York: Oxford University Press, 2005), 2:184, 185, 187.

23. Taruskin, *Oxford History,* 2:212, 213, 216.

24. Edward E. Lowinsky, "On Mozart's Rhythm," in *Music in the Culture of the Renaissance and Other Essays,* ed. Bonnie J. Blackburn (Chicago: The University of Chicago Press, 1989), 2:911–28; originally published in *The Musical Quarterly* 42 (1956), 162–86.

25. Laurence Dreyfus, *Bach and the Patterns of Invention* (Cambridge: Harvard University Press, 1996), 59–102.

PRELUDE

1. Claudio Monteverdi, *L'Orfeo* (Venice: Ricciardo Amadino, 1609), 81; facs. ed. in Monteverdi, *L'Orfeo: Favola in musica,* Archivium Musicum, Musica Drammatica 1 (Florence: Studio Per Edizioni Scelte, 1993).

2. For Orpheus in antiquity, see W. K. C. Guthrie, *Orpheus and Greek Religion* (New York: W. W. Norton & Co., 1966), and Emmet Robbins, "Famous Orpheus," in *Orpheus: The Metamorphoses of a Myth,* ed. John Warden (Toronto: University of Toronto Press, 1982), 3–23. For Virgil's and Ovid's Orpheus, see W. S. Anderson, "The Orpheus of Virgil and Ovid: *flebile nescio quid,*" in *Orpheus: The Metamorphoses of a Myth,* ed. Warden, 25–50, and Charles Segal, *Orpheus: The Myth of the Poet* (Baltimore: The Johns Hopkins University Press, 1989), 36–94. On the literary sources of Striggio's libretto, see most recently Philippe Canguilhem, "Les sources littéraires de l'*Orfeo* de Monteverdi," in *Du genre narratif à l'opéra au theatre et au cinema,* ed. R. Abbrugiati (Toulouse: Presses Universitaires du Mirail, 2000), 81–97.

3. Parenthetical quotations in this paragraph are from Monteverdi, *L'Orfeo,* 4, 65, 49, 52, 49–50, 64, 75, 78, 79, 80, 81, 85–86, and 91.

4. [Alessandro Striggio], *La Favola d'Orfeo* (Mantua: Francesco Osanna, 1607); facs. ed. in Claudio Monteverdi, *L'Orfeo: Favola in musica,* Archivium Musicum, Musica Drammatica 1 (Florence: Studio Per Edizioni Scelte, 1993).

5. For a critical edition, see Antonia Tissoni Benvenuti, *L'Orfeo del Poliziano con il testo critico dell'originale e delle successive forme teatrali* (Padua: Ed-

itrice Antenore, 1986). For a comparison of Poliziano's, Rinuccini's, and Striggio's dramas, see Barbara Russano Hanning, *Of Poetry and Music's Power: Humanism and the Creation of Opera*, Studies in Musicology 13 (Ann Arbor: UMI Research Press, 1980), 47–52. On the tradition leading from Poliziano's play and its music to early opera, see especially Nino Pirrotta and Elena Povoledo, in *Music and Theater from Poliziano to Monteverdi*, trans. Karen Eales (Cambridge: Cambridge University Press, 1982).

6. Silke Leopold, *Monteverdi: Music in Transition*, trans. Anne Smith (Oxford: Clarendon Press, 1991), 98.

7. On the male audience, see, e.g., Paolo Fabbri, *Monteverdi*, trans. Tim Carter (Cambridge: Cambridge University Press, 1994), 63–64. Only at the second performance, on 1 March 1607, were "all the ladies resident in the city" admitted, as Prince Francesco Gonzaga reported to his brother Ferdinando (Fabbri, *Monteverdi*, 64). For the cast at the première, see especially Tim Carter, "Singing *Orfeo*: On the Performers of Monteverdi's First Opera," *Recercare* 11 (1999): 75–118. See also Carter, *Monteverdi's Musical Theatre* (New Haven: Yale University Press, 2002), 91–108. Concerning the stage, Tim Carter suggests that "angusta" may have been a misprint for "augusta," in "Monteverdi's *Orfeo*: A Bibliographical Exploration," paper read at *Orfeo son io*, Convegno internazionale di studi su Claudio Monteverdi, Mantua, Teatro Accademico del Bibiena, 17 December 2005; I would like to thank Dr. Janie Cole for bringing this paper to my attention.

8. The idea has its source in Ovid, *Metamorphoses*, 10:79–85. It is present also in the ending of Poliziano's play.

9. I owe much of the information on visual representations of Orpheus in Italian Renaissance to the useful study by Giuseppe Scavizzi, "The Myth of Orpheus in Italian Renaissance Art, 1400–1600," in *Orpheus: The Metamorphoses of a Myth*, ed. Warden, 111–62.

10. Aby M. Warburg, "Dürer und die italienische Antike," in *Ausgewählte Schriften und Würdigungen*, ed. Dieter Wuttke (Baden-Baden: Valentin Koerner, 1979), 125–35. Useful recent studies are Betsy Rosasco, "Albrecht Dürer's *Death of Orpheus*: Its Critical Fortunes and a New Interpretation of Its Meaning," *Idea: Jahrbuch der Hamburger Kunsthalle* 3 (1984): 19–41; and Antoinette Roesler-Friedenthal, "Ein Porträt Andrea Mantegnas als *alter Orpheus* im Kontext seiner Selbstdarstellungen," *Römisches Jahrbuch der Bibliotheca Hertziana* 31 (1996): 149–86. (I would like to thank Joseph Connors for making me aware of the latter study.) Roesler-Friedenthal argues that Mantegna's lost *Death of Orpheus* was a self-portrait. The connection between Dürer's drawing and Poliziano's play is explored also in Edgar Wind, "*Hercules* and *Orpheus*: Two Mock-Heroic Designs by Dürer," *Journal of the Warburg and Courtauld Institutes* 2 (1939): 206–18.

11. On the word "puseran," see Rosasco, "Albrecht Dürer's *Death of Orpheus*," 36, n. 22; and Roesler-Friedenthal, "Ein Porträt Andrea Mantegna's als *alter Orpheus* im Kontext seiner Selbstdarstellungen," 151, n. 4, who refers to

a number of passages in Luther's works where the term is used, including this one: "auff welch Puseronen, nemlich, die Sodomitische und Gomorrische keuschheit."

12. Cf. Susan McClary, "Constructions of Gender in Monteverdi's Dramatic Music," *Cambridge Opera Journal* 1 (1989): 203–23.

13. For contrasting speculations as to why, when, and by whom the ending of the opera was revised, see Hanning, *Of Poetry and Music's Power*, 128–30; Nino Pirrotta, "Theater, Sets, and Music in Monteverdi's Operas," in *Music and Culture in Italy from the Middle Ages to the Baroque: A Collection of Essays* (Cambridge: Harvard University Press, 1984), 258–59; Iain Fenlon, "The Mantuan *Orfeo*," in *Claudio Monteverdi: Orfeo*, ed. John Whenham (Cambridge: Cambridge University Press, 1986), 16–18; Fabbri, *Monteverdi*, 66–67; Jon Solomon, "The Neoplatonic Apotheosis in Monteverdi's *Orfeo*," *Studi musicali* 24 (1995): 27–47. See also F. W. Sternfeld, *The Birth of Opera* (Oxford: Clarendon Press, 1993), passim.

14. Monteverdi, *L'Orfeo*, 93, 95, 3.

15. Franchino Gaffurio, *De harmonia musicorum instrumentorum opus* (Milan: Gotardus Pontanus, 1518), bk. 1, ch. 4.

16. Karl Kerényi, "Der Mythos von Orpheus und Eurydike," in *Claudio Monteverdi: "Orfeo"; Christoph Willibald Gluck: "Orpheus und Eurydike": Texte, Materialien, Kommentare*, ed. Attila Csampai and Dietmar Holland (Reinbek: Rowohlt, 1988), 9–15. For a claim that some of Monteverdi's instrumentation was designed to represent Orpheus's lyre, see Silke Leopold, "Lyra Orphei," in *Claudio Monteverdi: Festschrift Reinhold Hammerstein zum 70. Geburtstag*, ed. Ludwig Finscher (Laaber: Laaber Verlag, 1986), 337–45.

17. Monteverdi, *L'Orfeo*, 99.

18. Jacopo Peri, *Le musiche sopra L'Euridice del Sig. Ottavio Rinuccini* (Florence: Giorgio Marescotti, 1600); Giulio Caccini, *L'Euridice* (Florence: Giorgio Marescotti, 1600). A modern edition of the libretto can be found in Hanning, *Of Poetry and Music's Power*, 269–96.

19. For a comparison of the two operas, see especially Nino Pirrotta, "Monteverdi and the Problems of Opera," in *Music and Culture in Italy from the Middle Ages to the Baroque*, 233–53. See also Gary Tomlinson, "Madrigal, Monody, and Monteverdi's 'via naturale alla immitatione,' " *Journal of the American Musicological Society* 34 (1981): 60–108, and Fabbri, *Monteverdi*, 69–70.

20. Marco da Gagliano, *La Dafne* (Florence: Cristofano Marescotti, 1608). A modern edition of the original and revised versions of the libretto can be found in Hanning, *Of Poetry and Music's Power*, 245–67.

21. Marco da Gagliano, *La Dafne*, ed. James Erber (London: Cathedral Music, 1978), iii, iv–v.

22. Nino Pirrotta, "Early Opera and Aria," in *Music and Theater from Poliziano to Monteverdi*, 262–64.

23. Silke Leopold, "Orpheus in Mantua und anderswo: Poliziano, Peri und Monteverdi," in *Claudio Monteverdi: "Orfeo"; Christoph Willibald Gluck: "Orpheus und Eurydike": Texte, Materialien, Kommentare*, ed. Csampai and Hol-

land, 102: "Dies ist nicht, wie bei Rinuccini, der Triumph der Liebe, sondern die Apotheose der Musik—ein wahres Opernthema" (This is not, as with Rinuccini, the triumph of love, but rather the apotheosis of music—a true opera theme). Cf. a similar claim in Segal, *Orpheus: The Myth of the Poet*, 165–66: "This sublimation of grief into song, with the triumph of music, implicit or explicit, over sorrow and death, is also the basis for the operatic versions of the myth (Gluck's *Orfeo ed Euridice* and Monteverdi's *Orfeo*)."

24. See Solomon, "The Neoplatonic Apotheosis in Monteverdi's *Orfeo*," 27–28.

25. "It must be said that this Platonic apotheosis is musically and intellectually blank," writes Joseph Kerman. But he finds Striggio's ending even more deplorable, an "undramatic prevarication." Joseph Kerman, "*Orpheus:* The Neoclassic Vision," *Opera as Drama*, new and rev. ed. (Berkeley: University of California Press, 1988), 28.

26. Monteverdi, *L'Orfeo* [Dedicatory Letter].

27. Erwin Panofsky, *Idea: A Conception in Art Theory*, trans. Joseph J. S. Peake (New York: Harper & Row, 1968).

28. Maurice Blanchot, *The Gaze of Orpheus and Other Literary Essays*, trans. Lydia Davis (Barrytown, New York: Station Hill Press, 1981), 104, 99, 102.

29. Marcel Proust, *La prisonnière*, in vol. 3 of *À la recherche du temps perdu*, ed. Pierre Clarac and André Ferré (Paris: Gallimard, 1954), 182–88; trans. C. K. Scott Moncrieff as *The Captive* (New York: The Modern Library, 1929), 243–51.

30. See George D. Painter, *Marcel Proust: A Biography*, rev. ed. (London: Chatto & Windus, 1984), 319–21.

31. Proust, *The Captive*, 249, 250. In *La prisonnière:* "un petit pan de mur jaune . . . était si bien peint qu'il était, si on le regardait seul, comme une précieuse oeuvre d'art chinoise, d'une beauté qui se suffirait à elle-même" (186–87); "tableau qu'il adorait et croyait connaître très bien" (186); "la précieuse matière du tout petit pan de mur jaune" (187); "il attachait son regard, comme un enfant à un papillon jaune qu'il veut saisir, au précieux petit pan de mur. 'C'est ainsi que j'aurais dû écrire, disait-il. Mes derniers livres sont trop secs, il aurait fallu passer plusieurs couches de couleur, rendre ma phrase en elle-même précieuse, comme ce petit pan de mur jaune.' " (187); "il se répétait: 'Petit pan de mur jaune avec un auvent, petit pan de mur jaune'" (187).

32. Proust, *The Captive*, 250–51, 245, 251. In *La prisonnière:* "Tout se passe dans notre vie comme si nous y entrions avec le faix d'obligations contractées dans une vie antérieure; il n'y a aucune raison dans nos conditions de vie sur cette terre . . . pour l'artiste athée à ce qu'il se croie obligé de recommencer vingt fois un morceau dont l'admiration qu'il excitera importera peu à son corps mangé par les vers. . . . Toutes ces obligations . . . semblent appartenir à un monde différent . . . de ces lois inconnues auxquelles nous avons obéi parce que nous en portions l'enseignement en nous . . . —ces lois dont tout travail profond de l'intelligence nous rapproche" (187–88); "dans les générations futures . . . brillent les oeuvres des hommes" (184); "On l'enterra, mais toute la nuit funèbre, aux vitrines éclairées, ses livres, disposés trois par trois, veillaient comme des anges

aux ailes éployées et semblaient, pour celui qui n'était plus, le symbole de sa ré-
surrection" (188).

33. For Orpheus and Eurydice in the Italian Renaissance, see in particular
Konrat Ziegler, "Orpheus in Renaissance und Neuzeit," in *Form und Inhalt,
kunstgeschichtliche Studien: Otto Schmitt zum 60. Geburtstag am 13. Dezember 1950* (Stuttgart: W. Kohlhammer, 1951), 239–56. See also D. P. Walker, "Orpheus the Theologian and the Renaissance Platonists," *Journal of the Warburg
and Courtauld Institutes* 16 (1953): 100–120; Walker, *Spiritual and Demonic
Magic from Ficino to Campanella* (London: The Warburg Insitute, 1958); August Buck, *Der Orpheus-Mythos in der italienischen Renaissance* (Krefeld:
Scherpe, 1961). For Apollo and Daphne, see Wolfgang Stechow, *Apollo und
Daphne*, rev. ed. (Darmstadt: Wissenschaftliche Buchgesellschaft, 1965).

34. See Scavizzi, "Orpheus in Italian Renaissance Art," 125–28, 136–46.

35. Jaynie Anderson, *Giorgione: The Painter of "Poetic Brevity"* (Paris and
New York: Flammarion, 1997), 317f. For a study that sees a self-portrait of the
artist and a meditation on the artist's tragic situation as social outcast already
in the earlier 1494 Dürer drawing *The Death of Orpheus* mentioned above, see
Peter-Klaus Schuster, "Zu Dürers Zeichnung *Der Tod des Orpheus* und verwandten Darstellungen," *Jahrbuch der Hamburger Kunstsammlungen* 23
(1978): 7–24. See also Roesler-Friedenthal, "Ein Porträt Andrea Mantegnas als
alter Orpheus im Kontext seiner Selbstdarstellungen," cited in note 10, who
speculates that already Mantegna represented himself in Orpheus's role.

36. My reading of the events represented in the background differs somewhat from that in Scavizzi, "Orpheus in Italian Renaissance Art," 136–42.

37. Scavizzi, "Orpheus in Italian Renaissance Art," 142–43.

38. See my *A Theory of Art* (New York and Oxford: Oxford University Press,
2000), 120–33. The following paragraphs make use of material from my "Concepts and Developments in Music Theory," in *European Music 1520–1640*, ed.
James Haar (Woodbridge: The Boydell Press, 2006), 304–28.

39. "Fusse . . . non la soavità de le consonanze per contentar l'orecchio (con-
ciosiache del uso di queste nel lor cantare non si truova ne testimonio ne riscon-
tro alcuno appresso gli scrittori) ma lo esprimere interamente et con efficacia
tutto quello che voleva fare intendere . . . per il mezzo et ajuto de la acutezza e
gravità de la voce, . . . accompagnata con la regolata temperatura del presto et
adagio." Girolamo Mei, letter to Vincenzo Galilei, 8 May 1572, in Claude V.
Palisca, *Girolamo Mei: Letters on Ancient and Modern Music to Vincenzo Galilei
and Giovanni Bardi*, Musicological Studies and Documents 3 (N.p.: American
Institute of Musicology, 1960), 117.

40. "Il Musico, con la diversità degl'intervalli et particolarmente de conso-
nanti comunica al'intelletto tutte le passione dell'animo; et vie più informati
con i mezzi debiti dall'oratione." Vincenzo Galilei, *Discorso intorno all'uso del-
l'Enharmonio*, Florence, Biblioteca Nazionale Centrale, Ms. Galileiani 3, fol. 17v.

41. "Orphei hymnos exposuit, miraque, ut ferunt, dulcedine ad lyram an-
tiquo more cecinit." Giovanni Corsi, *Vita Marsilii Ficini*, in *Marsile Ficin
(1433–1499)*, by Raymond Marcel (Paris: Les Belles Lettres, 1958), 682. "Longe

felicior, quam Thracensis Orphei cithara, veram . . . Eurydicen, hoc est . . . Platonicam sapientiam, revocavit ab inferis." Angelus Politianus, *Miscellaneorum centuria prima*, ch. 100, in *Opera* (Venice: Aldus Manutius, 1498), sig. Kii^v.

42. Quoted from Ruth Saunders Magurn, introduction to *The Letters of Peter Paul Rubens*, trans. and ed. R. S. Magurn (Cambridge: Harvard University Press, 1955), 6.

43. For the *Apollo and Daphne* sketch, see Michael Jaffé, "Esquisses inédites de Rubens pour La Torre della Parada," *La Revue du Louvre et des Musées de France* 14 (1964): 312–22. For the *Orpheus and Eurydice* sketch, see the catalogue of the exhibition *Olieversfschetsen van Rubens* (Rotterdam: Museum Boymans, 1953), cat. no. 112.

44. *The Letters of Peter Paul Rubens*, no. 241, 406–8.

45. Hans Blumenberg, *The Legitimacy of the Modern Age*, trans. Robert M. Wallace (Cambridge: The MIT Press, 1983), 125–26.

46. Monteverdi, *L'Orfeo*, 2–3, 85–86, 93, 94.

47. Scholarly opinion today seems evenly divided among those who attribute the picture to Giorgione and those who think it is an early Titian. See, e.g., Terisio Pignatti and Filippo Pedrocco, *Giorgione* (New York: Rizzoli, 1999), 188–90.

48. Cf. Eleanor Irwin, "The Songs of Orpheus and the New Song of Christ," in *Orpheus: The Metamorphoses of a Myth*, ed. Warden, 51–62; and Patricia Vicari, "*Sparagmos:* Orpheus among the Christians," in *Orpheus: The Metamorphoses of a Myth*, ed. Warden, 63–83. For the medieval Orpheus, see, in particular, John Block Friedman, *Orpheus in the Middle Ages* (Cambridge: Harvard University Press, 1970).

49. See Scavizzi, "Orpheus in Italian Renaissance Art," 141.

50. Monteverdi, *L'Orfeo*, 81.

CHAPTER 1

1. For these dates, see especially Joshua Rifkin, "The Chronology of Bach's Saint Matthew Passion," *Musical Quarterly* 61 (1975): 360–87; and Yoshitake Kobayashi, "Zur Chronologie der Spätwerke Johann Sebastian Bachs: Kompositions- und Aufführungstätigkeit von 1736 bis 1750," *Bach Jahrbuch* 74 (1988): 50.

2. I follow the numbering given individual movements in Johann Sebastian Bach, *Matthäus-Passion BWV 244*, ed. Alfred Dürr, Neue Ausgabe sämtlicher Werke, series 2, vol. 5 (Kassel: Bärenreiter, 1972).

3. Alfred Dürr, *Kritischer Bericht* for Johann Sebastian Bach, *Matthäus-Passion*, Neue Ausgabe sämtlicher Werke, series 2, vol. 5 (Kassel: Bärenreiter, 1974), 72, 79.

4. Picander [Christian Friedrich Henrici], *Ernst-Schertzhaffte und Satyrische Gedichte*, vol. 2 (Leipzig, 1729), 101–12; facs. in Dürr, *Kritischer Bericht*, 73–78.

5. Facs. in Bach, *Matthäus-Passion BWV 244*, xii. In the autograph score,

the chorale melody, notated in red ink and without the text, is entrusted to the organs that accompany each choir (Berlin, Deutsche Staatsbibliothek, Mus. ms. Bach P 25; facs. in Johann Sebastian Bach, *Passio Domini nostri J. C. secundum Evangelistam Matthaeum*, Faksimile-Reihe Bachscher Werke und Schrift-stücke, ed. Bach-Archiv Leipzig, vol. 7 (Leipzig: VEB Deutscher Verlag für Musik, [1966]). In Johann Christoph Altnickol's copy of the early version of the score, the melody appears with the text but is labeled "Organo" (facs. in Johann Se-bastian Bach, *Matthäus-Passion Frühfassung BWV 244b*, ed. Alfred Dürr, Neue Ausgabe sämtlicher Werke, series 2, vol. 5a (Kassel: Bärenreiter, 1972), fol. 4v).

6. The most comprehensive investigation of the performing forces deployed in the Passion is Daniel R. Melamed, "The Double Chorus in J. S. Bach's *St. Matthew Passion* BWV 244," *Journal of the American Musicological Society* 57: (2004), 3–50. Melamed's paper appeared after I had completed this chapter, and the issues are somewhat different from the ones examined here, but his con-clusions basically agree with, and complement, mine. In particular, Melamed sug-gests that "the *St. Matthew Passion* owes a great deal to the usual division of singers into concertists and ripienists and that its singers can best be viewed as a principal group who are effectively concertists (Chorus 1) and a second group that functions in most of the work as a ripieno ensemble (Chorus 2)" (7). Throughout, Melamed stresses "the secondary status of Chorus 2. . . . In the dialogue movements { . . . } Chorus 1 always takes the lead, whereas Chorus 2 always interrupts or offers commentary. . . . This difference may be connected with the dialogue poetry itself in that Chorus 1 is associated with an individual allegorical character, the Daughter of Zion, whereas Chorus 2 represents a col-lective group of Believers. . . . This uneven division of labor between the two choirs almost certainly reflects the conceptual origin of Chorus 2 as a support-ing ensemble" (13f). Among earlier investigations of the matter, particularly noteworthy are: Lothar Steiger and Renate Steiger, "Die theologische Bedeu-tung der Doppelchörigkeit in Johann Sebastian Bachs *Matthäus-Passion*," in *Bachiana et alia musicologica: Festschrift Alfred Dürr zum 65. Geburtstag am 3. März 1983*, ed. Wolfgang Rehm (Kassel: Bärenreiter, 1983), 275–86; Ulrich Leisinger, "Forms and Functions of the Choral Movements in J. S. Bach's St. Matthew Passion," in *Bach Studies 2*, ed. Daniel R. Melamed (Cambridge: Cam-bridge University Press, 1995), 70–84; and John Butt, "Bach's Vocal Scoring: What Can It Mean?" *Early Music* 26 (1998): 99–107.

7. See, however, Elke Axmacher, *"Aus Liebe will mein Heyland sterben": Un-tersuchung zum Wandel des Passionsverständnisses im frühen 18. Jahrhundert*, Beiträge zur theologischen Bachforschung 2 (Neuhausen-Stuttgart: Hänssler-Verlag, 1984), 191, n. 44, who thinks that the missing "selber" in Picander's li-bretto might be a simple printer's error.

8. For an alternative typology of the Passion's da capo arias, see Emil Platen, *Die Matthäus-Passion von Johann Sebastian Bach: Entstehung, Werkbeschrei-bung, Rezeption* (Kassel and Munich: Bärenreiter and Deutscher Taschenbuch, 1991), 90–99. Bach's aria forms in general have been studied by Stephen A. Crist: *Aria Forms in the Vocal Works of J. S. Bach, 1714–1724*, Ph. D. diss., Brandeis

University, 1988; "Aria forms in the cantatas from Bach's first Leipzig *Jahrgang,*" in *Bach Studies,* ed. Don O. Franklin (Cambridge: Cambridge University Press, 1989), 36–53; "Bach, Theology, and Harmony: A New Look at the Arias," *Bach* 27 (1996): 1–30; and "J. S. Bach and the Conventions of the Da Capo Aria, or How Original Was Bach?" in *The Maymooth International Musicological Conference 1995: Selected Proceedings, Part One,* ed. P. F. Devine and H. White (Dublin, 1996), 71–85.

9. Only three, Nos. 8, 39, and 42, are not marked in this way, but in the two last-named the opening verses are printed again at the end, that is, the da capo is written out.

10. The repeats in Nos. 65 and 68 are written out in the Neue Bach Ausgabe but not in the composer's autograph.

11. For a very different reading of the opening chorus from the one presented below, see Platen, *Die Matthäus-Passion von Johann Sebastian Bach,* 104–5, 121–25, 244.

12. In 1935 Hans Joachim Moser heard in this pedal point an "*Ur*-beginning," like the one of the *Das Rheingold* Prelude. See Moser, *Johann Sebastian Bach* (Berlin, 1935), 205. In 2000 Martin Geck was still talking of an "Urlandschaft," but in doing so invoked the beginning of Brahms's First Symphony: "Vorstellungen von Natur ruft auch der anfängliche Orgelpunkt hervor—doch solche von Urlandschaft. Es ist der Impuls grundsätzlichen Beginnens, nach dem Johannes Brahms jahrzehntelang gesucht hat, bis er ihm in den ersten Takten seiner 1. Sinfonie neuen Ausdruck geben konnte." Geck, *Bach: Leben und Werk* (Reinbek: Rowohlt, 2000), 441.

CHAPTER 2

1. In the voluminous analytical literature on the fugues of *The Well-Tempered Keyboard* (WTC I and II, BWV 846–69 and 870–93), I have found two items to be particularly useful: Donald Francis Tovey, "A Preface; General Instructions for Using This Edition; Critical and Explanatory Notes to Each Prelude and Each Fugue," in J. S. Bach, *Forty-Eight Preludes and Fugues,* ed. D. F. Tovey, 2 vols. (New York: Oxford University Press, 1924); and Laurence Dreyfus, *Bach and the Patterns of Invention* (Cambridge: Harvard University Press, 1996). Other noteworthy studies include Hugo Riemann, *Analysis of J. S. Bach's Wohltemperirtes Clavier (48 Preludes & Fugues),* trans. J. S. Shedlock (London: Augner, n.d.); Ludwig Czaczkes, *Analyse des Wohltemperierten Klaviers: Form und Aufbau der Fuge bei Bach,* 2 vols. (Vienna, 1956, 1965); Johann Nepomuk David, *Das Wohltemperierte Klavier: Der Versuch einer Synopsis* (Göttingen, 1962); Hermann Keller, *The Well-Tempered Clavier by Johann Sebastian Bach,* trans. Leigh Gerdine (New York: W. W. Norton & Co., 1976); Alfred Dürr, *Johann Sebastian Bach: Das Wohltemperierte Klavier,* 2nd ed. (Kassel: Bärenreiter, 2000); David Ledbetter, *Bach's* Well-tempered Clavier: The 48 *Preludes and Fugues* (New Haven: Yale University Press, 2002); Ulrich Siegele, "Kategorien formaler Konstruktion in den Fugen des Wohltemperierten Klaviers,"

in *Bach, Das Wohltemperierte Klavier I: Tradition, Entstehung, Funktion, Analyse: Ulrich Siegele zum 70. Geburtstag*, Musikwissenschaftliche Schriften 38, ed. Siegbert Rampe (Munich-Salzburg: Katzbichler, 2002), 321–471.

2. A few examples of invertible counterpoint from Bach's C-Major Fugue were presented in Johann Philipp Kirnberger, *Die Kunst des reinen Satzes in der Musik*, vol. 2/2 (Berlin: Christian Friedrich Voss, 1776), 192f.

3. Another possibility would have been to adjust the lower voice rhythmically, and Bach may have toyed with this idea at some point; the latest stage of the only autograph source of *WTC* I preserves this reading of m. 15 (reproduced in Example 3). (See Johann Sebastian Bach, *Das Wohltemperierte Klavier I, BWV 846–869*, ed. Alfred Dürr, Neue Ausgabe sämtlicher Werke, series 5, vol. 6/1 (Kassel: Bärenreiter, 1989), 5, m. 15.) But by that time he had already decided not to complete the upper voice, so this final revision of the lower voice was redundant, probably an oversight on his part suggested by a memory of earlier thinking about the problem raised by this demonstration. Alfred Dürr, however, thinks otherwise, suggesting that the reason for the late revision lies "in a sensitivity of later Bach with regard to an irregular resolution of the seventh a'/B on the penultimate eighth of the measure." Dürr, *Johann Sebastian Bach, Das Wohltemperierte Klavier*, 103.

4. Quotations in this paragraph are from *The New Bach Reader*, ed. Hans T. David and Arthur Mendel, rev. Christoph Wolff (New York: W. W. Norton & Company, 1998), 397, 305, 399–400.

5. "So eine Bach'sche Fuge, das ist ein Kristall in der Schußbewegung, bis es auf dem Orgelpunt erstarrt." Cosima Wagner, *Die Tagebücher*, ed. Martin Gregor-Delin and Dietrich Mack, vol. 1 (1869–1877) (Munich: Piper, 1976), 480–81.

6. Georg Nikolaus Nissen, *Biographie W. A. Mozarts* (Leipzig, 1828), 655.

7. Donald Francis Tovey, *Essays in Musical Analysis*, vol. 5 (London, 1935), 25.

8. Dreyfus, *Bach and the Patterns of Invention*.

9. Dreyfus's own analysis of the C-Major Fugue, different from mine in some details but not in the general spirit, can be found in *Bach and the Patterns of Invention*, 150–55; his thinking on the fugue in general is found primarily in chs. 5–6, 135–88; his discussion of the concerto takes chs. 2–3, 33–102. As John Butt pointed out to me (private communication), the centrality of the ritornello to Bach's thinking was also shown (from the perspective of the compositional process) by Robert Marshall, who, in his *The Compositional Process of J. S. Bach: a Study of the Autograph Scores of the Vocal Works* (Princeton: Princeton University Press, 1972), repeatedly demonstrated that Bach expended much more effort on the ritornello than on the other sections of a movement.

10. Dreyfus, *Bach and the Patterns of Invention*, 94–101.

11. "Zwar sagt schon das einzelne Werk alles, was zu sagen ist—jedoch im Rahmen seines beschränkten Horizonts. Werkreihen oder Zyklen bieten die Möglichkeit, diesen Horizont gewaltig zu erweitern, ein und denselben Gedanken in unterschiedliche Formen des Ausdrucks zu gießen und damit in emphatischem Wortsinn erschöpfend zu behandeln. . . . In den *Inventionen* und

Sinfonien, dem *Wohltemperierten Klavier,* den *Sei Solo* für Violine, in den vier Teilen der *Clavier-Übung* und schließlich in der *Kunst der Fuge,* aber auch in der definitiven Gestalt der *h-Moll-Messe* ist dann das Bestreben spürbar, das universelle Moment der Musik in Zyklen von nicht erschöpfendem, aber ausschöpfendem Wesen aufscheinen zu lassen." Martin Geck, *Bach: Leben und Werk* (Reinbek: Rowohlt, 2000), 708–9.

12. "'Unendlichkeit' ist eine Assoziation, die einer Variationenreihe gut ansteht: Hoffmann/Kreisler will die *Goldberg-Variationen* weiterkomponieren." Geck, *Bach: Leben und Werk,* 672.

13. Christoph Wolff, *Johann Sebastian Bach: The Learned Musician* (New York: W. W. Norton & Co., 2000), 337.

CHAPTER 3

1. Elke Axmacher disagrees, pointing out that both the individual and communal points of view are present in both kinds of texts, the free poems and the chorales. This is true, if one considers the texts alone. But here the two different kinds of musical setting make all the difference. *"Aus Liebe will mein Heyland sterben": Untersuchung zum Wandel des Passionsverständnisses im frühen 18. Jahrhundert,* Beiträge zur theologischen Bachforschung 2 (Neuhausen-Stuttgart: Hänssler-Verlag, 1984), 197.

2. On the three hills, see M. Eliade and K. Galling, "Berge, heilige," in *Die Religion in Geschichte und Gegenwart. Handwörterbuch für Theologie und Religionswissenschaft,* 3rd ed., vol. 1 (1957), coll. 1043–44.

3. Elke Axmacher, *"Aus Liebe will mein Heyland sterben,"* 190, and Axmacher, "Die Deutung der Passion Jesu im Text der Matthäus-Passion von J. S. Bach," *Luther: Zeitschrift der Luther-Gesellschaft* 56 (1985): 62.

4. While I understand it, I cannot quite agree with Spitta's objection: "This mighty movement, saturated with the most intensified feeling of the divine Passion, has so long been universally regarded as an integral portion of the St. Matthew Passion, and it so admirably fits its place, musically speaking— particularly as it is a splendid finish to the first part—that we are scarcely conscious of the fact that, in one respect, it cannot conceal its original purpose; the poetical purport of the words refers almost exclusively to things which are antecedent to the Passion properly speaking. The verses ought to form an introduction to a rhymed narrative of it, and are therefore out of place here, where the history has already begun." Philipp Spitta, *Johann Sebastian Bach: His Work and Influence on the Music of Germany, 1685–1750,* trans. Clara Bell and John Alexander Fuller-Maitland, vol. 2 (London: Novello, 1884), 553.

5. Axmacher, *"Aus Liebe will mein Heyland sterben,"* 192.

6. Indeed, as Axmacher has demonstrated, Picander modeled a number of his poems directly on a cycle of Passion sermons, *Vom Leyden Christi,* by the seventeenth-century Rostock theologian Heinrich Müller; this may even have been at Bach's advice, given that the composer owned that volume of Müller's sermons. See Axmacher, *"Aus Liebe will mein Heyland sterben,"* 170–84, and

Axmacher, "Die Deutung der Passion Jesu im Text der Matthäus-Passion von J. S. Bach," 55–56. Axmacher's book is the fundamental and path-breaking study of the relationship between the texts of Bach's Passions and the Lutheran tradition of Passion sermons.

7. "Vielleicht wird viel zu wenig daran gedacht, daß die zeitgenössischen Hörer der Matthäuspassion Bachs nicht nur mehr oder weniger 'Ungläubige' sind, die Zugang zur 'Dogmatik' des Leidenden und Sterbenden verloren haben, vielmehr darüber hinaus 'Unverständige', die nichts von dem Eingeständnis verstehen können und wissen wollen, daß sie 'Sünder' sind und einer Erlösung bedürfen, sei es diese oder eine andere." Hans Blumenberg, *Matthäuspassion* (Frankfurt am Main: Suhrkamp Verlag, 1988), 127.

8. See, in particular, Elke Axmacher, "Die Deutung der Passion Jesu im Text der Matthäus-Passion von J. S. Bach;" Axmacher, *"Aus Liebe will mein Heyland sterben"*; Robin A. Leaver, *J. S. Bach as Preacher: His Passions and Music in Worship* (St. Louis: Concordia, 1984); Leaver, "The Mature Vocal Works and Their Theological and Liturgical Context," in *The Cambridge Companion to Bach*, ed. John Butt (Cambridge: Cambridge University Press, 1997), 86–122; Jaroslav Pelikan, *Bach Among the Theologians* (Philadelphia: Fortress Press, 1986); Martin Petzold, "Zwischen Orthodoxie, Pietismus und Aufklärung—Überlegungen zum theologiegeschichtlichen Kontext Johann Sebastian Bachs," *Bach-Studien* 7 (1982): 66–108; Petzoldt, "Die theologische Bedeutung der Chorale in Bachs Matthäus-Passion," *Musik und Kirche* 53 (1983): 53–63; *Bach als Ausleger der Bibel: Theologische und musikwissenschaftliche Studien zum Werk Johann Sebastian Bachs,* ed. Petzoldt (Göttingen: 1985); Petzoldt, "Zur Theologie der Matthäus-Passion in zeitgenossischer Perspektive," in *Johann Sebastian Bach, Matthäus-Passion, BWV 244: Vorträge der Sommerakademie J. S. Bach 1985,* ed. Ulrich Prinz (Stuttgart, 1990), 50–75; and Petzoldt, "'Bey einer andächtigen Musique ist allezeit Gott mit seiner Gnaden Gegenwart': Bach und die Theologie," in *Bach Handbuch,* ed. Konrad Küster (Kassel, Stuttgart, and Weimar: Bärenreiter and Metzler, 1999), 81–91.

9. Here I summarize Pelikan, *Bach Among the Theologians*, 91–101; see also Jaroslav Pelikan, *The Growth of Medieval Theology (600–1300),* vol. 3 in *The Christian Tradition: A History of the Development of Doctrine* (Chicago: The University of Chicago Press, 1978), 109–43.

10. "Du solt wissen und glauben . . . Das Christus solchs umb deiner sünden willen gelitten hab, das Gott die selben im auffgeladen und er sie in allem gehorsam getragen und dafür bezalet hab, auff das, wenn du erkennest, das du ein sünder seyst und habst Gott erzürnet, du dennoch nit verzagest, Sonder dich solches leydens und genugthuunh unsers Herrn Christi tröstest." Quoted from Axmacher, "Die Deutung der Passion Jesu im Text der Matthäus-Passion von J. S. Bach," 52.

11. Axmacher, *"Aus Liebe will mein Heyland sterben,"* 183–84 and 204–17.

12. Martin Geck, *Die Wiederentdeckung der Matthäuspassion im 19. Jahrhundert: Die zeitgenössischen Dokumente und ihre ideengeschichtliche Deutung,* Studien zur Musikgeschichte des 19. Jahrhunderts 9 (Regensburg: Gustav Bosse Verlag, 1967), 67–70.

13. "Sie ist ein einziges, in fast ununterbrochenem Moll gewiß wunderbar wogendes Wolkenmeer von Seufzern, Klagen und Anklagen, von Ausrufen des Entsetzens, des Bedauerns, des Mitleidens: eine Trauerode, die in einem regelrechten Grabgesang ('Ruhe sanft!') ihren Ausklang findet, die durch die Osterbotschaft weder bestimmt, noch auch begrenzt ist, in der Jesus der Sieger völlig stumm bleibt. Wann wird die Kirche sich darüber klar werden, und dann auch die Tausende und Tausende, die die evangelische Leidensgeschichte ausgerechnet nur in dieser Version kennen mögen, darauf aufmerksam machen, daß es sich in ihr um eine Abstraktion handelt, daß das bestimmt *nicht* die Passion *Jesu Christi* ist?" Karl Barth, *Die Kirchliche Dogmatik*, vol. 4/2 (Zollikon-Zürich: Evangelischer Verlag, 1955), 280.

14. Martin Petzoldt, *Bach und die Bibel: Katalog* (Leipzig: n.d.), 50.

15. Barth, *Die Kirchliche Dogmatik*, vol. 3/1 (1947), 464–65.

16. And, as Pelikan has demonstrated, Bach did put Christ the Victor at the center of the St. John Passion. Pelikan, *Bach Among the Theologians*, 106–13.

17. "Nur Leiden und Tod sind allen Evangelisten gemeinsam, sind durch die Kreuzesaffinität des ersten Theologen Paulus wie seiner Gefolgsleute Augustin und Luther zum Zentrum der christlichen Gedankenwelt geworden. Bach ist groß, weil er diese Zentrierung an sich genommen und zum Tönen gebracht hat." Blumenberg, *Matthäuspassion*, 78.

18. Axmacher, "Die Deutung der Passion Jesu im Text der Matthäus-Passion von J. S. Bach," 69.

19. According to Emil Platen, a text of this sort "corresponds quite closely to the diction of contemporary Passion sermons." See Platen, *Die Matthäus-Passion von Johann Sebastian Bach: Entstehung, Werkbeschreibung, Rezeption* (Kassel and Munich: Bärenreiter and Deutscher Taschenbuch, 1991), 49.

20. For another analysis of the Passion's temporal structure, see Platen, *Die Matthäus-Passion von Johann Sebastian Bach*, 45–49.

21. G. W. F. Hegel, *Aesthetics: Lectures on Fine Art*, trans. T. M. Knox, vol. 2 (Oxford: Clarendon Press, 1975), 1103–4.

22. Erich Auerbach, "Farinata and Cavalcante," *Mimesis: The Representation of Reality in Western Literature*, trans. Willard R. Trask (Princeton: Princeton University Press, 1953), 174–202. The remark on Hegel is on p. 191. The quotation following is on pp. 189–90 and 193.

23. Auerbach, *Mimesis*, 196.

24. Cf. Martin Petzoldt, "Hat Gott Zeit, hat der Mensch Ewigkeit? Zur Kantate BWV 106 von Johann Sebastian Bach," *Musik und Kirche* 66 (1996): 212–20.

25. Giuseppe Tomasi di Lampedusa, *Il Gattopardo* (Milan: Feltrinelli, 1969), 76.

26. Hans Blumenberg, *The Legitimacy of the Modern Age*, trans. Robert M. Wallace (Cambridge: The MIT Press, 1983), 467.

27. For Leibniz, God's point of view (which is the sum of all partial points of view) is timeless: the harmony among the preprogrammed monads is preestablished for all eternity. Temporality appears only for the partial points of view. For other parallels between Bach's and Leibniz's ways of thinking, a

persistent *topos* in Bach literature, see in particular Hans Heinrich Eggebrecht, "Bach und Leibniz," *Bericht über die wissenschaftliche Bachtagung der Gesellschaft für Musikforschung* (Leipzig, 1951), 431–47; John Butt, "'A mind unconscious that it is calculating'? Bach and the rationalist philosophy of Wolff, Leibniz and Spinoza," in *The Cambridge Companion to Bach*, ed. Butt (Cambridge: Cambridge University Press, 1997), 60–71.

28. Beethoven's characterization of Bach as "Urvater der Harmonie" occurs in a 15 January 1801 letter to Franz Anton Hoffmeister in Leipzig; see Ludwig van Beethoven, *Briefwechsel: Gesamtausgabe*, ed. Sieghard Brandenburg, vol. 1 (Munich: G. Henle, 1996), 63. The second characterization is quoted from Alexander Wheelock Thayer, *Life of Beethoven*, rev. and ed. Elliot Forbes (Princeton: Princeton University Press, 1967), 956.

29. *Briefwechsel zwischen Goethe und Zelter*, ed. Ludwig Geiger, vol. 3 (Leipzig, n.d.), 127.

30. Gioseffo Zarlino, *Le Istitutioni harmoniche* (Venice, 1558), pt. 1, ch. 5, 10.

31. Quoted from *The New Bach Reader*, ed. Hans T. David and Arthur Mendel, rev. Christoph Wolff (New York: W. W. Norton & Co., 1998), 16–17.

32. Johann Adolph Scheibe, "Letter from an Able *Musikant* Abroad," *Critischer Musikus*, May 14, 1737, in *The New Bach Reader*, ed. Hans T. David and Arthur Mendel, rev. Christoph Wolff, 338.

33. Johann Abraham Birnbaum, "Impartial Comments on a Questionable Passage in the Sixth Number of *Der Critische Musicus*," [1738], in *The New Bach Reader*, ed. Hans T. David and Arthur Mendel, rev. Christoph Wolff, 347. For Birnbaum's relationship with Bach, see Christoph Wolff, "'The Extraordinary Perfections of the Hon. Court Composer': An Inquiry into the Individuality of Bach's Music," *Bach: Essays on His Life and Music* (Cambridge: Harvard University Press, 1991), 391–97.

34. *The New Bach Reader*, ed. Hans T. David and Arthur Mendel, rev. Christoph Wolff, 305.

35. All quotations in this paragraph—the first two by Marburg and the third by Reichhardt—are from *The New Bach Reader*, ed. Hans T. David and Arthur Mendel, rev. Christoph Wolff, 375, 360, and 373.

36. Incidentally, Bach reception continued in Berlin without interruption until the time of Mendelssohn's revival of the St. Matthew Passion; Mendelssohn's copy of the score was a present from his grandmother, Babette Salomon, who had studied keyboard playing with Bach's son Friedemann. See Martin Geck, *Die Wiederentdeckung der Matthäuspassion im 19. Jahrhundert: Die zeitgenössischen Dokumente und ihre ideengeschichtliche Deutung*, Studien zur Musikgeschichte des 19. Jahrhunderts 9 (Regensburg: Gustav Bosse Verlag, 1967), 63.

37. Quoted from *The New Bach Reader*, ed. Hans T. David and Arthur Mendel, rev. Christoph Wolff, 367.

38. The harmonizations, published largely because of C. P. E. Bach's and Kirnberger's efforts, were the only publications of Bach's music between *The Art of*

Fugue in 1752 and *The Well-Tempered Keyboard* in 1801, although manuscript copies of the latter circulated widely.

39. This passage and the Reichardt quotation following are from *The New Bach Reader*, ed. Hans T. David and Arthur Mendel, rev. Christoph Wolff, 379–80 and 384.

40. In this paragraph I have summarized the excellent discussion in Michael Heinemann, "Paradigma Fuge: Bach und das Erbe des Kontrapunkts," in *Bach und die Nachwelt*, vol. 1, ed. Michael Heinemann and Hans-Joachim Hinrichsen, (Laaber: Laaber Verlag, 1997), 119–27. Laurenz Lütteken recently demonstrated another thread of continuity between the Berlin Bach tradition and the 1829 revival of the St. Mattew Passion, pointing to the philosophical debt that Kirnberger's ideal of *reiner Satz* owed Moses Mendelssohn, Felix Mendelssohn's grandfather; decades later Felix Mendelssohn was still reading Kirnberger. Laurenz Lütteken, "Zwischen Ohr und Verstand. Moses Mendelssohn, Johann Philipp Kirnberger und die Begründung des 'reinen Satzes' in der Musik," in *Musik und Ästhetik im Berlin Moses Mendelssohns*, ed. Anselm Gerhard (Tübingen: Max Niemeyer, 1999), 135–63.

41. Quoted from *The New Bach Reader*, ed. Hans T. David and Arthur Mendel, rev. Christoph Wolff, 399. The other quotations in this paragraph, all from Forkel's 1802 Bach biography, are likewise from *The New Bach Reader*, 443, 450, 455, and 456.

42. See Reinhold Bernhardt, "Aus der Umwelt der Wiener Klassiker. Freiherr Gottfried van Swieten (1734–1803)," *Der Bär: Jahrbuch von Breitkopf & Härtel 1929–30*, 74–166; Andreas Holschneider, "Die musikalische Bibliothek Gottfried van Swietens," in *Bericht über den Internationalen Musikwissenschaftlichen Kongreß Kassel 1962*, ed. Georg Reichert and Martin Just (Kassel: Bärenreiter, 1963), 174–78.

43. Lütteken, "Zwischen Ohr und Verstand," 163, n. 102.

44. *Briefwechsel zwischen Goethe und Zelter*, ed. L. Geiger, 2:481. The centrality of "harmony" for the Romantic understanding of Bach's music is emphasized in Carl Dahlhaus, "Zur Entstehung der romantischen Bach-Deutung," *Bach-Jahrbuch*, 64 (1978), 192–210.

45. Immanuel Kant, *Practical Philosophy*, trans. and ed. Mary J. Gregor, The Cambridge Edition of the Works of Immanuel Kant (Cambridge: Cambridge University Press, 1996), 255.

46. Quoted from *The New Bach Reader*, ed. Hans T. David and Arthur Mendel, rev. Christoph Wolff, 499. See also Friedrich Smend, "Goethes Verhältnis zu Bach," in *Bach Studien. Gesammelte Reden und Aufsätze*, ed. Christoph Wolff (Kassel: Bärenreiter, 1969), 212–36; Walter Wiora, "Goethes Wort über Bach," in *Hans Albrecht in memoriam*, ed. Wilfried Brennecke and Hans Haase (Kassel: Bärenreiter, 1962), 179–91.

47. Quoted from Albrecht Schöne, *Kommentare* to Johann Wolfgang Goethe, *Faust*, in Goethe, *Sämtliche Werke, Briefe, Tagebücher und Gespräche*, part 1, vol. 7/2 (Frankfurt: Deutscher Klassiker Verlag, 1994), 412.

48. E. T. A. Hoffmann, "Old and New Church Music," in *E. T. A. Hoffmann's Musical Writings: Kreisleriana, The Poet and the Composer, Music Criticism*, ed. David Charlton, trans. Martyn Clarke (Cambridge: Cambridge University Press, 1989), 355.

49. Anton Schindler, *The Life of Beethoven*, ed. Ignaz Moscheles, vol. 1 (London, 1841), 40, quoted from *The New Bach Reader*, ed. Hans T. David and Arthur Mendel, rev. Christoph Wolff, 490.

INTERLUDE

1. "Un discorso radicale sul nostro tempo dovrebbe partire dal riconosci-mento di un fatto: fino a *ieri*—e lo ieri può datarsi alla Rivoluzione francese o da quella russa, dalla prima guerra mondiale o dalla seconda, la differenza non è grande, ai fini del discorso—fino a *ieri*, dunque, vivevamo pur sempre nell'era cristiana. Oggi, non più." Nicola Chiaromonte, *Che cosa rimane: Taccuini 1955– 1971*, ed. Miriam Chiaromonte (Bologna: Il Mulino, 1995), 21–22.

2. This last is, by the way, the devil's favorite promise. What he neglects to spell out are the consequences. "Eritis sicut Deus scientes bonum et malum," writes Professor Mephistopheles, correcting the Vulgate's "dii," in an album of a prospective student. And out of the student's earshot he murmurs: "Folg' nur dem alten Spruch und meiner Muhme, der Schlange, / Dir wird gewiß einmal bei deiner Gottähnlichkeit bange!" (Just follow the old saying and my cousin the serpent, and some day your likeness to God will surely make you anxious!). Johann Wolfgang von Goethe, *Faust*, 2048–50.

3. My understanding of the content and development of the Christian teach-ing is based, first and foremost, on volumes 1, 3, and 4 of Jaroslav Pelikan's mag-isterial *The Christian Tradition: A History of the Development of Doctrine* (Chicago: The University of Chicago Press, 1971, 1978, 1984).

4. My understanding of the beginnings of Christianity is based primarily on Thomas Sheehan, *The First Coming: How the Kingdom of God Became Chris-tianity* (New York: Random House, 1986).

5. This aspect of Paul's message is at the center of Daniel Boyarin, *A Radical Jew: Paul and the Politics of Identity* (Berkeley: University of California Press, 1994).

6. Figural interpretation, Erich Auerbach has explained, "establishes a con-nection between two events or persons in such a way that the first signifies not only itself but also the second, while the second involves or fulfills the first. The two poles of a figure are separated in time, but both, being real events or per-sons, are within temporality." Erich Auerbach, *Mimesis [: The] Representation of Reality in Western Literature*, trans. Willard R. Trask (Princeton: Princeton University Press, 1953), 73.

7. Cf. Leszek Kolakowski, *God Owes Us Nothing: A Brief Remark on Pas-cal's Religion and on the Spirit of Jansenism* (Chicago: The University of Chicago Press, 1995).

8. This, however, is not the view of Elaine Pagels, who stresses Augustine's

radical originality and departure from earlier Christian tradition in her *Adam, Eve, and the Serpent* (New York: Random House, 1988), 98–150. I would like to thank Jonathan Schofer for bringing Pagels's book to my attention.

9. This middle-of-the-road position could even claim Augustine's authority, as the future saint had not denied the existence of free will: man was always free to choose evil—indeed, chose it whenever his will was on its own—but grace empowered the will to choose good; in other words, will was free under grace. However, given that Augustine also thought the gift of grace to be irresistible, it is difficult to see how I can be considered free if I cannot but do evil when on my own and yet cannot reject grace, either.

10. Quoted from Pelikan, *The Christian Tradition,* 4:287.

11. Saint Augustine, *The City of God,* trans. Marcus Dods (New York: The Modern Library, 2000). All quotations below are from this translation.

12. Here I follow Pagels, *Adam, Eve, and the Serpent,* 127–50.

13. Usually, but not always: for Goethe's awareness of the proximity of his own outlook to Pelagianism, see his autobiography, *Aus meinem Leben: Dichtung und Wahrheit,* bk. 15, in Johann Wolfgang von Goethe, *Werke, Hamburger Ausgabe,* vol. 10, ed. Lieselotte Blumenthal and Erich Trunz (Munich: Deutscher Taschenbuch Verlag, 1988), 43–44.

14. My summary of how the theory of free will came to be supplanted by the theory of autonomy is based primarily on the exceptionally illuminating account in Andrzej Rapaczynski, *Nature and Politics: Liberalism in the Philosophies of Hobbes, Locke, and Rousseau* (Ithaca: Cornell University Press, 1987). For a definitive history of the subject, see J. B. Schneewind, *The Invention of Autonomy: A History of Modern Moral Philosophy* (Cambridge: Cambridge University Press, 1998).

15. For Kant's considering Rousseau a second Newton, see Schneewind, *The Invention of Autonomy,* 491, and Susan Neiman, *Evil in Modern Thought: An Alternative History of Philosophy* (Princeton: Princeton University Press, 2002), 36. For the portrait, see Manfred Kuehn, *Kant: A Biography* (Cambridge: Cambridge University Press, 2001), 272, and Schneewind, *The Invention of Autonomy,* 490, n. 14.

16. Jean-Jacques Rousseau, *A Discourse on Inequality,* trans. Maurice Cranston (Harmondsworth: Penguin, 1984), 101.

17. See the discussion in my *A Theory of Art* (New York: Oxford University Press, 2000), 157–61.

18. On the persistence of the Jacobin-statist model in French politics, see Pierre Rosanvallon, *Le Modèle politique français: la société civile contre le jacobinisme de 1789 à nos jours* (Paris: Seuil, 2004).

19. Alexander Herzen, *My Past and Thoughts,* trans. Constance Garnett, rev. Humphrey Higgens, vol. 2 (New York: Knopf, 1968), 629.

20. Jean-Jacques Rousseau, *Emile, or On Education,* trans. Allan Bloom (n.p.: Basic Books, 1979), 37.

21. For Rousseau's (or his Savoyard Vicar's) views on the afterlife, see *Emile,* bk. 4, 282–85.

22. This and the following quotation are from Maurice Cranston, *The Noble Savage: Jean-Jacques Rousseau 1754–1762* (Chicago: The University of Chicago Press, 1991), 194, 321.

23. Jean-Jacques Rousseau, *A Discourse on Inequality*, trans. Maurice Cranston (Harmondsworth: Penguin, 1984), 136.

24. See the section on "Independence and dependence of self-consciousness: Lordship and Bondage," in G. W. F. Hegel, *Phenomenology of Spirit*, trans. A. V. Miller (Oxford: Oxford University Press, 1977), 111–19.

25. Rousseau, *A Discourse on Inequality*, 133.

26. Rousseau, *Emile, or On Education*, 213–14.

27. Immanuel Kant, "Conjectural Beginning of Human History," in *On History*, ed. Lewis White Beck (Indianapolis: Bobbs-Merrill, 1963), 61.

28. Jean-Jacques Rousseau, *The Social Contract*, trans. Maurice Cranston (Harmondsworth: Penguin, 1968), bk. 1, ch. 1, 49.

29. Both quotations in this paragraph are from Rousseau, *The Social Contract*, bk. 1, ch. 6, 60, 61.

30. Rousseau, *The Social Contract*, bk. 1, ch. 7, 64.

31. These are the subject of an important book by J. L. Talmon, *The Origins of Totalitarian Democracy* (London: Secker & Warburg, 1955).

32. Karl Löwith, *Meaning in History: The Theological Implications of the Philosophy of History* (Chicago: The University of Chicago Press, 1949), 1, 2–3.

33. Hans Blumenberg, *The Legitimacy of the Modern Age*, trans. Robert M. Wallace (Cambridge: The MIT Press, 1983), 35.

34. St. Augustine, *Confessions*, trans. William Watts, Loeb Classical Library, vol. 2 (Cambridge: Harvard University Press, 1912), bk. 11, ch. 20, 253.

35. See the discussion of the "transcendental aesthetic" in the *Critique of Pure Reason*, A17–49 (B31–73).

36. Friedrich Schlegel, "Athenäum Fragments," No. 216, in *German Aesthetic and Literary Criticism: The Romantic Ironists and Goethe*, ed. Kathleen M. Wheeler (Cambridge: Cambridge University Press, 1984), 48.

37. Immanuel Kant, "Idea for a Universal History from a Cosmopolitan Point of View," in *On History*, ed. Lewis White Beck (Indianapolis: Bobbs-Merrill, 1963), 11–26.

38. Kant, "Idea for a Universal History," 21.

39. "The aim of world history," Hegel claimed, "is that the spirit should attain knowledge of its own true nature [which is freedom], that it should objectivize this knowledge and transform it into a real world, and give itself an objective existence." Georg Wilhelm Friedrich Hegel, *Lectures on the Philosophy of World History: Introduction: Reason in History*, trans. H. B. Nisbet (Cambridge: Cambridge University Press, 1975), 64.

40. The two books of Hegel that most decisively shaped the posthumous reception of his philosophy of history are *Grundlinien der Philosophie des Rechts* [*Elements of the Philosophy of Right*] (1821) and *Vorlesungen über die Philosophie der Geschichte* [*Lectures on the Philosophy of History*] (1837).

41. See Immanuel Kant, "Perpetual Peace," in *On History*, ed. Lewis White Beck (Indianapolis: Bobbs-Merrill, 1963), 85–135.

42. My summary is based primarily on Rapaczynski, *Nature and Politics*, and on the Burtt and Rorty books referred to in the following notes.

43. For a classic statement of this interpretation, see Edwin Arthur Burtt, *The Metaphysical Foundations of Modern Physical Science*, rev. ed. (Garden City: Doubleday, 1954).

44. Burtt, *The Metaphysical Foundations of Modern Physical Science*, 308.

45. The book that played a key role in the revival of the pragmatic interpretation of modern science is Richard Rorty, *Philosophy and the Mirror of Nature* (Princeton: Princeton University Press, 1979).

46. Rapaczynski, *Nature and Politics*, 277.

47. The new dignity that the sphere of production acquires in modernity is a central theme in Rapaczynski's *Nature and Politics*.

48. Mircea Eliade, *The Myth of the Eternal Return*, trans. Willard R. Trask (New York: Pantheon Books, 1954).

49. Eliade, *The Myth of the Eternal Return*, 35.

50. Marcel Gauchet, *The Disenchantment of the World: A Political History of Religion*, trans. Oscar Burge (Princeton: Princeton University Press, 1997), 162.

51. Gauchet, *The Disenchantment of the World*, 28, 25.

52. Gauchet, *The Disenchantment of the World*, 176–77.

53. Reinhard Koselleck, *Futures Past: On the Semantics of Historical Time*, trans. Keith Tribe (Cambridge: The MIT Press, 1985).

54. Koselleck's view of what happened before 1500 is offered in a more recent collection, where he stresses the ever shorter duration of the three fundamental phases of human history. In the first phase, extending from ten million to six thousand years ago, natural conditions dominated human existence; this phase was marked by such milestones as the appearance of first documented tools two million years ago, first men-killing weapons and self-reflective art thirty thousand years ago, and the introduction of agriculture and domestication of animals twelve thousand years ago. In the second phase, which lasted until about two hundred years ago, humanity gradually mastered the natural determinants of its existence, developing high cultures on the basis of previous achievements. The present third phase is one of acceleration and globalization shaped by science, technology, and industry. Reinhart Koselleck, *Zeitschichten: Studien zur Historik. Mit einem Beitrag von Hans-Georg Gadamer* (Frankfurt am Main: Suhrkamp Verlag, 2000), 78–96.

CHAPTER 4

1. Adolf Nowak has traced the transition in eighteenth-century music theory from thinking primarily in terms of "invention" to thinking in terms of "disposition"; see his "Der Begriff 'Musikalisches Denken' in der Musiktheo-

rie der Aufklärung," in *Neue Musik und Tradition: Festschrift Rudolf Stephan,* ed. J. Kuckertz, H. de la Motte Haber, C. M. Schmidt, and W. Seidel (Laaber: Laaber Verlag, 1990), 113–22.

2. I am borrowing my terms here from Paul Ricoeur, *Time and Narrative,* 3 vols. (Chicago: The University of Chicago Press, 1984–1988).

3. Among the more recent English-language discussions of classical instrumental forms I have found the following to be particularly useful: Edward T. Cone, *Musical Form and Musical Performance* (New York: W. W. Norton & Co., 1968); Charles Rosen, *The Classical Style: Haydn, Mozart, Beethoven,* expanded ed. (New York: W. W. Norton & Co., 1997); Leonard G. Ratner, *Classic Music: Expression, Form, and Style* (New York: Schirmer Books, 1980); Mark Evan Bonds, *Wordless Rhetoric: Musical Form and the Metaphor of the Oration* (Cambridge: Harvard University Press, 1991); James Webster, *Haydn's "Farewell" Symphony and the Idea of Classical Style: Through-composition and Cyclic Integration in His Instrumental Music* (Cambridge: Cambridge University Press, 1991); William E. Caplin, *Classical Form: A Theory of Formal Functions for the Instrumental Music of Haydn, Mozart, and Beethoven* (New York: Oxford University Press, 1998); James Webster, "Sonata Form," in *The New Grove Dictionary of Music and Musicians,* 2nd ed. (2001), 23:687–701; James Hepokoski, "Back and Forth from *Egmont:* Beethoven, Mozart, and the Nonresolving Recapitulation," *19th-Century Music* 25 (2002): 127–54; and Hepokoski, "Beyond the Sonata Principle," *Journal of the American Musicological Society* 55 (2002): 91–154.

4. Frank Kermode, *The Sense of an Ending: Studies in the Theory of Fiction* (Oxford: Oxford University Press, 1967).

5. Carl Dahlhaus, "Der rhetorische Formbegriff H. Chr. Kochs und die Theorie der Sonatenform," *Archiv für Musikwissenschaft* 35 (1978): 155–76.

6. Heinrich Christoph Koch, *Versuch einer Anleitung zur Composition,* 3 vols. (Leipzig and Rudolstadt: Böhme, 1782–93).

7. Heinrich Christoph Koch, *Introductory Essay on Composition: The Mechanical Rules of Melody, Sections 3 and 4,* trans. Nancy Kovaleff Baker (New Haven: Yale University Press, 1983), 1.

8. Friedrich Nietzsche, *Der Fall Wagner,* 11.11–5, in *Werke: Kritische Gesamtausgabe,* vol. 6/3, ed. G. Colli and M. Montinari (Berlin: de Gruyter, 1969), 32.

9. We are indebted to Dahlhaus for a penetrating analysis of this change. See, in particular, his *The Idea of Absolute Music* (Chicago: The University of Chicago Press, 1989) and *Nineteenth-Century Music* (Berkeley: University of California Press, 1989).

10. Cf. Richard Rorty, "Texts and Lumps," *New Literary History* 17 (1985): 1–16.

11. "The First-Movement Punctuation Form in Mozart's Piano Concertos," in *Mozart's Piano Concertos: Text, Context, Interpretation,* ed. Neal Zaslaw (Ann Arbor: The University of Michigan Press, 1996), 239–59, as well as "Mozart's

Concerto Andante Punctuation Form," *Mozart-Jahrbuch 1998:* 119–38, where I attempted to reconstruct how Mozart thinks in a slow movement.

12. David Rosen, "The Composer's 'Standard Operating Procedure' as Evidence of Intention: The Case of a Formal Quirk in Mozart's K. 595," *Journal of Musicology* 5 (1987): 79–90.

13. For a different view of this relationship, see Peter Gülke, *"Triumph der neuen Tonkunst": Mozarts späte Sinfonien und ihr Umfeld* (Kassel-Stuttgart: Bärenreiter-Metzler, 1998), 54–68.

14. Jacques Handschin, *Musikgeschichte im Überblick* (Lucerne, 1948).

15. Leonard G. Ratner, *Classic Music: Expression, Form, Style* (New York: Schirmer Books, 1980).

16. This quotation and the one following are from Karl Barth, *Wolfgang Amadeus Mozart* (Grand Rapids: W. B. Eerdmans, 1986), 53 and 55f.

17. Emily Anderson, ed. and trans., *The Letters of Mozart and His Family,* 3rd ed. (London: Macmillan, 1985), 907.

18. Anderson, ed. and trans., *The Letters of Mozart and His Family,* 163.

19. Barth, *Wolfgang Amadeus Mozart,* 16.

20. The autograph (London, Royal College of Music, Ms. 402) shows that Mozart himself considered the appendix a real coda. Instead of writing out mm. 492–508, Mozart made a sign to use mm. 82–98 there. Before m. 99 he drew a double barline, topped it with fermatas, and wrote above and below the score, "Coda."

21. The autograph shows that this was something of an afterthought. Originally, Mozart went directly from m. 43 to the present m. 63, that is, composed no third phrase in the ritornello. But he changed his mind even before the ritornello was completed and wrote the second subject at the present m. 91.

22. Unexpected order reversals abound in Mozart piano concertos from early on. The obvious collorary here is the pleasure the composer took as a young man in jumbling proper word order in his letters and transforming perfectly correct but conventional sentences into slightly bizarre and absurd, though still recognizable, text. See, for instance, a letter of 21 August 1773, written from Vienna to his sister in Salzburg , which he signed "Gnagflow Trazom," or the message of 16 January 1773, written to his sister from Milan: "I for have the primo a uomo motet compose which to tomorrow at Church the Theatine perfomed be will." Anderson, ed. and trans., *The Letters of Mozart and His Family,* 239–40 and 226.

CHAPTER 5

1. This "was Mozart's favourite piece of the whole opera," says Michael Kelly—who had created the role of Don Curzio—in his 1826 *Reminiscences;* see Otto Erich Deutsch, *Mozart: A Documentary Biography,* trans. Eric Blom, Peter Branscombe, and Jeremy Noble (Stanford: Stanford University Press, 1965), 534. *Le nozze di Figaro* is based on Beaumarchais's *Le Mariage de Figaro,* which had

its public premiere at the Comédie-Française on 27 April 1784, a scant two years before Mozart's opera was premiered at the Viennese Burgtheater on 1 May 1786.

2. Jérôme-Joseph Momigny's interpretation of the opening movement of Mozart's String Quartet in D Minor, K. 421/417b, in his *Cours complet d'harmonie et de composition* of 1803–1806 is probably the best-known example.

CHAPTER 6

1. Both quotations are from Søren Kierkegaard, *Either/Or*, trans. Howard V. Hong and Edna H. Hong (Princeton: Princeton University Press, 1987), vol. 1, 85 and 92.

2. See, for instance, Wye Jamison Allanbrook, *Rhythmic Gesture in Mozart: "Le Nozze di Figaro" and "Don Giovanni"* (Chicago: The University of Chicago Press, 1983), 207–8.

3. Kierkegaard, *Either/Or*, vol. 1, 119.

4. Bernard Williams has written: "Those who survive Giovanni—not only the other characters, but . . . [we] ourselves—are both more and less than he is: more, since the conditions *on* humanity, which we accept, are also the conditions *of* humanity; and less, since one thing vitality needs is to keep the dream of being as free from conditions as his." Bernard Williams, "Don Giovanni as an Idea," in *W. A. Mozart, "Don Giovanni,"* Cambridge Opera Handbook, ed. Julian Rushton (Cambridge: Cambridge University Press, 1981), 91.

5. Denis de Rougemont, *L'Amour et l'Occident*, édition définitive (Paris: Plon, 1972), 234–38 and passim.

6. Kierkegaard, *Either/Or*, Part 1, 100.

7. Obviously he might have done otherwise: recall the difference that the music makes to our understanding of the "Viva la libertà!" For the most part, music is not very good at telling the audience *what* the personages are saying or doing, but it is expert at telling us *how* they are saying or doing whatever it is they are saying or doing. In opera, music performs the dramatic words and actions and, by doing so, reveals the attitudes of the personages toward their own words and actions and tells us something of their intentions, just as each one of us reveals something of our attitude toward our own words by the way in which we deliver them. It is not that "music knows best," or that it has "the capacity to convey the best truth," better than the one conveyed by the words and actions. This is the view that Carolyn Abbate attributes to the standard operatic hermeneutics and finds deplorable. (Carolyn Abbate, "Music—Drastic or Gnostic?" *Critical Inquiry* 30 [2004]: 520–22 and passim.) But neither is it the case, as she suggests, that music simply cloaks the words in "beautiful noise" of "emotional power." It is, rather, that the words and actions know one thing—they know, for instance, that the Count is asking for forgiveness—and the music knows another—that, for instance, at that moment at least, he really means it—and that we need both to make sense of what we see and hear.

8. Quoted from the "Notice" introducing the play in Beaumarchais, *Théâtre*, ed. J. P. de Beaumarchais (Paris: Garnier, 1980), 138.

9. E. T. A. Hoffmann, "A Tale of Don Juan (As It Happened to a Traveling Enthusiast)," in *Pleasures of Music: A Reader's Choice of Great Writings about Music and Musicians from Cellini to Bernard Shaw,* ed. Jacques Barzun (New York: Viking, 1960), 28 and 29f. The original story, "Don Juan: Eine fabelhafte Begebenheit, die sich mit einem reisenden Enthusiasten zugetragen," written in 1812, appeared in 1814–1815 in *Phantasiestücke in Callots Manier.*

10. All quotations in this paragraph are from Hoffmann, "A Tale of Don Juan," 30– 31.

11. All quotations in this paragraph are from Kierkegaard, *Either/Or,* Part 1, 45–135, specifically 64, 56, 70, 70, 57, 71, 94, 94–95.

12. Kierkegaard, *Either/Or,* Part 2, 169.

13. Kierkegaard, *Either/Or,* Part 1, 96.

14. This and the following quotation are from Kierkegaard, *Either/Or,* Part 1, 64 and 65.

15. Kierkegaard, *Either/Or,* Part 1, 68.

16. Kierkegaard, *Either/Or,* Part 1, 102.

17. Kierkegaard, *Either/Or,* Part 1, 49, 57, 65.

18. Kierkegaard, *Either/Or,* Part 1, 64–65.

19. Cf. Gernot Gruber, *Mozart and Posterity,* trans. R. S. Furness (London: Quartet Books, 1991), 97 and 128; and André Dabezies, "Faust et Don Juan," in *Dictionnaire de Don Juan,* ed. Pierre Brunel (Paris: Robert Laffont, 1999), 395–403.

20. "Werd' ich beruhigt je mich auf ein Faulbett legen: / So sei es gleich um mich getan! / Kannst du mich schmeichelnd je belügen / Daß ich mir selbst gefallen mag, / Kannst du mich mit Genuß betriegen: / Das sei für mich der letzte Tag!" (1692–97). Here and below I quote from Johann Wolfgang Goethe, *Faust: Texte,* in Goethe, *Sämtliche Werke, Briefe, Tagebücher und Gespräche,* vol. 7/1, ed. Albrecht Schöne (Frankfurt: Deutscher Klassiker Verlag, 1994); the translation is from Goethe, *Faust I & II,* trans. Stuart Atkins, in Goethe, *Collected Works,* vol. 2 (Princeton: Princeton University Press, 1984).

21. "Werd' ich zum Augenblicke sagen: / Verweile doch! du bist so schön! / Dann magst du mich in fesseln schlagen, / Dann will ich gern zu Grunde gehn! / Dann mag die Totenglocke schallen, / Dann bist du deines Dienstes frei, / Die Uhr mag stehn, der Zeiger fallen, / Es sei die Zeit für mich vorbei!" (1699–1706).

22. "Wie ich beharre bin ich Knecht, / Ob dein, was frag' ich, oder wessen" (1710–11).

23. ". . . geh er seinen Gang, / Im Weiterschreiten find er Qual und Glück, / Er! unbefriedigt jeden Augenblick" (11450–52).

24. "Solch ein Gewimmel möcht ich sehn, / Auf freiem Grund mit freiem Volke stehn. / Zum Augenblicke dürft' ich sagen: / Verweile doch, Du bist so schön! / Es kann die Spur von meinen Erdetagen / Nicht in Äonen untergehn. / Im Vorgefühl von solchem hohen Glück / Genieß ich jetzt den höchsten Augenblick" (11579–86).

25. Actually Mephisto does not say "if or when," just "Wenn" (when). "Ich

will mich *hier* zu deinem Dienst verbinden, / Auf deinen Wink nicht rasten und nicht ruhn; / Wenn wir uns *drüben* wieder finden, / So sollst du mir das Gleiche tun" (1656–59).

26. "Das Drüben kann mich wenig kümmern, / Schlägst du erst diese Welt zu Trümmern, / Die andere mag darnach entstehn. / Aus dieser Erde quillen meine Freuden, / Und diese Sonne scheinet meinen Leiden; / Kann ich mich erst von ihnen scheiden, / Dann mag was will und kann geschehn" (1660–66).

27. "Der Erdenkreis is mir genug bekannt. / Nach drüben ist die Aussicht uns verrant: / Tor! wer dorthin die Augen blinzelnd richtet, / Sich über Wolken seines gleichen dichtet; / Er stehe fest und sehe hier sich um; / Dem Tüchtigen ist diese Welt nicht stumm, / Was braucht er in die Ewigkeit zu schweifen, / Was er erkennt läßt sich ergreifen" (11441–48).

28. "'Die Beschäftigung mit Unsterblichkeits-Ideen,' fuhr Goethe fort, 'ist für vornehme Stände und besonders für Frauenzimmer, die nichts zu tun haben. Ein tüchtiger Mensch aber, der schon hier etwas Ordentliches zu sein gedenkt und der daher täglich zu streben, zu kämpfen und zu wirken hat, läßt die künftige Welt auf sich beruhen und ist tätig und nützlich in dieser.'" See Johann Peter Eckermann, *Gespräche mit Goethe in den letzten Jahren seines Lebens*, ed. Fritz Bergemann (n.p.: Insel Verlag, 1981), 85.

29. "Ich habe deines gleichen nie gehaßt. / Von allen Geistern die verneinen / Ist mir der Schalk am wenigsten zur Last. / Des Menschen Tätigkeit kann allzuleicht erschlaffen, / Er lieb sich bald die unbedingte Ruh; / Drum geb' ich gern ihm den Gesellen zu, / Der reizt und wirkt, und muß, als Teufel, schaffen" (337–43).

30. "Es irrt der Mensch so lang' er strebt" (317); "Wer immer strebend sich bemüht / Den können wir erlösen" (11936–37).

31. "Und so lang du das nicht hast, / Dieses: Stirb und werde! / Bist du nur ein trüber Gast / Auf der dunklen Erde."

32. "Ein Teil von jener Kraft, / Die stets das Böse will und stets das Gute schafft." (1335–36); "Ich bin der Geist, der stets verneint! / Und das mit Recht; denn alles was entsteht / Ist wert daß es zugrunde geht; / Drum besser wär's daß nichts entstünde. / So ist denn alles was ihr Sünde, / Zerstörung, kurz das Böse nennt, / Mein eigentliches Element" (1338–44).

33. "Ich bin nur durch die Welt gerannt. / Ein jed' Gelüst ergriff ich bei den Haaren, / Was nicht genügte ließ ich fahren, / Was mir entwischte ließ ich ziehn. / Ich habe nur begehrt und nur vollbracht, / Und abermals gewünscht, und so mit Macht / Mein Leben durchgestürmt . . ." (11433–39).

34. See Goethe's remarks of 24 February 1825 on Lord Byron in Eckermann, *Gespräche mit Goethe*, 134–39.

35. See, for instance, Robert Spaethling, *Music and Mozart in the Life of Goethe* (Columbia, SC: Camden House, 1987).

36. Eckermann, *Gespräche mit Goethe*, 365 (3 February 1830).

37. See, for instance, Goethe's remarks of 6 December 1829 in Eckermann, *Gespräche mit Goethe*, 350.

38. See Karl-Heinz Köhler, "Die Rezeption der Mozart-Opern unter Goethes

Theaterleitung im Jahrzehnt nach dem Tode des Komponisten: Ein Beitrag zur Wirkungsgeschichte des Mozartschen Schaffens im Spiegel der Weimarer Klassik," *Mozart-Jahrbuch 1991:* 231–36.

39. "Alles unser Bemühen daher, uns im Einfachen und Beschränkten abzuschließen, ging verloren, als Mozart auftrat. *Die Entführung aus dem Serail* schlug alles nieder, und es ist auf dem Theater von unserm so sorgsam gearbeiteten Stück niemals die Rede gewesen." Johann Wolfgang von Goethe, *Italienische Reise,* in *Werke, Hamburger Ausgabe,* vol. 11, ed. Erich Trunz (Munich: Deutscher Taschenbuch Verlag, 1988), 437; translation from Otto Erich Deutsch, *Mozart: A Documentary Biography,* trans. Eric Blom, Peter Branscombe, and Jeremy Noble (Stanford: Stanford University Press, 1965), 305. Cf. Goethe's private communication to Kayser in Deutsch, *Mozart: A Documentary Biography,* 258.

40. Quoted from Deutsch, *Mozart: A Documentary Biography,* 486.

41. "Die Musik müßte im Charakter des *Don Juan* sein; Mozart hätte den *Faust* komponieren müssen." Eckermann, *Gespräche mit Goethe,* 293 (12 February 1829).

42. "Des Denkens Faden ist zerrissen, / Mir ekelt lange vor allem Wissen. / Laß in den Tiefen der Sinnlichkeit / Uns glühende Leidenschaften stillen!" (1748–51); "Stürzen wir uns in das Rauschen der Zeit, / In's Rollen der Begebenheit! / Da mag denn Schmerz und Genuß, / Gelingen und Verdruß, / Mit einander wechseln wie es kann; / Nur rastlos betätigt sich der Mann" (1754–59); "Mein Busen, der vom Wissensdrang geheilt ist, / Soll keinen Schmerzen künftig sich verschließen, / Und was der ganzen Menschheit zugeteilt ist, / Will ich in meinem innern Selbst genießen, / Mit meinem Geist das Höchst' und Tiefste greifen, / Ihr Wohl and Weh auf meinen Busen häufen, / Und so mein eigen Selbst zu ihrem Selbst erweitern, / Und, wie sie selbst, am End' auch ich zerscheitern" (1768–75).

43. "Eröffn' ich Räume vielen Millionen, / Nicht sicher zwar, doch tätig-frei zu wohnen" (11563–64); "Im Innern hier ein paradiesisch Land" (11569); "Solch ein Gewimmel möcht ich sehn, / Auf freiem Grund mit freiem Volke stehn" (11579–80).

44. "Nur der verdient sich Freiheit wie das Leben, / Der täglich sie erobern muß" (11575–56).

45. "Und dem alten Gott vertraun" (11142); "Menschenopfer mußten bluten, / Nachts erscholl des Jammers Qual. / Meerab flossen Feuergluten; / Morgens war es ein Kanal" (11127–30).

46. "Vor Augen ist mein Reich unendlich / Im Rücken neckt mich der Verdruß" (11153–54); "Wie schaff ich mir es vom Gemüte! / Das Glöcklein läutet und ich wüte" (11257–58).

47. "Und das verfluchte Bim-Baum-Bimmel / Umnebelnd heitern Abendhimmel, / Mischt sich in jegliches Begebnis, / Vom ersten Bad bis zum Begräbnis, / Als wäre, zwischen Bim und Baum, / Das Leben ein verschollner Traum" (11263–68).

48. "Was willst du dich denn hier genierien, / Mußt du nicht längst koloni-

sieren" (11273–74); "So geht und schafft sie mir zur Seite!" (11275); "unbeson-
nenen wilden Streich" (11372); "Tausch wollt ich, wollte keinen Raub" (11371);
"Auf freiem Grund mit freiem Volke stehn" (11580); "Auf strenges Ordnen,
raschen Fleiß, / Erfolgt der allerschönste Preis; / Daß sich das größte Werk
vollende / Genügt Ein Geist für tausend Hände" (11507–10).

49. "Die wenig Bäume, nicht mein eigen, / Verderben mir den Welt-Besitz"
(11241–42).

50. "Das ist der Weisheit letzter Schluß: / Nur der verdient sich Freiheit wie
das Leben, / Der täglich sie erobern muß" (11574–76); "Bezahle, locke, presse
bei!" (11554).

51. Cf. Roberto Calasso, *The Ruin of Kasch*, trans. William Weaver and
Stephen Sartarelli (Cambridge: Harvard University Press, 1994), 4–8.

52. "Es ist nichts trauriger anzusehn als das unvermittelte Streben ins Unbe-
dinge in dieser durchaus bedingen Welt." I quote this and the following two remarks from Albrecht Schöne, *Kommentare* [to *Faust*], in Goethe, *Sämtliche
Werke, Briefe, Tagebücher und Gespräche*, pt. 1, vol. 7/2 (Frankfurt: Deutscher
Klassiker Verlag, 1994), 38.

53. On the idealizing reception of the tragedy, see Schöne, *Kommentare*, 709f
and elsewhere.

54. See Eckermann, *Gespräche mit Goethe*, 350 (6 December 1829).

55. On the derivation of Goethe's eschatological vision from the teaching
of Origen on the *Apokatastasis panton*, see the illuminating comments in
Schöne, *Kommentare*, 767 and 788–95. Toward the end of *Faust* the devil himself
feels some of the heat of divine love: "My head's on fire, and I've heart-and-
liver burn; / . . . My body is on fire everywhere" (Mir brennt der Kopf, das Herz,
die Leber brennt, / . . . Der ganze Körper steht in Feuer [11753, 11785]).

56. On Goethe's attitude to mythology, in particular with regard to the
Prometheus myth, see the subtle account in part 4 of Hans Blumenberg, *Work
on Myth*, trans. Robert M. Wallace (Cambridge: The MIT Press, 1985), 397–
557.

57. "Im Homer reflektiert sich die Menschenwelt noch einmal im Olymp
und schwebt wie eine Fata Morgana über der irdischen. Diese Spiegelung tut in
jedem poetischen Kunstwerk wohl, weil sie gleichsam eine Totalität hervorbringt
und wirklich Menschenbedürfnis ist. Daher auch in der katholischen Religion."
Quoted from Schöne, *Kommentare*, 164.

58. "Übrigens werden Sie zugeben, daß . . . ich, bei so übersinnlichen, kaum
zu ahnenden Dingen, mich sehr leicht im Vagen hätte verlieren können, wenn
ich nicht meinen poetischen Intentionen durch die scharf umrissenen christlich-
kirchlichen Figuren und Vorstellungen eine wohltätig beschränkende Form und
Festigkeit gegeben hätte." Eckermann, *Gespräche mit Goethe*, 471–72.

CHAPTER 7

1. The scholarly literature on various aspects of *Die Zauberflöte* is rich and
voluminous. In writing this chapter, I have particularly benefited from the fol-

lowing studies and editions: Peter Branscombe, *W. A. Mozart: "Die Zauber-flöte,"* Cambridge Opera Handbook (Cambridge: Cambridge University Press, 1991); Norbert Miller, "Die Erben von Zauberflöte und Glockenspiel: Peter von Winters *Labyrinth* und das Märchentheater Emanuel Schikaneders," in *Europäische Romantik in der Musik,* ed. Carl Dahlhaus and Norbert Miller (Stuttgart-Weimar: Metzler, 1999), 1:497–538; Wolfgang Amadé Mozart, *Die Zauberflöte, K. 620,* ed. Gernot Gruber and Olfred Orel, *Neue Ausgabe sämtlicher Werke,* series 2/5, vol. 19 (Kassel: Bärenreiter, 1970); Ivan Nagel, *Autonomy and Mercy: Reflections on Mozart's Operas,* trans. Marion Faber and Ivan Nagel (Cambridge: Harvard University Press, 1991); Jean Starobinski, *1789: The Emblems of Reason,* trans. Barbara Bray (Cambridge: The MIT Press, 1988); and Starobinski, "Sur l'argument d'*Idomeneo,*" *Critique* 56 (2000): 660–76.

2. For an illuminating study of the opera in the context of contemporary research on ancient mysteries, see Jan Assmann, *"Die Zauberflöte": Oper und Mysterium* (Munich and Vienna: Carl Hanser, 2005). I would like to thank the author for allowing me to read the manuscript prior to publication.

3. As late as 1878 Wagner complained that "here that which is eternal, valid for all times and all humanity . . . is so irretrievably bound to the veritably trivial tendency of the play, intended by the poet simply to please a suburban Viennese public." See "Das Publikum in Zeit und Raum," *Gesammelte Schriften und Dichtungen,* 2nd ed., vol. 10 (Leipzig, 1888), 98, trans. in, and quoted from, Branscombe, *W. A. Mozart: "Die Zauberflöte,"* 2.

4. The similarity between Mozart's first and last great operas is no accident: as Jean Starobinski has pointed out, they both rely on the example of Fénelon's *Aventures de Télémaque* of 1699. See Starobinski, "Sur l'argument d'*Idomeneo.*"

5. "Ich bin ein Teil des Teils, der Anfangs alles war, / Ein Teil der Finsternis, die sich das Licht gebar, / Das stolze Licht, das nun der Mutter Nacht / Den alten Rang, den Raum ihr streitig macht." (1349–52)

6. "Two Concepts of Liberty," *Four Essays on Liberty* (Oxford: Oxford University Press, 1969), 153.

7. *Collected Poems in English* (New York: Farrar, Straus and Giroux, 2000), 236.

8. Schopenhauer did not share these hopes, regretting in 1851 that, in effect, the misogyny of the priests was not that of the opera, and suggesting that Tamino should have been initiated alone, leaving the union with a woman to Papageno. "Aphorismen zur Lebensweisheit," *Parerga und Paralipomena I,* vol. 4 of *Sämtliche Werke,* ed. W. von Löhneysen (Stuttgart, 1963), 492.

9. To rethink the story of Orpheus was an ambition of the age. Goethe too talked of "Faust as a second Orpheus" (Faust als zweyter Orpheus) and planned to have him descend into the underworld to ask for Helen. See Albrecht Schöne, *Kommentare* [to *Faust*], in Goethe, *Sämtliche Werke, Briefe, Tagebücher und Gespräche,* part 1, vol. 7/2 (Frankfurt: Deutscher Klassiker Verlag, 1994), 493, 527, 548. To be sure, in the end Helen melts out of Faust's arms just as Eurydice did: he cannot hold on to the ancient ideal of beauty. But it is only after this

phantasmagoric encounter with classic antiquity that Faust is able to overcome his romantic-medieval past, his residual attachment to the Christian ideal of goodness, and, by putting power above either beauty or goodness, become, for better or worse, fully modern.

10. "Höret allerliebste Klange, / Macht euch schnell von Fabeln frei, / Eurer Götter alt Gemenge / Laßt es hin, es ist vorbei. / Niemand will euch mehr verstehen, / Fordern wir doch höhern Zoll: / Denn es muß von Herzen gehen, / Was auf Herzen wirken soll." (9679–86) One is tempted to recall Beethoven's dedication of *Missa solemnis:* "From the heart—May it return—to the heart!" (Von Herzen—Möge es wieder—zu Herzen gehen!).

11. I have explored the roots of artistic abstraction in the modern aspiration to absolute freedom in *A Theory of Art* (New York: Oxford University Press, 2000), 152–61.

12. Otto Erich Deutsch, *Mozart: A Documentary Biography*, trans. Eric Blom, Peter Branscombe, and Jeremy Noble (Stanford: Stanford University Press, 1965), 412.

13. Quoted from Peter Branscombe, *W. A. Mozart: "Die Zauberflöte,"* 89.

14. This and the following quote are from G. W. F. Hegel, *Aesthetics: Lectures on Fine Art*, trans. T. M. Knox (Oxford: Oxford University Press, 1975), 1191 and 946.

15. Hegel, *Aesthetics*, 934.

16. "The defect . . . in *The Magic Flute*," Kierkegaard observed, "is that the whole piece tends toward consciousness, and as a consequence the actual tendency of the piece is to annul the music." *Either/Or*, ed. and trans. Howard V. Hong and Edna H. Hong, 2 vols. (Princeton: Princeton University Press, 1987), 83.

17. See Emil Karl Blümml, "Ausdeutungen der *Zauberflöte*," *Mozart-Jahrbuch* 1 (1923): 109–46.

18. More persuasive than such concrete allegorizing is Jean Starobinski's recent attempt to see in *The Magic Flute* a version of "the solar myth of the Revolution": "Metaphors of light triumphing over darkness, life being reborn out of death, and the world being brought back to its beginning were to be found everywhere in the period leading up to 1789." Starobinski, *1789: The Emblems of Reason*, 43.

19. Among the parodists was Grillparzer, who in his 1826 satire on the paranoia of the political police in Vienna, *Der Zauberflöte zweiter Teil*, cast Monostatos as Metternich (whom contemporaries liked to call "Prince Midnight," or "Fürst Mitternacht"), now in the service of the Queen of the Night/Franz I, plotting the final destruction of a Sarastro and his followers who are already defeated and in sadly reduced circumstances.

20. *Thayer's Life of Beethoven*, ed. Elliot Forbes (Princeton: Princeton University Press, 1967), 776.

21. Quoted from Lewis Lockwood, *Beethoven: The Music and the Life* (New York: W. W. Norton & Co., 2003), 50.

22. Cf. Reinhold Brinkmann, *Late Idyll: The Second Symphony of Johannes*

Brahms, trans. Peter Palmer (Cambridge: Harvard University Press, 1995), 220–26.

23. On the difficulty of concluding the Revolution, see François Furet, *La Révolution française,* 2 vols. (Paris: Hachette, 1988), passim.

24. Karl-Heinz Köhler, "Die Rezeption der Mozart-Opern unter Goethes Theaterleitung im Jahrzehnt nach dem Tode des Komponisten: Ein Beitrag zur Wirkungsgeschichte des Mozartschen Schaffens im Spiegel der Weimarer Klassik," *Mozart-Jahrbuch 1991:* 231–36.

25. Johann Peter Eckermann, *Gespräche mit Goethe in den letzten Jahren seines Lebens,* ed. Fritz Bergemann (n.p.: Insel Verlag, 1981), 494f.

26. Hoffmann, in his "Seltsame Leiden eines Theater-Direktors" of 1818, mercilessly derided this generally hapless adaptation, but even so it dominated German stages until the late nineteenth century. E. T. A. Hoffmann, *Fantasie- und Nachtstücke,* ed. W. Müller-Seidel (Darmstadt, 1961), 668f. In Vulpius's version Sarastro in the end explicitly abdicates in favor of the young couple; this also happens in the two most prominent twentieth-century television adaptations, the 1956 version by W. H. Auden and Chester Kallman, and Ingmar Bergman's 1974 production.

27. On Goethe's sequel, see in particular Dieter Borchmeyer, *Goethe, Mozart und die Zauberflöte,* Veröffentlichung der Joachim Jungius-Gesellschaft der Wissenschaften Hamburg 76 (Göttingen: Vandenhoeck & Ruprecht, 1994); Nicholas Boyle, *Revolution and Renunciation (1790–1803),* vol. 2 of *Goethe: The Poet and the Age* (Oxford: Clarendon Press, 2000); Hans-Georg Gadamer, "Die Bildung zum Menschen: Der *Zauberflöte* anderer Teil," *Kleine Schriften,* vol. 2 (Tübingen: J. C. B. Mohr, 1967), 118–35; Johann Wolfgang Goethe, *Der Zauberflöte zweiter Teil: Fragment,* ed. Dieter Borchmeyer and Peter Huber, in *Sämtliche Werke,* vol. 1/6 (Frankfurt am Main: Deutscher Klassiker Verlag, 1993), 221–49; and, above all, Oskar Seidlin, *Von Goethe zu Thomas Mann: Zwölf Versuche* (Göttingen: Vanderhoeck & Ruprecht, 1963), 38–55.

28. See Goethe's conversation with Eckermann of 29 January 1827 in Eckermann, *Gespräche mit Goethe,* 206f.

29. See Maynard Solomon, *Mozart: A Life* (New York: HarperCollins, 1995), 3–18.

POSTLUDE

1. On the formal process in this much-discussed movement, see, in particular, Carl Dahlhaus, *Ludwig van Beethoven: Approaches to His Music,* trans. Mary Whittall (Oxford: Clarendon Press, 1991), 6–7, 89, 116–18, 169–71, 180. See also Janet Schmalfeldt, "Form as the Process of Becoming: The Beethoven-Hegelian Tradition and the *Tempest* Sonata," *Beethoven Forum* 4 (1995): 37–71.

2. See Thomas S. Grey, *Wagner's Musical Prose: Texts and Contexts* (Cambridge: Cambridge University Press, 1995), 100. Wagner's fascination with the first-movement fermatas furnishes a point of departure for Joseph Kerman's

attempt to recover the expressive significance of the symphony from the accumulated layers of twentieth-century academic formalist cover-up; see his "Taking the Fifth," *Write All These Down: Essays on Music* (Berkeley: University of California Press, 1994), 207–16.

3. Grey's perceptive comment (*Wagner's Musical Prose,* 100) deserves to be quoted here at length: "Wagner does not elaborate on the significance of this hermeneutic crux, but it is easy enough to suppose that it has something to do with the overt projection of a vocal persona by this declamatory interpolation, the oboe being typecast once again as a plangent vocal stand-in. The emergence of such an implied vocal presence is able to project the sense of a dramatic agent, a subject in which to ground all the hitherto abstract raging of the impersonal musical forces of fate. . . . With its tone of weary exhaustion it [the voice] seems to enter a feeble protest against the 'inexorable' process of recapitulation now underway, a protest rendered all the more pathetic and futile by the emphatic teleology of Beethoven's middle-period developmental procedures. (Apparently the same 'voice' returns momentarily in the closing measures of the movement, incidentally, to utter a couple of despairing semitone 'sighs' prior to the brutal conclusion: see the newly interpolated oboe part of mm. 486–87 and 490–91 as compared to the original close of the exposition.)"

4. Grey, *Wagner's Musical Prose,* 94.

5. See E. T. A. Hoffmann, "Old and New Church Music," in *Musical Writings: Kreisleriana, The Poet and the Composer, Music Criticism,* ed. David Charlton, trans. Martyn Clarke (Cambridge: Cambridge University Press, 1989), 351–76. In this essay of 1814 Hoffmann described Palestrina's style as follows (357–58): "Without adornment and without the impetus of melody, chord follows upon chord; most of them are perfect consonances, whose boldness and strength stir and elevate our spirits with inexpressible power. That love, that consonance of all things spiritual in nature which is promised to the Christian, finds expression in chords which only came into existence with Christianity; thus chords and harmony become the image and expression of that communion of spirits, of that bond with the eternal ideal which at once embraces and reigns over us. . . . Palestrina's simple, dignified works are conceived in the highest spirit of piety and love and proclaim godliness with power and splendour. His music can in fact be described by words with which the Italians have designated the work of many composers who are shallow and perfunctory beside him; it really is music from the other world (musica dell'altro mondo)."

6. See also William Kinderman, *Beethoven* (Berkeley: University of California Press, 1995), 219–20. For Kinderman, the movement "reflects Beethoven's intense interest at this time with parenthetical structures that enclose musical passages within contrasting sections. His use of such procedures assumes more and more importance in the last sonatas and seems to have increased as a result of his labours on the Credo of the *Missa solemnis* during the first half of 1820. . . . The opening movement of the sonata was composed at about the same time, and its unique formal design is evidently the product of similar techniques of parenthetical enclosure. . . . The entire *Adagio* section is thus po-

sitioned at the moment of the interrupted cadence, and the resulting paren-thetical structure gives the effect of a suspension of time in the contrasting section, or the enclosure of one time within another." See also Kinderman, "Thematic Contrast and Parenthetical Enclosure in the Piano Sonatas, Op. 109 and 111," in *Zu Beethoven,* ed. Harry Goldschmidt (Berlin: Verlag Neue Musik, 1988), 43–59. For Kinderman's reading of the Credo of the *Missa solemnis,* see his "Beethoven's Symbol for the Deity in the *Missa solemnis* and the Ninth Symphony," *19th-Century Music* 9 (1985): 102–18, and *Beethoven,* 240–52.

7. See Kinderman, "Thematic Contrast and Parenthetical Enclosure in the Piano Sonatas, Op. 109 and 111," 47.

8. See William Meredith, "The Origins of Beethoven's op. 109," *Musical Times* 126 (1985): 713–16.

9. "What follows is less an introduction to the fugal finale than a transi-tion from the slow movement, and to be understood it must be played with-out pause after the Adagio." Charles Rosen, *The Classical Style: Haydn, Mozart, Beethoven* (New York: W. W. Norton & Co., 1972), 426.

10. This is how the Largo makes use of what Rosen identified as the "gov-erning factors" in op. 106, "the descending thirds and the resultant clash be-tween B♭ and B♮," here transposed up a fifth; see Rosen, *The Classical Style,* 415. Rosen comments (429): "This transitional page is one of the most astonishing in the history of music. No other work until then, to my knowledge, combined the effect of almost uncontrolled improvisatory movement with such a totally systematic structure. . . . We have the sense of a contrapuntal texture taking shape, and growing organically out of unformed material."

11. Rosen (*The Classical Style,* 432) demonstrates that the episode "is formed freely from the main theme." The demonstration is convincing on pa-per, but the *effect* of the music is not one of a thought consciously derived from a thought entertained earlier, but rather of a thought coming from nowhere.

12. For Kinderman, "the music is focused on the duality of earthly pain and yearning aspiration." He talks also of "the consoling alternative embodied in the fugue" and concludes that "a central idea of this finale is the relation be-tween the earthly pain of the lament and the consolation and inward strength of the fugue." "Integration and Narrative Design in Beethoven's Piano Sonata in A♭ Major, Opus 110," *Beethoven Forum* 1 (1992): 114 and 127.

13. For Kinderman, by contrast, "the end of the sonata presents a precari-ous victory, barely sufficient to counteract powerful forces of dissociation, and it does not linger to celebrate its triumph, as do the Fifth and Ninth Sym-phonies." "Integration and Narrative Design in Beethoven's Piano Sonata in A♭ Major, Opus 110," 145.

14. "Self-contained, hermetic world . . . twice confronted with the ordinary world" is how Joseph Kerman characterizes the contrast in *The Beethoven Quar-tets* (New York: W. W. Norton & Co., 1979), 254. He writes further: "Beethoven's experiments with the church modes in those years . . . owe something to the vogue for medieval Catholicism expressed by Romantic poets like Brentano and

Novalis. . . . Already in Beethoven's lifetime, pious archeology was beginning to enshrine the great a-cappella school of church music. The *Heiliger Dankgesang* seems to anticipate the nineteenth-century Palestrina revival."

15. For contemplative "moments" in *Fidelio*, see Joseph Kerman, *"Augenblicke in Fidelio,"* in *Ludwig van Beethoven: "Fidelio,"* ed. Paul Robinson (Cambridge: Cambridge University Press, 1996), 132–44. For the tradition of "contemplative ensemble," see Carl Dahlhaus, "Über das 'kontemplative Ensemble,'" in *Opernstudien: Anna Amalie Abert zum 65. Geburtstag*, ed. Klaus Hortschansky (Tutzing: Schneider, 1975), 189–95.

16. Cf. the celebrated analysis of the opening movement of Mozart's String Quartet in D Minor, K. 421/417b, with a text added to the principal melodic part in Jérôme-Joseph Momigny, *Cours complet d'harmonie et de composition*, vol. 3 (Paris, 1803–1806).

17. According to Kinderman, *Beethoven*, 266, Beethoven's 1823 sketches (in Landsberg 8) for the recitatives and quotations from earlier movements in the opening section of the finale are supplied with verbal clues that "make clear the reasons for the rejection of each of the preceding movements." On the significance of this passage, see also Stephen Hinton, "Not *Which* Tones: The Crux of Beethoven's Ninth," *19th-Century Music* 22 (1998): 61–77.

Two other vocal works are relevant to our subject: *An die ferne Geliebte* and the *Missa solemnis*. On the former, see in particular Charles Rosen, *The Romantic Generation* (Cambridge: Harvard University Press, 1995), 166–74 and Joseph Kerman, "An die ferne Geliebte," in *Beethoven Studies*, ed. Alan Tyson (1973), 123–57. Rosen writes (166): "Beethoven is the first composer to represent the complex process of memory—not merely the sense of loss and regret that accompanies visions of the past, but the physical experience of calling up the past within the present" and goes on to demonstrate (169), among other features, "the use of a change of key with a mysterious hushed sonority to represent a movement away from reality [in the second stanza of the second song]. . . . Here it serves to portray the separation of present reality and past memory." On the *Missa solemnis*, see, in particular, William Kinderman, "Beethoven's Symbol for the Deity in the *Missa solemnis* and the Ninth Symphony," *19th-Century Music* 9 (1985): 102–18. In his recent *Beethoven*, Kinderman summarizes (219): "[in] the Credo of the *Missa solemnis* during the first half of 1820, . . . [Beethoven] devised an immense parenthetical structure separating the musical setting of the events on earth (from the 'et incarnatus est' to the 'Resurrexit') from the remainder of the movement; here, an abrupt interruption of the cadence at 'descendit de coelis' prepares a later resumption of the music at 'ascendit in coelum.'" And further (241): "The large interpolation in the musical form assumes a rhetorical or symbolic function, for it reflects musically the descent of Christ from heaven to earth, with his subsequent ascent after the crucifixion and burial being embodied in the return and continuation of music heard earlier in the movement. . . . In order to establish an audible musical relationship between descent and ascent, Beethoven employs a device prominent in other works from his later years—a grandiose interrupted cadence."

18. See Maynard Solomon, *Beethoven* (New York: Schirmer Books, 1977), 41. See also Solomon, *Beethoven*, 20: "Cäcilia Fischer recalled Beethoven 'leaning in the window with his head in both hands and staring fixedly at one spot.' He said: 'I was just occupied with such a lovely deep thought, I couldn't bear to be disturbed.'"

19. Here and below I quote from Solomon's translation of the Testament in *Beethoven*, 116–18; the emphasis is Beethoven's.

20. Solomon, *Beethoven*, 118.

21. Solomon, *Beethoven*, 155.

22. This and the following quotes are from Ludwig van Beethoven, *Tagebuch*, in *Beethoven Essays*, ed. Maynard Solomon (Cambridge: Harvard University Press, 1988), 246, 258, 274, 294.

23. Solomon, *Beethoven*, 113.

24. This and the following quotation are from Immanuel Kant, *The Critique of Judgement*, trans. J. C. Meredith, §49, 314, and §51, 320.

25. See, in particular, Ernst Theodor Amadeus Hoffmann, "Beethoven's Instrumental Music," *E. T. A. Hoffmann's Musical Writings: Kreisleriana, The Poet and the Composer, Music Criticism*, ed. David Charlton, trans. Martyn Clarke (Cambridge: Cambridge University Press, 1989), 96–103; and Arthur Schopenhauer, *The World as Will and Representation*, trans. E. F. J. Payne (New York: Dover, 1966), §52, 1:255–67, and ch. 39, 2:447–57.

26. *Ludwig van Beethovens Konversationshefte*, ed. Karl-Heinz Köhler, Grita Herre, and Dagmar Beck (Leipzig: VEB Deutscher Verlag für Musik, 1968), 1:235.

27. Friedrich Nietzsche, *Human, All Too Human*, trans. R. J. Hollingdale, vol. 1/2, No. 217 (Cambridge: Cambridge University Press, 1996), 366.

28. Friedrich Nietzsche, *Human, All Too Human*, vol. 1/2, No. 217, 366.

29. Friedrich Schiller, *On the Aesthetic Education of Man: In a Series of Letters*, trans. E. M. Wilkinson and L. A. Willoughby (Oxford: Oxford University Press, 1967), 9.

30. On this aspect of Schiller's *Letters*, see especially Martha Woodmansee, *The Author, Art, and the Market: Rereading the History of Aesthetics* (New York: Columbia University Press, 1994), 57–59.

31. Hans-Georg Gadamer, *Truth and Method* (New York: Continuum, 1975), 74. Gadamer refers to the last (the twenty-seventh) letter, in which the notion of the "aesthetic state" (*der ästhetische Staat*) makes its appearance; see Schiller, *On the Aesthetic Education of Man*, 215–19. The modern German history of the idea that Schiller's term identifies has been traced in Josef Chytry, *The Aesthetic State: A Quest in Modern German Thought* (Berkeley: University of California Press, 1989). It probably goes without saying that it is only in English translation that the term acquires the wonderful ambiguity that makes the title of my postlude possible.

32. Jean Starobinski, *1789: The Emblems of Reason*, trans. Barbara Bray (Cambridge: The MIT Press, 1988), 247–48.

33. Michael Oakeshott, *The Voice of Poetry in the Conversation of Mankind: An Essay* (London: Bowes & Bowes, 1959), 62.

34. Friedrich Nietzsche, *The Case of Wagner* in *Basic Writings of Nietzsche,* ed. and trans. W. Kaufmann (New York: Modern Library, 1968), 643.

35. For the most recent modulation of this image, see Scott Burnham, *Beethoven Hero* (Princeton: Princeton University Press, 1995).

36. On the significance of the Prometheus-Napoleon complex for the *Eroica,* see in particular Constantin Floros, *Beethovens Eroica und Prometheus-Musik* (Wilhelmshofen: Heinrichshofen, 1978), and Martin Geck and Peter Schleuning, *"Geschrieben auf Bonaparte"—Beethovens "Eroica": Revolution, Reaktion, Rezeption* (Reinbek: Rowohlt, 1989). For the significance of Goethe's intertwining of Napoleon with Prometheus, see Hans Blumenberg, *Work on Myth,* trans. Robert M. Wallace (Cambridge: The MIT Press, 1985), 465–522.

37. Mozart's explorations of inwardness are related to Rousseau's genre of reverie in Marshall Brown, "Mozart and After: The Revolution in Musical Consciousness," *Critical Inquiry* 7 (1980–1981): 689–706.

38. This and the following quotations are from Nicholas Boyle, *Revolution and Renunciation (1790–1803),* vol. 2 of *Goethe: The Poet and the Age* (Oxford: Clarendon Press, 2000), 324, 324, 325.

39. The conductor's desperate decision to substitute "Freiheit" for "Freude" must have been an attempt to mitigate this incongruence; this substitution, though there is not a shred of evidence in either Schiller's or Beethoven's intentions that might legitimate it, was contemplated as early as 1838 in Wolfgang Robert Grienpenkerl's novel *Das Musikfest: Oder, Die Beethovener,* and repeatedly thereafter. On the Freiheit-instead-of-Freude myth, see Christoph Bruckmann, "'Freude! sangen wir in Thränen, Freude! in dem tiefsten Leid': Zur Interpretation und Rezeption des Gedichts 'An die Freude' von Friedrich Schiller," *Jahrbuch der Deutschen Schillergesellschaft* 35 (1991): 108–12.

40. "Wem der große Wurf gelungen, / Eines Freundes Freund zu sein, / Wer ein holdes Weib errungen, / Mische seinen Jubel ein! / Ja—wer auch nur eine Seele / Sein nennt auf dem Erdenrund! / Und wer's nie gekonnt, der stehle / Weinend sich aus diesem Bund."

41. For a largely political reading of *Winterreise,* see Reinhold Brinkmann, "Schubert's Political Landscape," in *A New History of German Literature,* ed. David E. Wellbery (Cambridge: Harvard University Press, 2004), 540–46. "It seems that Wilhelm Müller conceived of *Die Winterreise* as allegorical diagnosis of his actual present," writes Brinkmann. "Indeed, Müller made many theoretical statements that point to his enlightened sense of political responsibility. They all suggest that his *Die Winterreise* was more than a private love story." As for Schubert, Brinkmann continues: "That Schubert likewise understood his own *Winterreise* as an encoded parable of the sociopolitical conditions of Austria under the restrictive Metternich System, can only be inferred." After listing the factors on which this inference is based, Brinkmann concludes: "The erratic wanderer's journey through an impenetrable landscape, an incommensurable world governed by powerful, anonymous, impersonal institutions, represents the situation of the individual longing for freedom and self-realization within the repressive police state of the Metternich era." See also Brinkmann,

"Monologe vom Tode, politische Allegorie und die 'heil'ge Kunst': Zur Land-schaft von Schuberts *Winterreise*," in his *Vom Pfeifen und von alten Dampf-maschinen: Aufsätze zur Musik von Beethoven bis Rihm* (Vienna: Paul Zsol-nay, 2006), 73–107. Brinkmann's political reading complements rather than contradicts the more existential-philosophical interpretation offered by Susan Youens in her *Retracing a Winter's Journey: Schubert's* Winterreise (Ithaca: Cor-nell University Press, 1991). For Youens, the cycle "goes far beyond grief over a sweetheart's infidelity to fundamental questions about the meaning of exis-tence." (50); the wanderer "probes his psychic wounds in a search for meaning conducted against the backdrop of a pervasive fear of meaninglessness" (52).

42. "Die Poeten schreiben alle, als wären sie krank und die ganze Welt ein Lazarett. . . . Das ist ein wahrer Mißbrauch der Poesie, die uns doch eigentlich dazu gegeben ist, um die kleinen Zwiste des Lebens auszugleichen und den Men-schen mit der Welt und seinem Zustand zufrieden zu machen. Aber die jetzige Generation fürchtet sich vor aller echten Kraft, und nur bei der Schwäche ist es ihr gemütlich und poetisch zu Sinne." Johann Peter Eckermann, *Gespräche mit Goethe in den letzten Jahren seines Lebens*, ed. Fritz Bergemann, 3rd ed. (Baden-Baden: Insel Verlag, 1987), 248.

Works Cited

Abbate, Carolyn. "Music—Drastic or Gnostic?" *Critical Inquiry* 30 (2004): 505–36.

———. *Unsung Voices: Opera and Musical Narrative in the Nineteenth Century.* Princeton: Princeton University Press, 1991.

Allanbrook, Wye Jamison. *Rhythmic Gesture in Mozart: "Le Nozze di Figaro" and "Don Giovanni."* Chicago: The University of Chicago Press, 1983.

Anderson, Emily, ed. and trans. *The Letters of Mozart and His Family.* 3rd ed. London: Macmillan, 1985.

Anderson, Jaynie. *Giorgione: The Painter of "Poetic Brevity."* Paris and New York: Flammarion, 1997.

Anderson, W. S. "The Orpheus of Virgil and Ovid: *flebile nescio quid.*" In *Orpheus: The Metamorphoses of a Myth*, ed. John Warden, 25–50. Toronto: University of Toronto Press, 1982.

Assmann, Jan. *"Die Zauberflöte": Oper und Mysterium.* Munich and Vienna: Carl Hanser, 2005.

Auerbach, Erich. *Mimesis: The Representation of Reality in Western Literature.* Trans. Willard R. Trask. Princeton: Princeton University Press, 1953.

Augustine, Saint. *The City of God.* Trans. Marcus Dods. New York: The Modern Library, 2000.

———. *Confessions.* Trans. William Watts. Loeb Classical Library. Cambridge: Harvard University Press, 1912.

Axmacher, Elke. *"Aus Liebe will mein Heyland sterben": Untersuchung zum Wandel des Passionsverständnisses im frühen 18. Jahrhundert.* Beiträge zur theologischen Bachforschung 2. Neuhausen-Stuttgart: Hänssler-Verlag, 1984.

———. "Die Deutung der Passion Jesu im Text der Matthäus-Passion von J. S. Bach." *Luther: Zeitschrift der Luther-Gesellschaft* 56 (1985): 49–69.

Bach, Johann Sebastian. *Matthäus-Passion BWV 244.* Ed. Alfred Dürr. Neue Ausgabe sämtlicher Werke, series 2, vol. 5. Kassel: Bärenreiter, 1972.

———. *Matthäus-Passion Frühfassung BWV 244b.* Ed. Alfred Dürr. Neue Ausgabe sämtlicher Werke, series 2, vol. 5a. Kassel: Bärenreiter, 1972.

————. *Passio Domini nostri J. C. secundum Evangelistam Matthaeum.* Ed. Bach-Archiv Leipzig. Faksimile-Reihe Bachscher Werke und Schriftstücke, vol. 7. Leipzig: VEB Deutscher Verlag für Musik, [1966].

————. *Das Wohltemperierte Klavier I, BWV 846–869.* Ed. Alfred Dürr. Neue Ausgabe sämtlicher Werke, series 5, vol. 6/1. Kassel: Bärenreiter, 1989.

Barth, Karl. *Die Kirchliche Dogmatik.* Zollikon-Zürich: Evangelischer Verlag, 1955.

————. *Wolfgang Amadeus Mozart.* Grand Rapids: W. B. Eerdmans, 1986.

Beaumarchais, Pierre-Augustin Caron de. *Théâtre.* Ed. J. P. de Beaumarchais. Paris: Garnier, 1980.

Beethoven, Ludwig van. *Briefwechsel: Gesamtausgabe.* Ed. Sieghard Brandenburg. Munich: G. Henle, 1996.

————. *Ludwig van Beethovens Konversationshefte.* Ed. Karl-Heinz Köhler, Grita Herre, and Dagmar Beck. Vol. 1. Leipzig: VEB Deutscher Verlag für Musik, 1968.

————. *Tagebuch.* Trans. and ed. Maynard Solomon. In Solomon, *Beethoven Essays,* 231–95. Cambridge: Harvard University Press, 1988.

Benvenuti, Antonia Tissoni. *L'Orfeo del Poliziano con il testo critico dell'originale e delle successive forme teatrali.* Padua: Editrice Antenore, 1986.

Berger, Karol. "The First-Movement Punctuation Form in Mozart's Piano Concertos." In *Mozart's Piano Concertos: Text, Context, Interpretation,* ed. Neal Zaslaw, 239–59. Ann Arbor: The University of Michigan Press, 1996.

————. "Mozart's Concerto Andante Punctuation Form." *Mozart-Jahrbuch 1998:* 119–38.

————. *A Theory of Art.* New York and Oxford: Oxford University Press, 2000.

Berlin, Isaiah. *Four Essays on Liberty.* Oxford: Oxford University Press, 1969.

Bernhardt, Reinhold. "Aus der Umwelt der Wiener Klassiker: Freiherr Gottfried van Swieten (1734–1803)." *Der Bär: Jahrbuch von Breitkopf & Härtel 1929–1930:* 74–166.

Birnbaum, Johann Abraham. "Impartial Comments on a Questionable Passage in the Sixth Number of *Der Critische Musicus* [1738]." In *The New Bach Reader,* ed. Hans T. David and Arthur Mendel, rev. Christoph Wolff, 347. New York: W. W. Norton & Co., 1998.

Blanchot, Maurice. *The Gaze of Orpheus and Other Literary Essays.* Trans. Lydia Davis. Barrytown, New York: Station Hill Press, 1981.

Blumenberg, Hans. *The Legitimacy of the Modern Age.* Trans. Robert M. Wallace. Cambridge: The MIT Press, 1983.

————. *Matthäuspassion.* Frankfurt am Main: Suhrkamp Verlag, 1988.

————. *Work on Myth.* Trans. Robert M. Wallace. Cambridge: The MIT Press, 1985.

Blümml, Emil Karl. "Ausdeutungen der *Zauberflöte.*" *Mozart-Jahrbuch 1* (1923): 109–46.

Bonds, Mark Evan. *Wordless Rhetoric: Musical Form and the Metaphor of the Oration.* Cambridge: Harvard University Press, 1991.

Borchmeyer, Dieter. *Goethe, Mozart und die Zauberflöte.* Veröffentlichung der

Joachim Jungius-Gesellschaft der Wissenschaften Hamburg 76. Göttingen: Vandenhoeck & Ruprecht, 1994.

Boyarin, Daniel. *A Radical Jew: Paul and the Politics of Identity.* Berkeley: University of California Press, 1994.

Boyle, Nicholas. *Revolution and Renunciation, 1790–1803.* Vol. 2 of *Goethe: The Poet and the Age.* Oxford: Clarendon Press, 2000.

Branscombe, Peter. *W. A. Mozart: "Die Zauberflöte."* Cambridge Opera Handbook. Cambridge: Cambridge University Press, 1991.

Brinkmann, Reinhold. *Late Idyll: The Second Symphony of Johannes Brahms.* Trans. Peter Palmer. Cambridge: Harvard University Press, 1995.

———. "Monologe vom Tode, politische Allegorie und die 'heil'ge Kunst': Zur Landschaft von Schuberts *Winterreise.*" In his *Vom Pfeifen und von alten Dampfmaschinen: Aufsätze zur Musik von Beethoven bis Rihm,* 73–107. Vienna: Paul Zsolnay, 2006.

———. "Schubert's Political Landscape." In *A New History of German Literature,* ed. David E. Wellbery, 540–46. Cambridge: Harvard University Press, 2004.

Brodsky, Joseph. *Collected Poems in English.* New York: Farrar, Straus and Giroux, 2000.

Brown, Marshall. "Mozart and After: The Revolution in Musical Consciousness." *Critical Inquiry* 7 (1980–81): 689–706.

Bruckmann, Christoph. "'Freude! sangen wir in Thränen, Freude! in dem tiefsten Leid': Zur Interpretation und Rezeption des Gedichts 'An die Freude' von Friedrich Schiller." *Jahrbuch der Deutschen Schillergesellschaft* 35 (1991): 108–12.

Buck, August. *Der Orpheus-Mythos in der italienischen Renaissance.* Krefeld: Scherpe, 1961.

Burnham, Scott. *Beethoven Hero.* Princeton: Princeton University Press, 1995.

Burtt, Edwin Arthur. *The Metaphysical Foundations of Modern Physical Science.* Rev. ed. Garden City: Doubleday, 1954.

Butt, John. "Bach's Vocal Scoring: What Can It Mean?" *Early Music* 26 (1998): 99–107.

———. "'A mind unconscious that it is calculating'? Bach and the rationalist philosophy of Wolff, Leibniz and Spinoza." In *The Cambridge Companion to Bach,* ed. John Butt, 60–71. Cambridge: Cambridge University Press, 1997.

Caccini, Giulio. *L'Euridice.* Florence: Giorgio Marescotti, 1600.

Calasso, Roberto. *The Ruin of Kasch.* Trans. William Weaver and Stephen Sartarelli. Cambridge: Harvard University Press, 1994.

Canguilhem, Philippe. "Les sources littéraires de l'*Orfeo* de Monteverdi." In *Du genre narratif à l'opéra au theatre et au cinema,* ed. R. Abbrugiati, 81–97. Toulouse: Presses Universitaires du Mirail, 2000.

Caplin, William E. *Classical Form: A Theory of Formal Functions for the Instrumental Music of Haydn, Mozart, and Beethoven.* New York: Oxford University Press, 1998.

Carter, Tim. *Monteverdi's Musical Theatre*. New Haven: Yale University Press, 2002.

———. "Monteverdi's *Orfeo*: A Bibliographical Exploration." Paper read at *Orfeo son io*, Convegno internazionale di studi su Claudio Monteverdi, Mantua, Teatro Accademico del Bibiena, 17 December 2005.

———. "Singing *Orfeo*: On the Performers of Monteverdi's First Opera." *Recercare* 11 (1999): 75–118.

Chateaubriand, François-René de. *The Memoirs*. Trans. Robert Baldick. New York: Alfred A. Knopf, 1961.

Chiaromonte, Nicola. *Che cosa rimane: Taccuini 1955–1971*. Ed. Miriam Chiaromonte. Bologna: Il Mulino, 1995.

Chua, Daniel K. L. *Absolute Music and the Construction of Meaning*. Cambridge: Cambridge University Press, 1999.

Chytry, Josef. *The Aesthetic State: A Quest in Modern German Thought*. Berkeley: University of California Press, 1989.

Cone, Edward T. *Musical Form and Musical Performance*. New York: W. W. Norton & Co., 1968.

Corsi, Giovanni. *Vita Marsilii Ficini*. In Raymond Marcel, *Marsile Ficin (1433–1499)*. Paris: Les Belles Lettres, 1958.

Cranston, Maurice. *The Noble Savage: Jean-Jacques Rousseau 1754–1762*. Chicago: The University of Chicago Press, 1991.

Crist, Stephen A. "Aria forms in the cantatas from Bach's first Leipzig *Jahrgang*." In *Bach Studies*, ed. Don O. Franklin, 36–53. Cambridge: Cambridge University Press, 1989.

———. *Aria Forms in the Vocal Works of J. S. Bach, 1714–1724*. PhD diss., Brandeis University, 1988.

———. "Bach, Theology, and Harmony: A New Look at the Arias." *Bach* 27 (1996): 1–30.

———. "J. S. Bach and the Conventions of the Da Capo Aria, or How Original Was Bach?" In *The Maynooth International Musicological Conference 1995: Selected Proceedings, Part One*, ed. P. F. Devine and H. White, 71–85. Blackrock, Co. Dublin: Four Courts, 1996.

Curtius, Ernst Robert. *European Literature and the Latin Middle Ages*. Trans. Willard R. Trask. New York: Harper & Row, 1963.

Czaczkes, Ludwig. *Analyse des Wohltemperierten Klaviers: Form und Aufbau der Fuge bei Bach*. 2 vols. Vienna, 1956, 1965.

Dabezies, André. "Faust et Don Juan." In *Dictionnaire de Don Juan*, ed. Pierre Brunel, 395–403. Paris: Robert Laffont, 1999.

Dahlhaus, Carl. *The Idea of Absolute Music*. Chicago: The University of Chicago Press, 1989.

———. *Ludwig van Beethoven: Approaches to His Music*. Trans. Mary Whittall. Oxford: Clarendon Press, 1991.

———. *Nineteenth-Century Music*. Trans. J. Bradford Robinson. Berkeley: University of California Press, 1989.

———. "Der rhetorische Formbegriff H. Chr. Kochs und die Theorie der Sonatenform." *Archiv für Musikwissenschaft* 35 (1978): 155–76.

———. "Über das 'kontemplative Ensemble.'" In *Opernstudien: Anna Amalie Abert zum 65. Geburtstag,* ed. Klaus Hortschansky, 189–95. Tutzing: Schneider, 1975.

———. "Zur Entstehung der romantischen Bach-Deutung." *Bach-Jahrbuch* 64 (1978): 192–210.

David, Hans T., and Arthur Mendel, eds., rev. Christoph Wolff. *The New Bach Reader: A Life of Johann Sebastian Bach in Letters and Documents.* New York: W. W. Norton & Co., 1998.

David, Johann Nepomuk. *Das Wohltemperierte Klavier: Der Versuch einer Synopsis.* Göttingen, 1962.

Deutsch, Otto Erich. *Mozart: A Documentary Biography.* Trans. Eric Blom, Peter Branscombe, and Jeremy Noble. Stanford: Stanford University Press, 1965.

Dreyfus, Laurence. *Bach and the Patterns of Invention.* Cambridge: Harvard University Press, 1996.

Dürr, Alfred. *Johann Sebastian Bach: Das Wohltemperierte Klavier.* 2nd ed. Kassel: Bärenreiter, 2000.

———. "Kritischer Bericht." In Johann Sebastian Bach, *Matthäus-Passion.* Neue Ausgabe sämtlicher Werke, series 2, vol. 5. Kassel: Bärenreiter, 1974.

Eckermann, Johann Peter. *Gespräche mit Goethe in den letzten Jahren seines Lebens.* Ed. Fritz Bergemann. N.p.: Insel Verlag, 1981.

Eggebrecht, Hans Heinrich. "Bach und Leibniz." In *Bericht über die wissenschaftliche Bachtagung der Gesellschaft für Musikforschung,* 431–47. Leipzig: n.p., 1951.

Eliade, Mircea. *The Myth of the Eternal Return.* Trans. Willard R. Trask. New York: Pantheon Books, 1954.

———, and K. Galling. "Berge, heilige." In *Die Religion in Geschichte und Gegenwart: Handwörterbuch für Theologie und Religionswissenschaft.* 3rd ed. (1957), 1:coll. 1043–44.

Fabbri, Paolo. *Monteverdi.* Trans. Tim Carter. Cambridge: Cambridge University Press, 1994.

Fenlon, Iain. "The Mantuan *Orfeo.*" In *Claudio Monteverdi: Orfeo,* ed. John Whenham, 16–18. Cambridge: Cambridge University Press, 1986.

Floros, Constantin. *Beethovens "Eroica" und Prometheus-Musik.* Wilhelmshaven: Heinrichshofen, 1978.

Friedman, John Block. *Orpheus in the Middle Ages.* Cambridge: Harvard University Press, 1970.

Furet, François. *La Révolution française.* 2 vols. Paris: Hachette, 1988.

Gadamer, Hans-Georg. "Die Bildung zum Menschen: Der *Zauberflöte* anderer Teil." In *Kleine Schriften,* 2:118–35. Tübingen: J. C. B. Mohr, 1967.

———. *Truth and Method.* New York: Continuum, 1975.

Gaffurio, Franchino. *De harmonia musicorum instrumentorum opus.* Milan: Gotardus Pontanus, 1518.

Gagliano, Marco da. *La Dafne.* Florence: Cristofano Marescotti, 1608.

———. *La Dafne.* Ed. James Erber. London: Cathedral Music, 1978.

Galilei, Vincenzo. *Discorso intorno all'uso dell'Enharmonio.* Florence, Biblioteca Nazionale Centrale, Ms. Galileiani 3.

Gauchet, Marcel. *The Disenchantment of the World: A Political History of Religion.* Trans. Oscar Burge. Princeton: Princeton University Press, 1997.

Geck, Martin. *Bach: Leben und Werk.* Reinbek: Rowohlt, 2000.

———. *Die Wiederentdeckung der Matthäuspassion im 19. Jahrhundert: Die zeitgenössischen Dokumente und ihre ideengeschichtliche Deutung.* Studien zur Musikgeschichte des 19. Jahrhunderts 9. Regensburg: Gustav Bosse Verlag, 1967.

———, and Peter Schleuning. *"Geschrieben auf Bonaparte." Beethovens "Eroica": Revolution, Reaktion, Rezeption.* Reinbek: Rowohlt, 1989.

Goethe, Johann Wolfgang von. *Aus meinem Leben: Dichtung und Wahrheit.* In Goethe, *Werke, Hamburger Ausgabe,* vol. 10, ed. Lieselotte Blumenthal and Erich Trunz. Munich: Deutscher Taschenbuch Verlag, 1988.

———. *Faust: Texte.* Ed. Albrecht Schöne. In Goethe, *Sämtliche Werke, Briefe, Tagebücher und Gespräche,* vol. 7/1. Frankfurt: Deutscher Klassiker Verlag, 1994.

———. *Faust I & II.* Trans. Stuart Atkins. In Goethe, *Collected Works,* vol. 2. Princeton: Princeton University Press, 1984.

———. *Italienische Reise.* In Goethe, *Werke, Hamburger Ausgabe,* vol. 11, ed. Erich Trunz. Munich: Deutscher Taschenbuch Verlag, 1988.

———. *Der "Zauberflöte" zweiter Teil: Fragment.* Ed. Dieter Borchmeyer and Peter Huber. In Goethe, *Sämtliche Werke,* vol. 1/6:221–49. Frankfurt am Main: Deutscher Klassiker Verlag, 1993.

———, and Karl Friedrich Zelter. *Briefwechsel zwischen Goethe und Zelter.* Ed. Ludwig Geiger. Leipzig, n.d.

Gould, Stephen Jay. *Time's Arrow, Time's Cycle: Myth and Metaphor in the Discovery of Geological Time.* Cambridge: Harvard University Press, 1987.

Grey, Thomas S. *Wagner's Musical Prose: Texts and Contexts.* Cambridge: Cambridge University Press, 1995.

Gruber, Gernot. *Mozart and Posterity.* Trans. R. S. Furness. London: Quartet Books, 1991.

Gülke, Peter. *"Triumph der neuen Tonkunst": Mozarts späte Sinfonien und ihr Umfeld.* Kassel-Stuttgart: Bärenreiter-Metzler, 1998.

Guthrie, W. K. C. *Orpheus and Greek Religion.* New York: W. W. Norton & Co., 1966.

Handschin, Jacques. *Musikgeschichte im Überblick.* Luzerne, 1948.

Hanning, Barbara Russano. *Of Poetry and Music's Power: Humanism and the Creation of Opera.* Studies in Musicology 13. Ann Arbor: UMI Research Press, 1980.

Hegel, Georg Wilhelm Friedrich. *Aesthetics: Lectures on Fine Art.* Trans. T. M. Knox. Oxford: Clarendon Press, 1975.

———. *Lectures on the Philosophy of World History: Introduction: Reason in History.* Trans. H. B. Nisbet. Cambridge: Cambridge University Press, 1975.

———. *Phenomenology of Spirit.* Trans. A. V. Miller. Oxford: Oxford University Press, 1977.

———. "Proceedings of the Estates Assembly in the Kingdom of Württemberg 1815–1816." In *Political Writings,* trans. T. M. Knox. Oxford: Clarendon Press, 1964.

Heinemann, Michael. "Paradigma Fuge: Bach und das Erbe des Kontrapunkts." In *Bach und die Nachwelt,* ed. Michael Heinemann and Hans-Joachim Hinrichsen, 1:119–27. Laaber: Laaber Verlag, 1997.

Hepokoski, James. "Back and forth from *Egmont:* Beethoven, Mozart, and the Nonresolving Recapitulation." *19th-Century Music* 25 (2002): 127–54.

———. "Beyond the Sonata Principle." *Journal of the American Musicological Society* 55 (2002): 91–154.

Herzen, Alexander. *My Past and Thoughts.* Trans. Constance Garnett, rev. Humphrey Higgens. New York: Knopf, 1968.

Hinton, Stephen. "Not *Which* Tones: The Crux of Beethoven's Ninth." *19th-Century Music* 22 (1998): 61–77.

Hoffmann, E. T. A. *Fantasie- und Nachtstücke.* Ed. W. Müller-Seidel. Darmstadt, 1961.

———. *Musical Writings: Kreisleriana, The Poet and the Composer, Music Criticism.* Ed. David Charlton, trans. Martyn Clarke. Cambridge: Cambridge University Press, 1989.

———. "A Tale of Don Juan (As It Happened to a Traveling Enthusiast)." In *Pleasures of Music: A Reader's Choice of Great Writings about Music and Musicians from Cellini to Bernard Shaw,* ed. Jacques Barzun, 21–34. New York: Viking, 1960.

Holschneider, Andreas. "Die musikalische Bibliothek Gottfried van Swietens." In *Bericht über den Internationalen Musikwissenschaftlichen Kongreß Kassel 1962,* ed. Georg Reichert and Martin Just, 174–78. Kassel: Bärenreiter, 1963.

Irwin, Eleanor. "The Songs of Orpheus and the New Song of Christ." In *Orpheus: The Metamorphoses of a Myth,* ed. John Warden, 51–62. Toronto: University of Toronto Press, 1982.

Jaffé, Michael. "Esquisses inédites de Rubens pour La Torre della Parada." *La Revue du Louvre et des Musées de France* 14 (1964): 312–22.

Jauss, Hans Robert. "Der literarische Prozess des Modernismus von Rousseau bis Adorno." in *Epochenschwelle und Epochenbewußtsein,* ed. R. Herzog and R. Koselleck, 243–68. Munich, 1987.

Kant, Immanuel. "Conjectural Beginning of Human History." *On History,* ed. Lewis White Beck. Indianapolis: Bobbs-Merrill, 1963.

———. *The Critique of Judgement.* Trans. J. C. Meredith. Oxford: Clarendon Press, 1952.

———. *Critique of Pure Reason.* Trans. Norman Kemp Smith. New York: St. Martin's Press, 1965.

————. "Idea for a Universal History from a Cosmopolitan Point of View." In *On History*, ed. Lewis White Beck, 11–26. Indianapolis: Bobbs-Merrill, 1963.

————. "Perpetual Peace." In *On History*, ed. Lewis White Beck, 85–135. Indianapolis: Bobbs-Merrill, 1963.

————. *Practical Philosophy.* Trans. and ed. Mary J. Gregor. The Cambridge Edition of the Works of Immanuel Kant. Cambridge: Cambridge University Press, 1996.

Keller, Hermann. *The Well-Tempered Clavier by Johann Sebastian Bach.* Trans. Leigh Gerdine. New York: W. W. Norton & Co., 1976.

Kerényi, Karl. "Der Mythos von Orpheus und Eurydike." in *Claudio Monteverdi: "Orfeo"; Christoph Willibald Gluck: "Orpheus und Eurydike": Texte, Materialien, Kommentare,* ed. Attila Csampai and Dietmar Holland, 9–15. Reinbek: Rowohlt, 1988.

Kerman, Joseph. "An die ferne Geliebte." In *Beethoven Studies,* ed. Alan Tyson, 123–57. New York: W. W. Norton, 1973.

————. "*Augenblicke* in *Fidelio.*" In *Ludwig van Beethoven: "Fidelio,"* ed. Paul Robinson, 132–44. Cambridge: Cambridge University Press, 1996.

————. *The Beethoven Quartets.* New York: W. W. Norton & Co., 1979.

————. "*Orpheus*: The Neoclassic Vision." In *Opera as Drama,* 18–38. New and rev. ed. Berkeley: University of California Press, 1988.

————. "Taking the Fifth." In *Write All These Down: Essays on Music,* 207–16. Berkeley: University of California Press, 1994).

Kermode, Frank. *The Sense of an Ending: Studies in the Theory of Fiction.* Oxford: Oxford University Press, 1967.

Kierkegaard, Søren. *Either/Or.* Trans. Howard V. Hong and Edna H. Hong. 2 vols. Princeton: Princeton University Press, 1987.

Kinderman, William. *Beethoven.* Berkeley: University of California Press, 1995.

————. "Beethoven's Symbol for the Deity in the *Missa solemnis* and the Ninth Symphony." *19th-Century Music* 9 (1985): 102–18.

————. "Integration and Narrative Design in Beethoven's Piano Sonata in A♭ Major, Opus 110," *Beethoven Forum* 1 (1992): 111–45.

————. "Thematic Contrast and Parenthetical Enclosure in the Piano Sonatas, Op. 109 and 111." In *Zu Beethoven,* ed. Harry Goldschmidt, 3:43–59. Berlin: Verlag Neue Musik, 1988.

Kirnberger, Johann Philipp. *Die Kunst des reinen Satzes in der Musik.* Berlin: Christian Friedrich Voss, 1776.

Kobayashi, Yoshitake. "Zur Chronologie der Spätwerke Johann Sebastian Bachs: Kompositions- und Aufführungstätigkeit von 1736 bis 1750." *Bach Jahrbuch* 74 (1988): 7–72.

Koch, Heinrich Christoph. *Introductory Essay on Composition: The Mechanical Rules of Melody, Sections 3 and 4.* Trans. Nancy Kovaleff Baker. New Haven: Yale University Press, 1983.

————. *Versuch einer Anleitung zur Composition.* 3 vols. Leipzig and Rudolstadt: Böhme, 1782–1793.

Köhler, Karl-Heinz. "Die Rezeption der Mozart-Opern unter Goethes Theaterleitung im Jahrzehnt nach dem Tode des Komponisten: Ein Beitrag zum Wirkungsgeschichte des Mozartschen Schaffens im Spiegel des Weimarer Klassik." *Mozart-Jahrbuch 1991:* 231–36.

Kolakowski, Leszek. *God Owes Us Nothing: A Brief Remark on Pascal's Religion and on the Spirit of Jansenism.* Chicago: The University of Chicago Press, 1995.

Koselleck, Reinhard. *Futures Past: On the Semantics of Historical Time.* Trans. Keith Tribe. Cambridge: The MIT Press, 1985.

———. *Zeitschichten: Studien zur Historik. Mit einem Beitrag von Hans-Georg Gadamer.* Frankfurt am Main: Suhrkamp Verlag, 2000.

Kuehn, Manfred. *Kant: A Biography,* Cambridge: Cambridge University Press, 2001.

Leaver, Robin A. *J. S. Bach as Preacher: His Passions and Music in Worship.* St. Louis: Concordia, 1984.

———. "The Mature Vocal Works and Their Theological and Liturgical Context." In *The Cambridge Companion to Bach,* ed. John Butt, 86–122. Cambridge: Cambridge University Press, 1997.

Ledbetter, David. *Bach's "Well-tempered Clavier": The 48 Preludes and Fugues.* New Haven: Yale University Press, 2002.

Le Goff, Jacques. *L'imaginaire médiéval.* Paris: Gallimard, 1985.

Leisinger, Ulrich. "Forms and Functions of the Choral Movements in J. S. Bach's St. Matthew Passion." In *Bach Studies 2,* ed. Daniel R. Melamed, 70–84. Cambridge: Cambridge University Press, 1995.

Leopold, Silke. "Lyra Orphei." In *Claudio Monteverdi: Festschrift Reinhold Hammerstein zum 70. Geburtstag,* ed. Ludwig Finscher, 337–45. Laaber: Laaber Verlag, 1986.

———. *Monteverdi: Music in Transition.* Trans. Anne Smith. Oxford: Clarendon Press, 1991.

———. "Orpheus in Mantua und anderswo: Poliziano, Peri und Monteverdi." In *Claudio Monteverdi, "Orfeo"; Christoph Willibald Gluck, "Orpheus und Eurydike": Texte, Materialien, Kommentare,* ed. Attila Csampai and Dietmar Holland, 83–109. Reinbek: Rowohlt, 1988.

Lockwood, Lewis. *Beethoven: The Music and the Life.* New York: W. W. Norton & Co., 2003.

Lowinsky, Edward E. "On Mozart's Rhythm." In *Music in the Culture of the Renaissance and Other Essays,* ed. Bonnie J. Blackburn, 2:911–28. Chicago: The University of Chicago Press, 1989; originally published in *The Musical Quarterly* 42 (1956): 162–86.

Löwith, Karl. *Meaning in History: The Theological Implications of the Philosophy of History.* Chicago: The University of Chicago Press, 1949.

Lütteken, Laurenz. "Zwischen Ohr und Verstand: Moses Mendelssohn, Johann Philipp Kirnberger und die Begründung des 'reinen Satzes' in der Musik." In *Musik und ästhetik im Berlin Moses Mendelssohns,* ed. Anselm Gerhard, 135–63. Tübingen: Max Niemeyer, 1999.

Magurn, Ruth Saunders. "Introduction." In *The Letters of Peter Paul Rubens,* trans. and ed. Ruth Saunders Magurn. Cambridge: Harvard University Press, 1955.

Marshall, Robert L. "Bach the Progressive." In *The Music of Johann Sebastian Bach: The Sources, the Style, the Significance*. New York: Schirmer Books, 1989.

———. *The Compositional Process of J. S. Bach: A Study of the Autograph Scores of the Vocal Works*. Princeton: Princeton University Press, 1972.

McClary, Susan. "Constructions of Gender in Monteverdi's Dramatic Music." *Cambridge Opera Journal* 1 (1989): 203–23.

Melamed, Daniel R. "The Double Chorus in J. S. Bach's *St. Matthew Passion* BWV 244." *Journal of the American Musicological Society* 57 (2004): 3–50.

Meredith, William. "The Origins of Beethoven's Op. 109." *The Musical Times* 126 (1985): 713–16.

Miller, Norbert. "Die Erben von Zauberflöte und Glockenspiel: Peter von Winters *Labyrinth* und das Märchentheater Emanuel Schikaneders." In *Europäische Romantik in der Musik*, ed. Carl Dahlhaus and Norbert Miller, 1:497–538. Stuttgart-Weimar: Metzler, 1999.

Momigny, Jérôme-Joseph. *Cours complet d'harmonie et de composition*. Vol. 3. Paris, 1803–1806.

Monteverdi, Claudio. *L'Orfeo*. Venice: Ricciardo Amadino, 1609. Facs. ed. in Monteverdi, *L'Orfeo: Favola in musica*. Archivium Musicum, Musica Drammatica 1. Florence: Studio Per Edizioni Scelte, 1993.

Moser, Hans Joachim. *Johann Sebastian Bach*. Berlin, 1935.

Mozart, Wolfgang Amadé. *"Die Zauberflöte," K. 620*. Ed. Gernot Gruber and Olfred Orel. *Neue Ausgabe sämtlicher Werke*, series 2/5, vol. 19. Kassel: Bärenreiter, 1970.

Nagel, Ivan. *Autonomy and Mercy: Reflections on Mozart's Operas*. Trans. Marion Faber and Ivan Nagel. Cambridge: Harvard University Press, 1991.

Neiman, Susan. *Evil in Modern Thought: An Alternative History of Philosophy*. Princeton: Princeton University Press, 2002.

Nietzsche, Friedrich. *Human, All Too Human*. Trans. R. J. Hollingdale. 2 vols. (Cambridge: Cambridge University Press, 1996); for the original, see *Menschliches, Allzumenschliches*. Kritische Studienausgabe. 2 vols. Ed. Giorgio Colli and Mazzino Montinari. Munich and Berlin: Deutscher Taschenbuch Verlag and Walter de Gruyter, 1988.

Nissen, Georg Nikolaus. *Biographie W. A. Mozarts*. Leipzig, 1828.

Nowak, Adolf. "Der Begriff 'Musikalisches Denken' in der Musiktheorie der Aufklärung." In *Neue Musik und Tradition: Festschrift Rudolf Stephan*, ed. J. Kuckertz, H. de la Motte Haber, C. M. Schmidt, and W. Seidel, 113–22. Laaber: Laaber Verlag, 1990.

Oakeshott, Michael. *The Voice of Poetry in the Conversation of Mankind: An Essay*. London: Bowes & Bowes, 1959.

Pagels, Elaine. *Adam, Eve, and the Serpent*. New York: Random House, 1988.

Painter, George D. *Marcel Proust: A Biography*. Rev. ed. London: Chatto & Windus, 1984.

Palisca, Claude V. *Girolamo Mei: Letters on Ancient and Modern Music to Vincenzo Galilei and Giovanni Bardi.* Musicological Studies and Documents 3. N.p.: American Institute of Musicology, 1960.

Panofsky, Erwin. *Idea: A Conception in Art Theory.* Trans. Joseph J. S. Peake. New York: Harper & Row, 1968.

Pelikan, Jaroslav. *Bach Among the Theologians.* Philadelphia: Fortress Press, 1986.

———. *The Christian Tradition: A History of the Development of Doctrine.* 4 vols. Chicago: The University of Chicago Press, 1971, 1978, 1984.

Peri, Jacopo. *Le musiche sopra L'Euridice del Sig. Ottavio Rinuccini.* Florence: Giorgio Marescotti, 1600.

Petzoldt, Martin, ed. *Bach als Ausleger der Bibel: Theologische und musikwissenschaftliche Studien zum Werk Johann Sebastian Bachs.* Göttingen: Vandenhoeck and Ruprecht, 1985.

———. *Bach und die Bibel: Katalog.* Leipzig: n.d.

———. "'Bey einer andächtigen Musique ist allezeit Gott mit seiner Gnaden Gegenwart': Bach und die Theologie." In *Bach Handbuch,* ed. Konrad Küster, 81–91. Kassel, Stuttgart, and Weimar: Bärenreiter and Metzler, 1999.

———. "Hat Gott Zeit, hat der Mensch Ewigkeit? Zur Kantate BWV 106 von Johann Sebastian Bach." *Musik und Kirche* 66 (1996): 212–20.

———. "Die theologische Bedeutung der Chorale in Bachs Matthäus-Passion." *Musik und Kirche* 53 (1983): 53–63.

———. "Zur Theologie der Matthäus-Passion in zeitgenossischer Perspektive." In *Johann Sebastian Bach, Matthäus-Passion, BWV 244: Vorträge der Sommerakademie J. S. Bach 1985,* ed. Ulrich Prinz, 50–75. Stuttgart Bärenreiter, 1990.

———. "Zwischen Orthodoxie, Pietismus und Aufklärung—Überlegungen zum theologiegeschichtlichen Kontext Johann Sebastian Bachs." *Bach-Studien* 7 (1982): 66–108.

Picander [Christian Friedrich Henrici]. "Texte zur Paßions-Music, nach dem Evangelisten Matthäo, am Char-Freytage bey der Vesper in der Kirche zu St. Thomä." *Ernst-Schertzhaffte und Satyrische Gedichte.* Vol. 2:101–12. Leipzig, 1729. Facs. in Alfred Dürr, "Kritischer Bericht," Johann Sebastian Bach, *Matthäus-Passion.* Neue Ausgabe sämtlicher Werke, series 2, 5:73–78. Kassel: Bärenreiter, 1974.

Pignatti, Terisio, and Filippo Pedrocco. *Giorgione.* New York: Rizzoli, 1999.

Pirrotta, Nino. "Monteverdi and the Problems of Opera." In *Music and Culture in Italy from the Middle Ages to the Baroque: A Collection of Essays,* 233–53. Cambridge: Harvard University Press, 1984.

———. "Theater, Sets, and Music in Monteverdi's Operas." In *Music and Culture in Italy from the Middle Ages to the Baroque: A Collection of Essays,* 258–59. Cambridge: Harvard University Press, 1984.

———, and Elena Povoledo. *Music and Theater from Poliziano to Monteverdi.* Trans. Karen Eales. Cambridge: Cambridge University Press, 1982.

Platen, Emil. *Die Matthäus-Passion von Johann Sebastian Bach: Entstehung,*

Werkbeschreibung, Rezeption. Kassel and Munich: Bärenreiter and Deutscher Taschenbuch, 1991.

Politianus, Angelus. *Miscellaneorum centuria prima.* In *Opera.* Venice: Aldus Manutius, 1498.

Proust, Marcel. *À la recherche du temps perdu.* Ed. Pierre Clarac and André Ferré. 3 vols. Paris: Gallimard, 1954. Trans. C. K. Scott Moncrieff as *Remembrance of Things Past* (New York: The Modern Library, 1929).

Rapaczynski, Andrzej. *Nature and Politics: Liberalism in the Philosophies of Hobbes, Locke, and Rousseau.* Ithaca: Cornell University Press, 1987.

Ratner, Leonard G. *Classic Music: Expression, Form, and Style.* New York: Schirmer Books, 1980.

Ricoeur, Paul. *Time and Narrative.* 3 vols. Chicago: The University of Chicago Press, 1984–1988.

Riemann, Hugo. *Analysis of J. S. Bach's Wohltemperirtes Clavier (48 Preludes & Fugues).* Trans. J. S. Shedlock. London: Augner, n.d.

Rifkin, Joshua. "The Chronology of Bach's Saint Matthew Passion." *Musical Quarterly* 61 (1975): 360–87.

Robbins, Emmet. "Famous Orpheus." In *Orpheus: The Metamorphoses of a Myth,* ed. John Warden, 3–23. Toronto: University of Toronto Press, 1982.

Roesler-Friedenthal, Antoinette. "Ein Porträt Andrea Mantegnas als *alter Orpheus* im Kontext seiner Selbstdarstellungen." *Römisches Jahrbuch der Bibliotheca Hertziana* 31 (1996): 149–86.

Rorty, Richard. *Philosophy and the Mirror of Nature.* Princeton: Princeton University Press, 1979.

———. "Texts and Lumps." *New Literary History* 17 (1985): 1–16.

Rosanvallon, Pierre. *Le Modèle politique français: La société civile contre le jacobinisme de 1789 à nos jours.* Paris: Seuil, 2004.

Rosasco, Betsy. "Albrecht Dürer's *Death of Orpheus:* Its Critical Fortunes and a New Interpretation of Its Meaning." *Idea: Jahrbuch der Hamburger Kunsthalle* 3 (1984): 19–41.

Rosen, Charles. *The Classical Style: Haydn, Mozart, Beethoven.* Exp. ed. New York: W. W. Norton & Co., 1997.

———. *The Romantic Generation.* Cambridge: Harvard University Press, 1995.

Rosen, David. "The Composer's 'Standard Operating Procedure' as Evidence of Intention: The Case of a Formal Quirk in Mozart's K. 595." *Journal of Musicology* 5 (1987): 79–90.

Rougemont, Denis de. *L'Amour et l'Occident.* Éd. définitive. Paris: Plon, 1972.

Rousseau, Jean-Jacques. *A Discourse on Inequality.* Trans. Maurice Cranston. Harmondsworth: Penguin, 1984.

———. *Emile, or On Education.* Trans. Allan Bloom. N.p.: Basic Books, 1979.

———. *The Social Contract.* Trans. Maurice Cranston. Harmondsworth: Penguin, 1968.

Rubens, Peter Paul. *The Letters.* Trans. and ed. R. S. Magurn. Cambridge: Harvard University Press, 1955.

[———.] *Olieversfschetsen van Rubens.* Rotterdam: Museum Boymans, 1953.

Scavizzi, Giuseppe. "The Myth of Orpheus in Italian Renaissance Art, 1400–1600." In *Orpheus: The Metamorphoses of a Myth,* ed. John Warden, 111–62. Toronto: University of Toronto Press, 1982.

Scheibe, Johann Adolph. "Letter from an Able *Musikant* Abroad." *Critischer Musikus,* May 14, 1737. In *The New Bach Reader,* ed. Hans T. David and Arthur Mendel, rev. Christoph Wolff, 338. New York: W. W. Norton & Co., 1998.

Schiller, Friedrich. *On the Aesthetic Education of Man: In a Series of Letters.* Trans. E. M. Wilkinson and L. A. Willoughby. Oxford: Oxford University Press, 1967).

Schindler, Anton. *The Life of Beethoven.* Ed. Ignaz Moscheles. London, 1841.

Schlegel, Friedrich. "Athenäum Fragments." In *German Aesthetic and Literary Criticism: The Romantic Ironists and Goethe,* ed. Kathleen M. Wheeler, 48. Cambridge: Cambridge University Press, 1984.

Schmalfeldt, Janet. "Form as the Process of Becoming: The Beethoven-Hegelian Tradition and the *Tempest* Sonata." *Beethoven Forum* 4 (1995): 37–71.

Schneewind, J. B. *The Invention of Autonomy: A History of Modern Moral Philosophy.* Cambridge: Cambridge University Press, 1998.

Schöne, Albrecht. *Kommentare* [to *Faust*]. In Goethe, *Sämtliche Werke, Briefe, Tagebücher und Gespräche,* pt. 1, vol. 7/2. Frankfurt: Deutscher Klassiker Verlag, 1994.

Schopenhauer, Arthur. "Aphorismen zur Lebensweisheit." *Parerga und Paralipomena I.* Vol. 4 of *Sämtliche Werke,* ed. W. von Löhneysen. Stuttgart: Wissenschaftliche Buchgesellschaft, 1963.

———. *The World as Will and Representation.* Trans. E. F. J. Payne. New York: Dover, 1966.

Schuster, Peter-Klaus. "Zu Dürers Zeichnung *Der Tod des Orpheus* und verwandten Darstellungen." *Jahrbuch der Hamburger Kunstsammlungen* 23 (1978): 7–24.

Segal, Charles. *Orpheus: The Myth of the Poet.* Baltimore: The Johns Hopkins University Press, 1989.

Seidlin, Oskar. *Von Goethe zu Thomas Mann: Zwölf Versuche.* Göttingen: Vanderhoeck & Ruprecht, 1963.

Sheehan, Thomas. *The First Coming: How the Kingdom of God Became Christianity.* New York: Random House, 1986.

Siegele, Ulrich. "Kategorien formaler Konstruktion in den Fugen des Wohltemperierten Klaviers." In *Bach, Das Wohltemperierte Klavier I: Tradition, Entstehung, Funktion, Analyse. Ulrich Siegele zum 70. Geburtstag,* Musikwissenschaftliche Schriften 38, ed. Siegbert Rampe, 321–471. Munich-Salzburg: Katzbichler, 2002.

Smend, Friedrich. "Goethes Verhältnis zu Bach." In *Bach Studien: Gesammelte Reden und Aufsätze,* ed. Christoph Wolff, 212–36. Kassel: Bärenreiter, 1969.

Solomon, Jon. "The Neoplatonic Apotheosis in Monteverdi's *Orfeo*." *Studi musicali* 24 (1995): 27–47.

Solomon, Maynard. *Beethoven.* New York: Schirmer Books, 1977.

———. *Mozart: A Life.* New York: HarperCollins, 1995.

Spaethling, Robert. *Music and Mozart in the Life of Goethe.* Columbia, SC: Camden House, 1987.

Spitta, Philipp. *Johann Sebastian Bach: His work and influence on the music of Germany, 1685–1750.* Trans. Clara Bell and John Alexander Fuller-Maitland. London: Novello, 1884.

Starobinski, Jean. *1789: The Emblems of Reason.* Trans. Barbara Bray. Cambridge: The MIT Press, 1988.

———. "Sur l'argument d'*Idomeneo.*" *Critique* 56 (2000): 660–76.

Stechow, Wolfgang. *Apollo und Daphne.* Rev. ed. Darmstadt: Wissenschaftliche Buchgesellschaft, 1965.

Steiger, Lothar, and Renate Steiger. "Die theologische Bedeutung der Doppelchörigkeit in Johann Sebastian Bachs 'Matthäus-Passion.'" In *Bachiana et alia musicologica: Festschrift Alfred Dürr zum 65. Geburtstag am 3. März 1983,* ed. Wolfgang Rehm, 275–86. Kassel: Bärenreiter, 1983.

Sternfeld, F. W. *The Birth of Opera.* Oxford: Clarendon Press, 1993.

[Striggio, Alessandro.] *La Favola d'Orfeo.* Mantua: Francesco Osanna, 1607. Facs. ed. in Claudio Monteverdi, *L'Orfeo: Favola in musica.* Archivium Musicum, Musica Drammatica 1. Florence: Studio Per Edizioni Scelte, 1993.

Talmon, J. L. *The Origins of Totalitarian Democracy.* London: Secker & Warburg, 1955.

Taruskin, Richard. *The Oxford History of Western Music.* 6 vols. New York: Oxford University Press, 2005.

Thayer, Alexander Wheelock. *Life of Beethoven.* Rev. and ed. Elliot Forbes. Princeton: Princeton University Press, 1967.

Tomasi di Lampedusa, Giuseppe. *Il Gattopardo.* Milan: Feltrinelli, 1969.

Tomlinson, Gary. "Madrigal, Monody, and Monteverdi's 'via naturale alla immitatione.'" *Journal of the American Musicological Society* 34 (1981): 60–108.

Tovey, Donald Francis. *Essays in Musical Analysis.* London, 1935.

———. "A Preface; General Instructions for Using This Edition; Critical and Explanatory Notes to Each Prelude and Each Fugue." In J. S. Bach, *Forty-Eight Preludes and Fugues,* ed. D. F. Tovey. 2 vols. New York: Oxford University Press, 1924.

Vicari, Patricia. "*Sparagmos:* Orpheus among the Christians." In *Orpheus: The Metamorphoses of a Myth,* ed. John Warden, 63–83. Toronto: University of Toronto Press, 1982 .

Wagner, Cosima. *Die Tagebücher.* Ed. Martin Gregor-Delin and Dietrich Mack. Munich: Piper, 1976.

Walker, D. P. "Orpheus the Theologian and the Renaissance Platonists." *Journal of the Warburg and Courtauld Institutes* 16 (1953): 100–120.

———. *Spiritual and Demonic Magic from Ficino to Campanella.* London: The Warburg Insitute, 1958.

Warburg, Aby M. "Dürer und die italienische Antike." In *Ausgewählte Schriften und Würdigungen,* ed. Dieter Wuttke, 125–35. Baden-Baden: Valentin Koerner, 1979.

Webster, James. *Haydn's "Farewell" Symphony and the Idea of Classical Style: Through-composition and Cyclic Integration in His Instrumental Music.* Cambridge: Cambridge University Press, 1991.

———. "Sonata Form." In *The New Grove Dictionary of Music and Musicians,* 2nd ed. (2001), 23:687–701.

Williams, Bernard. "Don Giovanni as an Idea." In *W. A. Mozart, "Don Giovanni,"* Cambridge Opera Handbook, ed. Julian Rushton, 81–91. Cambridge: Cambridge University Press, 1981.

Wind, Edgar. "*Hercules* and *Orpheus:* Two Mock-Heroic Designs by Dürer." *Journal of the Warburg and Courtauld Institutes* 2 (1939): 206–18.

Wiora, Walter. "Goethes Wort über Bach." In *Hans Albrecht in memoriam,* ed. Wilfried Brennecke and Hans Haase, 179–91. Kassel: Bärenreiter, 1962 .

Wolff, Christoph. "'The Extraordinary Perfections of the Hon. Court Composer': An Inquiry into the Individuality of Bach's Music." In *Bach: Essays on His Life and Music,* 391–97. Cambridge: Harvard University Press, 1991.

———. *Johann Sebastian Bach: The Learned Musician.* New York: W. W. Norton & Co., 2000.

Woodmansee, Martha. *The Author, Art, and the Market: Rereading the History of Aesthetics.* New York: Columbia University Press, 1994.

Youens, Susan. *Retracing a Winter's Journey: Schubert's "Winterreise."* Ithaca: Cornell University Press, 1991.

Zarlino, Gioseffo. *Le Istitutioni harmoniche.* Venice, 1558.

Ziegler, Konrat. "Orpheus in Renaissance und Neuzeit." In *Form und Inhalt, kunstgeschichtliche Studien: Otto Schmitt zum 60. Geburtstag am 13. Dezember 1950,* 239–56. Stuttgart: W. Kohlhammer, 1951.

Index

Page references in italics indicate figures, tables, and music examples.

Monophony: in Bach's work, 46, 54, 123; in Beethoven's work, 332; and early modern paradigm shift, 37

Monteverdi, Claudio, 5, 35–36; *L'Orfeo* by, 17, 19–26, 20, 28–29, 31, 32, 38, 39–42, 127, 285, 360–61n23

Moral law, Kantian, 128

Moral responsibility: Christian views on, 132–43, 158–59, 160; in Goethe's *Faust*, 271, 277–78; Kant's views on, 144, 145; Kierkegaard's views on, 262–63; and political modernity, 160–61; Rousseau's views on, 144–45, 154, 159

Mortality, Christian notions of, 131–33, 142, 171–72

Moser, Hans Joachim, 365n12

Moses, 137

Mozart, Wolfgang Amadeus: *The Abduction from the Seraglio* Singspiel by, 272, 281; Bach's influence on, 98, 121, 126; Barth on, 113, 189–90; correspondence of, 190, 212, 377n22; Goethe on, 271–72, 287; as performer, 186

—instrumental music of: cadence in, 183–86, 187, 190–91, 195–96; cadenzas in, 184–86, 187–88, 195; chromaticism in, 196; concerto allegro form in, 14, 185–86, 187, 188, 188, 192–93, 198; contraction in, 184, 185, 191; dissonance in, 288; harmony in, 183, 184, 187, 188, 198; Hoffmann on, 6; invention in, 193; masterpieces of, 183; modulation in, 192; Piano Concerto in C Minor as example of, 193, 194, 195, 197, 198; punctuation in, 183, 184–85, 187, 191, 198; recapitulation in, 14, 188, 192, 193, 194, 195–96, 198; reversals in, 196, 377n22; ritornelli in, 188, 188, 189, 192–93, 194, 195–96; sonata allegro form in, 188–89; temporality in, 8, 14–15, 179, 187, 189, 198; theme in, 180–82, 187–88, 192–93, 194

—operas of. See *Così fan tutte; Don Giovanni; Idomeneo; The Magic Flute; The Marriage of Figaro*

Müller, Heinrich, 112

Müller, Wilhelm, 352, 390n41

Nabokov, Vladimir, 31

Nagel, Ivan, 16, 281

Napoleon Bonaparte, 17, 259, 277, 340, 349

Nature: amorality of, 261; and modern salvation narrative, 161–62; in Mozart's works, 32, 261; in Rousseau's writings, 151–52, 153, 154, 162; scientific understanding of, 170–71

Neoplatonism, 28, 38

Nestroy, Johann Nepomuk, 289

Newton, Isaac, 145, 170

Nicean Creed, 111

Niedt, Friedrich Erhardt, 122

Nietzsche, Friedrich Wilhelm, 131, 182, 269, 279, 283, 293, 337–38, 339, 340

Nissen, Georg Nikolaus, 98

Le nozze di Figaro (Mozart). See *The Marriage of Figaro*

Oakeshott, Michael, 293, 339–40

Ockeghem, Jan van, 12

Opera, early Italian: ancient music in, 35, 37, 38, 39–40, 42; poet-musicians in, 28, 32, 37

Operas, Mozart's. See *Così fan tutte; Don Giovanni; Idomeneo; The Magic Flute; The Marriage of Figaro*

Original sin, 132, 140, 141

Orpheus and Eurydice story, representations of: by anonymous North Italian artist, 26; in Blanchot's writing, 30; in Carracci's fresco medallion, 21, 22; in Dürer's art, 24, 27; in Ficino's writing, 32, 38; in Giorgione's art, 32, 41; in Gluck's *Orfeo ed Euridice*, 361n23; and Goethe's *Faust*, 383–84n9; in Mantegna's art, 24, 25, 32; in Monteverdi's *L'Orfeo*, 17, 19–26, 28–29, 31, 32, 38, 39–42, 285, 361n23; and Mozart's *The Magic Flute*, 285; in Ovid's *Metamorphoses*, 21; in Poliziano's *Favola d'Orfeo*, 23, 24, 32; in Proust's writing, 30–32; in Rinuccini's *Euridice*, 21, 25–26, 361n23; in Rubens's art, 38–39; in Teniers's art, 32, 33; in Virgil's *Georgics*, 21

Ovid, 21, 26

Pagels, Elaine, 372–73n9

Palestrina, Giovanni Pierluigi da, 123, 318, 386n5, 388n14

Panofsky, Erwin, 29

Pascal, Blaise, 137

Passions, representation of, 35–37, 40–42, 285–86

Paul, Saint, 132–37

Peiresc, Nicolas-Claude Fabri de, 38

Text:	10/13 Aldus
Display:	Aldus
Music engraver:	Rolf Wulfsberg
Compositor:	Integrated Composition Systems
Indexer:	Andrew Joron
Printer/Binder:	Thomson-Shore